The Renaissance Man and His Children

The Renaissance Man and His Children

Childbirth and Early Childhood in Florence 1300-1600

Louis Haas

St. Martin's Press
New York, NY

THE RENAISSANCE MAN AND HIS CHILDREN: CHILDBIRTH AND EARLY
CHILDHOOD IN FLORENCE, 1300–1600

Library of Congress Cataloging-in-Publication Data
Haas, Louis, 1955-
    The Renaissance man and his children : childbirth and early
childhood in Florence, 1300-1600 / Louis Haas.
        p.   cm.
    Includes bibliographical references and index.
    ISBN: 978-0-312-17563-4
    1. Children—Italy—Florence—History. 2. Childbirth—Italy-
-Florence—History. 3. Family—Italy—Florence—History. 4. Father
and child—Italy—Florence—History. 5. Children—Italy—Florence-
-Social conditions.   I. Title.
HQ792.I8H3   1998
305.23'0945'51—dc21   98-12954
                                                                     CIP

First edition: August 1998

Transferred to Digital Printing 2011

Contents

Acknowledgments

As is usual with something of this scope, I have many people to thank for helping me along the way.

First, I would like to thank the members of Professor Donald Queller's medieval seminars at the University of Illinois at Urbana-Champaign: James Everett, John Hunt, Thomas Madden, James Roots, Patricia Wenzel, and others. I do need to single out one of the seminar members, Mark Angelos, who has remained a good and constant friend and invaluable critic since I first met him in 1983. Further thanks go to Professors O. Vernon Burton, Megan McLaughlin, Richard Mitchell of the University of Illinois, and Professor Barbara Hanawalt of the University of Minnesota, members of my dissertation committee who served as my first audience for this study. Other friends and colleagues at the University of Illinois who have now gone on to other places contributed in all sorts of ways, especially by offering comparative information and examples. These include Elizabeth Dunn, J. Thomas Murphy, Geoffrey Parker, Daniel Soloff, Terry Taylor, Stephen White, and even members of the Angry Wheezers.

Many thanks must also go to the Graduate College of the University of Illinois, which provided essential funds to deliver portions of this research at various conferences. In Florence, I owe a tremendous debt to the hardworking, competent, helpful, and patient staffs of the Archivio di Stato and the Bibioteca Nazionale. I also want to thank the various scholars I met in Florence who shared their expertise with me. Much of this occurred just in passing in the archives or walking to or from them or over cappucino taken quickly at the bar, since I am by nature shy and reticent. Nevertheless, scholars such as James Banker, Julius Kirshner, Carol Lansing, Timothy McGee, Anthony Molho, and many others of their kindness answered me when I dared to ask them questions. At the top of this list, however, go William Connell, expert in the *ricordanze* and all sorts of things Florentine, whom I met by chance while I was standing outside a *friggitoria* munching on a donut (my lunch for the day), and Lynn Lauffenberg, who knows so much and so many people.

More recently, I owe many thanks to thoughtful and helpful colleagues whom I have met at conferences. Among these are David Blanks, Michael Frassetto, Amy Livingstone, Larry Marvin, Linda Mitchell, and Michael Pedrotty. Professor Joseph Lynch of the Ohio State University has read two versions of the manuscript and offered much good advice, including the proverbial good word in season. Michael Cahall, Jonathan Dent, Sara Goelz, Thomas Greene, Holly Mayer, and Jean Hunter, colleagues at Duquesne University, read portions of the manuscript and contributed immensely to its clarity. Many thanks also go to the hardworking and energetic staff at St. Martin's, including my editor, Michael Flamini, who not only saw the potential and significance of this study but also allowed me to tell it the way I wanted to, and my production editor, Wendy Kraus.

All the above named people and many others too numerous to name, such as Pasha Greenfield, have made this a better study; none of them, however, are responsible for the errors that remain, which knowing me are legion.

Last, I must single out one individual above all without whom this study would not have been possible. That is Donald Queller, late Professor of History at the University of Illinois at Urbana-Campaign. It was under his tutelage and with his advice that I came to this study, and I learned so much from him while doing it. His professionalism, knowledge, work ethic, and personality made learning and doing history with him fun; and I really miss his presence. Thus, it is quite appropriate that I respectfully dedicate this study to him and his memory.

Historians and Childhood in Renaissance Florence

IT IS USUALLY THE LITTLE THINGS—for instance, the annoying details that do not fit—that trouble us the most about theories. With this in mind, let us begin with a letter. A simple but challenging letter:

> Your Eletta, my delight, greeted me with a smile although she did not know who I was. I was not only overcome with joy: I took her into my arms eagerly imagining that I was holding my own little girl. What can I say? If you think I exaggerate ask William of Ravenna or our Donato [degli Albizzi], for they both knew her. Your child has the identical aspect of the child who was my Eletta, the same expression, the same light and laughter in her eyes, the same gestures and walk, the same fashion of carrying her little self, save that my Eletta was somewhat taller for her age at five and a half, when I saw her for the last time. She has the same way of talking, the same vocabulary. She has the same simple manner. In truth there is no difference between them except that your little one has golden hair while mine had locks of chestnut. Ah, how often, holding your child in my arms and listening to her prattle, the memory of my own lost little girl has brought to my eyes tears that I conceal from all.[1]

The emotions described here, the sentiments expressed, the affection displayed are familiar to most of us in the modern Western world. In general, we love and care for our children and are interested in them and their activities. So too the writer. A chance encounter with a little girl had led him to recall his own daughter, long since dead. He had loved his daughter and he missed her. We empathize with this writer for his loss: we feel his grief, we understand his pain, and we recognize his love. Most of us could pen lines like these with the same exquisite detail and emotion given the same circumstances. But, who is this writer?

Writer is exactly correct, for these words come from the pen of the Florentine author, Giovanni Boccaccio—a voice from the distant past. Across the gulf of time his words touch and move us. These lines come from a letter he wrote to his friend Petrarch in 1366, just after meeting Petrarch's granddaughter. Discovering the identity of this writer, however, is not serendipitous but confusing—even troubling. To find attitudes and actions such as these expressed in the fourteenth century may surprise and puzzle some modern readers.[2] Part of this surprise and puzzlement rises out of our intuition about daily life in the past. We think that it looked and felt much like Thomas Hobbes's view of life in the state of nature—poor, nasty, brutish, and short—that is, devoid of any trace of humanity. More significantly, however, our surprise and puzzlement rise out of what we think we know about the quality of childhood in the European past.

Despite some recent studies to the contrary, one thesis still dominates the historical study of childhood in the European past: premodern childhood was a time of neglect and abuse since high infant mortality rates prevented people from forging close affective bonds with their children. Consequently, according to this theory, premodern Europeans failed to recognize childhood as a distinct stage in the development of the individual. If anything, adults saw children as just miniature versions of themselves; premodern paintings reflect this when they depict children garbed as adults and babies possessing adult features. The corollary to this thesis states that at some point (variously set somewhere in the seventeenth, eighteenth, or nineteenth century) these abusive and neglectful attitudes and practices changed for the better. People loved and cared for their children and recognized them as such. Childhood, according to historians, thus became "modern" because of this change. Developing and illustrating this thesis and its corollary is the aim of the standard work on childhood and family life in the European past: Philippe Ariès's *Centuries of Childhood* (1965). Other historians, such as Edward Shorter, Lawrence Stone, Randolf Trumbach; more recently Judith Lewis, Renate Blumenfeld-Kosinski, C. John Sommerville; and most recently Hugh Cunningham, have amplified this thesis.[3] Their views seem to permeate most other attempts to examine family life in the past. Reviewing Suzanne Dixon's *The Roman Mother* (1988), Sarah Pomeroy concluded that "Dixon's view provides support for theories advanced by Lawrence Stone, Lloyd deMause and others that the emotional affect among members of families in premodern Europe was low."[4]

Historians of modern Europe have adopted this thesis with a particular vengeance and use it as a foundation—or presupposition—for their studies of modern family life and childhood.[5] This thesis has been both pervasive and persuasive since it fits our feelings about life in the past as well as satisfies our belief in the existence of progress in history. Moreover, it fits some modern theories about society. For instance, many social scientists argue, based on works like these, that concepts such as mother-love are then only social constructs imposed upon women by modern, male-dominated society as a means of control and as such can therefore be changed, thus freeing women from the snares of patriarchal society.[6] A change in attitudes toward children had occurred in the past with the result being a narrowing of women's roles in the modern world.

Yet, the information and expressed sentiments in Boccaccio's letter stand outside the parameters of this general thesis and its corollary. Moreover, they do not particularly fit the specific picture of late medieval and Renaissance childhood that some historians have drawn for us. These historians have done much work on the Florentine family in general, emphasizing its political functions, its demographic composition, its economic and social roles, its ritual practices, and its dynastic policies.[7] There are even some particular studies on childhood in Florence.[8] Because of this body of work, historians of Florence are fairly definite about the picture they have drawn of Florentine childhood, and it is one that parallels the general thesis of childhood's being a progressive movement from abuse and neglect to care and affection, punctuated by a precise moment of change from the negative to the positive.

In her collection of essays, *Women, Family, and Ritual in Renaissance Italy* (1985), Christiane Klapisch-Zuber argued that after the turn of the fifteenth century attitudes toward children in Renaissance Florence became better—that is, more enlightened and more affective. The growth of the cult of the Christ child; the establishment of a foundlings' hospital (the Ospedale degli Innocenti) in 1445; the increase in the number of moralists' tracts that touch on the subjects of children and childhood; and the interest in *putti* and *bambini*, the so called holy dolls that show up in trousseaux and inventory lists, exemplified this change in attitudes and practices. Children in paintings even looked more lifelike.[9] Simply put, attitudes toward children became "modern" during the fifteenth century—children and childhood, therefore, had a renaissance.[10] Before this change, however, life for Tuscan children had been wretched, and some Florentine historians have described this wretchedness in all its lurid detail.

In *Tuscans and Their Families* (1985), David Herlihy and Christiane Klapisch-Zuber stated: "The behavior of Tuscan parents lends some support to Ariès's interpretation. Many of them did not really welcome the newborn baby into their hearths and hearts, at least not until it had survived the dangerous early years of life." The disasters of the fourteenth century, especially the demographic ones, exacerbated this negative attitude. Herlihy and Klapisch-Zuber asserted that "[t]he horrible mortalities in the early years of life discouraged parents, we believe, from forming deep emotional attachments with their newborn babies."[11] Herlihy elsewhere claimed that the high premodern infant mortality rate, as well as the high premodern mortality rate for children and adults, "undermined the durability and stability of the basic familial relations—between husband and wife, and parents and children." This demographic crisis led Florentine writers to investigate and then idealize the family because their own had been so disrupted.[12]

Herlihy discovered an interesting demographic fact of Florentine family life. Husbands, for various reasons, were considerably older than their wives (by approximately 14 years), and Florentine men on the average were almost 40 years old by the time they had their first child. Marital partners so widely separated in age and life experiences would have difficulty, so Herlihy believed, in forming close affective relations with one another. From this belief, Herlihy concluded that the late medieval and Renaissance family suffered an internal emotional crisis.[13] And, in Herlihy's opinion, this crisis exhibited itself very definitely in a father's relations with his children: "The mature, if not aged, fathers would have difficulty communicating with their children."[14] This is why, according to Sommerville, Florentine fathers composed so many advice books for their sons—they just could not communicate face to face.[15] Mothers, then, rather than fathers were the primary socializers of children.[16] Combined with the dreadful mortality rates of the time, this fact led Herlihy to observe that in late medieval and Renaissance Florence "of all domestic relationships, the bond between father and children was most fragile."[17] The result of this fragile bond was predictable: "Prevailing attitudes toward children, of both sexes, also led to oversight and confusion. Adults tended to ignore, neglect, and forget their offspring; infants in early life possessed a kind of transparency. It may be that their slim chances for survival prompted adults to keep a certain distance from them, to avoid cementing emotional attachments with them until their chances to survive substantially improved."[18]

Supposedly, salient proof of Florentine neglect and lack of concern for children can be found in the practice of sending children out to be breastfed by mercenary wetnurses. Diane Owen Hughes wondered at the effect this had on the children: "can we be confident that young children were socialized in the households, extended or otherwise, of Renaissance Florence when so many were sent out at birth to wetnurses, and when we are so ignorant of their later upbringing."[19] Richard Trexler seconded that observation. For him Florentine wetnursing practices represented an unstable "maternal numen" that had a devastating psychological effect on Florentines as they grew up. He saw this exemplified in Florentines' attachment to *bambini* and their tendency to call the Pope, saints, and Virgin Mary "*babbo*" and "*mammina*." All these, he concluded, were "the strong residual traces of manipulative instabilities in childhood."[20] Sommerville stated bluntly: "In short, wetnursing meant neglect for all children." After a brief description of Florentine wetnursing practices he concluded, "[o]bviously, women did not want children in order to enjoy them as infants."[21]

Some children suffered even harsher treatment at the hands of adults. While discussing Florence's foundling hospitals, Charles de la

Roncière observed that "infants, particularly girls, were so vulnerable that impoverished parents thought it better to part with them, assuming they cared about the child at all."[22] Klapisch-Zuber argued that Tuscan children tended even to be forgotten, especially if they were girls.[23] This fact displeased her, and she judged Tuscan parents harshly: "all this sad childhood that a document like the *Catasto* reveals in profusion is scandalous in our eyes."[24] There was, however, a bright side to all this as de la Roncière pointed out: "As soon as a child was old enough to walk and talk, attitudes changed."[25] Yet this was short lived according to Klapisch-Zuber: "In iconography as in vocabulary or in daily life, the child was no longer, after 7 years of age, any more than a second class individual, often passed over in silence or brutally thrown into the world of adults."[26]

Some historians, however, have seen the iconography of Florentine childhood as more a mask than a mirror. Barbara Kay Greenleaf pointed to the supposed hypocrisy in Renaissance Florentine art: "Artists' babies were always chubby and happy; in real life they were often underfed, unchanged, and quite miserable. While in reproductions a baby always held its mother's undivided attention, in real life the child would have been miles away from her sight and probably her thoughts as well."[27] Why then would Florentine patrons have accepted such truthless depictions? By having such scenes depicted, so Greenleaf concluded, they assuaged their own guilt as poor parents. Moreover, gazing at these scenes could also help them forget their own wretched childhood. The artist participated in this catharsis as well. Sommerville asked himself why da Vinci painted scenes of the Madonna and child so much and concluded that it was because he had been passed around from mother to wetnurse to wetnurse to stepmother. He never had—in Trexler's words—a stable maternal numen. Even if these artistic depictions were not true, they did serve as ideals for a new changing attitude toward children that developed during the High Renaissance, with artists as the apparent leaders in this movement.[28] Yet even here they had an ulterior motive for the change; as Sommerville noted, "[c]hildren were important, but primarily as family heirs and not as individuals."[29]

Where in these individual observations by historians, in this picture of Florentine childhood, in the more general thesis of childhood in history is there room for sentiments like those expressed by Boccaccio? Nowhere it seems. Yet, because of this letter, something seems wrong with this prevailing view of children in the past. Historians perhaps are not presenting the history of children and childhood in Renaissance Florence in all its true complexity.

There are other apparent anomalies within the traditional view of childhood in Florence. If Florentines supposedly had such a negative uncaring attitude toward children, why did the merchant elite have so many children? Some merchants had children from three different marriages—and not just one or two children from each of these marriages. It is not uncommon to stumble across merchants who listed more than half a dozen children in the records.[30] If Florentines supposedly cared so little about their children, why did they invest so much effort in and give importance to the introductory rituals that welcomed infants into the social and religious community that was Florence? Parents ensured that virtually all children born in Florence were baptized within three days of their birth and that they possessed godparents. Why did they perform these duties so diligently and so quickly? If wetnursing was supposedly such a wretched experience for all involved, why was it so widespread; and why did even the harshest critics of the practice advise it in certain circumstances? Few commentators ever criticized the wetnurses they had had as children; indeed many praised them. Because of its utility and ubiquity, wetnursing, rather than appearing as some form of abuse and neglect, was similar in function to daycare today. If Florentines, especially the humanists, supposedly failed to recognize childhood as a distinct stage of human life and development, why did they invest so much time and effort defining childhood and its special needs, especially regarding health and education, in tracts and treatises? If Florentines supposedly insulated themselves from the harsh realities of high infant mortality rates by becoming cold and distant to their children, why were so many of them emotionally shattered by the death of their children, even their newborns, and why did so many do so much to memorialize the death of their children and infants? As I have implied, sometimes evidence interferes with models.

In fact, in recent years studies have appeared that shed a different light on the general character of childhood in the past, and their conclusions imply that a new look at childhood in late medieval and Renaissance Florence is warranted. Overall, these studies demonstrate that people in general loved and cared for their children and recognized childhood as a distinct stage in the development of the individual. Moreover, these studies find no evidence of any radical switch from abuse and neglect to care and concern. According to this research, European childhood has always been, so to speak, "modern." Linda Pollock made just these points about childhood in early modern and modern England in *Forgotten Children: Parent-Child Relations from 1500 to 1900* (1983). Steven Ozment demonstrated the same points about childhood in Reformation era Germany in *When Fathers Ruled* (1983). David Nicholas made the same observations about childhood in fourteenth-century Ghent in *The Domestic Life of a Medieval City* (1985). Barbara Hanawalt came to the same conclusions about peasant childhood in late medieval England in *The Ties that Bound* (1986), and Shulamith Shahar reinforced these points in her more general *Childhood in the Middle Ages* (1990). Mark Golden plotted the same pattern of affective relations in Ancient Athens in *Children and Childhood in Classical Athens* (1990). Suzanne Dixon found how "modern" the Roman family really was in *The Roman Family* (1992). And Hanawalt again reiterated these points for urban childhood in late medieval London in *Growing Up in Medieval London* (1993).[31] How can historians like Ariès and Pollock arrive at such contradictory conclusions? Surprisingly, for all the work done on childhood in the past, we still just do not know all that much about it. And historians of childhood are the first to admit this paradoxical fact.[32] In addition, evidence contradicting the predominant thesis on the history of childhood, such as Boccaccio's letter, seems largely to be ignored rather than interpreted, and this willful neglect explains why we know little about childhood in the past—regardless of the era. Put simply, we need a new history of childhood that encompasses much more than a simplistic search for the advent of the modern domesticated nuclear family with its concomitant denigration of the premodern family. From my reading of the sources and the historiography I believe that there is far more continuity than change involved in the history of the family and affective relations. In fact, my work is one of the few works on family history that starts from a presupposition that I will not see any sort of fundamental change in attitudes toward children by adults.[33]

While it is certainly beyond me and my abilities to set out a new paradigm for the study of childhood, especially when we still need to clear away so much of the wreckage of the old, I am suggesting some new directions for researchers to take. We need to look at and analyze the contradictory evidence more closely and systematically. We need to look more closely for the simple, the commonplace, the recurring, the daily happenings within families historically. What exactly were the structures of everyday life regarding childhood?[34] For a proper understanding of childhood in the past we need more studies that are narrowly defined by either time or geography or both and based on personal evidence, such as letters and diaries, before we can draw any broad conclusions about the history of childhood.[35] In fact, whenever we have such rich and detailed studies of childhood in the past, our view of the quality of childhood and childcare in the past as a whole is altered. Hence this study of birth and infancy in late medieval and early Renaissance Florence.

Why just birth and infancy, and why late medieval and Renaissance Florence, 1300-1600?[36] Human infants require considerable care and attention from their biological parents and their society at large, if the species is to survive. Searching for the ways in which a society, and specifically the parents within it, ensure that care, then, is no irrelevant question. And understanding how past cultures ensured that care helps explain how and why present cultures do so. Understanding that parents in the past faced some of the same dictates and options regarding work and childcare that we in the modern Western world face can, through a recognition of their struggles and successes, help alleviate some of our own anxieties about this parental balance. If wetnursing was a form of premodern daycare, as I argue it was, this then reassures us today that we are not facing some new problem for the family but an age-old one, which humans like us have always known.

But human birth is much more than a biological event. It possesses religious, political, ritual, and dynastic significance that reflects the very structures of society. Moreover, birth involves more people than just the mother and infant—a birth weaves together immediate family members, more distant relatives, friends, and even strangers, as well as medical and religious professionals. In some ways a birth is like a *conjoncture* in an *Annaliste* sense—a point of tension that allows one to witness the underlying social layers—in which a nine-month-long biological occurrence reveals the dynamics of personal relationships, social perceptions, and symbolic rituals. My investigation tells us how people in the past—in this case Florentines during the fourteenth through sixteenth centuries—experienced and perceived this whole human process of birth and infancy.[37]

This investigation also has considerable historiographical significance. Although they have been constantly criticized, the ideas and conclusions of historians like Arie`s, Shorter, Stone, and their adherents regarding family life and childhood have not yet been dismissed.[38] One common problem with many of the works on childhood in the European past is that they examined too large an area, geographically or chronologically or topically. This may, to some extent, explain the paradox of much work having been done on childhood in the past but not much being known—most of the studies were too superficial and impressionistic. To examine all of childhood, through many eras in many countries, may be impossible within the scope of any one work. I therefore decided to narrow my geographic focus considerably to correct for the errors that can creep into these superficial and impressionistic studies, especially since a number of scholars have called for more studies like this one if we are ever to build a synthetic view of childhood in the past.[39] I chose to focus specifically on birth and infancy because we tend to know the least about how people experienced and society perceived these very crucial years throughout the ages. Moreover, the years of a child's life that encompass birth and infancy, which premodern people defined as the time from birth to age seven, seem to be the most susceptible to interpretation along the lines of the prevailing theory of childhood in the past. Regardless of how a society perceived its children—so this theory asserts—it tended always to see those at this early age in less favorable terms.[40] If the prevailing thesis on childhood in the past is based on a flawed concept and false assumptions, investigating specifically birth and infancy in the past is the way to prove that.

More importantly, I hope to correct some of our particular misperceptions about Florentine childhood, since all the works on

Florentine childhood suffer from one signal failing. They all were influenced by the model set out by Ariès, Shorter, and Stone. The authors accepted the validity of this model and couched their research and conclusions within its dictates.[41] But If this model is a false one, as I believe it is and as I believe many other authors have demonstrated, then the history of childhood in Florence desperately needs to be rewritten.[42] In some little ways, this has already happened. Many current Florentine social historians, in the course of other research, have rejected parts of this model whenever they have brushed up against it, or have provided brief glimpses of an alternative view of childhood in the course of other research.[43] But no one yet has attempted to synthesize this material and combine it with other evidence in an attempt to gain a more accurate picture of Florentine childhood. I hope I can be forgiven here not only for attempting merely this but also for relying at times on these brief glimpses—which their authors usually intended for other purposes—for my own goal of showing that the prevailing model of premodern childhood and its specific adaptation by many Florentine historians does not fit the historical experience of Florentine children.

I chose to focus on the period from 1300 to 1600, the late Middle Ages and Renaissance—a time period that many social historians call premodern as I shall do—for two reasons. First, the chronological span frames a fairly narrow window of time. Second, the range straddles two traditional historical eras, the Middle Ages and Renaissance, which have been the foci for part of the general historiographical debate on the status of children and childhood in the past. On the one hand most theorists and investigators have seen the Middle Ages as some sort of Dark Age for childhood. On the other hand, as we saw above, some have tried to argue that the Renaissance represented the first glimmerings of a new view of childhood.[44] A closer examination of birth and infancy during this time should test the truth of these hypotheses.

I chose Florence as the geographic site for this study likewise for some specific reasons. Florence as a premodern city-state presents a society (or culture if you will) narrowly defined by geography and unified by particular rituals and social practices.[45] More importantly, Florence, largely due to the humanist movement, had a number of moralists, preachers, educators, and physicians who described and theorized about birth and infancy. Two of the best known of these are Giovanni Dominici and Leon Battista Alberti.[46] Most importantly, the Florentine archives house hundreds of *ricordi* and *ricordanze*. These "remembrances" or "memories" form the largest collection of pre-seventeenth-century personal literature that describes the individual's private world in his or (on rare occasions) her own words. While not diaries in the modern sense of the word, they contain diary-like information. *Ricordi* contain maxims and personal reflections. The writers intended them for their posterity and sometimes for the public. The most famous collection of *ricordi* is that written by the historian Francesco Guicciardini. The *ricordanze* are account books that usually contain sections dealing with family history, business transactions, debits and credits, and household and miscellaneous costs. These records were intended solely for family members, primarily the writers and their sons and grandsons. They originated in the secret account books of Florentine merchants, the *libri segreti*, which themselves contain interesting autobiographical notes plus public and private information. Of course, as business records they will be biased toward trade and profit rather than emotion and family. But often these Florentine authors saw and recorded more than the bottom line. Giovanni Morelli, a Florentine merchant, wrote a book of *ricordi* that also includes the same information found in a *ricordanze*; he thus recorded his activities and described his feelings about them.

The Florentine archives are also rich in autobiographies and even diaries in the modern sense of the word. Unlike *ricordanze*, these memoirs were never intended for the instruction of future family members and usually did not include business transactions. The best known of these is Benvenuto Cellini's published autobiography, *La vita*. At age 58 that braggart, ruffian, and superbly talented artist recalled his life from birth in 1500 and continued the account to 1562. Despite the bombast, Cellini's *La vita* provides deep insight into the social and professional world of an elite Renaissance artist.[47]

As might be expected, *ricordanze*, *ricordi*, *libri segreti*, autobiographies, and diaries contain much personal information about childhood.[48] Moreover, since Renaissance Florence possessed a very literate society, personal letters abound. Finally, literature, such as Boccaccio's *Decameron*, and iconography can reflect both the theory and the reality of birth and infancy as well as correct for some of the biases that appear in the *ricordanze*.[49] Florence, perhaps more than any other premodern city, abounds with personal sources from the past, the best sort of records with which to study family and childhood.

My choice to include some sources and exclude others leads to a number of biases and limitations. First, although people from all social levels in Florence wrote *ricordanze*, the vast majority of those records that survive were written by the merchant and ruling elite of the city.[50] This is ever the case with premodern personal documents, and raises the question of how much their content reflects the beliefs and behaviors of Florentine and Tuscan society as a whole. There are, however, a few hints from the sources, as will be seen, that the values of the merchant and ruling elite regarding children were held by other elements in Florentine society as well. But caution is essential here.

Second, while both men and women wrote these kinds of materials, few by women have survived. Women wrote fewer letters than men, and participated less actively in the humanist movement and artistic flowering than did men. Thus, this study examines birth and infancy primarily through lenses held by men from the upper levels of Florentine society. In fact, a feminist study of birth and infancy in premodern Florence is a clear desideratum, but it is one that I, unfortunately, cannot satisfy with this study.[51] Perhaps because of this or perhaps because the sources tell us so much more about the Renaissance man than the Renaissance woman, I find myself not seeing the many anti-female tendencies in Florentine culture that Klapisch-Zuber has identified.[52] I think she has overemphasized these and because of this she has been somewhat mistaken in her analysis of the quality and tenor of Florentine childhood. I hope, therefore, with this work to offer a slight corrective to some of her particular conclusions regarding the influence of patriarchy in Florentine culture.

Third, I have deliberately excluded most legal sources from my considerations here. Premodern legal sources, because of their almost complete focus on inheritance and property, can give an indistinct and even overly patriarchal cast to a society. They highlight the "language of property" rather than the "language of sentiment," which is so essential to the study of the family.[53] Social historians of ancient Rome have become very wary recently regarding the utility of legal sources for explicating family life, and in fact have shied away from using them.[54] I have followed suit, especially since my concern is more the child within the family and not the child in public at the bar. I recognize that these two spheres overlap and that my attempt to separate them is, at some levels, artificial; but I hope that it is an artificiality that will allow us to see more of the intimate details of family life and childhood.[55] And certainly it will prevent the sort of error that Sommerville fell into in believing that Florentine children were only important as heirs and did not otherwise exist as individuals. Nevertheless, a study of Florentine children as seen by law is as requisite as a feminist study of children. But again, unfortunately, it is one that I cannot satisfy with this study. In fact, because of the peculiar biases that law brings to the study of society, a study of Florentine children as seen by law should follow this one, not precede it.

Despite these limits, I think this narrowly focused study sheds some light on premodern childhood in general and will be of interest to social historians, especially those interested in the historical family. Moreover, I think I can speculate about the inaccuracy of the dominant thesis on childhood and its corollary based on my Florentine evidence, especially since so many of the general works on childhood have drawn upon Florentine evidence to support the dominant thesis on childhood and its corollary. More importantly though—and this is its main purpose—this study sheds detailed light on how Florentine parents (primarily fathers) viewed, reared, and cared for their children as they did, and why they did so. What was birth and infancy like for Florentines and their children? A question, I hope, whose answer will be of particular interest to social historians interested in the medieval and Renaissance family as well as specialists interested in the history of Florence.[56] In the process of answering this question, I will resolve the apparent anomalies I identified earlier. Thus, this study should not only compliment the revisionist studies by Pollock, Ozment, Nicholas, Golden, Dixon, and Hanawalt but in the process also hang some flesh on the bare demographic skeleton of family life that David Herlihy and Christiane Klapisch-Zuber so ably constructed in *Tuscans and Their Families: A Study of the Florentine Catasto of 1427* (1985).[57] I hope to accomplish this last goal in particular by letting premodern Florentines speak to us in their own words as often as I can. Doing this, I hope, will make this work interesting and fun for the non-specialist to read as well.

Lastly, through the pages of this study perhaps we, too, if only for a moment, will be able to join people like Boccaccio and his daughter while they hug, laugh, walk, talk, and live and love again—if only on these pages and in our mind's eye. By doing so we understand more about our own humanity through realizing that they too were human. Maybe that is my real purpose here.

Di Mateo Naque Molti Figli:

Florentines Think about Having Children

COMMENTS AND OBSERVATIONS about the love of children consistently served Florentines as points of reference or comparison:

Who would believe, except by the experience of his own feelings, how great and intense is the love of a father toward his children. . . . I am sure that no love is more unshakable, more constant, more complete, or more vast than the love which a father bears to his children.

—Leon Battista Alberti[1]

[May 24, 1413] . . . our homeland [*patria*] is more precious than our children. . . .

—Messer Rinaldo Gianfigliazzi[2]

Everyone says that small children are the comfort and delight of their fathers and of the old people of the family. . . .
When you pick your wife, you choose your children.

—Alberti[3]

Don't you see that a woman who has no children has no home?

—Madonna Sostrata[4]

There are four great loves: the first is that for your soul, the second
is that for your children. . . .

—Paolo da Certaldo[5]

No one can censure the desire to have children, for it is natural.

—Francesco Guicciardini[6]

Furthermore, natural law has ordained that the human species
should multiply. . . .

—Anonymous[7]

Protect your fortune and your children from that which fate at the
moment has tested me with.

—Iacopo Acciaiuoli[8]

Have you given more love to Him [God] than you have to your
children?

—Anonymous[9]

Moreover, anytime Florentine authors wished to describe the absolute
horror of an event they noted that it particularly affected children.
Luca Landucci, for instance, recorded in his diary for 12 February
1499 that the French sacked Tortona and "pillaged the place, slaying
even the children."[10]

Points of reference such as these make no sense unless we assume
that Florentines recognized children as something special in and
valuable to Florentine society. Some of these comparisons, such as the
one made earlier by Rinaldo Gianfigliazzi, make no sense unless we
assume that Florentine parents loved their children. And most did.
Despite the importance Florentine society put on friendship for social,
political, and economic advancement and advantage, Leon Battista
Alberti pointed out that the bonds of friendship were subordinate to
and of a lesser quality than those engendered between parents and
children.[11] Most Florentines would have agreed. No wonder then that
Florentine fathers recorded the birth of their children in such a
distinctive fashion in their *ricordanze*. According to Tommaso
Guidetti, "I had from Lisa my wife and born to me (*minaque*) one little

girl."[12] Virtually all of the writers of *ricordanze* recorded the birth of a child with some variant of the phrase, "minaque." In an exception that perhaps proves the rule, Lapo Niccolini included his wife's role in this process by noting that their son, Giovanni, had been born from both of them.[13] We can forgive Tommaso and other Florentine men for their eccentric and egocentric turn of phrase—born to me—since they were understandably proud of this event and perceived it first in how it related to themselves.

Women as well boasted about birth. In a letter dated 20 April 1517 Clarice Strozzi wrote her husband, Filippo, informing him of the birth of a little girl to Gostanza d'Alfonso. She reminded her husband that Gostanza had given birth (literally, born fruit—*ha frota*) just as she, meaning herself, had so many times before.[14] She was proud of her own accomplishments and compared Gostanza's to hers.

Humanists and moralists in Florence spent considerable time discussing children and family life. Some, such as Paolo da Certaldo and San Bernardino, made general statements about them in the course of their works.[15] Others developed specific tracts dealing with children and family life. Giovanni Dominici (1356-1419) wrote his *Regola del Governo di Cura Familiare* for Bartolomea Alberti, whose husband was exiled in 1400, leaving her to raise four children alone. One of the reasons he wrote this, he told her, was because "these children of yours are subject to fortune and to changing circumstances," and she would need help in rearing them. His work is characterized by a sympathy and understanding for the child and emphasized loving childrearing.[16] His ideas influenced someone else. He corresponded frequently with Francesco Datini, the fantastically wealthy merchant of Prato whose legacy founded the *Innocenti*, the foundlings hospital in Florence. They discussed matters of the spirit, including charity, as well as those of the flesh, including the family.[17]

Other Italian authors devoted attention to childrearing in their works. The Venetian humanist Francesco Barbaro (1390-1454) made a trip in 1415 to Florence where he met Lorenzo de'Medici, the uncle of Lorenzo the Magnificent. He then wrote a tract on family life, *De re uxoria* (1416), for Lorenzo's marriage to Ginevra Cavalcanti. He designed it as a guidebook on family life for the new bride, and included much information on childrearing practices, including how to deal with wetnurses.[18]

Premodern medical authors likewise paid attention to the needs of children in their general works, and by the fifteenth century many were writing treatises dealing in particular with the care of children and childhood diseases. The summa of Bartholomaeus Anglicus, *De proprietatibus rerum*, included a section on childcare that was written in less scholarly tones, indicating that it was intended for practical application by the general, not scholarly, population. This work was popular in Italy, and had even been translated into the vernacular. In fact, Italian medical authors led European scholars in the study of childcare and childhood diseases, probably because they relied heavily on classical authors, many of whom had devoted attention to the family and childrearing practices. Two Paduans, Michele Savonarola (the grandfather of the Dominican Girolamo Savonarola) and Paulus Bargellardus, wrote such treatises; the Sienese Aldobrandinus likewise did so. Many translations of the relevant sections on family and childrearing practices from the works of Rhazes and Avicenna freely circulated among the Italian medical community. Florentine physicians—thus their young patients' parents—and some humanists had access to this material.[19]

Humanists frequently exchanged ideas on family life and childrearing practices amongst themselves. Giovanni Rucellai used Agnolo Pandolfini's *Trattato del governo della famiglia* and sections of Matteo Palmieri's *Della vita civile* for the portions of his *Zibaldone Quaresimale*, which dealt with children and the family. Matteo Strozzi let Matteo Castellani borrow his copy of Barbaro's *De re uxoria*. Some causal relationship between these works and civic action may have existed since Pandolfini's sons served as consuls of the silk guild, which monitored the *Innocenti*.[20] Children and their care, therefore, were intellectual and practical topics amongst the elite in premodern Florence.

Historians have long recognized that premodern Florence teemed with children.[21] In his *ricordanze* Ugolino Martelli listed the births of his children, and this particular record indicates how prolific the merchant elite of Florence—both male and female—could be:

Nicholo	7 March 1435
Filippo	21 February 1437 (d. 30 December 1437)
Filippo	17 April 1438 (d. 9 November 1443)
Charlo	10 June 1439
Gionbattista	11 January 1441
Ginevra	11 October 1443 (d. before 12 November 1444)
Ginevra	12 November 1444
Allesandra	2 August 1447 (d. 10 August 1480)
Chosimo	26 September 1448
Lodovicho	18 August 1451
Luigi	13 December 1452
Lorenzo	21 November 1454 (d. 21 February 1455)
Lena	10 January 1456
Filippo	not recorded (d. 16 July 1476)[22]

Luca Landucci and his wife had 12 children; Gregorio Dati recorded that he was one of 17 children that his mother and father had; Catherine of Siena's mother had 25 children.[23] Not to be outdone, Checcha Masi, the wife of an artisan, had 36 children. On the other hand, Alessandra Macinghi Strozzi, married in 1422 to one of the richest men in Florence, had 8 children between 1426 and 1436.[24] Examples such as these could be multiplied endlessly for the merchant elite. No wonder a popular image of Florence for writers and commentators was that of a woman in childbirth.[25]

Multiple marriages, extramarital affairs, and the advent of a new generation could give a packed and layered appearance to a Florentine household. By 1470, Otto Niccolini had nine children from his previous marriage living at home with the four children from his current marriage, his illegitimate child, and two grandsons. As he was away, his second wife, Bartolomea, supervised this brood, which ranged in age from 24 years to one-and-a-half. Bartolomea was also pregnant.[26]

Many Florentines from the merchant and ruling elite seemed to want swarms of children. In 1427, 11 percent of Florence's population lived in households with ten or more members; 50 percent lived in households with six or more members.[27] According to Lionardo in

Alberti's *Libri della Famiglia* a woman's beauty was based on her charm, her grace, and her "aptitude for bearing and giving birth to many fine children." He also said, "One takes a wife, in fact, mainly to have children by her."[28] And in fact, the second book of Alberti's dialogue places having children as the first purpose of marriage.[29] In this, Alberti was only following common Christian attitudes about the purpose of marriage.[30] Most Florentines accepted this concept of marriage.[31] Niccolò Machiavelli's play, *La Mandragola,* touched on this popular perception that part of a woman's utility for society stemmed from her fertility by revolving around the theme of a husband and wife's frustrated desire to have children. A widow's fertility or lack thereof was therefore an obvious concern for men in any marriage negotiation. Florentines even believed that having children solidified and sanctified conjugal love.[32] In addition children supported their parents in their old age: they were "a staff to sustain our old age," as one of the characters in the *Mandragola* stated.[33] Cellini's mother and father spent 18 long years wanting and trying to have children, but failing. Francesco Datini's major requirement from his wife Margherita was a house filled with children. She wanted this too.[34] Having children was a shared desire and activity for many elite Florentine couples. In Alberti's *Libri della famiglia* Gianozzo told his wife that "the children to be born to us will belong to us both, to you as much as to me, to me as much as to you."[35]

Florentine marital patterns, hence birthing patterns, provide something of a paradox for the historian. Florentines of the merchant elite married late (though the men usually married women much younger than themselves) yet had many children. Florentines of the rural and urban poor married early (here the couples were closer in age) yet had few children. A limit, or structure, existed then to the desire for many children; and usually only the wealthier segments of Florence's population could fulfill or indulge in this desire. In 1427, for instance, the richest one thousand households contained 873 children; the poorest thousand only 648. In Florence wealth and the number of children were highly correlated: in general the higher one's tax assessment the more children there were living in the household.[36] The average household from the poorer half of Florence contained half as many people as did that from the richer. Half of the poor were 25 years of age and older; half of the wealthy were 17 years or younger.[37] In 1526 when Bernardo Masi, a Florentine coppersmith, died, his son Bartolomeo, also a coppersmith, recorded that neither he nor his seven brothers (their ages ranged from 17 to 48 years of age) had married or had children, though three of the four younger brothers had become monks.[38] None of these men apparently had been sufficiently able to establish themselves to contemplate marriage let alone fatherhood.

Like people elsewhere in premodern Europe, some Florentines undoubtedly tried to control their fertility through contraception and abortion. Perhaps they were too poor to have children at all or to have many of them, they felt they had too many children already, they wanted greater spacing between children, or they simply disliked children. Regardless of the reason, Florentine sources note the use of abortifacients, coitus interruptus, anal intercourse (which the moralists referred to as conjugal sodomy) and other positions in order not to have children. The extent of family limitation in Florentine society is unknown, however, just as it seems to be for the rest of premodern European society.[39] Nevertheless in Florence, "the rich show[ed] the least inclination to limit births," and the *ricordanze* reflect that fact.[40]

Regardless of wealth, premodern Florence had a young society. In 1427, 15.8 percent of the population was aged four years or younger. At neighboring Prato in 1371-72 38 percent of the population was aged eight years or younger.[41] If numbers and percentages mean anything, therefore, premodern Tuscany by the weight of population was a child-centered and child-dedicated society. And much more than numbers and percentages will indicate this, as I hope to show.[42] But nothing for the moment illustrates this better than the tendency of many Florentines to take in and raise children who were not their own. Legitimate and illegitimate children shared space together with the children of relatives and servants, as well as with children taken from the streets or foundling hospitals.[43] In their tax statement of 1427, for instance, Tomasso di Francesco Davizzi and his mother, Catelana, declared the presence of Checca in their household, "a girl who Monna Catelana vowed to raise for the love of God since she has neither daddy nor mama to raise her. . . ."[44]

This adoption could be made formal with a notary's drawing up a contract or, more usually, remained informal—that is, arranged privately between families.[45] Despite the arrangements, Florentines saw the act itself as worthy and virtuous, especially since the Romans had used adoption. Alberti urged families that adopted children to treat and consider them as they would their own.[46] And this attitude could be reciprocal. Francesco Datini had considerable affection for the woman who adopted him and she for him; he even told her that he would treat her like his own mother until her dying day. This experience must have had considerable effect upon him since he formally adopted his illegitimate daughter. His wife, Margherita, also accepted her into their household, especially when it became apparent that Margherita could not have any children. She became quite attached to the little girl, and years later at her wedding Margherita, the adoptive mother, performed the fertility rituals usually performed by the natural mother—the placing of a child in the bride's arms and a florin in her shoe.[47] Margherita, like the woman who reared her husband, Francesco, had fallen in love with an adoptive child—her husband's illegitimate daughter.

Friends and family would, at times, let others raise their children. These quasi-adoptive arrangements were usually temporary. Raffaello Sinbaldi recalled that when he was a schoolboy his uncle, who lived at Empoli, asked his father if he could come to stay and live with him, his wife, and his daughters. The reason for this request, he said, was because his family did not have any sons. Raffaello went off for two years. He returned to Florence, but left at age 12 to live again with his uncle and his family, much to their delight he noted. Margherita Datini's sister, Francesca, offered to let Margherita raise one of her four sons, since Margherita had no children of her own. The Datinis eventually took a niece, Tina, into their household. In addition they reared Piero Mazzei, the son of their good friend Lapo Mazzei, from an early age in their home.[48] Nothing seemed unusual about these arrangements to either those offering or those accepting. Many Florentines seemed happy to oblige their less fortunate neighbors and family members when it came to having and rearing children.

Florentines would take in children literally off the streets. Filippo Strozzi wanted his younger brother Matteo (who was 11 years old) to leave home and come with him to Rome to learn the family business. He knew that this would upset their mother, Alessandra, so he suggested to her that she might want to take a poor child into the house and raise it. Others took in waifs too.[49] Bartolomeo Valori recalled in 1452 that he and his future wife Caterina Pazzi had been raised together until the age of twelve.[50] Boccaccio's *Decameron* has a few stories that revolve around the theme of children taken into someone's household to be raised, which highlights that this was a culturally accepted practice.[51] In one of the stories, a soldier searches a house during the sack of Faenza when a two-year-old who had lost her parents saw him and "while he was climbing up the stairs called out 'Father' to him. This aroused his compassion and he took her in."[52] Thus, fiction reflected a reality of Florentine daily life. A typical source for such foster children was, of course, the *Innocenti,* and Florentine couples promised to bring these children up as they would their natural children.[53] Moreover, many of these people provided such children with all sorts of goods and services, such as dowries, even though there was no legal requirement for them to do so.[54] At least here, regarding property, which may be a real and material expression of the sentiment of emotion, they treated them like their natural children.

Some historians have argued that instances of fosterage, like those I describe, indicate how "little importance was attached to actual parentage" in the premodern world.[55] I think, however, these instances indicate more how some premodern people wanted to have many children in the household and how much they wanted to be parents. Many premodern Florentines, especially those from the merchant and ruling elite, wanted to fill their households with children and would do it naturally or artificially. Why, though, would these Florentines want to fill their house with children?

Leon Battista Alberti wrote his *Libri della famiglia* (1434-43) in dialogue form to discuss the pros and cons of family life. His characters described how rearing children could be a negative experience. They noted, for instance, how much anxiety and trouble children caused a father. Florentines recognized these facts of family life.[56] Discussing his siblings and father, Francesco Guicciardini observed that "all things considered, we were more trouble to him than we were solace. Think what must be the plight of those whose children are crazy, evil, or unfortunate." Guicciardini noted a particular problem for Florentine fathers. Children reflected the honor of the family and the father in particular. They were an ornament and credit to the family if good; a blemish and deficit if bad.[57] "Every errant child," according to Lionardo in Alberti, *Libri della famiglia*, "in many ways brings shame on his father."[58] In such an honor-bound society as Florence, a child like this could be a considerable source of anxiety and even a liability for a father.

Another liability for fathers, one certainly recognized by the poor, was that children cost money to have and rear—regardless of one's status or wealth. Sant'Antonino, Archbishop of Florence, 1446-59, warned parents not to have more children than they could support.[59] Nicolò Ammanatini certainly spoke for many when he claimed that the cause of his poverty was "the taxes and babies which we have every year."[60] Lapo Mazzei, though he loved his children immensely, could still note in a letter to Francesco Datini that he had too many—when he wrote this he had eight and feared his wife was pregnant with twins—and it was much trouble keeping them clothed and shod.[61] No wonder St. Joseph became an ever more popular figure in the premodern era. As David Herlihy observed, "Harassed fathers needed a patron, a powerful figure in heaven who knew and understood the difficulties they confronted."[62] And the difficulty of rearing children was real for women as well, since many aspects of childrearing fell to them automatically as head of the domestic sphere. Cristofanno di Giovanni was able to keep his mistress from marrying someone else by telling her that the fellow had children from a previous marriage and that she would have to take care of them. It worked; she did not marry him.[63]

Alberti based his dialogue on the real concerns and observations of Florentine society. But his highlighting of the negative was not necessarily an argument against having children. In typical rhetorical fashion Alberti used his characters as devil's advocates for why Florentines should have children. Alberti betrays this purpose when he has Adovardo admit, "I am ashamed to keep saying all the time that sons are not a pleasure to their father."[64] In the flow of the arguments and counter-arguments he sketched a real picture of Florentine family life and what it meant for parents. Having children and rearing them required hard work, sacrifice, money, and love.

In fact, Alberti tried to present a balanced portrait of family life and childrearing in Florence. Adovardo noted elsewhere that "The older they grow, I won't deny it, the greater the joys your children give you, but also the more griefs."[65] Alberti made a simple statement of fact here: children are a mixed blessing. But it is clear where his sympathies lay. Overall, children were a great joy and pleasure to their parents, a fact reflected as well in many of Boccaccio's descriptions of parents and children in the *Decameron*.[66] Florentine parents were accustomed to use terms of endearment when writing about their children or addressing them, reflecting the great joy and pleasure their children gave them.[67] Alberti pointed out how children were a comfort and even an escape to fathers burdened with civic and business affairs. He remembered how Cato the Elder would interrupt his business affairs to spend time with his children and return refreshed to his daily tasks.[68] Alberti recognized a simple fact: most premodern Florentines had children to enjoy them as children.

Despite what some historians have thought, Alberti and other commentators on the family did not see children first and foremost as heirs. Their reasoning for having children is very complex, and shows that there were a number of motives. For instance, although Alberti's work begins with noting the decline in the number of children in present day Florentine families, his first book begins with discussing the duty and love a father owes his children. In the second book, which is a more explicit and detailed examination as to why parents had children, he noted that they first and foremost "act as pledges and securities of marital love and kindness." He then noted how children serve as heirs but also continue the lineage in general, and the father and his hopes in particular. Yet he also observed how children help their parents, how they are a comfort, and how they "make us happy and give us great joys and satisfactions."[69] The decision to have children, therefore, was a much more complex process for Florentines than just the assurance of inheritance; a family grew numerically, and emotionally, and the love between those members ensured that emotional growth.

On the other hand, in as patriarchal a society as Florence a major reason to have male children was to provide descendants for the family and heirs to the property. Moreover, sons carried the family name into the future. Florentines feared for their lineage's survival, and, considering the demographic disasters of the premodern era, justifiably so. Alberti said it bluntly: "families diminish when men die without heirs."[70] In fact, as Anthony Molho has pointed out, one of the motives—or functions—of marriage, besides reproduction and the legitimation of children, was the creation of a means to convey property from the older generation to the younger. In other words, marriage created a system for the development of legally recognized heirs—that is, legitimate children.[71] But there could be more immediate and personal goals in having children than just the survival of the patriline. Alessandra Strozzi constantly pressured her sons to marry and have children because she wanted descendants not for her husband's lineage so much as for the immediate family she and Filippo had built.[72] Men, however, also saw descendants as a way to perpetuate themselves in particular. At his son's marriage, Giovanni Chellini prayed for various benefits for his son, including children to increase "my house and me."[73] One of the goals of marriage, according to Alberti, was then to literally perpetuate the husband through his children.[74] In a patriarchal society men valued sons over daughters—though not excessively—for this purpose, and we do see some disappointment—though also not excessive—over the birth of girls.[75] These reactions should be expected since the birth of a male heir had so much riding upon it. In addition, the self-interest of Florentines in the survival of their family and fortune promised that parents would do their utmost to guarantee the safe development and survival of the heir.

One way to guarantee an heir was to have many children. This mitigated the effects of the high infant mortality rates of premodern Europe. Florentines of course recognized the premodern demographic threat hanging over their family and fortune, and this may help explain why an extraordinary number of births occurred after passes of the plague through Florence—what Herlihy and Klapisch-Zuber have identified as "baby bubbles" in the demographic record.[76] Sometimes this policy of having a large number of children to offset the cost of premodern mortality and ensure an heir and descendent succeeded too well. Lapo Niccolini and his wife had 13 children, 10 of whom survived to adulthood; Paolo Niccolini had five children by his second wife, all of whom survived.[77] Some Florentine houses could be packed with children, as I noted above.

Other reasons existed to have children; duty, for instance, called people to become parents. According to Matteo Palmieri having children both increased the population and provided citizens for the state.[78] The Florentine Catasti provided exemptions (200 florins in 1427) for each child in an attempt by the state to promote a larger population.[79] Having children was a civic duty. Having children was also a Christian duty. Florentines commonly recognized that a woman who became pregnant "will acquire a soul for our Lord."[80] According to Giovanni Dominici, parents carnally made children in the flesh through procreation and spiritually in the faith through religious education. And because of this, he concluded, "God has committed to you nothing so precious as children whether He has given you one or more." From this stemmed the attitude that children were a loan from God to the parents, and many *ricordanze* writers specifically stated this.[81] Having children also helped parents achieve salvation since children had a duty to pray for their parents' souls after death. Gregorio Dati introduced the section of his *ricordanze* listing his children thus: "I shall record the fruits that his grace will grant us, and may He in His mercy vouchsafe that they be such as to console our souls eternally, amen." Many Florentine sons wrote prayers to God asking for forgiveness for their fathers and mothers in the *ricordanze*. Some noted payments to have prayers said for their mothers' and fathers' souls.[82]

Having children, though, could also be hazardous to a Florentine's spiritual well-being. According to a Florentine confessor's manual, one of the sources of vainglory was having many children and being excessively proud in that fact.[83] Having children, and especially many children, was therefore perceived by Florentines as an accomplishment of sorts, even a source of honor as noted above, especially if they were legitimate.[84] Lionardo in Alberti's *Libri della famiglia* stated that children, "whose character is excellent are proof of the diligence of their father and an honor to him."[85] Lapo Mazzei was told he should love and honor his wife because she had given him so many children. In fact, in their announcements of the death of their wives, writers of *ricordanze* consistently listed the number of children they had borne.

They did the same for their daughters and even daughters-in-law.[86] At his mother's death on 20 June 1522, Piero Bonaccorso noted that one of her accomplishments, or legacies (ristiano doppo lei), were her children including "io Piero."[87] Moreover, in noting the deaths of their male relatives, particularly those of their fathers, writers of *ricordanze* made sure to list the number of children they had had.[88]

This accounting was not just a statement of fact but an evaluation of worth. In addition writers of *ricordanze* also listed who had died "sanza figliuoli." Giovanni Morelli noted that before the death of her husband in 1384 his sister Sandra had one child but "she had no more, neither male nor female."[89] Again, this is more than just a statement of fact, in this instance it is almost an insult, as if these individuals had somehow failed. At times Francesco and Margherita Datini's friends and family criticized them and even made fun of them because they had not had any children together.[90] Having children was a source of accomplishment, and Florentines had pride in their children and in the number of them that they had. Valorino Curianni identified himself as the son of his father, Lapo, and a man who had two children, a boy and a girl, with a wife who was pregnant. No wonder neighborhood gossip networks buzzed with information about who was pregnant and who had given birth.[91] Margherita Datini's friends and relatives constantly communicated news of her impending pregnancies, none of which ever materialized. Despite her desire for children, she never conceived, and this fact exasperated her.[92]

There were many remedies in Florentine society for childless couples like the Datinis and many solutions for those who just wanted to increase their fertility. Some writers prescribed the proper time for intercourse in order to have children. Alberti advised late May, at night, specifically the hour after supper as the best time for procreation.[93] He and others insisted that the woman had to be fully aroused to ensure a successful pregnancy. On the other hand, after the act, the woman was supposed to lie in bed quietly, in complete relaxation, if she wanted children. Neither parent was to be drunk during the sexual act, for this resulted in deformed children or a failed pregnancy. And parents were to have the purest of motives in wanting children. Giovanni Dominici stated that if parents wanted children just to make themselves important or to create legacies, they would fail in the attempt. But if they just wanted to have honest, good children then they would succeed.[94] In his opinion, perhaps, the Datinis may have wanted children for the wrong reasons.

Nevertheless, other means besides tinkering with the sexual act were available for Florentines wanting children. One of the most publicly visible, and therefore perhaps most accepted, was the ritual of a new bride's holding a small child in her arms during her wedding ceremony, just as Datini's illegitimate daughter had done at her wedding. When his son Tommaso married Bartolomea Sacchetti on 2 July 1452, Giovanni Chellini recorded that Gino Capponi's little boy, Tommaso, was placed in her arms during the ceremony. The little boy was four months old at the time. Sometimes the new bride was supposed to kiss the child as part of the ritual. Writers of *ricordanze* noted that this act cost them a small sum paid to the child, or more properly its parents, perhaps more as a memorial rather than for services rendered. On the other hand, since the child had rendered a gift ritually, perhaps it deserved one as a form of ritual reciprocity. Certainly, though, the idea behind this ritual was that close association to the thing desired would lead to its being realized. But the ritual also could become an occasion for display by choosing the small children of important Florentines, and the communal government tried to prevent this in its 1388 sumptuary statutes by prohibiting the ritual.[95]

Many women and men prayed for children; Boccaccio reflected this practice when he had a wife hope, "perhaps God will grant me the grace of becoming pregnant."[96] Most, if not all, Florentine couples prayed for children before going to bed.[97] Others went to sacred sites and prayed for children; a childless couple went to Monte Gargano and prayed to the archangel Michael for a child. He answered their prayers.[98] In particular St. Margaret was a favorite patron saint of childless women who wanted to remedy that condition.[99] Florentine women who wanted to have children visited the picture of the Annunciation at Santissima Annunziata. In Machiavelli's *Mandragola* a character recalled a neighbor's advice that if she heard first mass 40 days in a row at Santissima Annunziata, she would become pregnant. Reverence of and worship before an image of the most important birth announcement in history undoubtedly would help women attain and experience the same joy and glory that Mary had at the announcement of the conception of her child. This must have been a powerful ritual belief since Florentine brides today still leave their wedding bouquets before the painting of the Annunciation at Santissima Annunziata.[100]

Others thought that heavenly powers needed other supernatural aid to ensure pregnancy. Francesca Tecchini, Margherita Datini's sister, told her that many women she knew had become pregnant because they had worn a certain foul-smelling poultice with writing on it made by a certain woman. She told Margherita the poultice cost very little to make and then added that with this and God, the Virgin Mary, and St. John the Baptist she would have a child.[101] Florence in fact was filled with fertility devices. Witches and sorcerers provided women and men with amulets for having children. One Iacopo di Francesco of San Miniato desired "to practice this illegal art of sorcery and magic according to the instructions in these books, and being importuned by a woman, he inscribed certain characters upon a locket . . . and gave it to the woman, instructing her to carry the locket without her husband's knowledge and thus she would become pregnant."[102] Niccolò dell'Ammannato told Francesco Datini that his wife knew of a magic belt that, if placed on a woman by a virgin boy after three repetitions of the Lord's Prayer and the Hail Mary, would ensure pregnancy. But he then added that Margherita Datini would have a better chance of getting pregnant if she fed three beggars on three successive Fridays.[103] Christian and other supernatural beliefs then existed side by side in the popular imagination and even intermingled in the attempts to have children. Figures of the Christ child (the so called *bambini*), which represented all babies and the most important baby at the same time, and even figures of Mary Magdalene served as fertility devices. These could be made of wax, sugar, plaster or wood. Like the ritual of praying before the picture of the Annunciation at Santissima Annunziata, these *bambini* must have been powerful tools for fertility since in Italy today women still receive dolls when they marry.[104]

Florentines, like other premodern Europeans, believed that certain foods aided in fertility; consuming potions made from the mandrake or eating elder leaves supposedly increased fertility. Eating bread stored away on New Year's Day, which in Florence was the day after the Annunciation (25 March), brought fertility. Margherita Datini sent a friend a barrel of Venetian wine, telling her that drinking it would produce boys.[105] While these Christian and other supernatural beliefs could coexist in the popular imagination, the Church sometimes intervened if the results desired appeared too deliberate or seemed to violate (and not just facilitate) the natural order of things. For instance. a Florentine confessor's manual condemned those who ate special substances specifically to have male children.[106]

Some Florentines even believed that just living in Tuscany increased fertility, and some added that these lands were especially propitious for giving birth to males.[107] Sometimes particular places in Tuscany were noted for their ability to increase fertility. According to Buonaccorso Pitti:

> On 5 January [1406], my brother Bartolomeo and I brought our wives to Bagni di Pateriolo. Bartolomeo's wife, Lisa, had been ill for a long time and the doctors, being unable to diagnose her illness, had advised her to take the baths. She was cured, returned to Florence and shortly thereafter became pregnant with her first son, for her nine previous children were girls. It therefore seemed to us that those waters had good properties and I note the fact here.[108]

Florentines in general thought that baths in particular had special powers to increase fertility, since the belief appears elsewhere in popular literature.[109]

Most if not all of these attempts to encourage or increase fertility were directed at or involved women—the wife or the mother-to-be. Rarely did popular belief single out the male as being solely responsible for increasing fertility as it did women. Rarely did men have to participate in the various activities and rituals to encourage or increase fertility. Women—not men—had to visit sacred or propitious places; women had to possess "holy dolls;" women had to participate in rituals at their marriage to ensure fertility. Not men. This is an interesting gender bias; despite the fact that children were born to men, as the writers of *ricordanze* would have it, it seems that Florentine culture placed responsibility for conceiving them predominately on women. And in this patriarchal society, where so much depended on the presence of a male heir, this must have been both an awesome and burdensome responsibility to have.

Remembering his son Alberto, Giovanni Morelli recalled "when, the hour, and the instant and the place and how he was generated by me; how much consolation he was to me and his mother; then his movements in his mother's stomach which I diligently sought out with my hand, awaiting his birth with the greatest desire."[110] Like Morelli, many Florentines knew something of the physiology of conception and pregnancy. They knew, for instance, that pregnant women had cravings. Cellini referred to "those strange longings which are so powerful in pregnant women."[111] They recognized morning sickness for what it was, and knew that pregnant women tired more easily than those who were not pregnant. Medical belief held that menstrual blood nourished the fetus (an Aristotelian idea), which explained why pregnant women did not menstruate.[112]

Blood was essential for conception, as Dante explained, relying upon scholastic authors such as Aquinas. In fact in *The Purgatorio* he popularized the scholastic view of conception, giving average Florentines a description of "nascimento nostro," as Antonio Pucci called it.[113] A substance called `perfect blood' that resided in the male's heart possessed the formative power for all human organs. This substance changed into sperm in the heart and passed to the sexual organs—"that place the better left unmentioned," according to Dante. Through the sexual act the perfect blood mingled with the female's blood in the uterus. This combination "has now become a soul/like that of a plant, but with the difference/that this begins where that achieves its goal." Conception had occurred. Dante noted further stages. The fetus began to move, to quicken (the movement that Morelli recalled), and to develop sensory powers. Limbs developed next, "as nature's plan commands." Just as the body was developing so was the soul. At conception the soul was like that of a plant, meaning it lived. As the body developed sensory powers, the soul did as well. Body and soul developed in tandem. Once the fetus' brain developed, "the First Mover turns to it./ And there, rejoicing at such art in nature,/ breathes into it a new and powerful spirit." The soul had gained human reasoning. While not a physiologically accurate description, Dante gave Florentines a description that was plausible and that conformed to scholastic doctrine.[114]

On the other hand, there was much about pregnancy that baffled Florentines, especially the men. A common element in both literature and other records is how easy it was for women to initially conceal their pregnancies if they so chose. And men were usually the ones fooled here. A Monna Francesca, who was four months pregnant, married one Cecco Arrighi, who was not the baby's father. When he questioned her about her swollen stomach, she replied that she had stomach cramps, which caused the swelling. Cecco believed her.[115] Bernardo Machiavelli's wife, however, suspected their servant girl of being pregnant because of "certain signs." She was right. On the other hand some women were able to fake pregnancy; moreover many did this not so much to snare a husband but, as they were married, to quiet the carping of neighbors, friends, and relatives—all of whom thought that it was about time for them to have children and wanted to know when they would give birth.[116] As mentioned above, not only did Florence teem with children, but it also buzzed with gossip about having them.

In Florentine society then, at least for the merchant elite, not only were children the inheritors of property and guardians of the family name and honor, they were also the recipients of their parents' emotional investments, the "focus of all a man's hopes and desires," as Alberti noted.[117] Having a child and rearing it properly conferred a positive status on men and women from the merchant elite in Florentine society. Many of these Florentines saw great personal satisfaction in the simple fact of being parents. Being perceived as sterile or dying without children conferred a negative image on men and women from the merchant elite in Florentine society. For many this was such an odious thing that they resorted to all sorts of devices to improve upon nature and God's will. Some even lied about having children. Margherita Datini has wandered through the pages of this chapter, as she did Tuscany, childless. Francesco too has suffered in these pages, as he did in real life, without having a child from her. Iris Origo identified their childlessness as the root of the considerable tension that filled their marriage. Somehow their family life was incomplete. Florentines knew that children formed an essential part of the Florentine family—one leg of the triad as it were. Florentine family life was inconceivable without them:

> LIONARDO: What do you mean by family?
>
> GIANNOZZO: Children, wife, and other members of the household, both relatives and servants.
>
> LIONARDO: I understand.[118]

Per La Grazia Di Dio Partori Uno Babino: The Birth Process

A FLORENTINE COUPLE had been trying to have a child for 18 years when much to their surprise and joy the wife became pregnant. But she miscarried, losing twin boys. Right after this she became pregnant again and delivered a little girl, whom they named Cosa, in honor of the father's mother. Two years after the birth of Cosa the wife again became pregnant, and from all indications (she had the same cravings as before) everyone thought she would have another girl. The couple had already picked a name, Reparata, in honor of the mother's mother. This birth was special, however, so special that years later the child, relying for the most part on the family's oral tradition, could describe it in some detail:

The child was born during the night after All Saints' Day, at exactly half past four, in the year 1500. The midwife knew that they were expecting a girl and as soon as she had washed the baby she wrapped it up in some fine white linen and then she came up very, very, softly to my father and said: "I've brought you a wonderful present—and one you didn't expect."

My father was a true philosopher; he had been pacing the room and when the midwife came to him he said: "Whatever God gives is dear to me." Then drawing back the swaddling clothes, he saw with his own eyes the son that no one had expected. He clasped his old hands together, and with them lifted his eyes up to heaven, and said: "Lord, I thank You with all my heart. This is a great gift, and he is very welcome." Everyone there began talking happily and asking him what he was going to call the boy. But Giovanni kept on repeating: "He is Welcome [Benvenuto]." So that was the name they decided on. I was baptized with it, and by the grace of God I carry it to this day.[1]

Thus Benvenuto Cellini characteristically announced his entrance into the world. But this familiar passage does much more than introduce the reader to the subject of Cellini's autobiography. It provides some details—brief but glittering—about the process of birth in premodern Florence. We find expectant parents, a birth assistant, an audience (presumably family and friends) to comfort and witness, a description of infant care after the birth (wash and swaddle), presentation to the head of the household, and naming. Giovanni Cellini's pride and joyful surprise at the birth of his first son is apparent. The audience too was pleased. Twenty-one years was a considerable length of time to wait for the arrival of the heir. Giovanni's behavior is almost a caricature of the expectant father. The midwife found him outside the room where the birth occurred, pacing. He seemed to go into shock on seeing his son, thanking God and repeating over and over again the same short phrase. He was stunned, pleasantly to be sure, but stunned nevertheless. Birth for premodern Florentine parents was a momentous occasion.[2]

    This momentous occasion occurred at home for the most part, but not necessarily one's own. Lapo da Castiglionchio recorded that his first two sons were born in the house of Bernardo di Bernardo, his brother-in-law.[3] Choosing to have a child away from one's own home might represent nothing more than a family's not possessing a fixed domicile or the exigencies of the moment. Yet having a child in someone's house—because of the familial as well as the ritual significance of birth—could also be a way to demonstrate as well as reinforce ties of kinship or friendship. A careful check through the *ricordanze* looking for birth location could show the webs of friendship a Florentine possessed. And that is one reason the writers of *ricordanze* included the birth location in their description of the birth. They wanted their descendants to know who their allies were—and this was perhaps a little reminder for themselves as well.

Alberti, however, in his tract on the family advised parents to have the child born at home, and by this he meant the father's house.[4] Florentines for the most part followed this advice: many of the writers of *ricordanze* recorded the birth location simply but proudly as "in mia casa."[5] Sometimes though, achieving this could be a long time coming. Giovanni Morelli noted that finally, for his seventh child, his fifth boy, Iacopo, that "this one was the first of them born in my house in the district [*borgo*] of Santa Croce."[6]

Sometimes for these urban Florentines of the merchant and ruling class the birth of their children occurred at their country estates. In fact, the family would often plan for this. One of Boccaccio's stories reflects that; Niccoluccio's wife, "because she was pregnant, had gone to stay at one of his estates about three miles outside the city."[7] A country birth possessed a bucolic mystique about it, and probably was a little less hectic for all involved, being away from the hustle and bustle—and heat (if it were summer)—of Florence. But even in this circumstance, proximity to Florence was still important. For one thing, it made the journey out for the mother less rigorous. Moreover, the parents were close enough to the city to enjoy the benefit of family and friends during the birth as well as contact with a most important religious ritual site—the baptistery at San Giovanni. Bartolomeo Sassetti recorded the birth of his son, Lorenzo, on 10 August 1462 at his villa. But this place was close enough to Florence that he was baptized on 12 August "in firenze in san giovanni."[8]

The place parents chose to have their children also could bind them to larger associations, such as the lineage or *consorzerie*. The birth of Marco Parenti's first son, Piero, occurred in the Mugello near the village of Aronta at a relative's house—the Parenti family's ancestral home.[9] While Marco's family had arrived at this place to escape the plague, having a birth there helped seal a bond between the generations in the Parenti lineage. Past and present, through births under the same roof, maybe in the same room, were closer. Certainly for Parenti and his wife, participating in this biological experience in the same place other Parentis had given birth forged a tie to the lineage.[10] In 1380 Niccolò Baldovinetti noted that his wife gave birth to their son,

Santi, in the tower at Chalicharea.[11] Perhaps this action represents recognition of a once significant tower association or the existence of a later version of a *consorzeria*.[12]

Historians do not know much about the activities inside the room in which birth occurred, since the male writers of *ricordanze* were kept outside. Renaissance paintings depicting the birth of the Virgin or of St. John commonly place the expectant father outside the room in which the birth had occurred. Domenico Beccafumi's *Birth of the Virgin* (1540-43) shows the father seen through a doorway sitting head in hands waiting for news of the birth of his child. In some cases fathers were even absent from the home. This last piece of information is not so astounding since the Florentine elite was fairly mobile. Merchants and diplomats were frequently absent, and family affairs went on without them. In 1503 Machiavelli missed the birth of his first son because he was on a mission to Rome for the Signoria. He was also away from home during the early part of his son Totto's life. One writer of *ricordanze* missed the birth of his daughter Cassandra because he was taking the waters for his own health.[13] He did, however, return in time for her baptism two days later.

Yet, the sense from these *ricordanze* is that for the most part fathers were present for the birth. Their preciseness in recording the exact time of their child's birth—sometimes to the half-hour—certainly implies that they were close enough at hand to note the time of birth. In fact, most of their birth entries were written right after the event. Moreover, historians know that elsewhere in the premodern world husbands were present throughout the birth process, and one German village, Wallis, even required them to be there.[14]

But being present did not mean that they were entirely privy to what went on inside the birth sanctuary. In fact, some elite Florentine homes had separate bedrooms for husband and wife where either could retire from the rest of the household on account of illness, or, in the mother's case, pregnancy and delivery.[15] Most of them, like Cellini's father, probably spent the time waiting outside. Benedetta Carlini was born in a difficult birth. So much so that at one point the midwife came out and told her father that both mother and daughter were in peril. At that point he fell to his knees praying for God to spare their lives.[16] What is important here is first that he was outside the room and had to be told of the poor progress of the birth. But he was not just an idle bystander; he was also performing a function. He sought divine aid for the birth: for premodern Florentines prayer in times of peril was essential and helpful. Also by sitting outside he could represent the family to other visitors, both kin and friends. Sebastiano del Piombo's *Birth of the Virgin* (1525) illustrates this by showing the father outside the room shaking a well-wisher's hand. This fellow clasps the father's shoulder as well.

Premodern birth at home could be a hectic affair, with servants running hither and yon fetching things, with the wife's and husband's friends and relatives circulating about, and with people arriving to assist in the delivery. In fact, there was a special cohort of birth professionals present at births—midwives, *guardadonne,* and doctors. These people were expected.[17]

Midwives were the most visible people there, since they were in charge of the birth. Bartolomaeus Anglicus had mentioned that a midwife was "a woman who knows the art of soothing a woman in labor, so that she can give birth more easily and the child will not incur any danger at the moment of birth."[18] She was simply the woman who delivered (literally lifted) children, "che leva i fanciulli" as the Tuscan idiom indicates, hence her title "levatrice."[19] Piombo's *Birth of Adonis* (early sixteenth century) shows the infant coming out of a tree headfirst into the waiting hands of a nymph—she is lifting him out.

The process by which one became a midwife is unclear. Certainly, there was no formal training, and a woman may have just fallen into to it by accident or luck of the draw. In 1272 the young Margaret of Cortona became a servant to the patrician Moscani family. For some reason, she began to assist at the births of Cortona's patricians and eventually became much in demand among them as the midwife to have. They rewarded her not only monetarily but spiritually by having her stand as godmother to the children she had delivered. Moreover, she could always count on taking meals with her patient's family during the birth.[20]

In medieval England, medical advice books stated that it was the mother's duty to hire the midwife.[21] On 26 May 1490, Tribaldo dei Rossi recorded that his wife, Nanina, paid the midwife two lire and two soldi for delivering their child three days before.[22] In Florence men also did this. Bernardo Machiavelli and his male relatives and friends had to find someone to take care of his pregnant servant girl. They decided to place her with a midwife. They made the arrangements with her and promised to pay her five lire a month until the birth occurred. To secure her services one of them gave her "fiorino uno largo" (a gold florin worth about 6.5 lire).[23] The next day Bernardo packed the pregnant servant girl off to the midwife's house. These men knew exactly where the midwife lived and how to strike a deal with her. So, when the time came Florentines—male or female—knew where and how to contact a midwife.[24]

Previous service that had been satisfactory could ensure a repeat performance for a midwife. Matteo Strozzi recorded that his son Piero and his daughter Andruola had the same midwife. For Piero's delivery he paid her two lire, for Andruola's he paid her two lire, fifteen soldi. In fact, for Piero's birth, Matteo was specific enough to note that while the delivery itself cost him two lire, the entire confinement of his wife cost him ten lire.[25] Niccolò Strozzi on 17 April 1478 paid one lira to the midwife of his daughter Maria. Filippo Strozzi paid the midwife who attended his sister at the birth of a still-born child one lira, seven soldi, six denari.[26] Payment then for the services of a midwife varied. And more than one midwife could be employed at a time, especially for a difficult birth. In telling of the birth of a deformed child (in his words, a monster) at Volterra Luca Landucci mentioned that the midwives present had been terrified by the birth.[27] And midwives could be busy. Merry Wiesner has noted for premodern Nuremburg that some midwives participated in three to five births a week.[28] No doubt, a competent and successful midwife in Florence—considering how prolific the merchant elite were—could make a viable living at this.

Aside from the delivery itself, midwives could and did do other things associated with the birth. As we saw in the description of Benedetta Carlini's difficult birth, the midwife could be the first person to convey bad news to the father. As we saw in the description of Cellini's birth, the midwife also could be the first person to convey good news to the father. Undoubtedly for an expectant father the appearance of the midwife next to him at any point in the birthing process could provoke all sorts of emotions ranging from fear to expectant joy. Midwives too might perform a more heart-rending task.

Agostino Capponi sent the twin daughters of his slave girl, Polonia, to the Innocenti, but the midwife was the one who took them there.[29] Because midwives were so intimately associated with birth, they were often called upon to treat newborns and mothers who had just given birth if and when they became ill.[30]

The midwife was not the only professional at a birth. Another woman helped at the birth—the *guardadonna*, whose duties or role are not quite as clear as the midwife's even though she too was a paid specialist. From her title she must have been present specifically for the mother's benefit.[31] She is simply the woman who "looks after" the mother during birth as these writers of *ricordanze* noted about their wives: "monna Gemma guardava la Caterina in parto"[32] or "Monna Maria ghuarda donna che . . . ghuardano la fiametta nel parto."[33] Her role seems to have been similar to that of the lying-in nurse that the English aristocracy hired in the eighteenth century, whose duty it was to ease the mother's travail, give medicine, and help the doctor during birth.[34] Apparently some in Florence aided the midwife, since writers of *ricordanze* noted that *guardadonne* at times helped deliver children. And both midwives and *guardadonne* were mentioned in the same records as having been present for the same births.[35]

Expenses for the services of *guardadonne* varied too. Manno Petrucci paid his wife's *guardadonna* two lire and four soldi; Filippo Strozzi paid his wife's *guardadonna* one lira, seven soldi, four denari; Matteo Strozzi waited a little more than a month to pay his wife's *guardadonna* four lire.[36] In this case, because of the high sum paid, the *guardadonna* may have been retained for some time after the birth to help the mother recover.

It is difficult to define precisely the role of these *guardadonne*. In fact, they may have acted more like servants than birth professionals such as midwives. Paintings of birth from the Renaissance consistently show the scene of the mother in bed being tended to and cleaned (or cooled down?) after the birth by a woman, who is either a servant or perhaps the *guardadonne*. On 31 July 1478, Bernardo Machiavelli recorded that the sister of two of his sharecroppers was employed in his house as a servant specifically to tend to his wife and children. He also noted that she had been in the household since the first of the month when she had originally functioned as a *guardadonna*.[37] What-

ever the *guardadonne* did in relation to the midwife, they seemed to
have been paid about the same amount for their services. Niccolò
Strozzi paid the midwife five lire and five soldi for his son Carlo's birth
in 1471. The *guardadonna* received the same amount.[38]

Although they did this infrequently, physicians attended births.
Cellini noted that his mother "had a miscarriage because of the
doctor's bungling, and she lost twin boys."[39] In August 1476, Filippo
Strozzi noted that a physician (*medico*) saved his wife's life when she
gave birth.[40] Giovanni Corsini tells us that the doctors (*i medici*) who
attended his wife during the birth in which she died in 1409
considered that a fall down some stairs some days before was the
reason why she died.[41] In the cases in which a physician was called,
either the child, the mother or both died or were in grave peril.
Perhaps the doctor was the birth professional of last resort, used only
when things were going badly during the birth process. In Germany it
was only in the late sixteenth century that doctors began to be called
to births. Perhaps the frequency of their appearance at births in
premodern Florence reflects simply the large number of physicians
available in the Florentine population relative to other premodern
populations.[42]

Aside from the birth professionals, other people could attend and
assist at births. Boccaccio tells a story of how a lover, one Messer
Gentile, arranged the lying-in for his beloved: "she felt the time for her
childbirth had arrived; and so, assisted tenderly by Messer Gentile's
mother, not long afterward she gave birth to a handsome male
child."[43] Servants too could aid in birth, not only for their own
mistress, but for others. Bernardo Strozzi, for instance, sent his servant
girl to at least six different women to help them in their childbirth.[44]
Perhaps like Margaret of Cortona she later became a midwife; or
maybe she became a *guardadonna*.

Things could be hectic with the comings and goings of so many
people—so hectic that someone could use this time to escape the
master's eye. When Bernardo Machiavelli's wife was in labor their
servant girl used her masters' distraction and preoccupation to go to
a neighbor's house to consort with her lover.[45] With everything else
going on around her, she must have thought her absence might not
be noticed. Renaissance birth paintings of the Virgin or John the

Baptist, where there was not such a record of who was in attendance as at Christ's birth, all show swarms of people around the mother. While these paintings depict the time just after the child has been born, they certainly hint at the hustle and bustle that was present during labor. Mariotto Alberighi noted that the men who stood as godfathers for his daughter, Maria, had been present for the birth, undoubtedly a circle of friends to keep him company through his wife's labor and celebrate in his joy.[46]

In a letter to Francesco Datini on 7 November 1388, a Saturday, Niccolò del Ammannato hinted at the hustle and bustle of birth as well as something that was probably foremost in everybody's mind—the pain of childbirth. He told him that six women had been attending his (Francesco's) maid, who had been in labor since Tuesday. Her pain was so great that she had to be held down to keep from killing herself. He and everyone else in the household were terribly saddened by her predicament, especially since they thought the child had died inside her.[47] Bartholomaeus Anglicus had noted that birth for young girls took longer and was more dangerous because their limbs were stiff, by which he meant the birth canal, womb, and peritoneum had never been stretched out before. He also noted that the delivery of the afterbirth as well was particularly painful for women.[48] Even uncomplicated labors could be prolonged. Ser Antonio Bartolomei in 1470 noted that his wife's labor lasted from the morning of 13 January to the evening of 14 January. She delivered a healthy baby boy.[49]

Boccaccio was observant enough to note the pain of childbirth in one of his stories: "The time was near for the girl to give birth, and she was screaming as women usually do at these times." By saying that screaming was usual, Boccaccio illustrates a commonplace of premodern life. In another of his stories Calandrino, convinced by some wags that he is pregnant, wailed: "When women are about to give birth, I've heard them make such a racket, and even with the large thing they have to do it with." He is convinced that he will die in birth from the pain.[50] One can imagine then the helplessness a husband could feel knowing that in the next room his wife was suffering and could even die of the process. With Florence's narrow streets and the prolific merchant elite, passersby as well could feel pathos for the travail the mother was going through—mothers would be reminded of their own labor; men would be reminded of something they were not really privy too, and perhaps were glad not to be. Nevertheless, the sounds of women in childbirth were part of the normal cacophony that made up the premodern city of Florence. A French poem perhaps summarized the feelings of Florentine women about labor—a woman during childbirth will curse her own birth and wonder why she did not abort.[51] Considering the pain and exertion attendant upon birth, this was probably not an unusual feeling.

No wonder Florentines sought divine aid for women in birth. Piero Masi noted that the birth of his siblings was always accomplished with the grace of God. His brother Bartolomeo recorded the same aid for other births.[52] Divine aid was sought by other means too. The legend of St. Margaret was read aloud to women in childbirth, especially if the labor was difficult. At times the copy would even be placed on the woman's stomach. In these instances the book itself served as medicine and the telling of the legend would help the mother identify with St. Margaret (who had been swallowed by a dragon but emerged later unharmed, as one hoped the child would) and thereby concentrate on her own body during labor. This would effect a "talking cure" in a Lévi-Strauss sense in which a ritual communicates with a patient and hence helps her.[53]

There were other aids for premodern birth. A German treatise of 1513 on midwifery described a special birthing chair, which the author noted was very popular in Italy.[54] As late as the nineteenth century in England wine was still used to ease a mother's labor. In fact she shared it with her friends who were attending her.[55] In many of the birth paintings of the Renaissance, wine is always shown being brought to the new mother.

Surrounded by friends, relatives, and the guardadonna, and under the midwife's direction, the mother delivered a child. The guardadonna helped the mother here, soothing and encouraging her. According to Bartholomaeus Anglicus, when necessary the midwife applied unguents and bandages to the stomach to soothe the womb during contractions and labor. And at the moment of birth itself, "She takes the newborn child out of the uterus by surrounding its umbilical cord with four fingers."[56] Most likely this means that she cut the cord some four fingers from the infant's navel or that she tied it off between the infant and the mother with four fingers separating the two knots.

After the delivery, the birth professionals had other duties. According to Bartholomaeus Anglicus, the midwife was to wash away the blood, to soothe the child with salt and honey on its limbs, and then to cover the child.[57] At times at the Innocenti they received virtual newborns, and what they did for them reflects what midwives did as well for regular births: "We did everything to warm her head and dry out all her parts. We had her umbilical cord tied and we washed away all the blood with warm white wine."[58] A prominent feature of Renaissance birth paintings is a round basin in which the child is to be washed, and these paintings usually show this activity: the child is either about to be bathed, is being bathed, or has just been bathed. As we noted above, Cellini's midwife had washed and wrapped him before taking him to the father. Giotto's *Birth of the Virgin* (1305-06) shows a woman cleaning the infant's eyes with a cloth. Carpaccio's *Birth of the Virgin* (1504-08) shows in the background a woman standing before a fire warming a cloth. In fact, all these pictures depict an abundance of cloth present at the birth for washing, swaddling, and cleaning. An anonymous *Birth of St. John the Baptist* (fourteenth century) shows him partially swaddled with one of the women offering him a little trinket. If these paintings are any reflection of reality, a considerable amount of care and attention was given to the new arrival.

Certain oddities could be noticeable in a birth. In one of his stories Boccaccio acknowledged the existence of birthmarks. By chance a young fellow was recognized by his long-lost father because he had on him "a large bright red birthmark on his chest, not painted on but rather implanted naturally upon the skin, the kind women there would call 'roses.'"[59] This type of marking seems to have been common enough in premodern Florence or at least noticed enough in the popular mentality to be identified with an idiomatic expression. Other biological quirks as well could call attention to themselves. Bernardo Strozzi either witnessed or more likely was told that when his daughter, Antonia, was born, her amniotic sack had not yet burst. As he put it, she was born "dressed."[60] In other parts of Italy being born with the caul carried with it ritual import—those who had it were seen as different, special, even magical. They would keep the dried caul as an amulet or magical charm.[61] Christiane Klapisch-Zuber has noted how these people could be identified by the specific name of Santi or Santa.[62] Antonia's second name was Santa. Despite all the popular beliefs surrounding one born so, Bernardo never mentioned this facet of Antonia's birth again in his *ricordanze*. Perhaps there was no need to do so since because of her name all in Florence would realize her significance—or the special circumstances of her birth—just from her name.

After the child had been delivered it was time to comfort and congratulate the mother. Here is where Renaissance birth paintings give us a bit of colorful exactitude since this was the moment of depiction—after the fact. These paintings do portray an understandable lack of men.[63] Women surround the infant, women tend to the mother, women come to visit the mother and infant. Men, if they are depicted, are outside the room. As Madelaine Jeay has noted, during premodern childbirth a wife escapeed from her husband. Adrian Wilson has expanded on this to argue convincingly that the absence of men at birth meant that women not only were in control of the birth process but that they actually created its social process as well.[64] The Florentine evidence supports that proposition. Giovanni da Milano's *Birth of the Virgin* (1365) shows the mother in bed being cleaned—or cooled down—by other women after the birth. In Domenico Ghirlandaio's *Birth of St. John the Baptist* (ca. 1485) the mother is in bed while a servant brings her wine on a platter. Uccelo's *Birth of the Virgin* (1436) shows a servant hurrying down the stairs carrying a plate on which there is a chicken wing for the mother. Cimabue's mosaic *Birth of the Virgin* (1291) also shows a woman serving the mother food, consisting of cookies (what looks like *lingue di gatti*) and a chicken in a bowl. Iacopo Ottavanti recorded what he provided for the mother of his brother's illegitimate son. After the birth she was to have four eggs a day, biscuits and jam—and capons.[65]

Birth, as we have seen above could, be a hazardous affair—for either the mother or the child. David Herlihy and Christiane Klapisch-Zuber have noted from the Florentine Books of the Dead that about 20 percent of all female deaths were attributed to the rigors of childbirth. For the years 1424-25 and 1430 these books record 52 women having died in childbirth. This works out to about 17 per year for a total of 14.4 mothers' deaths for every 1000 births.[66] In a study of Nuremberg midwives, Merry Wiesner noted that they were advised to let women rest three to six weeks after the birth to recover from the rigors of birth. Two of the largest causes of death that were attributed to the midwives came from infection (puerperal fever), probably from the midwives' unclean hands, and puncture of internal organs due to the clumsy handling of instruments. Alberti too recognized that a mother needed rest after the birth, and she should not go out "until her health is fully restored and all her limbs have fully regained their strength." The English upper class was cognizant of the real dangers associated with birth in the premodern era. Moreover, apparently even the artisan class recognized these. Nehemiah Wallington, a London lathe worker, was especially concerned that birth could and did put his wife's and his child's life in danger. Ser Bartolomeo Dei, a Florentine notary temporarily in Milan in 1489, was kept apprised of the progress of his daughter's (or daughter-in-law's?) pregnancy and delivery in a series of letters. The family expressed some concern for her health since her legs had been badly swollen throughout the pregnancy. And it was only after the birth that the letter writer informed Dei that he had downplayed the seriousness of her condition to ease his friend's mind.[67] The perils of childbirth may explain why slave girls who were pregnant or became pregnant lost value relative to non-pregnant slave girls.[68]

Multiple births—usually twins—were potentially hazardous, especially since there was no sure way for premodern Florentines to predict them, and their arrival could take birth professionals as well as family members by surprise. Boccaccio noted this type of surprise in one of his stories. He described a countess who "became pregnant with two children as was clear when the time for her delivery arrived."[69] In 1505, Cristofano Guidini recorded the birth of twin sons. And he used a descriptive idiomatic expression common in Tuscany—his wife delivered two sons born from one body ("ebbi due figliuoli maschi, nati a uno corpo").[70] Boccaccio used much the same idiom when he described elsewhere that someone delivered two children "born in the same childbirth" ["a un medesimo parto nate"].[71] Writers of *ricordanze* observed how sometimes after the birth of one child, sometimes hours afterwards, another child came. Usually these later children were born dead.[72]

Twins meant other dangers too. They were more susceptible to premature birth than single births were. Cellini, as we saw above, noted the death of twin siblings who were premature.[73] In 1505, at the birth of twins, Giovanni Buongirolami observed that they appeared to be only seven to eight months old. Both subsequently died, one at three weeks, the other at fifteen months.[74] Bartolomeo Salvetti recorded the birth of twins to his wife on 4 November 1484. The first, a girl, was either stillborn or died very soon after the birth for he noted that God immediately took her back to himself. Moreover, he arranged to have her baptized inside the house. The second child out of the womb was a boy. Most likely under the influence of the rapid death of his infant daughter, he wrote in his *ricordanze*, beseeching God to give the little boy a long life and holiness and sanctity of both body and soul for his [the father's] sake. He also asked that God let him get the little boy properly baptized.[75]

Single births could be premature as well. Giovanni Morelli recalled the birth of his second son: "He was seven months old, and because he was very small and malformed we believed that he would not live so we baptized him at the middle of the day at San Giovanni."[76] He surprised them by living 20 years. Morelli and his wife obviously miscounted the months as well, since a child born two-months prematurely would hardly have been viable in the premodern world.

Writers of *ricordanze* also recorded stillbirths. They were common enough that the Florentine books of the dead carried a separate category for these children.[77] The Florentine physician Antonio Benivieni, in a treatise published in 1507, *De abditiis non nullis ac mirandis morborum et sanationum causis Florentiae*, gave an obstetrical description of how one was to extract a dead fetus or infant from a womb. This was not only a Florentine problem in the premodern world. German and English handbooks for midwives described the grisly procedure as well.[78] Before physicians or midwives attempted this extraction, they could administer some sort of anesthesia or soporific (elixir of sage was said to be one such medicine) to the mother. A sixteenth-century handbook of prescriptions has one to be given to women who have a dead fetus or child inside. After it was administered, the corpse was to be extracted.[79]

While this procedure was perhaps fatal for the mother, it was certainly galling emotionally for the father and the other family members:

> November 5, 1445. I record that my wife Lucrezia, from whom I have eleven children alive today, died this day, Friday evening, two and one-half hours after sunset. This has caused me as much grief as though I were dying, for we have lived together for twenty years, one month, and eleven days. I pray to God most fervently that he pardon her. She died from the effects of labor; she delivered a boy said to have died inside the womb. And yet, because others said it had breathed, it was baptized at home and given the name Giovanni. We buried it in the church of S. Simone in the church yard.
>
> The loss of this woman was a grievous blow; she was mourned by the entire populace of Florence. She was a good woman, sweet-tempered and well mannered, and was loved by everyone who knew her. I believe that her soul has gone to sit at the feet of God's servants. For she bore her final sufferings with patience and humility. She lay ill for two weeks after delivering the child, whom God through his great mercy accepted among his angels.[80]

Six months later Luca da Panzano arranged for 30 masses of St. Gregory to be said on 30 consecutive mornings for the salvation of his wife's soul. He also arranged for two candles to be lit for her during the masses.[81]

Other mishaps could occur at birth. Because of the low level of prenatal care in the premodern world, even for the elite, the most frequent of these were miscarriages.[82] Gregorio Dati witnessed a number of miscarriages, one of which killed his first wife, Bandecca:

> My beloved wife, Bandecca, went to Paradise after a nine-month illness started by a miscarriage in the fifth month of pregnancy. It was eleven o'clock at night on Friday, 15 July 1390, when she peacefully returned her soul to her Creator in Buonaccorso Berardi's house. The next day I had her buried in S. Brancazio; she had received the last sacraments.

At the third hour of Thursday, 19 March 1405, Ginevra gave birth to a female child of less than seven months. She had not realized she was pregnant, since for four months she had been ailing as though she were not, and in the end she was unable to hold it.

Caterina, my fourth wife, miscarried after four months and the child did not live long enough to receive baptism. That was in August 1421.[83]

His and Ginevra's next child was described as "a fine full-term baby girl."[84]

Writers of *ricordanze* recorded birth defects as well. Otto Niccolini, the son of Lapo Niccolini, was born on 26 December 1410 without a left hand. Luca Landucci filled his diary with accounts of deformed children. In 1474 a friend sent his family a letter describing what he saw as a monstrous birth:

> there had been born in Volterra a boy (that is a monster [*cioe` un mostruo*]) which had the head of a bull, and three teeth, with a lump of skin on the head like a horn, and the top of the head was open like a pomegranate with fiery rays coming out. Its arms were all hairy, and its feet were like a lion's with lion's claws. Its body was of the nature of that of a female of the human race, but its legs down to its feet were those of a bull like the head.

While this description is certainly fanciful—even mythological—there may be a basis of fact here. Certainly something happened at this birth; something was not right. As the letter-writer noted, "The midwives and the other women half died of fright."[85] The description of the top of the head may describe an anacephalic child, one born without the top of the head or most of the brain with only the brain stem functioning to sustain life at a very low level. The writer also told the Landuccis that the child died almost immediately, and the mother died four days after the birth. Elsewhere in his diary, Landucci recorded the birth of children with cleft palates and the existence of Siamese twins, some of whom he saw as young children.[86]

Morelli mentioned a different form of birth defect—hydrocephalism. His brother Morello had a daughter, Bartolomea, born with a swelling of the head ("e nacque costei con uno infiato nel capo"). They took her to a physician, one Master Francsco, where he proceeded to lance the swelling in numerous places. Both blood and pus (fluid) came out, and the child died in a few days. Morello had another daughter born right after this, Antonia, who had the same condition. This time the Morelli brothers did not make the same mistake and take her to Maestro Francesco. They wrapped the infant's head in a turban to keep it warm and the swelling went down and she was better. She lived seven years before dying of the plague, though Morelli made no mention whether the girl had suffered any form of mental retardation.[87] Medieval doctors discussed hydrocephalism in their treatments of infant and childhood diseases.[88] Maestro Guglielmo da Piacenza, a fifteenth-century Florentine surgeon, addressed this condition in his treatise *La Cirugia,* under the rubric "Concerning water remaining on the head of new-born infants." In this section he only offered reasons for the existence of this condition.[89] From the title of his work, however, there is little doubt that his solution to the problem was the same as Maestro Francesco's.

Premodern birth was deadly and fraught with peril, and Florentines realized that. Paradoxically birth could mean premature death for either the mother or child, or for both.[90] We saw the despair Benedetto Carlini's father exhibited when the midwife came out in the process of his daughter's birth and told him that both mother and child might die. Clearly at that moment his world or at least the domestic part of it was about to perish. We also saw how Francesco Datini's maid had a prolonged pregnancy with the result being a dead infant inside her.

Gregorio Dati noted that "At eleven o'clock on Friday, 24 April 1416, Ginevra gave birth to a baby girl after a painful and almost fatal labor." She was lucky here, but not so lucky in 1420:

After that it was God's will to recall to Himself the blessed soul of my wife Ginevra. She died in childbirth after lengthy suffering, which she bore with remarkable strength and patience. She was perfectly lucid at the time of her death when she received all the sacraments: confession, communion, extreme unction, and a papal indulgence granting absolution for all her sins, which she received from Master Lionardo [Gregorio's brother, who must have been in attendance at the birth], who had been granted it by the Pope. It comforted her greatly, and she returned her soul to her Creator on 7 September, the Eve of the Feast of Our Lady, at nones: the hour when Our Blessed Lord Jesus Christ expired on the cross and yielded up his spirit to our Heavenly Father. On Friday the 8th she was honorably buried and on the 9th, masses were said for her soul. Her body lies in our plot at S. Spirito and her soul has gone to eternal life. God bless her and grant us fortitude.

Her death saddened him, but it also left him deserted by his helpmate. He and Ginevra had had 11 children in the course of their marriage, and while a number had died and others were adult, 3 were still under the age of eight and presumably lived at home. Gregorio wrote in his *ricordanze*: "Her loss has sorely tried me. May He [God] help me to bring up the unruly family which is left to me in the best way for their souls and bodies."[91] Other Florentine families experienced such a loss. The death of Giovanni Corsini's wife ten days after she bore their son Andrea in 1409 left him with six children—ages six, five, four, two, one, and ten days old. He ruefully noted that "too many small children were left to me" by this occurrence. He was not totally alone in this circumstance, however. His father, Matteo, as well had recorded this occurrence in his own *ricordanze*, and he ended the passage in the same way, stating that these six children were left to him too. Undoubtedly, as their grandfather, Matteo felt some obligation to help care for them. The death of a mother in childbirth touched more than just her husband and children.[92] The Corsini, one of the richest families in Florence, were unlucky in birth—a fact that highlights how common or frequent the death of a wife in childbirth must have been. Death in birth took women of the lower, middle, and upper classes.[93]

Something stoical or at least fatalistic seems to exist in some of these husbands' accounts of the death of their wives in birth. This is probably a reflection of the likelihood that a Florentine husband could expect such an event as well as his helplessness once it happened. During birth he was not in control—not even present in the birth room—and all he could do was pray. In a sense, he did not really know or understand the process. Of all the things involved in having children, the actual biological process belonged only to the mother.

Oderigo d'Andrea di Credi's short note about the death of his wife, Caterina, reflects the stoic fatalism. In 1404, Caterina delivered "a girl child on the 25th of October; and in that birth, as it pleased God, the said Caterina my wife died."[94] When this could happen so frequently and unexpectedly, how else was one to deal with it? This stoical or fatalistic attitude toward the hazards of birth—which the women undoubtedly shared since they lost sisters, mothers, relatives, friends, as well as risked their own lives—does point up a difference between the attitudes of premodern and modern Westerners to birth. We do not understand how they could function in a process so fraught with immediate and real dangers; they would not understand how much safer the process has become.

The liklihood that a newborn infant could quickly die, sometimes right after the birth, was also one of those facts of existence to which premodern Europeans had to adjust. The *ricordanze* note this suddenness: "On 23 July 1562, a Thursday, at 9 3/4 hours, Bernardo was born to me and was baptized that same day at 15 hours; Messer Giulio dei Nobili, Piero d'Avanrati and Tommaso Primesendi were godfathers. He died the same day at 23 1/2 hours and was buried on the 24th at 14 hours in Santa Maria Novela in our crypt."[95] The Corsini *ricordanze* record not only the suddenness but also the frequency:" + Naque Giovana dì . . . MCCCLXXXVII. e morì subito (quickly)" or "+ Naque Giovanni dì xxv di magio .MCCCLXXXVIII. e morì subito" or "+ Naque la giovana dì .xii. di luglo ani .MCCCLXVIIII. e nacque in vila al nostro luogho. Rendevola [I returned her] a Dio e sosterosi a Santa Iacopo a Muciano, pioviere di Decimo, dì deto."[96] Died quickly; died quickly; returned . . . the same day.

But this does not necessarily mean that these people were unaffected by the eventuality, that they became inured to the experience of the death of their newborns. It does not mean they did not grieve and grieve deeply. The guild regulations for Florentine undertakers (*becchini*) emphasized that members should be discreet in setting prices for the burial of newborns to account for the families' sensibilities.[97] Undertakers even recognized that the death of a newborn was traumatic for families.

Matteo Corsini noted how he returned the second Giovanna, just one day old, to God and buried her in a church. Writers of *ricordanze* seemed to accept the idea that children were a temporary gift from God and that all life was in God's hands. Paliano Falcucci recorded how on 27 March 1383 "it was pleasing to God, our Lord, to call to himself the above mentioned Antonio, my son."[98] He was five months old. At the death of his stepsister, who was only four days old, Bartolomeo Masi hoped in 1513 that God would bless her ["che Iddio la benedica"].[99] In 1420, Bernardo Strozzi asked God's forbearance and grace on either side of his son's earthly sojourn—at his birth and at his death seven days later. At the birth he asked that God grant his son Francesco a good life and salvation from death of both the body and the soul. At the death he asked that God have mercy on his son and receive his soul in paradise.[100] Writers of *ricordanze* made sure that their dead infants—even the stillborn ones—received what they spiritually deserved.

While it is certainly banal to state that life in the past, following Hobbes, was poor, nasty, brutish, and short, we of the modern Western world are sometimes amazed at how premodern Europeans could have remained functioning human beings with all they saw, experienced, and felt in their daily lives, especially the mortality. But the whole point is that they did. Like other things so different from our own existence, they dealt with and accepted the frequent deaths of their newborn children. We might feel that we could not do so, which is what makes the past such a foreign country to us. It is in the little touches of how they dealt with such an occasion that we recognize that they too were human. In March 1388, Francesco Datini's five-month-old illegitimate son died, and Datini provided five *braccia* of unbleached woolen cloth for his shroud. His *ricordanze* noted that the boy was buried at San Francesco at the end of his own tomb.[101] When the time came, they would be together, lying on the threshold between the material and spiritual world.

That birth was such a dangerous and chancy proposition for premodern Florentines helps explain why they reacted so joyfully at a successful birth. Certainly, dynastic security, alliance- building, and simple maternal and paternal pride figured in here as well. Bernardo Velluti's father toasted his arrival in 1330. He was the first boy to be born after four girls. Afterwards, his father put on a great feast.[102] In August 1430, Manno Petrucci bought five soldi, six denari worth of confections with which to celebrate the birth of a daughter. He also listed the expenditure of twelve grossi, presumably for the feast celebrating her birth.[103] The joy and sense of celebration in birth can be seen in the letters that were sent out announcing the new arrival. Catherine dé Medici wrote to her cousin, the Florentine Grand Duke, Cosimo I: "my cousin . . . it pleased God to give my lord and me a second son newly born."[104]

We have an even better example, which is a letter addressed to the father, who was away from home on the republic's business, by the baby's mother. The father is a most unlikely father in modern popular opinion—Niccolò Machiavelli. On 24 November 1503, 16 days after the birth of their first son, Bernardo, Marietta wrote Machiavelli, apologizing for the delay, but said she had been recovering from the effects of the birth:

> My very dear Niccolò: You make fun of me, but you are not right. I should be more courageous, if you were here. You well know that I am never in good spirits when you are away, and less than ever now that I hear there is plague in Rome. Imagine if I can be happy, when I can rest neither by night nor day. Please, write more frequently than you do now; I have received only three letters from you. Do not be surprised, if I have not written to you; it was impossible; I was sick in bed with fever [puerperal fever?]. The baby is well and resembles you. He is as white as snow, but his head is like a bit of black velvet and he is hairy as you are. His resemblance to you makes me think him beautiful, and he is as lively as though he were a year old, and he opened his eyes before he was quite born and made his voice heard all over the house. But the little girl [meaning herself] is not at all well. Do come back. Nothing else. God be with you and bless you.
>
> I am sending your night cap, two shirts, two handkerchiefs and a towel. Yours, Marietta, in Florence.[105]

Marietta just had to describe the baby to him in detail, noting his liveliness, his cries, how much he looked like his father, his complexion, and his dark thick hair. She seems to have become attached very quickly and easily to this child. Machiavelli did return home within a month. Machiavelli's friend, Biagio Buonaccorsi, had written him on

15 November about the baby, and he too noticed his dark hair: "We shall do our best to ensure that this sprig shall turn out well and do us [Biagio was the child's godfather] credit, do not doubt it. But he looks like a little crow, he is so dark."[106] Biagio too seems proud that his friend had the birth of a son. Both of these letters try to convey some of the sense of what the child looks like, for Machiavelli, being away in Rome, is cut off from this family affair. Any information was welcome. The first news of this birth, however, had reached Machiavelli from a relative, Battista Machiavelli, in a letter dated 9 November 1503. In this letter Battista mentioned that the child was both sound and lively and that he had been baptized with honor that same day. He also invoked a blessing from God for the child.[107] Battista provided Machiavelli with the essentials: the child was safe, healthy, and Christian. Curiously, Battista made no mention of Marietta's condition in this letter. Perhaps this was supposed to be a good sign for Machiavelli, considering the dangers of premodern birth: no news was good news. And if these interchanges between Machiavelli and his friends and family at home are any indication, much information about births in Florence did travel to those who were away.

Friends and family who were away also sent congratulatory letters to new parents. The Cardinal of Bologna, a personal friend of Francesco Datini, sent one such letter to Datini's illegitimate daughter, Ginevra, on the birth of her first child. Pius V sent a letter dated 28 January 1569 to the Grand Duke's wife congratulating her on the birth of a child.[108]

Of all the means to show one's joy and appreciation of the birth of a child, the foremost seems to have come in the form of gifts, both to the child and to the mother and father. In 1375, Francesco Datini had an illegitimate child. His foster mother wrote to him telling him that she gave "a thousand blessings" to the child. Domenico di Cambio wrote to Francesco Datini and told him that a box of *zuccate* (pickled pumpkin) was the best gift for a new father. Margherita Datini and her circle of friends (*brigate*) would bring gifts of water and linen for the newborn baby of one of their friends and other gifts for the new mother.[109] This giving of gifts and the gifts themselves also maintained friendship and group solidarity among their circle. In fact, while I am emphasizing the celebratory nature of the gift here, I do not mean to preclude the possibility that these gifts could also demonstrate subservience, patronage, or social reciprocity between individuals.

Husbands, of course, gave gifts to their wives. Lapo Castiglionchio made an entry for 1363 in his *ricordanze:* "Next, to give to Margherita, my wife, for the birth of Bernardo, my son, five florins."[110] Perhaps the most appropriate present for a new mother was a *desco da parto*. This was a small painted plate depicting weddings, births, or banquets that was a customary childbirth gift, though usually these were given by women to other women.[111] The artist Neri di Bicci recorded in 1461 that he painted one for Domenico Pietrasanta. The same year he also painted one for Ser Bastiano, a notary.[112] While these were gifts specifically to celebrate a childbirth, some may have seen in them some sort of aid for fertility. The Datinis, who had such trouble having children and never succeeded, kept a *desco da parto* in their bedroom. Was it just a gift or something more? Considering all her other attempts to get pregnant, it would seem that for her this plate represented much more than just an elegant gift. Whether through luck or through some other higher level of magic, for the Datinis a *desco da parto* may have been a tool for conception.[113]

A *desco da parto* by Masaccio (1427) depicts a scene with trumpeters heralding the arrival of a number of men carrying gifts and women entering the room where the mother and child lie. One of the men is carrying a *desco da parto*. Fra Carnevale da Urbino's *Visitation* (fifteenth century) shows a *brigata* of women bearing gifts trooping off to visit a new mother.[114] Cloth and utensils, such as silver forks and spoons, were the most common gifts to celebrate birth that writers of *ricordanze* recorded.[115] Lisa Guidetti in May 1483 received a cape and four pieces of damask cloth from a female friend for the birth of her son, Giovanni Battista. In February 1489 when she delivered another son, Rinieri, four women, one of whom was a cousin, gave her gifts, such as 12 forks. One of the women gave her marzipan candy. On 21 December 1494 the Guidetti sent Chanora(?) Ricelleni, who had just delivered a boy, 12 gilded forks and a marzipan cake.[116]

Parents gave gifts to their adult children who were parents. Filippo Strozzi sent his daughter, Mariotta, a silver cup with pine nut cookies inside on the news that she had delivered her first child. The arms of the Strozzi and her husband's families were inscribed on the cup. This cup had originally been sent to Filippo's wife by Mariotta's husband when she had given birth to a daughter. According to Klapisch-Zuber, the giving of silver cups with the coats of arms of both families was a common birth gift amongst the merchant elite.[117] Parents sent other gifts as well. Monna Magdalena, the mother of Lisa Guidetti, sent her 12 spoons when she gave birth to Giovanni Battista.[118]

Other relatives beyond the immediate family participated in this cycle of gift giving. Andrea Minerbotti's wife received a silver cup from her brother-in-law when she gave birth sometime in 1500.[119] Giovanni Rucellai recorded the complex web of ties of family gift-giving for the birth of his grandson, Cosimo, on 1 June 1468. The godfathers as a group presented the new mother, who was a Medici, with red cloth for a surcoat, brocaded damask cloth for the sleeves, and a cake. Her father, Piero di Cosimo de'Medici, gave her a silver basin and a silver mug full of cookies. Her second cousin, who had been brought up in the same household as her father, gave her a goblet full of cookies. Her brother-in-law, Guglielmo Pazzi, also gave a silver goblet full of pinenut cookies. One sister gave a bolt of white cloth; and the other gave cloth for a gown and a chemise, and a cloth to make a cloak for the baby. The Tornabuoni brothers, her maternal uncles, gave her cloth for a surcoat.[120] At a birth, then, one could expect kin, friends, and neighbors—the familiar *parenti, amici, e vicini* of Florentine formulas—to help celebrate the occasion by gift-giving.

Thus, as we have seen, most Florentines of the merchant elite spent much time, effort, and worry awaiting and preparing for the arrival of their children. Moreover, they were very cognizant of the real risks attendant in the birth process, and tried within the parameters of the premodern world—that is, the structures of their daily life—to best alleviate those dangers. Birth was much more than just a family affair, with birth professionals, kin, friends, neighbors, and servants all helping out and celebrating in the joy—or sometimes participating in the sorrow of the death of a child or mother or both. These Florentines of the merchant elite seemed spare no expense in the preparation for the birth as well as its celebration. But the celebration of the birth was just the first step in a number of rituals intended to welcome the newborn into the world and the Christian community as well as to protect it and give it an identity. Within hours after the birth, a number of other rituals surrounded the infant and made him or her welcome—*benvenuto*.

III

Alle Fonte Del Santo Battesimo: The Rituals of Birth

Children—1404

Glory, honor and praise be to Almighty God. Continuing from folio 5, I shall list the children which He shall in his grace bestow on me and my wife Ginevra.

On Sunday morning at terce, 27 April of the same year, Ginevra gave birth to our first-born son. He was baptized at the hour of vespers on Monday the 28th in the church of S. Giovanni. We named him Manetto Domenico. His sponsors in God's love were Bartolo di Giovanni di Niccola, Giovanni di Michelozzo, a belt-maker, and Domenico di Deo, a goldsmith. God make him good. . . .

At terce on Tuesday morning, 8 June 1406, Ginevra had her third child, a fine full-term baby girl whom we had baptized on Friday morning, 9 June. We christened her Elisabetta Caterina and she will be called Lisabetta in memory of my dead wife, Betta. The sponsors were Fra Lorenzo, Bartolo, and the blind woman.

On 4 June 1407, a Saturday, Ginevra gave birth after a nine-month pregnancy to a little girl whom we had baptized on the evening of Tuesday the 7th. We named her Antonia Margherita and we shall call her Antonia. Her godfather was Nello di Ser Piero Nelli, a neighbor. God grant her good fortune. . . .

On 1 May 1415, at the hour of terce on a Wednesday, God granted us a fine little boy, and I had him baptized at four on Saturday morning. Jacopo di Francesco di Tura and Aringhieri di Jacopo, the wool merchant, were his godfathers. May God grant that he be healthy, wise, and good. We named him after the two holy apostles, Jacopo and Filippo, on whose feast day he was born and we shall call him Filippo.[1]

Immediately after its birth, as these *ricordanze* entries note, an infant participated in a series of rituals all centered around the baptismal font—baptism, baptismal kinship, and naming.[2]

In premodern Christian society the ritual of baptism was highly significant, since it introduced a new soul into the Church and a new member to both the family and the larger community.[3] Moreover, a child received its name—hence its social identity—at baptism. A child thus became a Christian and in a sense a human there.[4] Premodern Florentines from the merchant elite clearly recognized these religious and social benefits. In *Il Paradiso*, Dante had a distant ancestor, Cacciaguida, recall the significance of his baptism: "and in your ancient Baptistery I became a Christian—and Cacciaguida there on earth."[5] Describing his birth in the third person, Giovanni Morelli pointed out that his godfathers "made him a Christian [fecolo cristiano]."[6] Cellini recounted how he received his name Benvenuto: "Holy Baptism gave me this name and by it I am still living with the grace of God."[7] In the early fifteenth century the popular preacher San Bernardino taught that a child received its soul only after baptism, a point that runs contrary to contemporary theology.[8] Nevertheless, Paolo Sassetti had anticipated this sentiment in 1376. His niece, Giovanna, was baptized at his house immediately after her birth; and this ceremony, according to him, gave her a soul.[9] She died the same day.

Florentines knew what happened to children who died before receiving baptism. They went to the Limbo of Children-a place separate from Heaven with no future.[10] In Dante's *Inferno*, Virgil said this was for those that "lacked Baptism's grace, which is the door of the true faith you were born to." In *Il Purgatorio*, Virgil further explained that Limbo was "a place below where sorrow lies in untormented gloom. Its lamentations are not the shrieks of pain, but hopeless sighs. There do I dwell with souls of babes whom death bit off in their first innocence, before baptism washed them of their taint of earth."[11]

To rescue children from this Florentines recognized that they had a duty to baptize them. Matteo Corsini began the page of his *ricordanze* that listed his children by noting that he was writing about his children whom he had had baptized. A fifteenth-century Florentine confessor's manual condemned those who, through neglect or mistake, allowed a child to die without baptism.[12] The first task of the foundlings hospital in Florence when it received a child was to baptize it.[13] In Florence diocesan law recognized this duty and allowed the laity to baptize in an emergency, when the death of the child was feared. To control this, however, Florentine confessors were to ask their parishioners whether they had performed a baptism through necessity and what the situation had been that prompted them to take such action. Done correctly and properly, though, this was an act of spiritual mercy. Pagolo Morelli's last child was baptized at home by the *guardadonna* immediately after its birth. It died shortly thereafter.[14]

Writers of *ricordanze* often described hasty baptisms followed by the death of the child.[15] In fact, in these cases, they went out of their way to stress that the child received baptism before death. Bartolomeo Valori made sure to record that his two-month-premature daughter lived long enough to receive baptism and that she then went to heaven.[16] Matteo Corsini recorded the birth, baptism, and death of a three-month-premature daughter. Luca Panzano noted that his wife gave birth to a stillborn child, which was then baptized because some of the attendants thought it had breathed.[17] Florentines took no chances; they knew what happened to unbaptized infants and whom to blame for the infant's fate. Imagine then the anguish that Gregorio and Caterina Dati must have felt in August 1421 when they lost a child before they could have it baptized.[18]

Even if a newborn was not ill and in peril, speed was essential in baptism. The Episcopal Constitutions of Fiesole (1306) warned parents that their children should be baptized as soon as possible. The Episcopal Constitutions of Florence (1310) reiterated this.[19] Parents generally followed this advice. Matteo di Giovanni Corsini recorded: "Gostanza e Aghata was born on the fifth of February at the 11 and 1/2 hour on the Sunday after the Annunciation. She was baptized the following Tuesday morning at the 1/3 hour." Gregorio and Ginevra Dati's first son was born at terce 27 April 1404 and baptized the next day at vespers. Ser Antonio Bartolomei recorded that his daughter Margherita was "baptized the same day." Overall, the vast majority of Florentine children received baptism within three days.[20] This haste in baptism showed, if nothing else, that Florentines recognized the necessity of baptism for one's soul.

God forgave original sin through the ceremony. Moreover, a child received grace and salvation at baptism. This meant that baptism was a singular gift, different from the other sacraments, and hence more important. Giovanni Morelli said it simply enough: baptism meant salvation for the soul. As a consequence, according to Sant'Antonino, the fifteenth-century Archbishop of Florence, infanticide before a child was baptized was more odious than that occurring afterwards. Baptism also represented the beginning of infantile innocence.[21] No wonder baptism created a moment of high religious drama for premodern people.

It also gave occasion for a highly visible display of social significance. Attending baptismal services at the local church demonstrated, for instance, a family's solidarity.[22] Despite the humanist movement, premodern Florence was still, in Lauro Martines' words, "more a visual than a literate society."[23] The stages of the baptismal ceremony, such as the procession to and from the baptistery, the ceremony outside the baptistery's doors, the ceremony around the font, and the visual images they evoked were important to Florentines.[24] Parents displayed themselves, their social connections, and their social status during the baptismal ceremony. Their visual act created a text, in a sense, for the rest of the community to read.

Godparents were quite visible during this ritual. Sant'Antonino stressed that godparents had to touch the infant during the ceremony. Usually the godmother or a servant held the infant during the procession, but Antonio Rospiglioso considered the honor so significant that he insisted on his child's being carried by one of its godfathers.[25] An idiom for becoming a godparent highlights the importance of touching during the baptismal ceremony. Morelli wrote that at the baptism of his second son "Telda, my mother, and Catellana, Morello's wife, held him at baptism [tennelo a battesimo]."[26] Other writers of *ricordanze* emphasized the specific ritual location in their idiom. Filippo Strozzi recorded that "on 20 April 1469 at the nineteenth hour my first daughter was born to me and baptized on the 21st. Franco Sasette and Morallo Moralli held her at the font."[27]

In the city of Florence parish churches did not have baptismal fonts. The baptistery of San Giovanni, located in the approximate center of the city just east of the Duomo, the cathedral at Florence (Santa Maria del Fiore), was the site for most baptisms.[28] Such an arrangement, perhaps, weakened neighborhood ties and emphasized the idea that "there was but one public stage in Florence, the city stage."[29] On the other hand, this arrangement meant that all Florentines were united with each other by San Giovanni, since he was the patron saint of Florence, and at San Giovanni, since this was where they were baptized.

Having only one location for baptism in a city the size of Florence could be troublesome. During the fifteenth and early sixteenth centuries an average of between five and seven baptisms took place each day. In the year 1453, for instance, the baptismal registers of San Giovanni recorded 2,046 baptisms. In 1338, before the mortality of the Black Death, a priest at San Giovanni told the chronicler Villani that he had recorded some 6,000 babies baptized that year, an average of 16 a day.[30] The baptistery at San Giovanni must have been a busy place,[31] and baptismal processions through the city must have been common sights.

The procession winding its way through the narrow urban canyons presented the infant, its father and family, and its godparents to the greater Florentine community.[32] Giovanni Dominici described a procession composed of family and friends, all decked out in colored and gilded clothing with embroidered capes flapping in the wind and banners held aloft flying towards the sky.[33] On a more prosaic note, Bartolomeo Sassetti recalled how cold it was the morning of his son's baptism—Christmas Day 1457. The little boy was wrapped in flannel and carried to the Church by a woman—though not his mother.[34]

Because of the rigors of birth, most premodern mothers did not participate in the baptismal ceremony, which occurred shortly after birth. And if the rigors of birth were not cause enough for the mother to be absent, adherence to the Mosaic law of ritual female impurity after a birth would have kept most mothers from participating in the baptismal ceremony. In his Confessionale, Sant'Antonino stated that women could enter a church before the forty days of purification had passed if they so desired. On the other hand, he said that it was not a sin for women to observe this 40-day period and stay away from church. He referred to the observance of this ritual purification as a custom of the country ["consuetudo patrie"] rather than a rigid Church rule. Nevertheless, it seems that Florentines respected the custom of the country. Tribaldo dei Rossi, for instance, recorded two churchings of his wife, during which she reentered the church a month after the birth (he was less than exact on his dates here), presented candles at the altar of the Virgin Mary, and had a mass said for her there.[35] Therefore, because of the confinement or for religious reasons, another woman (or several women in some cases)—such as a servant, wetnurse, godmother, relative, or family friend—would carry the child to and from the baptistery. In December 1473, Niccolò Strozzi paid 16 soldi to the women who had carried his son to the baptistery.[36]

Spectators along the way played their role in welcoming the infant into society and recognizing the social boundaries of its natural and baptismal kinship ties.[37] Luca Panzano recalled the many families who participated in his son's baptism and the citizens who viewed the procession. In one of Agnolo Firenzuolo's stories a fellow named Niccolò invites the general public to the baptismal feast following the ceremony. This act might reflect a desire to reward the spectators for their role in creating this social space, or a desire to have them continue that role after the procession, or both. The Datinis even sent their young niece Tina in their place to witness a baptism when they could not attend.[38] Spectators at baptism were important and even crucial.

Perhaps nothing indicates the significance Florentines attached to baptism and the baptistery better than Boccaccio's comment about Dante: "In Florence alone, and over the font of San Giovanni, was Dante disposed to take the crown, to the end that, where he had taken his first name by baptism, in the same place he might take his second name by coronation."[39] The ceremonial aspects of baptism were so significant and useful for families that the state tried to regulate them. Sumptuary legislation of 1355/6 limited parents' expenses to one florin and tried to limit the purchases to candles and confections.[40] Writers of *ricordanze* noted these purchases of candles and torches for the baptism.[41] These were necessary expenses for the ceremony, since a candle was used in the ritual at the font and the torch would be useful for illumination and ornamentation inside the baptistery. In April 1473 the government of Florence put a ceiling on the sumptuousness of display exhibited during the baptismal ceremony. The previous month the government had also set limits on the amount of money spent on the celebratory dinner after baptism.[42] Attempts at control came from other quarters. Giovanni Dominici enjoined his audience not to seek ostentation in the baptismal ceremony. Richard Trexler called these limits an "attack upon the right of the good families of Florence to display their honor," which demonstrates that baptism served many social and religious goals.[43] Because of this, most Florentines ignored these injunctions.

The Church also tried to limit the ritual gift-giving that occurred at baptism. The Constitutions of Fiesole stated, on pain of excommunication, that no one could give presents at baptism worth more than ten soldi. The Constitutions of Florence also set the limit at ten soldi for gifts, except for candles, exchanged at baptism. The Constitutions of Florence expanded this limitation to the gift-giving that occurred at other Christian ceremonies, such as catechism or confirmation. The Constitutions did not explain why gift-giving should be limited, but it may reflect the same attitude that led the Florentine government to attempt to prevent families from displaying wealth in order to acquire and display prestige and friends. The Constitutions of Florence did state that the gift-giving stemmed from the *cognatio spiritualis* newly contracted among baptismal kin, not from any previous bond of friendship.[44] Baptismal kin were those people ritually joined by the rite of baptism. Baptism, through the *cognatio spiritualis,* generated a religious and social bond between the godparents and the godchild, called godparenthood and a similar bond between the godparents and the parents, called coparenthood. Godparent and coparent, then, are terms that can identify the same individual.[45] Luca Landucci reflected this by denoting his godfather as both the fellow who baptized him and "compare di mio padre."[46]

The *cognatio spiritualis* worried the Church. The Constitutions of Fiesole prohibited the laity from choosing secular clergy as baptismal kin. In 1517 the Provincial Council of Florence reiterated this.[47] These are significant prohibitions. While Canon Law held that monks and nuns could not become baptismal kin, it never prohibited secular clergy from engaging in baptismal kinship.[48] These prohibitions represent a strong—perhaps uncharacteristically strong—attempt on the part of the Florentine ecclesiastical hierarchy to control and protect its priests. The Constitutions of Florence explained that secular clergy should not become godparents because the friendship arising out of the *cognatio spiritualis* could become twisted and corrupted by unprincipled people who would use the bond to gain undue influence over the clergymen. It was not just that the Church did not want its priests too closely associated with lay friends; the Church feared that people would use the *cognatio spiritualis* and the special closeness it implied as a pretext for gaining special, perhaps illegal, favors from priests. The Church wanted to protect its personnel, and indirectly its property, from such chicanery. Violators were subject to a twenty-soldi fine.[49] Despite this, Florentines of the merchant elite consistently picked priests as their baptismal kin; they also chose religious.[50]

The 1517 Provincial Council of Florence defined the *cognatio spiritualis* as "that spiritual relationship originating in respect of baptism or confirmation, when there are cofathers and comothers."[51] People who married their baptismal kin committed spiritual incest since the *cognatio spiritualis* had made them spiritual relatives. And these spiritual ties were stronger even than family ties, since the spirit was more important than the flesh. The 1517 Provincial Council explained who was not allowed to marry among baptismal kin, thus defining the baptismal kinship nexus. Godparents could not marry their godchildren or their godchildren's parents. Godchildren could not marry their godparents' children, either natural or adoptive, or their godparents' spouses, even after their godparents had died. Parents could not marry their coparents' spouses. The 1517 Provinical Council did point out that a godchild's siblings could marry his or her godparents' children.[52] San Bernardino reminded his listeners that if they had held children at baptism they could not marry them. Considering the wide age differential between husbands and wives in premodern Florence (an average of 12 years), this was not just empty advice. Seven of Boccaccio's stories mention baptismal kinship, and three of these note the prohibition against intermarriage among baptismal kin, which rose out of the *cognatio spiritualis*. Boccaccio's stories, therefore, indicate a popular perception of this religious, social, and sexual boundary to baptismal kinship as well as a sense of awe, expressed through humor, about the taboo.[53] And Florentine confessors warned people that having sex with baptismal kin was a spiritual sin, sacrilegious, and incestuous.[54] Premodern Florentines were quite aware of spiritual incest and its consequences.

The incest taboo could cause another problem. If parents held their own children at baptism—as in an emergency—would they become baptismal kin and thus would their marriage become incestuous and hence invalid? To solve this problem the Constitutions of Fiesole and Florence and the Council of Florence all asserted that parents should not become godparents to their own children, even though canon law allowed parents in an emergency to serve as godparents for their children, since their marriage had been contracted before the ritual act.[55]

Some scholars have concluded that Renaissance elites thought it fashionable to have large numbers of coparents.[56] More importantly, in the rambunctious political and economic world of premodern cities, the elite saw large numbers of coparents as being socially useful. Nevertheless, the 1517 Provincial Council of Florence prescribed only three godparents for children.[57] San Bernardino had previously narrowed even this and stated that people should choose one coparent, not a hundred, when they baptized their children. Giovanni Dominici likewise criticized people who collected swarms of coparents around the font.[58] Florentine sumptuary legislation of 1355/6 set a limit of three godparents-counting both men and women-and violators were subject to a 25-lire fine.[59]

The Church had a practical reason for limiting the number of godparents. If people had too many baptismal kin, then they might forget who they were: godchildren in particular might forget who their godparents' children were. People in modern Latin America sometimes forget who their baptismal kin are for much the same reason. And if Florentines forgot, they might unwittingly then marry a baptismal kin, thus committing spiritual incest. This was the reason why the Council of Florence ordered those churches within the bishopric that had fonts to begin recording the names of godparents in the baptismal registry.[60]

Florentines, however, rarely adhered to this limitation of three godparents. Matteo di Giovanni Corsini for instance, chose 11 godfathers for his first child. Some children even had a town for their godparent. Undoubtedly, a point of tension existed between the Church's desire to limit the number of godparents and the people's desire to expand as widely as possible their baptismal kinship network.[61]

That Florentines rarely adhered to a three-godparent rule is apparent in Cellini's description of baptismal kinship practices in France. While in the employ of the king of France, Cellini had hired a 15-year-old pauper as a model:

> This young girl was untouched, and a virgin, and I got her pregnant. She bore me a daughter on the seventh of June, at the thirteenth hour of the day, 1544; and that was just the forty-fourth year of my own life. I gave her the name Costanza: she was held at her baptism by Guido Guidi, the King's physician and, as I have written before, a very good friend of mine. He was the only godfather, since that is the custom in France, to have one godfather and two godmothers. One of these latter was Signora Maddalena, the wife of Luigi Alamanni, a Florentine gentleman and a marvelous poet. The other godmother was the wife of Ricciardi del Bene, the wife of one of our Florentine citizens and a substantial merchant in Paris. She was a high-ranking French lady.[62]

Canon law decreed not only a maximum number of godparents (three) but also the specific composition of this number. A girl had one godfather and two godmothers; a boy two godfathers and one godmother. In premodern France and England custom usually paralleled the canonical regulations.[63] Cellini evidently mistook the specific arrangement in France for a girl for all children. That he felt compelled to explain the arrangement in his account implies that Florentine custom did not parallel Canonical regulations.

Cellini's account also reveals a little of baptismal kinship's utility for the parents. His cofather and his comothers' husbands were

Florentines as was one of the comothers. For Florentines living abroad baptismal kinship was an excellent device for maintaining their immigrant community's group solidarity and for preserving friendship.[64] The acquisition and maintenance of friendship was a common theme throughout Florentine society. This is not surprising considering the turbulent and exciting urban politics in Florence, especially during the late fourteenth and early fifteenth centuries.[65] In Rome, Cellini's first master was a goldsmith known as Firenzuolo. When Cellini switched masters, he and Firenzuolo argued, partly over his abrupt departure, partly over money. Cellini prevailed, but the two parted bitterly. In the course of time, Cellini related, "Firenzuolo and I became friends again; when he asked me I stood as godfather to one of his children."[66] What better way did premodern European culture have for demonstrating the depth of friendship than a public, religious ceremony? Baptismal kinship, therefore, offered Florentine parents opportunities to gain or reward friends.[67] In their *ricordanze* Florentines recorded many friends honored with this spiritual connection. Florentines likewise recorded that they had become godparents to their friends' children. Bartolomeo Masi, for instance, recorded becoming a godparent 43 times between 1505 and 1526. Those who stood as godparents for others' children also noted who the other godparents were. While canon law held that fellow godparents were not spiritually related, in the popular imagination these fellow godparents saw themselves somehow bound together. Bartolomeo Masi frequently referred to this group as his companions.[68] Who were these baptismal kin?

Florentines rarely chose natural kin or affines as coparents.[69] Sometimes a special circumstance or need prompted the choice of a blood relative as a coparent. Morelli's brother asked his mother, who had remarried after his father's death, to be godmother to two of his children. Leonida Pandimiglio suggested that in this case Morelli's brother used baptismal kinship to reaffirm familial bonds.[70] More normally, friends, especially neighbors, comprised the bulk of Florentines' baptismal kinship network.[71] Morelli mentioned that some of his godparents were good friends of his father and came from the same quarter as did his father.[72] Six of Lapo Niccolini's eight identifiable cofathers came from the same quarter as did he.[73] Twenty-four of

Matteo Corsini's twenty-six cofathers that can be geographically plotted came from the same quarter as Matteo, seventeen from the same *gonfalone*.[74] Giovanni Morelli's brother's godmothers were next-door neighbors of the Morelli.[75] From the account book of Cambio di Tano Petrucci (d. 1430), a goldsmith, Dale and Francis William Kent discovered that his children

> were held at the font by such familiar neighbourhood characters as Ser Tommaso di Ser Luca Franceschi, Ser Tommaso Carondini (the busy notary often used by Petrucci), by Carondini's wife Mea, and even by his mother! The cobbler Antonio di Cieco, from whom Petrucci bought his shoes, also took part in the baptisms of most of his children, and a daughter born in 1409 was 'given to God' by the doublet-maker Manno di Bonuccio di Manno, who was the gonfalonier of Lion Rosso in 1427.[76]

On a more practical note, considering the speed with which some baptisms were accomplished, neighbors made a convenient choice.

The neighborhood connection may explain why most coparents only appear once in the *ricordanze*—the day of the baptism.[77] These baptismal kin were not business associates, who would tend to appear more frequently in the commercially oriented *ricordanze*. But business associates too became coparents. Matteo Corsini's notary, Bartolomeo Segnorini, who in the course of his lifetime drew up more than 40 contracts for Matteo, became his cofather in 1380. Lapo Niccolini's banker, Franciesco Cavalcanti, became his cofather in 1386. Ser Antonio Bartolomei, a notary, had three fellow notaries stand as godfathers to his daughter, Magdalena, on 30 July 1461. One of these he referred to specifically as "mio notai." Piero Strozzi also at one point had three notaries as coparents. Rossello Strozzi made business deals with his cofathers. Buonaccorso Pitti's renter, a woman named Ginevra, became his comother, not once but twice.[78]

Some coparents then made return trips to the font. This choice signified a double honor but could also imply that parents did not have enough friends.[79] Since the death of a child dissolved the *cognatio spiritualis*, parents would also have former coparents repeat the performance to continue the bonds of baptismal kinship.[80] This is what Gregorio Dati attempted with his business partner, Nando di Lippi. Thrice he made him a coparent, and thrice the child died within a year. After the death of the last child Dati did not ask him again. Perhaps Dati thought Nando brought bad luck to the coparenthood relationship or even brought bad luck down on the child. In 1405, Dati made Bartolo Niccola, his banker, and Margherita, a blind woman, his coparents; but the child died. The next year, he made the same individuals his coparents for his daughter, Elisabetta.[81] With the high infant-mortality rate in premodern Florence, securing friendships with baptismal kinship could have been problematic at times and would have needed to be redone frequently.

Dati recorded that Margherita became his comother "for the love of God [per amor di dio]."[82] This phrase, denoting an act of charity, appears frequently in the *ricordanze* accounts of baptism.[83] Dati chose 15 of his 52 coparents (or 28.8 percent) "for the love of God." While becoming a coparent was the occasion for exchanging gifts, sometimes quite lavish ones, here a coparent "for the love of God" contributed no gifts though the parents did. Having a coparent "for the love of God" then represented an act of charity on the parents' part. Margherita, who was blind, needed aid. Matteo Corsini listed a pauper, Salvagia, as a comother "for the love of God."[84] What could a pauper give a Corsini except an excuse for an act of charity?[85]

Many priests and religious likewise served as godparents "for the love of God."[86] These coparents served as an excuse for charity and much more. The celibacy of such individuals meant that choosing them as godparents eliminated future marital impediments arising from the *cognatio spiritualis,* if parents wished to place marital strategies with social peers before baptismal kinship strategies with social peers. Priests in particular formed the hub of a parish's gossip network; they represented, therefore, an excellent source for news of one's neighbors. Moreover, access to priests outside one's parish meant access to another parish's gossip network. Priests, therefore, were good friends to have. Ronald Weissman observed that Florentines chose priests outside their parish to be cofathers because they feared that confession to their own priest meant that their neighbors would hear about them. Florentines saw advantage in knowing a priest outside their parish for religious purposes too.[87] On a more positive note, since one of the duties of a godparent was the religious education of the godchild, a priest or religious was an excellent choice to fulfill this duty.[88]

Florentines rarely chose coparents whose social status was much above their own. For instance, Bartolomeo Masi, a fifteenth-century coppersmith, was chosen to be a cofather mostly by fellow artisans and shopkeepers. A practical utility beyond working-class solidarity may have existed in having a fellow artisan as coparent. Simone d'Giovanni Ferrini, a blacksmith, had Domenico di Bernardo and Agniolo di Baccio d'Agniolo, both woodcutters, as his cofathers. Simone perhaps sought to assure his supply of fuel. Half of Lapo Niccolini's cofathers fell below his social and economic status. And many of the coparents for the other *ricordanze* writers likewise fell below the writer's social and economic status. This phenomenon reflects Klapisch-Zuber's contention that baptismal kinship in Florence served to tie well-to-do people to the neighborhood. She calls these lower-status coparents "a local clientage."[89] In the countryside landlords asked their peasants and sharecroppers to be their coparents. For instance, one of Morelli's share-croppers was his cofather. David Herlihy saw this as evidence of close ties of friendship and association between these families. These instances may not represent close family ties so much as ties of patronage along the lines of Latin American baptismal kinship (*compadrazgo*), in which landlords use the bonds of godparenthood and coparenthood with their peasants to soften the tension generated by an exploitive economic system and to intensify further the web of clientage.[90]

Sometimes Florentines chose coparents to ease the strain of politics. In Florence it was common to have fellow office members become coparents, sometimes all together, and other times represented by a procurator.[91] Having fellow office-holders as cofathers could temper debates, facilitate decisions, and generally make bureaucratic life a bit easier. Having officials as godfathers could inculcate in a child a sense of civic loyalty and pride and may represent one of the seeds of an individual's sense of civic humanism. They were excellent role models, therefore. Lorenzo de'Medici's godparents were the very institutions of Florence: representatives of each quarter, the priors of the Signoria, nine of the *accopiatori* (the officials who qualified candidates for office and the specific instruments for Medici control of Florence), the archbishop of Florence, and the priors of San Lorenzo, the family church.[92]

Many Florentines serving as officials of the Florentine imperial government made coparenthood ties with the people they governed, sometimes with the whole town.[93] This behavior seems to fly in the face of Brunetto Latini's advice that an administrator, and by implication any Florentine imperial official, should not have friends among those he governed.[94] It seems, though, that once they arrived in the field Florentine imperial officials found that baptismal kinship provided some leverage with which to turn the wheels of imperialism.[95] Conversely, parents from subject towns came to San Giovanni to make baptismal kinship ties with Florentines.[96]

Baptismal kinship aided Florence's foreign policy as well. In 1390, Milan and Florence made a pact only after Maso degli Albizzi became godfather to a Visconti child. According to Trexler, this did not represent a seal to the bargain but the initial step: a friendly overture.[97] Baptismal kinship also wove the heads of state together. Louis XI insisted on becoming the godfather of Lorenzo de' Medici's daughter, Lucrezia, in 1470. Lorenzo, however, had wanted Galeazzo Sforza to fill that role. Here Lorenzo bumped into the biological constraints on networking via baptismal kinship. Lorenzo had two possible choices for his cofather, yet only one child. He probably could not have had both men as cofather since that would have diminished the honor of being sole cofather. Louis XI prevailed, and on 4 November 1470 his representative stood at the font for him. Two years later Galeazzo asked Lorenzo to be the godfather of his newborn child, thus reaffirming their earlier promise to forge baptismal kinship bonds.[98]

Baptismal kinship also helped one to acquire local political allies and build a neighborhood faction.[99] Morelli recorded how his father acquired rich and powerful friends by toadying to them and offering to become their coparent. With these contacts Morelli's father had "friends not relatives," which to Morelli were more valuable for social climbing.[100]

Protection from the judicial or bureaucratic apparatus of the state was also a reason to seek out influential coparents. Coparents could and did protect each other from high assessments when district officials met to discuss taxes. In a trial before the Signoria (the Florentine executive body) Buonoccorso Pitti paraded forth a host of witnesses, but the testimony of his cofather swayed the court to rule in his favor. On the other hand, Florentine judges were aware that baptismal kin would support each other before the court based on that relationship. Therefore, one of the questions they put to witnesses was whether or not they were related spiritually to defendants, accusers, or other witnesses.[101]

Protection and reward were also reasons Florentines chose certain comothers. Many of the comothers whom Morelli listed for his relatives had one thing in common. All had been present at the birth as midwives, *guardadonne,* or were companions of the new mother.[102] Women who aided in the birth of a child would have been obvious choices for this honor. Wetnurses, too, became comothers. Cellini, for instance, had his illegitimate son's wetnurse stand as his godmother.[103] Like choosing a midwife or *guardadonna* as comother, perhaps this also represented one way to reward people who had aided the family. Sometimes the wetnurse for another child became a godmother to the new child, again perhaps as a gesture of reward.[104] Moreover, since wetnursing was a hazardous affair for the child,[105] perhaps this was one way to ensure the safety of the child, by binding the nurse closer to the child and family through baptismal kinship. In Cellini's case this did no good, for the wetnurse—his comother, his son's godmother—accidentally smothered his infant son.[106]

Choosing a godparent for a child and a coparent for oneself was a complicated and complex issue. Despite the element of calculation implicit in such a choice, a coparent was someone with whom premodern Florentines were in close and usually frequent contact.

Besides the sexual prohibitions, Florentines enmeshed in the baptismal kinship nexus had certain specific duties toward each other that arose out of the *cognatio spiritualis,* the close friendship the ceremony reflected, and the sense of protection it implied. San Bernardino preached that all people should honor their godfathers. In a sermon of 20 March 1424 he listed, in order of importance, the seven fathers to whom one owed obligations. The first was God, the second was one's natural father; the "third father is your godfather." The fourth was one's confessor, the fifth was one's benefactor, the sixth was any governmental official, and the seventh was any elderly man. Godfathers thus ranked high in San Bernardino's scheme.[107]

He further explained why godchildren should honor their godfathers, and as a consequence indicated what a godfather did for a godchild. A Florentine godfather held his godchild at baptism, a sign of society's acceptance of the child. He responded in the child's place during the ceremony, a religious obligation, and, in San Bernardino's words, pledged the child's faith to the Church. He befriended the child's father as *compare*, and he acted as a grandfather to the child. This last item, meaning the nurturing and kindly attitude of a godparent to a godchild, along with the honor godchildren were supposed to show their godfather, implies that the bonds in Florentine godparenthood were close.[108] In one of his stories, Boccaccio sketched a godfather's duty to his godchild: holding him publicly at baptism; giving him a name; and, lastly, teaching him about Christianity.[109] San Bernardino stressed that a godparent had the responsibility to force an erring and sinful godchild to return to confession and penitence and to lead a good life.[110] Godparents were not only responsible for their godchildren's religious education; they were specifically responsible for getting them confirmed.[111] Florentine godfathers also performed their popularly perceived duty, becoming the real father of their orphaned godchildren. Bernardo Masi lost his father in 1458, and his godfather, Giusto di Antonio di Giusto, an ironworker, approached his mother and offered to take him into his house as a son.[112]

Between coparents other duties existed. They were to treat each other with honor. This is exemplified in the special title they called each other. No longer was a friend or associate just that; he was "mio compare," as Lapo Niccolini said. Cellini, telling of a journey with his cofather, referred to the man as "mio compar Tribolo." The humanist Francesco Filelfo referred to his cofather as "mio amatissimo compare." Lapo Mazzei referred to Margherita Datini as "comare carissima," and he even referred to his own wife, Tessa, as "your comother" whenever he talked about her with Francesco Datini. Coparents used this address in written communication to each other. Galeazzo Sforza addressed a letter to Lorenzo de' Medici, his cofather: "Spectabilis Compater noster carissime." Francesco Nero frequently addressed

Filippo Strozzi as "Compare mio," and signed himself as "vostro Compare."[113]

The honorific title even extended into non-baptismal kinship relationships, similar to the way in which the Spanish word for cofather—*compadre*—is used today. One evening Cellini sneaked up on the house of a woman whom he loathed, intending to surprise her and her current lover. Francesco Bachiacca, Cellini's friend, tried to dissuade him from performing any mischief. "In a loud voice," recalled Cellini, "he called out to me, 'Compare,' for so we used to call ourselves for fun."[114] One of Boccaccio's stories also reflects the popular extension of this term to mean any sort of special friend. The characters refer to each other as *compare,* even though they are not baptismal kin, as a sign of friendship.[115]

A special terminology existed for godchildren too. Complaining about past taxes, Lionardo di Antonio de' Nobili wrote Cosimo de' Medici: "You could say that I and my son, *tuo figlioccio* [your godson], have become complete peasants." Lapo Mazzei referred to his son as "your godson" whenever he mentioned him to Francesco Datini, his godfather. In *Decameron* VII:3, Rinaldo at one point is told to pick up his godson: "recatevi in braccio vostro figlioccio." In his *ricordanze* Francesco Castellani wrote that he gave gifts to "mio figlioccio" and his mother, Castellani's comother. In an anonymous *ricordanze* from the early sixteenth century the author listed in his index entries for three *padrini*—godfathers.[116] The use of coparenthood and godparenthood terminology reflected on the part of those using them an "expression of reciprocal and affectionate respect."[117]

Gift-giving was a highly developed duty among baptismal kin. In fact, it was just as customary for them to bring gifts to the baptism as it was for other relatives. Domenico di Cambio wrote a letter to Francesco Datini on 20 January 1390 detailing for him the proper gifts with which "to make a child a Christian." He included two types of cake, red and white confections, candles, and torches. He added that the cost varied depending on how much a godfather wanted to do honor to himself.[118] Sometimes the godparents presented gifts the day of the baptism, sometimes later. Luca Panzano recalled how one of his fellow coparents, who represented the other coparents, delivered gifts and money to the parents' house four days after the baptism.[119]

Florentine sumptuary legislation of 1355/6 tried to limit this gift-giving to one florin-to no avail.[120]

Writers of *ricordanze* noted that cofathers gave presents to their comother: that is, the child's mother.[121] Bartolomeo Masi called this duty a uniquely Florentine custom.[122] Godparents brought gifts for their godchildren too. One of Luca Panzano's children received a practical gift from his godparents—diapers.[123] Godparents gave a particular gift to their godchildren in a particular way that was more ritual than gift. At the font one of the godparents would place a coin or several coins into the swaddling cloth of the child. A godfather of Lisabetta Chellini, for instance, "placed in her swaddling cloth at San Giovanni three coins worth one florin."[124] Since guests at a wedding placed a florin in the bride's shoe to represent her hope of riches, a coin in a child's swaddling cloth also represented its hope of riches.[125] Coins, therefore, had a close symbolic relationship to baptism; a coin around the neck of a foundling meant that it had already been baptized.[126]

Beyond gift-giving, baptismal kin were also expected to aid each other. In 1478, for instance, when Lorenzo de' Medici went to war with the papacy in the aftermath of the Pazzi conspiracy, he wrote his cofathers, the king of France and the duke of Milan, seeking aid. Trexler noted that "he did not, be it noted, do this by demanding his credits, but by protesting his humble servitude."[127] While he may not have demanded his credits, he expected his due. He stressed his service to them to remind them that they too, as cofathers, had a responsibility to him. Lapo Niccolini's cofather, Ser Antonio dall'Ancisa, a notary, helped Lapo settle a flawed business deal. Later, Lapo loaned him money without interest due, "for the love that I have for that family." Another of Lapo's cofathers, a wool merchant, gave Lapo's son—who was not his godson—much advice about the business world.[128] Palla Rucellai was asked by his comother if he would have Lorenza Rucellai, Palla's cousin's wife, sit with her and help during childbirth. And Catherine of Siena supposedly restored breast-milk to her comothers.[129]

Considering baptismal kinship's social significance and utility, no wonder Giovanni Dominici complained about the "worldliness" of baptism. He pointed out the hypocrisy in some baptisms. On the one hand, baptism was supposed to represent the cleansing of original sin. On the other hand, he said, parents sought glory in the ceremony and influential godparents. These godparents might even be notorious sinners. He was so upset with the hypocrisy in some baptisms that he crossed the line into the heresy of Donatism. He thought some baptisms were ineffective, meaning that the child received the sacrament but not the grace, because the fathers and godparents went to the ceremony without contrition, desiring only to make a festival of the affair.[130]

Godparents performed one more religious and social duty for their godchildren: they gave them their names. This too occurred at the font, as many *ricordanze* writers noted.[131] More specifically, a child received its second name first—in the ceremony preceding the actual baptism held outside the baptistery. It then received its first name, while everyone stood around the font. For both occurrences, as part of the liturgy, the priest would ask the godparents what name the child had.[132] A Florentine, then, had more than one name. In fact many had three names besides their last name. Bernardo and Maddalena Masi had a little girl on 2 November 1513 whom they named "Margherita e Rafaella e Romola." It was more common, however, for children to have two names. Piero and Catrina Strozzi had a little boy on 11 September 1460, whom they named "Girolamo e Raffaello." And in the *ricordanze* the writers specify that one is the first name ("el primo") and the other is the second ("il secondo"). Sometimes the writers specify which of the two names the family will use. Antonio Rustichi recorded his ninth child's names as Pippa and Ganola but noted that the family would call her Pippa. Bartolomeo Valori's daughters all had the same second name—Maria—except one, whose first name was Maria.[133] Regardless of how many they had, names were important to Florentines. According to Leon Battista Alberti, "Beautiful and magnif- icent names, by the same token, seem to be propitious. They somehow add luster to our virtues and our dignity, and make them still more splendid and admirable. . . . They cost little and they often help us do a lot of good."[134] Unlike godparents in England and France, Floren- tine godparents did not give their godchildren their own names. In fact, they did not have any freedom in the choice of the name given. Godparents simply transmitted the parents' wishes. Florentine parents expected their coparents to follow explicitly their instructions in naming. Luca Panzano hastily corrected the godparents when they accidentally inverted his son's name at the font. Moreover, writers of *ricordanze* recorded explicitly that they gave the name to their child—no one else. They usually wrote some variant of "I put the name to him or her [puosigli]."[135]

In a recent survey of first names from Tuscan official records between 1200 and 1530 (including over 60,000 names of household heads drawn from the 1427 Catasto) David Herlihy noted a wide variety of sources for Tuscan names: classical, nonsensical, geographic, heroic, weather- or time-related, religious, and familial.[136] Although the *ricordanze* reflect this diversity, family and religious names predominate whenever the writer saw fit to explain the choice; in fact, a general tendency seems to have been to pair the familial name with a saint's name, usually the name of the saint on whose day the child was born. Tommaso Guidetti named his son Manelo because it was an ancient family name and, as he recorded, he wished to remake it.[137]

This name remade has been the subject of investigation by Klapisch-Zuber. Because so many ancestors and dead siblings were the source for so many names, Florentines thought that by giving a child a deceased's name that they could figuratively—if not literally—remake the individual. There was something apparently even taboo about this process. According to Klapisch-Zuber, "Giving the name of a living relative would be equivalent to making him enter prematurely into the group of ancestors and would threaten the child."[138] While this is an interesting idea, Klapisch-Zuber may be reading the idiom too literally. Herlihy, for instance, questioned whether `to remake' referred to the person or just the name.[139] In most cases remaking referred to only the name. On 13 February 1489, Tommaso and Lisa Guidetti named their son Rinieri "to remake the name of Rinieri, her father."[140] There were other reasons to reuse a name: "per rispetto, per memoria, per fare honore" [for the respect one had for another, to remember another, to give another honor].[141] And there was no taboo about using a living relative's name for a new child. Tribaldo Rossi, for instance, named his son, who was born 23 May 1490, Amerigho in honor of his father, Amerigho, who died 8 April 1491. Marco Parenti recorded that his son Piero named his son Marco.[142] There is, however, a simple reason why most names of the previous generation that were used by the present generation for their children originally belonged to dead relatives. Considering the late age of marriage for Florentine couples, and especially Florentine men, few if any relatives of the previous generation were alive to be honored in naming. Nevertheless, giving a child the name of a living relative or ancestor was a way to tie generations together, to tie past to present.[143] Moreover, a child would perhaps be loved even more by recalling another loved one.

Although in naming practices the eldest children favored the paternal line, both sides of a family were represented.[144] Some sons were named after their paternal great-grandfather, others after their paternal grandfather or father.[145] Some Florentines named their children to honor their own uncles or aunts or their own brothers or sisters.[146] Florentine men also memorialized their maternal grandmother or their mother.[147] Women chose names too.[148] Cellini recounted how his parents had picked the names of their children out ahead of time. His older sister, Cosa, was named after her father's mother. Cellini, who was thought by all to be a girl while in the womb, was to be named Reparata, after his mother's mother. This arrangement appears to have been the result of a compromise between husband and wife on naming practices. Tribaldo Rossi's mother died in 1495; and when a daughter arrived in 1500 he wanted to memorialize his mother by giving the little girl her name. But his wife wanted to memorialize her mother. Tribaldo did not remake the name of his mother.[149] On 27 March 1394, Ser Iacopo da Prato recorded the birth of a daughter, "Peina e Selvaggia." He noted that the first name memorialized his aunt, his mother's sister, and the second name memorialized his grandmother, his father's mother.[150] Despite a recognized male bias in Florentine society, the maternal side of a family was well represented in Florentine naming practices.[151]

A particular naming practice existed, however, that was solely the father's province, and may have been a source of marital friction. Lapo Curianni noted on 15 November 1385 that he named a daughter Tessa "for my first wife."[152] Gregorio Dati recorded memorializing two dead wives in this fashion.[153] Biagio Buonaccorsi was so eager to remake his dead wife that he had a son given the male version of her name—

Alessandro for Alessandra.[154] No writer of *ricordanze*, however, recorded that he remade the name of his wife's dead husband. Sometimes, though, a female child bore the name of her mother who had just died in childbirth.[155]

Herlihy noted another apparent taboo in the naming practices of premodern Florence. Florentines remade a name only once. To do it again, to rename a child with a name held by two dead relatives, implied bad luck.[156] Yet there were some exceptions to this rule. The Durante family tried to have the name Bianca represented among their children thrice. And thrice they failed. The Valori family tried to get the name Pichina (the name of Bartolomeo Valori's mother) represented among their children. Finally the third child to possess it lived.[157]

Aside from family considerations, saints' names were popular choices for Florentines in the naming of their children. According to Herlihy, by the fifteenth century a change had occurred in Florentine naming practices to make saints' names the most popular choice for naming children. Thirteen of the leading fifteen first names in Tuscany in 1427 were those of saints.[158] This change may be part of the same religious phenomenon that led Tuscans to add a second name, since about 75 percent of Florentine children had a second name that was a saint's name. This addition had occurred by the end of the fourteenth century.[159]

Why give a child a saint's name? First, in the liturgy for baptism, in confessor's handbooks, or Summae, the Church had always advised that children's names should be those of saints and not pagans. Sant'Antonino reiterated this in his *Summa Theologica*.[160] A more important reason would be to establish a guardian relationship for the child; considering the many threats to society in the Late Middle Ages, children needed divine protection.[161] Names benefitted the recipient through the agency of the namesake, and giving children the name of the saint on whose feast day they were born or baptized reflects this. According to Gregorio Dati, "We named him after the two holy apostles, Jacopo and Filippo, on whose feast day he was born and we shall call him Filippo."[162] Sometimes, if the birth or baptism occurred on the feast day of an obscure saint, the parents would then choose a more powerful or more personal saint to gain greater protection for their child.[163]

Certain saints' names were more popular than others. Romolo or Romola for the patron saint of the cathedral of Fiesole was a frequent choice, sometimes even for the third name.[164] Children born or baptized on Sunday received a second name of Domenico or Dominica.[165] Children baptized hurriedly for fear of death received a second—or sometimes a first—name of Giovanni or Giovanna, for St. John the Baptist, the particular patron saint of Florence and a most powerful spiritual protector.[166] Matteo Corsini recorded the birth of a daughter, who was three months premature, on 22 February 1383. He noted that she was baptized at home and given the name Giovanna. She had no godparents listed and died that day.[167] Benedetto or Benedetta (Blessed) was a common saint's name to celebrate a miracle associated with the child. Benedetta Carlini's father was so happy that she and her mother lived through the birth that he named her so, and decided that she should become a nun. Boccaccio, in the *Decameron,* made a pun out of this particular naming practice. Playing a joke on a fellow in order to make love with his wife, an abbot makes him believe he is in Purgatory. He eventually decides to release him and tells him that he will have a son (conveniently fathered by the abbot in the poor fellow's absence). The abbot also tells him that "you shall name him Benedetto, for through the prayers of your holy abbot and your wife and through the love of St. Benedict, this grace is given you by God."[168]

A third reason to give the child the name of a saint, according to Herlihy, was to reflect the parents' own devotion. Parents also hoped that the child would grow up in imitation of the saint they favored or admired. This motive reflects the lay piety of the Late Middle Ages. Preachers, especially the mendicants, had been very successful in popularizing the lives, and as a consequence the names, of many saints in Tuscany.[169] Cristofano Guidini claimed that he gave his son the name Francesco because he was especially devoted to Saint Francis, whom he referred to as "mio divoto," and he also did this to honor Saint Francis ["a onore Santo Francesco"].[170] According to Gregorio Dati, "On 5 July 1402, before the hour of terce, Betta gave birth to our eighth child . . . and we called him Piero Antonio because of Betta's special devotion to S. Antonio."[171] Francesco Giovanni had made a vow to name a child in honor of Saint John the Evangelist, and Mea, his wife, had years before vowed to name a child in honor of Saint Peter. On 26 March 1443 they fulfilled these vows in their son Piero e Giovanni. Ser Iacopo di Lando da Prato named a son Niccolò and a daughter Niccolosa for the reverence in which he held Saint Nicholas. The devotion or reverence a parent had for a saint could stem from a particular occurrence. Elsewhere Iacopo noted that he named a child for Saint Paul because the saint had aided him when he was ill.[172] Children then, in their names, could help their parents pay back spiritual debts while having exemplary models for their own lives. Moreover, they had a heavenly protector.

Regardless of the name received, children sometimes went by other names—nicknames. According to Boccaccio, "Once there was a man named Fresco de Celatico who had a niece whose pet name was Cesca, a term of endearment."[173] Most nicknames were short-ened versions of the first name: Giano for Giuliano, Mea for Bartolomea, Mone for Simone, Nana for Giovanna, Pippo for Filippo, Lisa for Lisabetta.[174] Sometimes they were diminutives. Lionardo Guiccio recalled that he was called Lioncilio.[175] Sometimes children went by their second name rather than their first. Niccolò Bal-dovinetti's son, Tommaso Ettore, was known as Ettore.[176] Most Florentines did not mind turning names into nicknames or having their names turned into nicknames. Catherine dé Pazzi, however, was called Lucrezia (her grandmother's name) by her parents when she was a child. This upset her greatly.[177] But this was not a nickname; this was a name change. She saw this—even as a child—as a "denial of her baptismal name." Names were important to Florentines; names were identity for Florentines.

The whole ceremony and ritual surrounding baptism was impor-tant. This entry by Christofano Guidini, a Sienese, relates that importance:

In the year of our lord 1389 on the 18th of July, I had a daughter from Mattia, my wife: she was born in my house at Uvile and baptized on the 20th of July. She had the name of Catherine to revere Blessed Catherine . . . the godmother was Catherine di Ghetto . . . who was the only goddaughter [figliuola spirituale] of the said Venerable Catherine.[178]

With all this care, concern, and attention regarding birth and baptism Florentines should have been attentive to every need of their newborns. But in a seeming paradox most of these children left the bosom of the family, some the same day they were born, others at later points, to go off to the wetnurse.[179] How then do we explain this apparent contradiction? Florentines really did delight in the birth of their children, and they invested a considerable amount of time, effort, and money in rituals to welcome and protect them. Yet they eventually sent these infants away for months, if not years, at a time—Giovanni Morelli's father, Pagolo, stayed with his wetnurse for 12 years. Or is the contradiction more apparent than real, and do we just not understand the premodern practice of wetnursing? Who was this wetnurse, and how did wetnursing function in premodern Florence?

Demo a Balia: Wetnursing 1—Structures and Dimensions

ENTRIES LIKE THE FOLLOWING abound in the *ricordi* and *ricordanze*:

29 September 1493. We sent to the wetnurse (*balia*) Alesandra, our daughter. We sent her to Monna Chaterina, wife of Matteo del Soldato living in the district of Santo Spirito at a rate of 3 lire a month.[1]

The little girl did not return home to live with her parents for a year and nine months. Who were these wetnurses? Why did parents hire them? How did parents find them? Since wetnursing is foreign to the modern Western World its prevalence in the premodern Western world is thus surprising.[2] Many historians seem disturbed by the concept and confused about the practice, commonly describing wet-nursing as an infanticidal practice adopted largely by the wealthier classes as a means to avoid raising their own children.[3]

According to James Bruce Ross, "immediate separation from its mother" was the fate of a Florentine child from the merchant or ruling class. She doubted that these children were well cared for by the wetnurse and noted that there "is little evidence that parents visited the child" at the wetnurse. As a consequence of this neglect the child was returned "to a stranger in an alien home, to a person with whom no physical or emotional ties had ever been established."[4] For the most part historians of Florence who have touched on wetnursing have followed Ross' lead in interpreting it as a wretched practice for all involved.[5] Richard Trexler emphasized an even nastier side to wetnursing: it "fed on death. The only good *balia* was one whose child had died and made her milk available."[6] Christiane Klapisch-Zuber made a detailed statistical survey of wetnursing practices from the *ricordi* and *ricordanze*. Assuming that wetnursing represented neglect, she discovered an anti-female bias to wetnursing, finding that Florentines had a greater tendency to send little girls to wetnurses, and that they kept them there longer than they did little boys. She concluded, "The girl's life and physical development were deemed of lesser importance." On closer examination, however, her statistics do not really warrant that conclusion. She found that of her sample—68.5 percent of the girls were sent to outside nurses as compared to only 55 percent of the boys. But this distinction between these percentages is not statistically significant since she does not have a representative sample—and her sample size is woefully small. The surviving *ricordi* and *ricordanze* simply do not provide a statistically unbiased and representative sample of the Florentine population, since their survival was anything but random. The differences between her percentages for boys and girls out to wetnurse is then more apparent and meaningless than real and significant.[7]

Yet the modern critique of wetnursing in premodern Florence has a seemingly solid foundation. Many moralists and humanists decried the practice that they saw around them, and modern historians have been quick to pick up on this opposition and even amplify it. And these Florentine commentators were not shy about voicing their opinions regarding wetnursing. San Bernardino harangued crowds about it. "Though he be your own child, and you be wise and pretty-mannered and discreet, yet you give him to be nursed by a sow. . . . And when he comes home and you say: 'I know not whom you resemble! You are not like unto any of us!' And so I say to you, women, who send your child out to nurse: he will take on the condition of the woman who feeds him."[8] He added elsewhere that children who went off to the wetnurse did not grow as large as those who were breastfed by their mothers.[9] The humanist Leon Battista Alberti wrote a dialogue about wetnursing in which the character Lionardo bemoaned all the problems inherent in finding and employing competent wetnurses. His solution was simple: have the mother nurse her own child. And he found an excellent precedent for this since the Romans (so he thought) had done it this way.[10] In fact, much of the rhetoric of the Renaissance discussion and critique of wetnursing came from classical sources.[11] The Venetian humanist Francesco Barbaro adopted Plutarch's explanation for why women's breasts were located where they were on her body. Nature placed them high so that the mother could embrace her child.[12] Alberti even emphasized a positive effect of maternal breastfeeding, noting that a woman would love her child more if she breastfed it.[13]

Despite their invective, commentators such as San Bernardino and Alberti did not oppose the practice itself. What concerned them most was the question of who was actually raising the children, an observation that implies that wetnursing was much more than just hired breastfeeding.[14] San Bernardino told parents that "the child acquires certain of the customs of the one who suckles him."[15] Echoing this sort of attitude, Michelangelo believed that he had gained his skill at sculpture from having been wetnursed by the wife of a stonecutter.[16]

The humanist critique of wetnursing delved more into the question of the character of the wetnurse and the suitability of her environment for these infants.[17] The humanist critique also reflected an urban dislike for the peasantry, from whom many wetnurses were drawn.[18] There also may have been some aspect of social-status conflict since women of lower status breastfed children from a higher social status. Here then we see the points of conflict affecting Florentine society's perceptions of wetnursing: elite versus non-elite culture, rich versus poor, urban versus rural.

There may even have been an element of sexism in the humanist critique of wetnursing, since a woman who had sent her children off to a wetnurse was more independent, more free, to pursue her own interests and duties.[19] Moreover, most humanists and moralists directed their criticism of the practice not so much at the father as at the mother. One author claimed that breastfeeding her young was the only worthwhile accomplishment a woman could make. A sixteenth-century English chaplain believed that women hired wetnurses out of modesty or for their own leisure, and with the latter he perhaps intended a veiled attack on women's freedom.[20] Despite this widespread literary criticism, wetnursing continued unabated. David Hunt asked a good question: if all the premodern literature was so against wetnursing, why did so many families use it so widely? Jack Goody, in noting the premodern Catholic Church's opposition to wetnursing, said it was of little avail "given the widespread nature of the practice." Obviously, wetnursing was useful to premodern parents. Moreover, not all of the humanist literature was critical of the practice; some humanists, such as Francesco da Barberino (1264-1348), even advised wetnursing. In his *Del reggimento e de' costumi delle donne* he devoted an entire section, some 524 lines of Tuscan poetry, to a discussion of the *balia*. And most humanists and moralists alike took the time and effort to explain the physical characteristics one should look for in a competent wetnurse. In fact, regardless of how they felt about wetnursing, the humanists and moralists all accepted the practice as commonplace in their day.[21]

Wetnursing was commonplace elsewhere in the premodern world. In eighteenth-century Paris, for instance, four bureaus regulated the wetnursing trade. Unfortunately, only one of these bureaus' records have survived; nevertheless, in 1751 alone over 12,000 women came to this one bureau seeking employment as wetnurse. Over the course of the next half-century these numbers increased. Sussman estimated that 50 percent of Parisian infants went out to a nurse in the country; 25 percent went to a nurse living in the city; 20 percent were abandoned to the foundling hospitals; and the rest were nursed by their mothers. Out of a population of some 90,000 in Hamburg during the eighteenth century some 5,000 women listed their occupation as wetnurse. In his detailed study of Imperial Russian foundling homes David Ransel discovered that during the late nineteenth century the foundling homes in Moscow and St. Petersburg could have upwards of 30,000 women per year applying to be wetnurses. In 1885 the Moscow foundling home employed some 15,000 women as wetnurses, the St. Petersburg foundling home 9,000. Around 1900, St. Petersburg had five separate agencies handling the wetnursing business for the public. Over 10,000 women were under contract as wetnurses at this time. Linda Pollock found that nineteenth-century English aristocrats were still hiring wetnurses for their children; and while maternal breast-feeding was more popular, it was not that much more popular than hiring a wetnurse. In fact, a century earlier in England maternal breastfeeding among the aristocracy was proof that the family faced hard financial times. Only poor mothers nursed their own children. Yet even the poor hired wetnurses. In premodern and modern France the majority of nurslings came from the ranks of the urban artisans. From the list of fathers' occupations Sussman noted that roughly 60 percent of a sample of nurslings came from the artisan class, 15 percent from the shopkeeping class, 10 percent from the servant class, and only 10 percent from the ranks of the bourgeois. In France wetnursing was a vibrant business until World War I, though its heyday was during the period of the Enlightenment.[22] Florentine wetnursing patterns seem to parallel those of Enlightenment Paris; wetnursing was common in Florence.[23]

In 1466, for instance, the *Innocenti* had 456 wetnurses on the payroll. Noting the increase in foundlings and orphans in Florence during the time of the Italian wars, Trexler observed that the "country-side was increasingly turned into a milk farm for the Innocenti." Of some 281 absolutions granted by the episcopal court of Florence for the supposed accidental smothering of children, only 23 needed to be granted for the natural parents. Between 1531 and 1540 only 14 of the 128 children supposedly accidentally smothered were done so by their natural parents. Most likely these other accused couples were the wetnurses and their husbands.[24] The disparity between the number of strangers and natural parents accused of overlaying children hints at the wide extent of wetnursing in Florence. And the presence of the *Innocenti* and other foundling hospitals in Tuscany certainly put pressure upon the wetnursing system in the area, making it harder for citizens to find and employ their own wetnurses and consistently driving up the cost. By the midnineteenth century, for instance, Tuscan foundling homes enrolled over 5,000 children a year; and the bureau-cracy of these homes had to control thousands of wetnurses.[25]

Other things hint at wetnursing's ubiquity in Florence. It appeared as the subject of legislation. The Florentine urban statutes of the late thirteenth century specified a nursing time of three years. In addition Florentine sumptuary laws in 1355/56 regulated the wetnurse's dress.

In Boccaccio's *Decameron* one of the first things the characters do after a birth is arrange for a wetnurse for the child. One of Alberti's characters, Gianozzo, asked his wife to guess the age of a toothless, gray-haired woman they had encountered. His wife answered that "the woman seemed about the age of her mother's wetnurse." This witty answer, couched in an idiom of its time and place, reflects the commonness of wetnursing in Florence. The humanist monk Aliotto, discussing Leonardo Bruni, Poggio Bracciolini, Carlo Marsuppini, and Benedetto Accolti—all Florentine chancellors but born or reared in Arezzo—complemented Arezzo's educational system by calling it "the wetnurse of the best minds." In a letter to Cristofano di Bartolo sometime in the 1390s, Francesco Datini criticized him for allowing his concubine to breastfeed their illegitimate child. What irritated Francesco about this was that Cristofano allowed her to do this inside the Datini business compound overseas, thus interrupting (at least in Francesco's mind) the smooth flow of his business. Francesco told him that in Prato and Florence few parents, including those who were wealthy, kept a nursing child at home. Richard Goldthwaite commented that the wetnurse was "the other woman" in the lives of the Florentine elite, and she appears frequently in their records. Aside from the *ricordanze,* wetnurses appear in both wills and letters. Alessandra Strozzi left a wetnurse shoes and a gown in her will, a copy of which she recorded in her *ricordi.* In a letter to her husband Luigi, dated 19 June 1537, Isabella Guicciardini mentioned their wetnurse. Diane Owen Hughes found references to Genoese wetnurses in wills in which testators remembered both their own and their children's wetnurses.[26]

Christofano Guidini had a separate section of his *ricordanze* devoted to "all of my children that were sent to the wetnurse, the salary I gave, when, to whom, and where." The records therein could be remarkably detailed:

> The first child I gave to a wetnurse was my first son, that is Francesco, on 7 November 1380. He went to Monna Andrea the wife of Feio living at Brolio in the contado at a salary of 50 soldi a month. On the last day of the said month I went to see my son at Brolio, and I gave Monna Andrea, his wetnurse, two fiorini.

On the last day of May 1381 Monna Andrea, the wetnurse, brought the child back, because she said that she was pregnant. She had been paid periodically.

Then on 3 June 1381 I gave the child to Monna Mina, wife of Biagiuolo of Rapolano at a cost of 3 lire a month. She kept him for a year and was periodically paid by Monna Agnesa, my mother (may God pardon her). And because the wetnurse became pregnant, she did not wish to keep him any longer. I then no longer gave him to a wetnurse, and we kept him at home without a wetnurse and weaned him.[27]

Marco Parenti, likewise, kept meticulous records of his children's tenure at the wetnurse, their transfer to other wetnurses, their weaning, and their return.[28]

Not only was wetnursing common in Florence it was also intensive, considering how prolific the merchant elite were. Antonio Masi noted that of his and his wife's 36 children, 28 went to the wetnurse. Matteo Strozzi in 1433 made a copy of his Catasto account in his *ricordanze,* which listed five children, ages one through seven, four of whom (Filippo, 5; Piero, 4; Lorenzo, 3; Caterina, 1) were still at the wetnurse, for he noted his expenses to the wetnurse as a possible tax credit. In the index to his *debitori e creditori* account book he listed a total of 11 wetnurses for his 6 children over a period of ten years. Giovanni Morelli's father at one point had three children at the wetnurse.[29] The wetnurse, therefore, added a different dimension to the family schematic in the premodern era, as did the nurseling. Klapisch-Zuber described it as a triangular relationship in which the parents relate to the child and the wetnurse, the wetnurse relates to the child and the parents, and the child relates to the parents and the wetnurse.[30] As many urban families temporarily decreased in size with the removal of the nurseling, many rural families temporarily increased in size with the addition of the nurseling.[31] The presence of the wetnurse in the composition of the premodern family could also reflect a parallel relationship. Niccolò Busini recorded that between 1395 and 1401 three of his children had the same wetnurse.[32] As his family increased so did hers, and both were linked by wetnursing.

Why did premodern parents hire a wetnurse? Florentines and other premodern people were well aware of the contraceptive value of wetnursing for mothers—lactating women are less likely to conceive.[33] But, as we have seen, the merchant elite of Florence wanted more children, so sending their children out to wetnurses was a crude form of reverse birth control, an attempt to increase fertility. They could also manipulate this to some extent. Cambio Petrucci and his wife sent their first two children and their fourth child immediately to the wetnurse. Their other children remained at home for a while, nursed by the mother.[34] As the Petrucci family grew the desire for more children declined and they manipulated wetnursing to accommodate this.

Perhaps the most frequent reason given for hiring wetnurses was to preserve the health of the mother—especially if she had had a difficult delivery, a not-too-uncommon occurrence in the premodern era—or of the child, especially if the mother's milk was bad or insufficient. In his treatise on the family, Alberti has one of his characters, Lionardo, remark that "these doctors nowadays will assert that giving the breast weakens the mother and makes her sterile for a time." In this dialogue about wetnursing Lionardo strongly favored maternal breastfeeding—unless the mother had experienced a difficult birth. Then, the hiring of a wetnurse was imperative. Giovanni Rucellai advised maternal breastfeeding if it could be done without danger (senza pericolo). The humanist Maffeo Vegio, who advised women to breastfeed only if they were healthy, recalled that after his own birth his mother was too ill and did not have enough breastmilk to feed him, even though she had wanted to. Describing a birth, Boccaccio specifically noted, "after giving her small son to a wet-nurse, she began recuperating."[35] Commentators throughout the premodern era described nursing for a woman who had just given birth as draining.[36] While they were certainly making a crude analogy between the mother's expressing milk and losing energy, commentators recognized that breastfeeding is physically demanding for the mother and that it is hard work.

Some thought the initial fluid put out by a lactating woman, the colostrum, was unhealthy for a child since it appeared thinner and more yellow than breast milk proper.[37] Commentators, therefore, thought it better to hire a wetnurse rather than subject a child to something suspect and of doubtful nutritive value. And Florentines recognized that not every mother could suckle. Oderigo di Credi recalled how in 1400 his wife gave birth to a son in July but in December she became ill and lost her milk.[38] In 1442, Niccolò Ammanatini, expressing his poverty to the tax officials, noted that "[m]y wife has no milk and we must hire a wet nurse."[39] Catherine of Racconigi's (b. 1486) family was so poor that when her mother was unable to breastfeed her, her brother was sent door to door with her to beg the other village mothers to nurse her.[40] Sometimes mothers were not even present to nurse their children; considering the high mortality rate for mothers, their absence right after birth was a real possibility. In cases like these, since there was no efficient or suitable artificial feeding in the premodern world, a wetnurse was essential.[41]

There was a male-specific reason for sometimes hiring a wetnurse—bastardy. Some of these children, especially those who were children of slave mothers, ended up in a foundling home. Men who did not want to place their illegitimate children in a foundling home found them a wetnurse whenever their mother could not nurse them.[42] Luca da Panzano had a son born from another man's wife, and he arranged for a rural wetnurse.[43] A cuckold, for obvious reasons regarding honor, would not want the physical reminder of his shame around. A bastard, therefore, could create a delicate and tense situation, though the child had to be cared for somehow. One of Francesco Datini's associates found himself in an equally complicated situation. One of his slave girls became pregnant. When he could not discover who the father was, he arranged for a wetnurse himself. When his wife discovered this, she became enraged, suspecting that he was the father. She kicked the slave girl out of their home, and he pleaded with Datini to have Margherita Datini intercede on his behalf with his wife.[44] In 1475, Bernardo Machiavelli had to find a wetnurse for the son of his new servant girl, though without the suspicion that Datini's associate suffered.[45]

A number of humanists opined that mothers did not nurse their own children because the act offended them. Giovanni Rucellai in fact ranked it equally with health as a reason for mothers not to breastfeed.[46] This sense of offense might reflect a cultural belief that only the poor breastfed.[47] Or it could relate to a belief that breastfeeding, like other bodily functions, ought to be hidden.[48] Moreover, this offensiveness might relate to the mother's sense of her own beauty. A French commentator, Bernard de Gordon, said women hired wetnurses for their own vanity.[49] Some evidence indicates that women were concerned about keeping their breasts looking attractive and that they saw breastfeeding as detrimental to that goal.[50] In their diaries, English aristocratic women noted that one of the reasons they hired a wetnurse was to preserve their figures.[51] Thus John Sommerville claimed that wetnursing during the Renaissance was "one of the first luxuries women demanded."[52] Judith C. Brown added a twist to this, stating that couples in the Renaissance adopted wetnursing so they could avoid a sexual taboo for nursing women. Lawrence Stone, however, found no evidence that this sort of taboo ever existed. Moreover, the numbers of women who became pregnant while nursing in the premodern period (both mothers and wetnurses) implies the weakness of such a taboo—if it ever existed in the popular mentality.[53]

Regardless of the reason, women who did hire wetnurses were considerably freer than those who did not. Klapisch-Zuber concluded that these women possessed "complete liberty."[54] Liberty, however, did not mean mere leisure. Women, even of the aristocratic and wealthier classes, had considerable household responsibilities. Some of these, if Margherita Datini is any example, even related to the family's commercial affairs when the husband was away.[55] There was then an economic reason for a mother to hire a wetnurse. Women of the lower classes worked in industry. In 1396, for instance, Francesco Datini employed 96 women for a period of six months as spinners for a particular shipment of wool.[56] Women, as we are just finding out, were more active in and essential for the premodern economy than we once thought. Jean-Louis Flandrin concluded that the premodern economy would have collapsed without women's contribution, and elite society would have been a different entity if women had not been able to devote themselves to their social obligations.[57] Wetnursing allowed this to happen. Even peasant women, as Le Roy Ladurie discovered at Montaillou, would hire wetnurses if their work was necessary or desired for the family economy.[58] In the premodern world the mother's contribution to the household economy and management was thought crucial and profitable enough by all social classes to justify the cost of wetnursing.[59]

Yet for some the cost of wetnursing was prohibitive. Tribaldo Rossi recorded that his poverty was the reason he had to recall a child from the wetnurse before he wanted to. Boccaccio, in describing a poor villager, shows him with a child almost a year old still nursing at his mother's breast. The urban poor also found it hard to pay for a wetnurse. Poverty more than any other reason might explain why Benedetta Carlini's mother nursed her.[60]

Nevertheless, whenever they could, the lower classes hired wet-nurses for their children, and for the same reason that the more well-to-do hired wetnurses. Some evidence from the 1427 Catasto seems to support this. Of some 234 infants listed at the wetnurse from the Catasto 90 come from a status below what Herlihy and Klapisch-Zuber defined as rich. The vast majority of petitions to have nursing costs reimbursed came from the poorer countryside rather than the wealthier urban area of Florence.[61] Just as artisans in ancien regime France hired wetnurses so the wife could continue to contribute to the family economy, so did Florentine artisans. On 13 June 1428, for example, a grocer Francesco di [last name unreadable] sent his son out to an urban wetnurse.[62] A simple parish priest, Iacopo Melocchi, sent all his children out to a wetnurse.[63] On 16 December 1403 the parents of Giovanni di Miniato, who later grew up to become a leatherworker, sent him to the wetnurse some seven months after his birth.[64] In fact, one of the reasons the lower classes may have sent their children to foundlings hospitals was so both parents could work. In a sense they received government- sponsored day care, since both parents had to work.[65]

Why would someone become a wetnurse? For some the reasons mirror the reasons women hired wetnurses. Herlihy and Klapisch-Zuber noted that the lower a family's income in Florence the fewer children they had. If wetnursing, whose contraceptive value was well known, was as widespread as I think it was, it was a prime agent behind that statistic. This represents a conscious decision by the poor to limit their offspring. Wetnursing also represented income for women, especially if they had already weaned their own children and were still lactating.[66] If a woman had lost her own child in birth or right after, she was still lactating and hence had a product to market. In a situation like this perhaps offering to wetnurse someone else's child could serve the grieving mother as a psychological comfort.

Sometimes, lower-class women would send their children off to wetnurse so they could wetnurse the child of someone of the upper class and still make a profit.[67] This was why some Tuscan women left their newborns at a foundling hospital. In 1433 one woman gave up her daughter because she "could not feed her, and she would have to hire herself out as a wet-nurse to be able to live." Another's problem in 1435 was that "the father did not want to do anything. It was necessary for her to hire out as a wet-nurse if she wanted to live, because she was dying of hunger."[68] Trexler saw examples such as these as evidence of the inhuman character of wetnursing and how foundling hospitals exploited poor women who otherwise would have nursed their own children.[69] This is too one-sided and ignores the harsh realities of the premodern economic world. For people living on or near the margin of society and existence, even a paltry income could mean the difference between success and failure of the family.[70] Although I have emphasized the economic motivations for someone's deciding to become a wetnurse, I do not wish to ignore some human impulses. Some women must have become wetnurses because they liked infants and enjoyed being around them.

Wetnurses were hired in two ways: *in casa*, in which the wetnurse came and stayed in the parents' house, and outside, in which a couple sent their child outside the family home, sometimes miles away and sometimes for years, to be nursed.[71] From the evidence that Klapisch-Zuber drew from the *ricordi* and *ricordanze* about 20 percent of Florentine wetnurses were *in casa,* and some of these were even slaves.[72]

An *in casa* nurse was more expensive than an outside nurse. According to Klapisch-Zuber's figures drawn from the years 1400-1480, the yearly cost of an *in casa* nurse was between 18 and 20 fiorini per year plus expenses, such as shoes, food, and clothing. An urban outside nurse cost between 18 and 20 fiorini per year, without expenses; a rural outside nurse cost between 9 and 15 fiorini per year, without expenses. Klapisch-Zuber thought that the reason an *in casa* nurse cost so much more than an outside nurse was also related to the reason why people used an *in casa* nurse. They could have more control over her life. Specifically, parents would want to make sure that she did not become pregnant, thus in their minds spoiling the quality of the milk and terminating the contract prematurely.[73] There might, however, have been a simpler and less manipulative reason to hire an *in casa* nurse, which is related to why an outside urban nurse cost more than an outside rural nurse. Parents could have greater access to their children with an *in casa* wetnurse than with an outside nurse. They could also have greater access to their children with an urban nurse than with a rural nurse. The price differentials from these three categories of nurses reflects the demand that Florentine parents placed on the available pool of wetnurses so they could keep their infants as close to them as possible yet work within the confines of the structures of their premodern world.

The eldest child, usually the most favored, was more likely than younger ones to have an *in casa* nurse.[74] In 1463, after five years of waiting, Marco Parenti's wife gave birth to his ninth child, the second son after seven girls. The birth seemed to surprise him pleasantly. He had an *in casa* nurse for him whereas the other children had not had one, perhaps because he wanted to see more of the child. On 5 November 1484, Bartolomeo Salvietti sent his son Lionardo off to a wetnurse, but on 10 October 1485 he brought him back to the house and hired an *in casa* nurse for him. In August 1486 he hired another *in casa* nurse for him. Maybe the parents just wanted their son at home. Cipriano Guidicci did the opposite. For eight months he and his wife kept their son at home with them, having hired an *in casa* nurse, then they sent him to an outside nurse for ten more months.[75] This may have been a more common pattern of nursing since many people would hire a temporary urban nurse (either *in casa* or outside) to span the gap between birth and the trip to the rural wetnurse.[76]

An *in casa* nurse sometimes had another function, which may help explain why she was the most expensive form of nurse. She might end up doing double duty as a regular servant. Niccolò Baldovinnetti recorded that Bartola, the wife of Guido d'Ugolino, "came to stay with me as wetnurse for my son Francescho Boreghini and as house servant."[77] Francesco Datini's brother-in-law killed two birds with one stone by firing his lazy maid and having his *in casa* wetnurse assume her duties.[78]

Not only was an *in casa* nurse paid more than an outside nurse, but she had other needs that her employers had to consider. Sometimes this involved finding a wetnurse for her child, since part of the contract was the inclusion of her expenses as part of her salary. This would result in dual accounts in the *ricordi* and *ricordanze*, the writer listing the expenses for child and for the child of the wetnurse.[79] At other times, an *in casa* wetnurse's child could come to live with her.[80] In cases like these the cost for having a *in casa* wetnurse could be high.

Having a slave as an *in casa* wetnurse could also be expensive. In May 1447, Giovanni Strozzi purchased a slave with "latte frescho" to serve as a wetnurse for his newborn son, Piero. She cost him 47 florins, but Giovanni may have had a particular reason for expending such a sum for a wetnurse. In 1444 he had sent his first son to a wetnurse, where he subsequently died. In 1445 he had sent another son to a wetnurse where he subsequently died. In 1447 he may have wanted to oversee matters a little better for his third son, and this son did live. Yet Giovanni also saw profit in this scheme since by July 1447 he was hiring her out to nurse someone else's child. On 4 October 1447 he hired her out to someone else and she returned to him in April 1448.[81] Two days after his son's birth in 1464, Bartolomeo di Ser Antonio recorded the arrival in his house of a slave woman who nursed the child for two months. He then sent the child to a regular wetnurse. Guido Antella recorded that he hired a number of slave women to serve as *in casa* wetnurses for his children.[82] Slaves as wetnurses apparently were very common in the Mediterranean world. At Ragusa, for instance, they appear in wills with orders to be manumitted as a reward for their service.[83] A Florentine merchant based in Majorca, Niccolò Giovanni, agreed to free his slave girl if she nursed his son for two years.[84] Like other aspects of slavery, however, slave wetnursing could be gruesome and inhumane. In 1618 at Pisa, for instance, a slave wetnurse ran away from her master because he beat her whenever his child cried. Moreover, some masters forced their slave women to serve as wetnurses right after they had given birth, thus denying nutrition to their own children, and in many, if not most, cases these children were abandoned to the Innocenti.[85]

In some of the above examples the *in casa* nurse, either slave or free, served only temporarily, and the child eventually went off to an outside wetnurse, either urban or rural. Perhaps these parents wanted to keep their children as close as possible to them but the cost of an *in casa* nurse prevented this from being permanent. Klapisch-Zuber discovered that for every child sent to an outside urban nurse, six children went to outside rural nurses. Moreover, 45 percent of these outside nurses lived more than 15 kilometers from Florence.[86] There were three main areas near Florence where parents sent children to the wetnurse: the Mugello, north of Florence; the Casentino, east of Florence; and the countryside around Prato. In fact, Prato had an excellent reputation as a choice area for finding wetnurses.[87] The rural area around Florence proper also was a popular choice, most likely because the family could keep in close contact with their child. Lapo Mazzei, who was devoted to his children, sent 13 of his 14 children into the hills surrounding Florence for their wetnursing.[88] A rural wetnurse was not necessarily a poor choice for Florentines, since humanists extolled the virtues of country air, albeit while decrying the inhabitants. One of Alberti's characters, Lionardo, even asserted that country air was better for children than urban air. Morelli, whose father was wetnursed in the Mugello, referred often to the "bel paeso di Mugello." And even though he is a harsh critic of the Florentine wetnursing system, Trexler did admit that with "optimal conditions, the rural *balie* saved lives."[89]

A wetnurse's geographical location also tells us something about her social status. Most rural wetnurses were the wives of farmers. Sometimes these were laborers for the family whose child was being wetnursed, and at times the location of the wetnurse was near the family's villa or lands. Giovanni Amica recorded that the wetnurses for his daughters were the farmhands, *lavoratori,* of a relative who was a Rucellai. Giovanni Strozzi sent one of his children to the wife of "nostro lavoratore" for wetnursing. Tribaldo Rossi noted that he owned a farm near the house of the wetnurse for his first son.[90] Leah Lydia Otis found that the vast majority of municipal wetnurses in Montpellier during the fifteenth century were the wives of artisans or urban workers.[91] Urban nurses from premodern Florence reflect that same composition, a composition that must have been prevalent enough to appear in fiction.[92] In one of Boccaccio's stories Madame Beritola hired a wetnurse who "[t]hough she was a woman of low station she was nevertheless sensible and prudent."[93] The rural and urban lower classes, therefore, furnished the urban middle and upper classes with their wetnurses, so wetnursing as a practice was very much class based and biased. This should not be interpreted as any hard-and-fast rule, since the rural and urban lower classes utilized wetnursing themselves whenever necessary.

Boccaccio's description hints at what must have been a crucial question: just what qualities should an ideal wetnurse possess? According to Barberino she should be:

> between twenty-five and thirty-five years, as much like the mother as possible, and let her have good color and a strong neck and strong chest and ample flesh, firm and fat rather than lean, but by no means too much so, her breath not bad, her teeth clean. And as for her manners, guard against the proud and wrathful and gloomy, neither fearful nor foolish, nor coarse. . . . Let her breasts be between soft and hard, big but not excessive in length, the quantity of her milk moderate, and the color white and not green, nor yellow and even less black, the odor good and also the taste, not salty nor bitter, but on the sweet side, and uniform throughout, but not foamy, and abundant. And note that the best is one who has her own male child. And beware of one who "goes bad" such as one whom her husband won't leave alone, and one whom you find gravid. . . .[94]

Barberino speaks volumes here. First he wanted the wetnurse to be as similar to the mother as possible, in age (according to Florentine demographic statistics he is quite accurate in his age range) and looks. Most likely Florentines believed that having a nurse look like the mother would ease the transition of the child from mother to nurse and back to mother. Antonio Rustichi's wife, Caterina, even ensured that the wetnurses for her first two children were named Caterina.[95]

In an age when not everyone, especially in the lower classes, was well fed, finding a fleshy, healthy wetnurse with good color was significant. It meant that this woman was eating well enough to nurse safely without endangering the child. Margherita Datini, a broker for parents seeking wetnurses, looked for women with good color and strong necks when she searched for suitable wetnurses. Giovanni Rucellai likewise warned his sons to find healthy wetnurses for their children.[96] Barberino mentioned breast size; so did Margherita Datini.

She thought large-breasted women were unsuited for wetnursing because they would give the child a flat nose.[97]

The wetnurse's character, as Barberino emphasized, was crucial, and his description recalls Boccaccio's sensible and prudent woman. Alberti had one of his characters describe the perfect wetnurse as good, knowledgeable, moral, and clean.[98] The underlying reason for their concern with the wetnurse's character recalls the humanists' opposition to wetnursing. They knew a wetnurse did more than just breastfeed a child. A wetnurse was a child's first educator. More specifically and less correctly, they believed that her qualities were contained in the milk and passed on to the child. A nurse, according to Alberti, was supposed to be "free, clean, and clear of those vices and defects which infect and corrupt the milk and the blood." Later in this passage he elaborated by stating that "leprosy and epilepsy and other serious diseases are passed on by the breast, it is said." Paolo da Certaldo likewise thought the character of the wetnurse was directly passed to the child. He even said that a drunkard's qualities would be passed on by the wetnurse, so he cautioned parents not to hire them.[99] The transfer between wetnurse and child was not a one-way street. While the observations of the humanists appear fanciful, syphilis was one disease that a child could pass on to a wetnurse (who likewise could pass it on to another charge). As the fifteenth century turned into the sixteenth, foundling homes faced a quandary with the rise and rapid spread of syphilis. How could they feed syphilitic foundlings without endangering the wetnurses and eventually other children? Foundling homes adopted both bottle feeding and direct animal feeding, using goats, with poor results for the most part.[100]

Lastly, Barberino went into an elaborate description of the breast milk, including how it should taste. For others the quality of the breast milk was equally important. Paolo da Certaldo sensibly noted that while other characteristics were important one had to have a wetnurse "who had an abundance of milk." Paolo Sassetti in recording a wetnursing deal made a marginal note that she seemed to have enough milk.[101] Certaldo feared that wetnurses who did not have enough breast milk would resort to using farm animal milk (which tells us as well something about the location of Florentine wetnurses). Humanists as a group expressed considerable doubts about using farm animal milk for feeding infants. Believing that just like human milk it could transfer qualities, they did not want dull, brutish, bestial children.[102] Barberino did say that in cases of necessity a wetnurse could feed a child ewe's milk, but no other animal's milk.[103]

Parents also did not want a wetnurse who was pregnant to continue nursing their child, since they believed that pregnant women's milk was bad for the infant.[104] (In addition, they must have realized that pregnant women will eventually cease lactating.) Milk quality was thus an important issue in choosing a wetnurse. Luca da Panzano counted himself lucky in 1423 for finding a wetnurse with milk only 15 days old.[105] On the other hand, Antonio Rustichi complained about the quality of milk given his daughter Pippa and son Lionardo.[106] From what Barberino said about choosing a wetnurse, but especially regarding the quality of a wetnurse's milk and how someone ascertained that, parents were obviously supposed to undertake an elaborate inspection of the wetnurse.

Considering the various limitations of the premodern world, such as poor communications, it must have taken some time and effort to bring together a parturient woman and a lactating woman. According to Alberti:

> It would take a long time to tell you how careful we fathers have to be about these things, and how much trouble there is each time before one has found an honest, good, and competent nurse. Nor would you believe, perhaps, how much anxiety, trouble, and remorse of spirit results if she is not found in time or if she is not adequate. Yet this sort of person always seems to be unavailable just when you need her the most.[107]

Timing was essential here, as Alberti noted, for with all the other concerns a father had about a wetnurse "he must with much effort get hold of one who will be ready in time."[108] Other humanists, such as Palmieri and Rucellai, likewise echoed these concerns.[109] That they did indicates that the process of arranging for a wetnurse was one fraught with worry and full of difficulties. Paolo da Certaldo advised parents not to leave children with a substandard wetnurse just because she was available and the price was right.[110]

Despite the difficulties, certainly one thing made wetnursing work—it was a business venture, which even involved the wetnurse's husband, whose role was signified by the masculinization of his wife's title. He was the *balio*. He usually collected payments and transported children between their home and his.[111] Klapisch-Zuber discovered the *ricordanze* of a *balio*. He was Piero di Francesco Puro da Vecchio, a sometime—servant for various corporate groups including the Parte Guelfa, living in the first half of the fifteenth century. In fact, his position as a servant for these corporate groups may have given him excellent contacts for the wetnursing business. He and his wife would send their children out to a rural wetnurse for three to four lire a month and charge their own clients seven lire a month. Parents brought their children to him and he also collected the payments.[112]

Sometimes a third party arrived at the parents' house to take their infants to the wetnurse. Marco Parenti recorded that on 9 August 1451, two days after his daughter's birth, a Mona Lisa, who was not the wetnurse, arrived to take her to the wetnurse.[113] Other people also could receive the payment. On 21 July 1483, Bartolomeo Salvetti recorded that the aunt of the *balio* came to pick up his payment to the wetnurse. One Piero, whom Salvetti identified as the wetnurse's brother-in-law, also came periodically to receive payment for the wetnursing.[114] Even children of the *balio* and wetnurse came to receive the payments.[115] Wetnursing was a family business in the premodern world.

This business even involved Francesco Datini, the fantastically wealthy merchant of Prato, and his wife Margherita. He served as a broker, lining up clients, and she tracked the wetnurses down. They frequently communicated about this business, and she was constantly sending messages to the farms around Prato asking if any woman was available to wetnurse.[116] At times, if she were lucky, she could offer a potential client an assortment of good nurses. Sometimes she had nurses available but was dissatisfied with them for one reason or another. At one point she wrote Francesco that she had three women lined up but that one, while a "good milk-giver," was scatterbrained; another was mean (and had only one eye); and the third wanted to keep her child with her. In fact, Margherita suspected that most of the wetnurses she placed under contract who had a child less than one year old still nursed it and the client's child. At other times, Margherita complained, wetnurses just could not be found.[117] The experiences of Francesco and Margherita Datini certainly reflected the experiences, on a larger or smaller scale, of other couples involved in the wetnursing business.

If professionals such as Margherita Datini had trouble locating wetnurses at times, it must have been that much harder for parents to locate a good wetnurse. Having a good network of family, friends, and neighbors certainly helped in this search. The parish priest probably also served as a good source of information about who might need a wetnurse or who might be available to wetnurse, since he usually served as center of the parish's gossip network.[118] Klapisch-Zuber pointed out that women themselves, with their circle of friends, served as excellent sources of information on who might be available to wetnurse.[119] Regardless of the source, gossip about who needed a wetnurse and who could wetnurse undoubtedly formed part of the everyday discourse between inhabitants of Florence. Moreover, counting *balie, balii,* messengers, and collectors there must have been a large network of individuals associated with the wetnursing industry.[120]

According to Klapisch-Zuber, fathers "usually" decided the wetnursing arrangements and contract "alone."[121] This is doubtful, just from the perspective of common sense. My sense from reading the records is that Florentine parents usually made joint decisions. Her conclusion may just reflect the bias of the *ricordi* and *ricordanze* in that they are male records and the husband usually handed over the wetnurse's salary. Moreover, we get hints from the *ricordi* and *ricordanze* that both parents were involved in the choice of a wetnurse. On 12 March 1411, Cambio Petrucci and his wife invited a prospective wetnurse to their house for an inspection because "we wished to see if she had milk."[122] Marco Parenti recorded that his wife arranged a wetnursing contract with the wetnurse.[123] Other writers used the first person plural possessive in their *ricordi* and *ricordanze* at times to refer to the wetnurse or the wetnursing contract.[124] Considering that these are such highly individual and personal accounts, this is significant and meaningful, indicating that wetnursing involved a joint decision by the parents. The *balio* Piero Puro noted that he received children from both fathers and mothers.[125] And wives did deliver payments to the wetnurse.[126]

As I mentioned, *ricordi* and *ricordanze* writers meticulously recorded their deals with the wetnurse. While the records were not

notarized, they have the physical appearance of formal contracts.[127]
Bartolomeo Sassetti recorded his arrangements in the business section
of his *ricordanze* rather than the *memoria* section, where he recorded
other family records—such as births.[128] The typical record lists the
wetnurse, the *balio*, the length of the stay, the location of the wetnurse,
the monthly cost, the schedule of payments (Manno Petrucci said he
would pay his wetnurse every month), and the return of the child.[129]
Guido Antella recorded that on 12 January 1381 he and Monna
Giovanna, the wetnurse of his son Alessandro, closed their wetnursing
contract and he drew up the final payment.[130] Sometimes the account
was in arrears at the final accounting, as Luca Panzano discovered; he
was behind in his payments by two months.[131] These contracts
frequently noted certain conditions, that the deal was valid while the
wetnurse furnished suitable milk or that if the wetnurse became
pregnant she had to inform the parent and return the child.[132] Marco
Parenti informed Mona Mattea that she would continue to receive her
salary as long as she nursed his son.[133] Wetnursing was a business,
something that Florentines knew well how to organize.

But it represented childcare and family maintenance too. According to Diane Owen Hughes, "Without the nurses the bourgeois family
might not have been as large nor the bourgeoisie so stable."[134] The
wetnursing system also helped artisan and peasant families, providing
them with chances to increase their household earnings, and, specifically in the case of families that took in nurslings, providing a
mechanism with which to limit family size. Wetnursing was a useful
and valuable tool for implementing family strategies in the premodern
era. Let us not, however, forget the children in this system:

> Antonio, my son at the wetnurse.
>
> I recall that at last on 8 December 1426 [he was born 6 November 1426] I sent to the wetnurse Antonio, my son, to a place four
> miles from Florence, to Monna Antonia, the wife of Nanni di
> Lorenzo. He stayed in the parish of San Martino at the rate of 4 lire
> 10 soldi for every month of the wetnursing.[135]

What happened to these children once they went off to the wetnurse?

Demo a Balia: Wetnursing 2—Care And Emotion

WE KNOW SOMETHING about what was supposed to happen to Florentine children at the wetnurse from two Renaissance carnival songs about wetnurses:

> Here we come, *balie,* from the Casentino,
> each one looking for a baby,
> and here are our husbands
> who lead us on the way,
> whoever has a baby, show him to us,
> male or female, it doesn't matter.
> We shall take good care of him,
> and he will be well fed,
> that we'll soon have him standing straight
> like a proud knight.
> If the baby falls sick
> or is a bit run down,
> we'll take such good care of him
> that he will soon recover;
> but we must help him out
> in changing him frequently;
> when he's wet, we must dry him
> and wash him with a little wine.
> We're fine in our way of life,

prompt and skillful in our trade,
always when the baby cries
we feel our milk returning:
acting with energy and speed,
we do our duty,
we take him out of the cradle
drying his little face.
When he has a sore eye
we go clear up to Poppi:
a woman puts him on her knee
and gives him back his health,
and then she wants us to hold him
sometimes for days on end, so naked,
behind the bake oven,
playing with him in the sunshine.
In every matter, we know what to do,
so that the baby grows up quickly;
as long as he stays straight and hard
we don't mind getting tired;
and he'll never leave us
until his nursing is finished:
so you can be quite confident
in sending him to the Casentino.

With lots of good fine milk
our breasts are full.
To avoid all suspicion,
let the doctor see it,
because in it is found
the life and being of the creature,
for good milk nourishes
with no trouble and makes the flesh firm. . . .
We're young married women,
well experienced in our art,
we can swaddle a baby in a flash
and no one has to show us
how to use the cloth and bands;

while caring for him we arrange them carefully
because if he catches cold,
the baby is harmed and the *balia* blamed.
We change three times a day
the wool and linen cloths and white bands,
and we never get tired or cross
being with him so he won't cry. . . .[1]

These songs indicate that wetnurses did much more than just breastfeed children. Wetnurses were the primary child-care providers for many Florentine children during the first years of their life. And if these songs were any reflection of reality, Florentines could be confident sending their children into the Casentino.

On 20 March 1457 the painter Neri di Bicci recorded that he sent his son, Bicci, to the wetnurse two days after his birth. How soon after the birth Florentine parents sent their children to the wetnurse varied widely. Some, like Giovanni Buongirolami, consistently sent their children off to the wetnurse the day after baptism. Others, like Niccolò Baldovinetti, brought an *in casa* wetnurse in right after the birth. In 1515, Ser Piero Bonaccorsi brought an outside wetnurse and her husband into his house the day after his son was born. They stayed for five weeks and then left, taking the child with them.[2] For another child, however, Piero waited weeks without having a nurse *in casa* before sending her out to the wetnurse. He recorded that his daughter, Clemenza, was born 20 August 1524 and that on 29 September 1524 "I sent to the wetnurse that Clemenza, my daughter, to Ponte Anfredi to Agnolo di Bartolomeo di Nencio, blacksmith . . . and to Mona Cattrina, his wife, at 5 lire a month, on account, commencing this day and that Agnolo and Mona Cattrina carried her there."[3]

From Christiane Klapisch-Zuber's data drawn from the *ricordi* and *ricordanze* from 1320 to 1530 and comprising 180 examples, the vast majority (over 90 percent) of Florentine children who went off to the wetnurse did so during the first month after birth. Tables 5.1 and 5.2 show a more exact breakdown of these figures.

While her sample is neither representative nor large, her data, and the above examples, show that children did not go immediately to the wetnurse. Some stayed at home for a week or more. This is an important

TABLE 5.1

MONTHS BETWEEN BIRTH AND WETNURSING	PERCENTAGE
1	92.8
2	3.9
3-6	2.2
7-12	1.1

point that suggests two questions. First, why did infants remain at home for this initial period? Second, who fed these children while they stayed at home for this period? Some of the infants were kept at home until the baptism. Others stayed longer. Certainly, the arrangements for the wetnurse and the precise timing for the delivery to her explains some of this delay. Moreover, parents did want to enjoy their infants and perhaps realized that the first days or weeks of an infant's life are helpful for forming a bond of love. Paolo Sassetti emphatically stated, "Monday, Tuesday, Wednesday, and Thursday, Lisabetta [his daughter] remained at home; and then Friday the 18th she went into the hands of the wetnurse, whose name was Lena."[5] Her mother must have nursed her, just as the mothers for these other children also nursed them (despite the humanists' fears that colostrum was unhealthy). Cristofano Guidini's wife consistently breastfed her children two weeks to two months before turning them over to a wetnurse.[6] Catherine of Siena chided her brothers for their lack of duty and obligation to their mother by reminding them that their mother had nursed them for a while before sending them to a wetnurse. Francesco da Barberino even considered it normal that the mother would temporarily breastfeed her own child before sending it out to the wetnurse.[7]

If mothers initially began breastfeeding their children and then switched to sending them to a wetnurse, this left them with a particular and potentially painful problem. They would continue to lactate, a physiological fact that Florentines recognized. In one of Boccaccio's stories, for instance, a woman is stranded on an island after

TABLE 5.2

DAYS BETWEEN BIRTH AND WETNURSING	PERCENTAGE
1-2	17.2
3-14	61.7
15-30	14.5
31	7.2[4]

pirates had stolen her children, one of whom was newborn but with a wetnurse. By chance the woman happened to find two newborn deer, which had lost their mother. "And as the milk from her own breasts had not yet dried up after her recent childbirth," she nursed them.[8] For women who wanted to cease lactating, Florentine apothecaries had pharmaceutical remedies for drying up breastmilk, just as they had remedies for increasing breastmilk (the latter of these would have been of particular interest to wetnurses).[9]

In their parent's arms, or the arms of the nurse or *balio*, or at times in a basket on the back of a donkey, Florentine infants went out to the suburbs or country for their stay at the wetnurse.[10] Considering the extent of wetnursing, there must have been considerable traffic in infants on Tuscan roads in the premodern era. Yet when these infants finally did go off to the wetnurse, they did not just disappear from the hearts and minds of their parents. Subsequent contact occurred. James Bruce Ross argued, however, that urban parents who sent their children to a rural wetnurse "did not see them for long periods." She based this conclusion on an oft-cited passage by Giovanni Morelli, who reminded his readers that his father as a child had spent 12 years at the wetnurse and never received a visit from his father, who died while he was still at the wetnurse. While this incident certainly happened, Morelli's point was that a Florentine father should not behave so.[11]

If nothing else, the regular payment entries to the *balia* or *balio* in the *ricordi* and *ricordanze*, some of which were "mese per mese" as one writer put it, imply that subsequent contact occurred.[12] Carlo Strozzi, for instance, made payments to the wetnurse of his son Marchone on the following dates: 15 January 1516, 16 February 1516, 15 March 1516, 12 April 1516, 17 May 1516, 23 August 1516, 6 September 1516, 15 October 1516, 12 November 1516, 3 December 1516, 31 December 1516, 6 February 1517, 4 March 1517, 18 April 1517, and 9 May 1517.[13]

While parents and wetnurses used intermediaries, such as the *balio*, for transporting payments, they also made the deliveries themselves or came to get them themselves. Tommaso Guidetti recorded that his wife made trips to the village where their son was at wetnurse to pay her. On 17 August 1495, for instance, their daughter Maria went off to the wetnurse; on 24 November 1495 he gave his wife 11 soldi to go the wetnurse and buy shoes for the child.[14] In fact, his wife handled all the dealings with the wetnurse for this child. Alessandra Strozzi handled some of her children's wetnursing payments, though in most these cases the wetnurse or *balio* came to her. Biagio Buonaccorsi recorded on 25 July 1512 that he carried a payment to the *balio*. At other times the *balio* or the wetnurse came to him to receive payment.[15] Whenever parents went to pay the wetnurse they saw their children. Cristofano Guidini said this exactly. He sent his son, Francesc, to a wetnurse on 7 November 1380. "On the last day of the said month [November] I went to see the said child at Brolio, and I gave to the said Monna Andrea, his wetnurse, two fiorini."[16] Likewise, whenever the wetnurse came to receive her payment from the parents she may have brought their child. Filippo Manetti recorded that a month after he sent his son to the wetnurse she came to his house for her first payment.[17] Sometimes a wetnurse would bring the child to the parents specifically for a visit. Luigi Tansilo, a sixteenth-century Neapolitan poet, mentioned in his poem *La balia* such an occasion.[18] Parents also had a chance to see their children whenever they delivered extra clothing, such as diapers and swaddling cloths. Neri di Bicci had a son at wetnurse outside of Prato, whom he had sent there 4 October 1458 with a substantial trousseau. On 31 December 1458, in the dead of winter, he took more clothing and diapers to her house for his son.[19]

In fact these installments may also reflect the growth of the child, who now needed larger items; and visits to the child or communication with the wetnurse at least would indicate when these were needed and what exactly was needed. Two months after he sent his son to the wetnurse, Luca Panzano purchased a new cradle and sent it to the wetnurse for his son, Ridolfo.[20] Most likely the child had been in a smaller basket and was now ready for a wooden cradle. In the monthly payments list to wetnurses, other *ricordi* and *ricordanze* writers frequently noted deliveries of extra goods. Manno Petrucci, for instance, sent extra diapers to his son's wetnurse two months after he had been delivered there and again three months later.[21] Shoes also were a frequent delivery in these subsequent installments.[22]

Parents had reasons other than financial for maintaining contact with their nursing children. Many wanted to be kept informed of their child's health. Francesco Datini had a friend in Prato who kept him apprised of a son's illness while at the wetnurse. In another instance the *balio* kept Niccolò Machiavelli's family apprised of his son's illness at the wetnurse. In a series of letters dating from 1527 while away from Florence, Machiavelli discovered that his youngest son, Totto, had an eye infection. He wrote to his family, "I wish with all my heart that I knew that Totto's eyes were recovered." His older son, Guido, assured him, "You were not informed about Totto, because he is not home, but the husband of the wetnurse told us that his eyes are not yet recovered; he says, however, that he is improving; so you must be of good cheer."[23]

Parents also visited their children at the wetnurse, because they missed them and visiting them made them feel better. While working on his *Perseus,* Cellini was frequently depressed because of the technical difficulties with which the piece presented him as well as his sense of having fallen in status after having transferred from the court of King Francis I of France to that of the grand duke of Florence. To cheer himself up, he tells us:

> On one occasion, when I was in that mood, I mounted my handsome little horse, and with a hundred crowns in my pocket rode off to Fiesole to see a natural son of mine, whom I was keeping at nurse with my *comare,* the wife of one of my workmen. When I arrived I

found the boy in very good health: sad at heart, I kissed him; and
then when I wanted to leave he refused to let me go, holding me fast
with his little hands and breaking into a storm of crying and screaming. Seeing he was only somewhere around two years old, this was
beyond belief. . . . I detached myself from my little boy and left him
crying his eyes out.[24]

In a surprising discovery, Philip Gavitt found that mothers and
fathers who had abandoned infants at the foundling hospital frequently visited these children after the hospital officials had placed
them at the wetnurse. In fact, they interfered with the hospital's
operation by paying the wetnurse themselves and even changing
wetnurses without informing the *Innocenti*. Wetnurses in these circumstances would themselves bypass the *Innocenti* officials and deal
directly with the parents or parent of the foundling. In addition
Richard Trexler has noted that some parents who abandoned infants at
the Innocenti left written messages telling the officials where to place
the children at the wetnurse so that they could be close together,
presumably to make it easier for the parents to visit their children at
the wetnurse.[25] If this evidence from the *Innocenti* is any indication of
a general societal trend, Florentines most certainly visited their
children at the wetnurse. And Florentine moralists had consistently
urged these visits on parents; Paolo da Certaldo, for instance, stated
that parents should always visit their children at the wetnurse. Ross,
however, doubted that Florentine parents followed this advice.[26] The
above examples show that some—if not most—did.

Parents had a practical reason to visit their children at the
wetnurse beyond delivery of payment and emotional contact. Parents
should visit their children, so Certaldo stated, to evaluate their health
at the wetnurse and to monitor the care the wetnurse was giving their
children. If the parents were not pleased with how the nurse was
caring for their children he advised that they should transfer them
quickly from one wetnurse to another.[27] In fact changing wetnurses
was a fairly likely proposition for many Florentine children. Between
1300 and 1530, of 318 Florentine children on whom Klapisch-Zuber
has information 104 (or 33 percent) went to a second nurse, 24 (or 8
percent) went to a third nurse, 10 (or 3 percent) went to a fourth

nurse, 5 (or 2 percent) went to a fifth nurse and, 1 (or .3 percent) went to a sixth nurse.[28] Tommaso Guidetti's daughter Maria went through six wetnurses during a period of 14 months. In December 1496 he sent her to a seventh. He had no better luck with his next child, a son, who also went through a number of wetnurses, with what must have been considerable despair and frustration for his parents. Antonio Rustichi encountered much the same problem. He had two sons at the wetnurse, and the wetnurse of his younger son no longer could nurse. He had the older child, Lionardo, weaned and sent back home in exchange for the younger child, Stefano.[29]

Besides the parent's displeasure with the nurse's performance, other reasons existed as to why a wetnursing contract might be broken. Not every *ricordi* and *ricordanze* writer noted why a contract was broken, but of those that did most stated that it was because the wetnurse had become pregnant.[30] On 11 November 1466, Neri di Bicci matter of factly recorded that he received his daughter, Nanina, back from the wetnurse and her husband "because she was pregnant."[31] In most cases, the pregnancy of the nurse and subsequent termination of the contract seem not to have engendered hard feelings of the parents for the wetnurse, for the writers of the *ricordanze* made little or no comment about this. But in the cases in which the parents discovered that the wetnurse was still giving "pregnant milk" to their child, the parents could be very critical of the nurse.[32] Virgilio Adriani discovered that the wetnurse of his son was pregnant by two months. He instantly fired her and got another.[33]

Changing wetnurses replicated all the problems encountered in finding the initial wetnurse and added another—the need for extreme haste. Where parents did have (potentially) nine months or more to seek out an available first nurse, finding subsequent nurses, especially within the first few months of their children's lives, meant the parents had to move quickly enough to satisfy their children's hunger. Most likely the mother could not nurse, since her breast milk had already dried up, though this was not always the case. Cristofano Guidini recorded the birth of twins on 28 December 1385. One, Manno, went to the wetnurse on 12 January 1386; the other, Gherardo, went to the wetnurse on 6 February 1386. On 17 March 1386, Manno's wetnurse returned him because she was pregnant.

Cristofano recorded that his wife breastfed him until they could find another wetnurse; or, as he put it, "finally we found a wetnurse."[34] In this instance, they were lucky that the wife had continued to nurse the other twin into February.

Wetnurses ended contracts early for reasons other than their own pregnancy. In some cases they had become ill or even died, or their milk had dried up. According to Klapisch-Zuber, 15 percent of contracts ended because of the wetnurses' illness, 16 percent because of the wetnurses' milk drying up, and 20 percent because of the poor care by the nurse (including drunkenness) or because of the child's illness.[35] Or the wetnurse may have just grown tired of caring for someone else's child. Neri di Bicci recorded on 7 July 1458 that the *balio* of his son, Bicci, returned him, two months before they had agreed to in the initial contract. Neri was not pleased (he said it was against his wishes), and noted that the wetnurse simply did not want to care for his son (who was over two years old) any longer.[36]

Some historians have criticized the practice of changing wet-nurses; Klapisch-Zuber, for instance, referred to Florentine children's "being tossed from nurse to nurse." They have wondered at the supposedly negative psychological effects that this would have on the child.[37] Others, such as Valerie Fildes and George Sussmann, who have made more extensive study of the practice of wetnursing in the premodern world, tend to discount the negative psychological effects, especially since wetnursing, including the rotation, "was so normal a part of the life cycle." Miriam Slater argued that trying to see trauma in wetnursing is anachronistic, since separation anxiety in the modern era is not understood well and especially since the premodern era was one "in which psychological trauma was hardly understood to exist."[38] The fact that no commentators on family life in their critique of wetnursing mentioned separation anxiety—or anything approximating it—reinforces the idea that scholars err in trying to find psychological trauma in changing nurses. It was a normal part of childhood.

This is not, however, to argue that horrible and tragic things could not happen to children at the wetnurse, for they did. The common folk belief in changelings certainly reflects parents' anxieties that their infants would be away from them for long periods of time and that they could lose them.[39] And parents never could be positive that something might not happen to their children while at the wetnurse. Gene Brucker's delightful telling of the marital dispute of Giovanni and Lusanna hints at this. At one point Lusanna confessed to a friend that she was unhappy because she did not have any children. Her friend, Fiora, suggested that they visit a wetnurse to find her a baby. She approached a wetnurse with this idea, only to have the wetnurse instantly turn it down. "You know what will happen with this business," the wetnurse told Fiora, "someone will lose his head." Fiora must have had second thoughts after this, because she told Lusanna's sister-in-law, "I do not wish to be involved in this affair because the penalty is death."[40]

As Klapisch-Zuber has stated, "A Florentine could fear the worst if the *balio* came knocking at his door." She found that 17.4 percent of the wetnursing examples she has studied ended in death for the child; three-quarters of these were by illness, the rest by supposed accidental suffocation by the nurse. She noted, however, that foundlings out to nurse had a higher death rate than the children of the writers of *ricordanze*. Jean-Louis Flandrin had hypothesized the same for other geographic areas of the premodern world, and like other historians used this hypothesis as a basis to criticize wetnursing. This is perhaps misguided, as we ought to expect a higher death rate for foundlings off to nurse than any other group of children in any premodern society since these children were at greatest risk. For the most part foundlings came from mothers who were impoverished, enslaved, and even diseased (especially if the mothers were prostitutes). Moreover, they may have gone through the rigors of a secret birth, which would have put them even more at risk.[41] Nevertheless, Klapisch-Zuber's numbers compare favorably with figures from premodern France that indicate a death rate of 31-32 percent for children at the wetnurse—a percentage that matches the generally accepted death rate of infants (0-12 months) in the premodern world. While some historians, such as Flandrin, have argued that wetnursing guaranteed a higher death rate of infants in the premodern world than did maternal breastfeeding, Sussmann's more detailed evaluation has shown there is no statistical significance between the death rates of infants who were breastfed by their mothers and those who were wetnursed.[42]

Francesco Datini was in Pisa on business when his five-month-old illegitimate son became ill at the wetnurse. The *balio* went to Niccolò di Giunta, Datini's associate, to tell him that the child was sick. Niccolò sent for three doctors, but to no avail as the boy died. Niccolò wrote to tell Francesco the bad news; what made this more poignant was that three days before he had written Francesco a positive review of the child's health at the wetnurse. Death could occur suddenly for children at the wetnurse. Giovanni Morelli's brother, Morello, lost a daughter to the plague while she was at the wetnurse, which must have been a common experience for Florentine parents after 1348.[43]

Many times, because the child was at such a distance, it would be buried in a church close to the wetnurse.[44] Biagio Buonaccorsi, for instance, noted that his son, Filippo, "was buried in the church of Santa Maria in the Mugello in the tomb of the Cini (who employed the *balio* as a laborer)."[45] Sometimes the parents did not receive word of the death till after the burial. Fathers usually recorded the death in the same place in their *ricordanze* that they had listed the birth. Moreover, the death entries for their infants off to nurse show no difference from their death entries for other family members. If, for instance, a *ricordanze* writer was in the habit of memorializing relatives' deaths with little crosses drawn in the margin, he did the same for his children—male and female—who died at the nurse.[46]

In 1433, Terrino Manovetti asked, as he had asked for his deceased brother and father, that God pardon his one-year-old daughter who died in the wetnurse's bed. But she had not died of natural causes. She died accidentally through the carelessness of the nurse, he thought, who had taken his daughter into her bed, fallen asleep, and suffocated her, perhaps by rolling over on top of her. And this was an *in casa* nurse as well, a fact that should have provided a safer circumstance for the little girl since the wetnurse was under closer family scrutiny than an outside nurse would have been.[47] This case and others like it pose a problem. Of all deaths at the wetnurse about 25 percent were attributed to accidental suffocation, what we can call overlaying. The writers of *ricordanze* clearly specify that the wetnurse suffocated the child. Morelli, in noting the death of his brother's son Andrea, stated, "we think she suffocated him."[48] Suffocation in bed by a parent or a substitute was not an unusual cause of death in the premodern world.

Barberino advised parents and nurses not to allow children to sleep in bed with them for fear of smothering them.[49] But Bernard de Gordon, in his *Regimen Sanitatis* (1309) said that wetnurses should not let their charges sleep in bed with them, not for their safety but because they would get too used to the nurse's warmth and would cry when removed.[50] He was unconcerned about the problem of overlaying.

Nevertheless, the Church recognized the problem of overlaying by forbidding parents to sleep in bed with their children to prevent this from happening.[51] Regulations like this pose a problem of interpretation, for if children went off to the wetnurse for a year or two, how old then were these children that the Church was talking about? Moreover, some of the children in these overlaying cases from the *ricordi* and *ricordanze* were not newborns. Filippo Strozzi's daughter, Lianore, for instance, was suffocated by the wetnurse in her bed, but she was a-year-and-a-month old.[52] Some have seen the wetnurse's (or parents') claim of overlaying as an excuse to cover up a real crime—the deliberate murder of the child. But why would a wetnurse do this? She could quit anytime without any real penalty or loss, excepting the loss in income. So why deliberately kill the child? Moreover, since she was paid by installment, deliberately killing the child meant an end to income.[53] A premodern record of overlaying a child might mean something else. It might be an attempt to explain an inexplicable death, such as crib death, for sometimes the circumstances surrounding the death appeared odd or suspect.[54] Biagio Buonaccorsi noted that the wetnurse of his son suffocated him while nursing him.[55] On the surface this seems implausible, though perhaps the child somehow choked to death while nursing. Life for infants in the premodern world was precarious. But parents and others would want an explanation for a sudden and even mysterious death. The claim of accidental overlaying would be convenient, and would avoid a more serious charge of homicide. Perhaps a claim of overlaying hides an accident of a different sort caused by a wetnurse's negligence, such as dropping a child. Nevertheless, parents did not seem to blame the nurse for the death of their child whenever overlaying was listed as the cause in the *ricordanze*. Or at least they did not record that they blamed the nurse. They did not even appear to get angry, though Matteo Corsini bluntly scribbled that the wetnurse of his son Orlando murdered him.[56]

Andrea Minerbotti's wetnurse refused payment for the eight months she had kept his daughter since she claimed she had overlaid her, which may reflect the blame she felt for the child's death.[57] One wonders whether the frequent listing of overlaying as a cause of death for children in the premodern world might be a sort of fiction, a way to explain an inexplicable death.

Certainly, death at the wetnurse's home was the worst Florentine parents could expect for their children, but what they normally could expect for their children at the wetnurse's home was considerably better. In his encyclopedia, Bartholomaeus Anglicus claimed:

> The nurse (*nutrix*) is so named because of her nourishing (*nutriendo*) power, since she is suitable for feeding the newborn child. A nurse, says Isidore, feeds the child in place of the mother. Like a mother, the nurse is happy when the child is happy, and suffers when the child suffers. She lifts him up if he falls, gives him suck if he cries, kisses him if he is sick, binds and ties him if he flails about, cleans him if he has soiled himself, and feeds him, although he struggles with his fingers. She instructs the child who cannot speak, babbling, practically breaking her tongue, in order to teach him speech more readily. She uses medicines in order to cure a sick child. She lifts him up on her hands, shoulders, and knees, and relieves the crying child. She first chews the food, preparing it for the toothless child so he can swallow it more easily, and thus feeds the hungry child. Whistling and singing, she strokes him as he sleeps and ties the childish limbs with bandages and linens, which she adjusts, lest he suffer some curvature. She refreshes his disfigured body with baths and unguents.[58]

This advice from an intellectual on what wetnurses should do parallels the more popular account from the carnival songs of what wetnurses did.

Little is known about the care infants were supposed to receive or did receive in the premodern era.[59] And here the *ricordi* and *ricordanze* are mostly silent. Nevertheless, advice books and other incidental sources can give us some hints on this. Both the carnival songs and Bartholomaeus Anglicus highlight the suckling, but that is to be expected, since the prime function of the wetnurse was to breastfeed a child. The physician Michele Savonarola noted the calming effect a nipple had on a baby by calling it a "quieta-puti."[60] St. Catherine of Siena used a breastfeeding analogy in explaining her relationship to God. "Do you know father [her confessor], what God did for my soul today? He did as a mother does to the child she loves the most. She shows her breast, but keeps it out of reach until he begins to cry; then she smiles benignly and takes him to the breast and, kissing him, presents the food happily and abundantly."[61] She described here a playful scene. In fact, a number of commentators on wetnursing practices in the premodern era complained that wetnurses overfed babies by suckling them every time they cried. Some also complained that the wetnurses rocked them too frequently whenever they cried.[62] Both complaints, however, reflect a caring attitude on the part of the wetnurses toward their charges. Since milk quality was an issue, Paulus Bagellardus and others advised nurses on what they should eat while nursing and what foods to avoid, including spicy and salty foods and beans.[63] One physician, Piero di Giovanni, in his medical treatise claimed that cradle cap on infants was caused by their drinking breastmilk that was affected by an imbalance in bodily humors, perhaps caused by the nurse's bad diet.[64] Commentators noted other aspects of an infant's feeding. One told the parents that to "protect his clothes from slobber," they ought to tell the nurse to make their child a bib.[65]

Surprisingly for an era not noted for its attention to personal hygiene, wetnurses were enjoined to bathe infants frequently. There seems to have been some debate over using salt water or fresh water for this, with physicians favoring salt and common people favoring fresh.[66] And a bath was even an occasion for play.[67] According to the carnival songs, wetnurses were supposed to rub the child down with a little wine after they removed a wet diaper, which may have had a sanitizing effect, since the skin would dry quicker, preventing the development of a rash.

In fact, these wetnurses claimed they could expertly swaddle a baby in a flash.[68] Like wetnursing, swaddling is an aspect of premodern childcare that modern Westerners neither understand very well nor sympathize with very much. Why were premodern infants—many of whom appear this way in artwork from the past—wrapped from shoulders to toes? Historians have been critical of the practice, sometimes soaring to absurd heights of psychological theorizing on the supposed effects of this. According to Lawrence Stone:

> the practice of tight swaddling in the first months or even year of life is believed to isolate the infant from its surroundings and to give it a sense of both frustrated rage and yet helpless acceptance of the cruelty and duplicity of the world. Thus there could be, and often was, a combination of sensory deprivation, motor deprivation, and emotional deprivation—to say nothing of oral deprivation—in the first critical months of life, of which the consequences upon the adult personality are now known to be very serious and long-lasting in reducing the capacity for warm social relationships.[69]

Yet there is no evidence that swaddling caused these deprivations. Luke Demaitre minimized the negative effects of swaddling, since about half of all infants depicted in artwork from the premodern period appear naked or loosely clothed, implying that being swaddled was not a round-the-clock phenomenon. According to the vita of Francesca Romano (d. 1440), as an infant in the cradle she could not stand for any man to touch her naked body. While this information is designed to focus on her modesty and chastity, it shows that infants were not swaddled all the time.[70] Medical books that dealt with swaddling all emphasized that the wrap should not be too tight. From his studies of premodern English family life, Ralph Houlbrooke concluded that children were at most swaddled for only three months of their lives.[71] Moreover, modern pediatric advice even recommends swaddling to calm fretful newborns, since the closeness and warmth of the wrap simulates the closeness and warmth of the womb.

John Sommerville argued that premodern children were swaddled to immobilize them and get them out of the way of their caretakers.[72] This reasoning, however, does not appear in the literature of the premodern era, though the advice books do have some specific reasons for swaddling. Overall, commentators recognized swaddling's calming effect on infants in easing their transition from the womb to the world. Swaddling also had a practical benefit, since this kept an infant from scratching its eyes. Since physicians, following Galen, believed that life was a constant process of the human body's drying out, swaddling also helped retain the body's moisture—or so they thought.[73] This also might explain why babies were bathed so frequently. In general commentators believed that swaddling helped protect an infant. Swaddling in their opinion also helped form an infant's arms and legs.[74] Twice in the songs from the Casentino, the nurses mention how they will make the child stand straight. The Dominican Girolamo Savonarola, grandson of the physician Michele Savonarola and himself a student of medicine, used an interesting metaphor for why Florence needed reforms: "Like a child he has soft arms, and they have to be swaddled so as to anchor the members."[75] Lastly, swaddling may have been simply the means with which to keep a diaper on a baby. At one point the childless Margherita Datini borrowed a friend's baby for a sleepover. The baby wet the bed. Its mother chided her for not swaddling the baby properly, and pointed out that at home the baby did not wet the bed.[76] Margherita Datini, unlike the nurses from the Casentino, could not expertly swaddle a baby in a flash. Florentines believed that swaddling was in the best interests of their infants' lives, and they probably saw proof of that in its calming effect upon them; they probably slept better if swaddled.

Physicians and moralists considered sleep important for infants. According to Leo Battista Alberti, for "children who are weak on account of their babyhood and can hardly hold themselves up, much rest and long periods of inactivity are proper. When they are kept up and made overtired, they only grow weaker." Where did these children sleep? Certainly all the injunctions against taking infants into bed imply that people did this. We also have evidence that cradles would be parked next to the bed. Boccaccio described a couple going to bed: "and he and his wife got into the other bed, by the side of which she placed the cradle in which she kept her infant son." Some of the writers of *ricordanze*, who list a trousseau of goods sent to the wetnurse with the child, neglect to include a cradle. But this is logical, since the wetnurse had at least one child of her own (or at least had prepared for one child).[77]

While getting the proper amount of sleep was important for infants, play was just as important. The moralists and physicians advised it for the development of the child; the wetnurses did it probably because it was fun. No wonder so many female mystics and saints in their visions and dreams wanted to play with the infant Jesus.[78] Michele Savonarola wanted wetnurses to exercise infants' eye-to-hand coordination by holding a pebble or a bone in front of their eyes and letting them try to grab it. He also wanted them to move the infants' arms and legs and tickle them to encourage growth and coordination. After this workout, he said they ought to nurse them. Alberti noted that people often would snap their fingers to attract an infant's attention. Both Barbaro and Alberti thought it good to have a wetnurse sing and babble to an infant. A child, therefore, learned its first words from its wetnurse. A story by Agnolo Firenzuolo illustrates this. To become acquainted with a young woman, Fulvio Macaro was convinced by a friend, Menico, to dress up like a servant girl from a country village. Menico told Fulvio he thought this plan would work because "as your nurse belonged to that village, I think you will be able to talk like a native."[79]

One of the key things wetnurses were supposed to do for their charges was to keep them from danger. Barberino specified these dangers: "pits, horses, rivers, fire, dogs, knives and other sharp instruments, snakes and poisonous plants."[80] No wonder children went off to the wetnurse protected with all sorts of amulets, especially red coral. The premodern world was laced with dangers for children. Red coral also had a more practical use as it was used by teething infants to chew on. Nevertheless, despite the best intentions of the amulets, when something unfortunate happened to the child, the wetnurse was supposed to be there to care for and comfort the child. And the carnival songs imply that she would be there and do this. Barberino said a wetnurse should give a child a gift whenever it got hurt, and should even pretend to punish whatever object, such as a stone, had hurt the child. And of course she was to bandage the injury.[81] Wetnurses would also treat sick children, as both Bartholomaeus Anglicus and the carnival songs from the Casentino state. In fact, one of the songs from the Casentino noted how a wetnurse could go to a village healing-woman to cure an ailing child—in this case it was for an eye infection, a common problem for children. Both Paulus Bagellardus and Bartholomaeus Anglicus advised physicians that whenever they treated an ailing infant they should treat its wetnurse, as medicine passed through a nurse's system and distributed in the breastmilk was easier, in their opinion, on the child's system.[82] Bernard de Gordon even included instructions on how to make "astrological-medicinal" amulets and images in his treatise on childcare. An amulet or image of Capricorn, for instance, placed on an infant's stomach supposedly quieted its crying.[83]

Another aspect of the wetnurse's job, obviously, was weaning the child and introducing it to solid foods. Bartholomaeus Anglicus saw this as the dividing line between *infans* and *pueritia*.[84] Paolo da Certaldo advised wetnurses to give nothing but breastmilk for the first year of a child's life, and then "little by little" introduce other foods with the breastmilk. Barberino had advised waiting two years before doing this. Paulus Bagellardus advised waiting until the child's body was well formed and sturdy.[85] All these authors advised waiting a while until the child was healthy and able to eat solid food before attempting weaning. This graduated policy of introducing solids and weaning implies that the authors understood the special needs of these young children and were concerned for their well-being. Klapisch-Zuber found from the *ricordi* and *ricordanze* that the average age for weaning was 18.7 months.[86] The actual act of weaning was simple, and apparently effective. Catherine of Siena used it as a metaphor in discussing with Gregory XI his imminent return to Rome—a holy man had warned him of an assassination attempt. She wrote, "I think he wants to do with you as the mother does to her child when she wants to take away the milk from his mouth. She puts something bitter on her breast so that he tastes the bitterness before the milk, so that for fear of the bitter he abandons the sweet."[87] For this metaphor to work, Gregory XI also had to know something about weaning practices. Barberino advised the same practice, and said that this should be followed by giving the child bread soaked in milk or apple juice. Bagellardus advised honey water by itself or mixed with solid food. He also thought one could use diluted wine as the liquid here. Alberti mentioned cereal and soup as a baby's first solid foods. Nurses were also encouraged to prechew a baby's first food—a practice still seen today in primitive tribes.[88]

Premodern parents and wetnurses had some concern for the child's health and well-being during the weaning process.[89] Bartolomeo di Lorenzo, a bannermaker, complained in 1534 because his daughter's wetnurse had left early "when she had promised to remain with us until September, so that we could avoid having Cecchina weaned during the great heat and before she has all her teeth."[90] His concern here may be related more to his and his wife's putting up with a cranky kid in the heat of summer than the existence of a health hazard for their daughter. Bartholomaeus Anglicus had observed that weaning "causes much grief," but did not say for whom.[91] On the other hand, early weaning did pose risks in the premodern world. Diarrhea or rickets were two of the more common problems associated with this. In England, for instance, rickets became commonly associated with weaning only because the age of weaning (and subsequent cessation of all milk-drinking) dropped to nine months.[92] Diarrhea, however, resulted from the young child's problems with digesting solid food, especially food that was spoiled. This would explain why weaning during summer could be troublesome and even fatal. So Bartolomeo da Lorenzo and his wife did have reason to be concerned with their wetnurse's defection. Waiting till the child was about one-and-a-half years old, though, as most Florentines did, could mollify the irritation to the digestive system from receiving solid food. Florentines would not have to worry about rickets either, since they had their children weaned at such a late date. Moreover, there is fairly strong evidence that children continued to drink milk after being weaned since glass breast pumps and cow horns fashioned for drinking have been found from premodern Italy.[93]

Klapisch-Zuber mentioned the dangers and deaths associated with weaning in premodern Tuscany.[94] Moreover, she thought the process was psychologically traumatic for the child because it seemed to occur so abruptly, and she mentioned the "evidence of this brutality in formulas" the writers of *ricordanze* used to record the weaning of their children. Francesco Durante in 1343 noted that his child was weaned with the phrase "che si spopò questo dì" (who was weaned this day).[95] But how else was he to record it; how else were writers of *ricordanze* to record it? Niccolò Busini, like all the other *ricordi* and *ricordanze* writers, matter of factly recorded that the wetnurse of his son, Buono, nursed him from 27 September 1401 to 15 June 1402, when she began feeding him solids. I see no brutality here, just a simple statement of fact.[96] Lawrence Stone even argued that weaning in the premodern era most likely was not traumatic, since it took place at such a late date in the child's life.[97]

Weaning did not necessarily terminate a contract. While Klapisch-Zuber found that the average age of weaning for a Florentine child was 18.7 months, the average age of a child on its return home was 20.4 months.[98] Wetnursing was much more than hired breastfeeding. In fact, this period after weaning is referred to as drynursing in the premodern world, and usually cost less than wetnursing.[99] But eventually, at some point close to the weaning, the child did return home to its parents. The humanist Giovanni Rucellai saw this as a special occasion. Lapo Mazzei rejoiced whenever any of his many children returned from the wetnurse. The *ricordanze* abound with notification of children's returns.[100] On 21 May 1469, Giovanni Dinoamico opened his door to find the wetnurse and the *balio* standing there with his daughter, Brigida, and her trousseau and cradle. Three days after he and his wife lost a newborn daughter, Paliano Falcucci recorded that their son, Antonio, returned from the wetnurse. In the company of a servant, Rosello Strozzi's daughter, Chaterina, returned from the wetnurse—11 years after she had left. She had been gone for quite a while, but there were extenuating circumstances; he was a widower and needed someone to help him raise his daughter. The death of Pagolo Morelli's mother and the large brood with which his father was left certainly helps explain why he was at the wetnurse for 12 years. Manno Petrucci noted at the end of his son's tenure at the wetnurse that "I was content," though he does not specify whether he was content to have his son home or he was content with the service or both.[101]

Certainly, the end of a wetnursing contract was a bittersweet experience. We tend to concentrate on the child's family, forgetting that the child had entered into another family and stayed for almost two years.[102] Undoubtedly, this stay generated strong feelings in the wetnurse and her family for the child. And they would be sad at the child's departure. In 1385, Francesco Datini decided to have his illegitimate daughter, the child of his slave, come and live with him and Margherita. She was six years old at this time. The wetnurse's husband sent him a note telling him how much he and his wife loved the little girl. And they hoped that she would be treated well, because "she is fearful and we love her dearly, and therefore we beseech you, be gentle with her."[103]

VI

A Chasa: Children at Home

IN 1510, Niccolò Machiavelli made his third trip to France as a representative of the Florentine state. During his stay there he took time out from his diplomatic chores to chastise the Florentine chancery for not sending him news of his family. On 29 August 1510, Biagio Buonaccorsi wrote back, "Your wife is here and she is living; the children are on their feet; no smoke has been seen from the house."[1] Machiavelli wanted to know what was happening at home, including how the children were. His questions are our questions. What happened to Florentine children of the merchant elite after they returned from the wetnurse? What was their homelife like? Who cared for them?[2]

Benvenuto Cellini retained vivid yet kaleidoscopic memories of his childhood:

> When I was already about three years old my grandfather Andrea was still alive and over a hundred. One day they were changing a cistern pipe when a large scorpion which they had not noticed crawled out of it, slipped to the ground, and scuttled away under a bench. I caught sight of it, ran over, and picked the thing up. It was so big that when I had it in my little hand its tail hung out at one end and both claws at the other. They say that laughing happily I ran up to my grandfather and said: "Look grandpapa [nonno mio], look at my lovely little crab." He recognized what it was and almost dropped dead from shock and anxiety. Then he tried to coax me into giving it to him, but the more he did so the more I screamed tearfully, refusing to give it to anyone.

My father was also in the house and, hearing the noise, he ran in to see what it was all about. He was so terror-stricken that his mind refused to work and he could not think up any way of stopping the poisonous creature from killing me. Then his eyes fell on a pair of scissors and he managed to wheedle me into letting him snip off the scorpion's tail and claws. When the danger was past he regarded it as a good omen.

Another time, when I was about five, my father was sitting alone in one of our small rooms, singing and playing his viol. Some washing had just been done there and a good log fire was still burning. It was very cold, and he had drawn near the fire. Then, as he was looking at the flames, his eye fell on a little animal, like a lizard, that was running around merrily in the very hottest part of the fire. Suddenly realizing what it was, he called my sister and myself and showed it to us. And then he gave me such a violent box on the ears that I screamed and burst into tears. At this he calmed me as kindly as he could and said: "My dear little boy, I didn't hit you because you had done wrong. I only did it so that you will never forget that the lizard you saw in the fire is a salamander, and as far as we know for certain no one has ever seen one before."

Then he kissed me and gave me a little money.

When my father began teaching me to play the flute and to sing, although I was at the tender age when children love blowing whistles and playing with toys of that kind, I hated every moment of it and would only sing or play the flute to obey him. . . .

It was at that time, when I was still very young, that my father had me carried to the signory and made me play the flute as a soprano accompaniment to the palace musicians. I played away at my music and was held up by one of the palace officials. Afterwards the Gonfalonier, that is Soderini, made me talk to him and, delighted at my chatter, gave me some sweets.[3]

Cellini was a precocious child and headstrong to be sure, or so he would have us believe. He was also a loved child, most especially by his father, who figures prominently in Cellini's childhood memories. These vignettes suggest a question: who was supposed to rear the children in premodern Florence: the father, the mother, or both?

Modern historians disagree on the answer to this question. Some, such as James Bruce Ross and Christiane Klapisch-Zuber, have argued that for children aged two through seven the mother played the predominant role. In fact, Klapisch-Zuber insisted that fathers were hardly ever available for their children after they returned from the wetnurse. Others, such as Richard Trexler, have argued that fathers did their best to supplant their wives in the childrearing process—they took a predominant role. Judith C. Brown reflected this apparent confusion in a book about a mystic nun, Benedetta Carlini. She noted that compared to other Tuscan fathers Benedetta's was "unusually" active in caring for her, and Brown seemed surprised by that.[4] Humanists, however, would not have been surprised by the part Benedetta Carlini's father played in her upbringing. They believed that both parents had a responsibility to rear their children. In general humanists thought that men were better suited for public life and women for private life because of various perceived physical differences between the sexes and the conclusions of ancient authors about the differences between the genders. Yet whenever it came to rearing children, men, according to the humanists, were even to intrude into the women's arena of private life. One of Leon Battista Alberti's characters in his *Libri della Famiglia*, Gianozzo, noted that while he did not discuss his business affairs with his wife, he did talk—and often—with her about household affairs, especially childrearing.[5] Giovanni Dominici and Giovanni Rucellai addressed their childrearing advice to both parents.[6] Nevertheless, Alberti mentioned that there were certain aspects of childrearing, "which are women's domain and properly fall to the nurse and the mother much more than the father." He was especially concerned about a father's not being dexterous and gentle enough to handle an infant or small child without injuring it.[7] But what did fathers and mothers do; what exactly were their areas of concentration?

A petition from 23 December 1422 to the priors for the release of a prisoner from the Stinche, the communal jail, stated that "[n]ot only does his detention harm himself, but it deprives his children of their bread and guidance."[8] According to the humanists, sustenance and education—bread and guidance, if you will—were the primary childrearing responsibilities of a father.[9] Of the two, the first was an accepted responsibility, a given; the second, comprising more than just book learning, was more essential, but more difficult to define clearly and to achieve. One of Alberti's characters stated that a father had a duty to do much more than just "stock the cupboard and the cradle." He owed counsel and moral guidance to his children. A child should "learn virtue rather than vice."[10] A father, according to Giovanni Morelli, ought to teach his children good manners amongst other things.[11] Cellini's father told him that a father was one "who brought you into the world and looked after you, and sowed the seeds of all your splendid talents."[12] While the humanists defined this counsel and moral guidance somewhat vaguely, they clearly understood that it contributed significantly to a child's successful development into an adult, with all the status, honor, and responsibilities that meant in premodern Florence. They considered it no easy task inculcating cultural values in a child. After listening to Lionardo discuss a father's duties in this respect, Alberti had Adovardo retort, "beware lest you give us fathers too much to do." Lionardo then stated that fathers had to work hard at counseling and guiding their children and noted that Adovardo was a good example of a father who could succeed at this.[13]

A mother's sphere was more directly related to the day-to-day feeding and caring for a child than the father's, or so Alberti thought. In the *Libri della Famiglia* when Lionardo pushed Battista to tell him everything relating to birth and childrearing, Battista sarcastically asked him whether he wanted to know how even to make cereal and soup for babies.[14] He implied with this crack that feeding a child was a mother's task. In fact, Bartholomaeus Anglicus had made feeding a child one of the distinguishing characteristics of a mother.[15] Morelli too believed that the mother was best suited for this aspect of childrearing.[16] But mothers also helped counsel and guide their children. Luca Panzano, for instance, remembered his mother's early influence on him.[17] Boccaccio, while condemnatory, did mention that mothers taught their daughters their womanly wiles.[18] Francesco da Barberino noted that little girls learned much from imitating and listening to their mothers. And Michele da Savonarola emphasized that the mother was as equally responsible as the father and teacher for her child's moral guidance.[19]

In Alberti's *Libri della Famiglia* Adovardo asserted that it was the father's duty not only to shape the character of the child but also to educate the child.[20] But education, like moral guidance, was a shared duty for Florentine parents. This should not be too surprising since parents, with the help of their communes, were responsible for the organization of schooling throughout Renaissance Italy. Some parents began this pursuit of knowledge for their children early. They carved the letters of the alphabet out of fruit to quiz their young children when they were about two years old. A correct guess meant the child got to eat the letter as a reward. Parents were enjoined to begin this practice even while the child was at the wetnurse.[21] Parents also read to their children. Lapo Mazzei sent a letter to Margherita Datini, telling her to return his copy of *The Little Flowers of St. Francis* so he could read it to his children. When he was a child, Michele Verini had the Bible and even Euclid read to him after supper.[22]

Oral tradition played a role in a child's education, especially in maintaining family solidarity, pride, and awareness. Cellini recalled as a child being told much about his father's life. Mothers told stories to their children, and in the course of this furthered their learning of the vernacular, which the wetnurse had begun, and taught them some of the simple codes of Florentine social mores.[23] Memory-training was essential for education and in particular for the oral components of Florentine culture. In *Libri della Famiglia* Lionardo mentioned that his "own father often used to send us as messengers to various people on unnecessary errands, just to train our memory." He added that his father also used to ask his children their opinion of matters "to sharpen and awaken our intellect and mind."[24]

Adovardo had noted that while a father might himself like to teach his children how to read, the demands of public and private life usually prevented that. In those cases a tutor had to be hired—but only the best. Both the *ricordanze* and *Decameron* note the presence of these individuals in Florentine households. Sometimes despite the parents' best intentions the tutors were inadequate. In February 1470, Bartolomea Niccolini hired one for her son Lodovico, aged five. In April she discharged him, and told her husband, Otto, that this tutor had fewer brains than a goose. She added that they had to hire another one since Lodovico knew little and was not studious and that their other son

Jacopo, aged four, needed to learn how to read.[25] Because they were in the household more often than fathers, mothers probably had considerable control over the tutors and considerable responsibility for monitoring them.

Children learned religion and religious ritual from their parents; mothers, for instance, taught them their prayers. Margaret of Cortona, for instance, learned how to pray from her mother. According to Giovanni Dominici, a child's first prayers should be the *Ave Maria*, the *Pater Noster*, and the *Miserere*. When older they were as well to learn the seven Psalms for the safety of the state. He said that parents should take their young children to church, so they could learn about it in their early years. He added that they should not take them during peak hours, so they neither disturbed the crowd of worshipers nor were disturbed by them.[26] Little girls, according to Francesco da Barberino, could learn much from imitating their mothers at church, especially gender-specific behavior:

> And if with her mother
> She goes perhaps to church,
> Little by little she learns
> To stand respectably and ornately
> And to pray, and say Our Fathers
> As she sees her mother
> And the other women act.[27]

Giovanni Dominici even thought parents should encourage children to confess their sins to them: "While they are young you should teach them to tell you the faults that they commit, to strike their breast, say an *Ave Maria*, take some punishment due them or perform some similar act." This was to prepare them for the habit of confessing to a priest when they became older. Parents could even use figs or other fruits as a reward to encourage this practice confession.[28] In his *Confessionale*, Sant' Antonino condemned mothers who failed to take their daughters to mass and confession.[29] His harsh stricture reinforces the perception that mothers were primarily responsible for their children's religious education. At home children were to ask their parents for a blessing when they woke, when they went to sleep, and sometime in between. A child asked simply: "Bless me." A parent answered: "May God bless you with an eternal blessing." The child then kissed the parent's hand, and according to Giovanni Dominici, went off "secure in the belief that nothing will harm [it] so far as the salvation of the soul was concerned." Children learned other religious rituals. For instance, whenever they began some new activity, they were to kiss a cross scratched in the ground or on a piece of furniture. Children also learned religion from visual images. Paintings, according to Dominici, were an excellent device parents could use to teach children about religion and other things. He noted that paintings of the massacre of the Holy Innocents would teach children to fear weapons and armed men.[30] Inculcating nonviolence in children, then, is no new practice. Other visual aids existed for religious education. Boccaccio observed that children learned feast days from calendars.[31]

Rearing children was difficult for Florentine parents, and tension and disagreement could exist between fathers and mothers regarding childrearing since both were involved in educating their children. Sant' Antonino compared the intercessory powers of the Virgin Mary to that of a mother when a child wants something from its father.[32] Undoubtedly, Florentine children, like children everywhere, understood well how to play off one parent against the other. This tension and disagreement between parents could arise in particular from the father's periodic absences. While in Rome in 1470, Otto Niccolini received a letter from his wife, Bartolomea, in which she wrote that she did not appreciate being left by herself to deal with the children. She also reminded him that she missed him. But, she warned, a situation like this would not occur again: either she would go to Rome with him or he had to make better preparations for help at home. Otto did neither: he died that same year.[33]

Since Florentine males who were engaged in commercial or state business were frequently absent from home husbands and wives kept in contact with each other by letter. Many of these letters contain accounts of their children's growth, the state of their health, and the cute things that they did. Clarice de'Medici wrote Lorenzo to tell him that their son, Giovanni (the future Pope Leo X), at three years of age, was wandering around the house asking when he would be home (he pronounced his father's name as "Loencio"). He was still at this sort of game three years later, this time spouting off a long series of Os and then asking where Lorenzo was. One of the Medici retainers wrote Lorenzo at another point to tell him that his six-year-old son, Giuliano, was "as fresh as a rose."[34] The writers of these missives obviously thought that the recipients would be quite interested in the mundane activities of their children, and they probably were. But epistolary communication was no substitute for physical presence when it came to childrearing.

Others helped with the childrearing, which certainly eased the strain on the mothers caused by absent fathers. The wealthier families had servants. In 1469, Fiametta Strozzi wrote to her husband, Filippo, telling him that as soon as their son returned from the wetnurse they ought to buy a slave girl to look after him or a little Moorish boy to be his buddy.[35] Boccaccio tells us of "Messer Amerigo Abate da Trapani who, with other worldly goods he possessed, was well furnished with many children. Therefore, he was in need of servants."[36] The writers of *ricordanze* sometimes hired servants whenever their children returned from the wetnurse.[37]

Another set, potentially two sets, of parents might also be present to help rear the children, and Cellini even alluded to them in his patchy memories of childhood—grandparents. On the other hand, because of premodern mortality rates, coupled with the late age of marriage for Florentine males, the chances were probably not good that most Florentine children experienced the presence of a grandparent. Nevertheless, in Tuscany, according to Charles de la Roncière, it was customary for mothers to visit their married daughters. A visit to their grandchildren was a possible motive for this. In one of Boccaccio's stories a bandit discussed nonsensical devotional prayers with a traveling merchant: "recite the *Dirupisti* or the *Intemerata* or the *De profundis,* all of which, according to what my grandmother used to say, are quite effective." Alessandra Strozzi described a granddaughter: "She is a beautiful child, and a double of [her mother] Fiametta: white like her and with all her features. . . . May God lend her a long life." There is perhaps no better depiction of a grandfather's attachment to a grandson than Domenico Ghirlandaio's *Portrait of a Man with his Grandson* (ca. 1480). Boccaccio described this sentiment in one of his stories. The count of Antwerp is separated from his children and years later returns, unrecognized because of his penury, to see his married daughter, who has a number of children. The eldest is eight years old. "When they saw the Count eating some food there, all of them gathered around him and began to make a fuss over him, almost as though some hidden power inside them allowed them to sense he was their grandfather. Recognizing his grandchildren, he began to show his affection and to caress them." He frequently played with these children, and by the story's end, his real identity had been established and all lived happily ever after.[38] Through fiction Boccaccio sketched a Florentine truth—the existence of intergenerational affection.

Klapisch-Zuber noted from the Florentine *Catasti* that 48 percent of the households headed by men aged 67 or older had a child between the ages of one and five living there. Grandchildren would likely be underfoot in many Tuscan households, including that of the Medici. Cosimo de'Medici at one point was conducting business at his villa with some ambassadors from Lucca. He stopped to play the bagpipe with one of his grandsons, and then told the astounded ambassadors that they were lucky he did not sing as well. Grandparents were especially important for helping integrate children into a home and caring for them. Giovanni Morelli called his grandfather, Matteo da Quaranta, "our second father," because he played such a significant role in his life after his father died. Gianozzo, in Alberti's *Libri della Famiglia*, told his audience they should work hard in the present for their grandchildren's sake in the future. Most Florentine grandparents enjoyed and loved their grandchildren. Allessandra Strozzi wanted her children to have children so she could enjoy grandchildren.[39]

Other relatives also took a hand in helping to rear children. As a child Marco Parenti lived in a joint household shared by his father; uncle; and cousin, Giovanni.[40] The humanist Michele Verini was very attached to his uncle. Despite the widespread belief among historians that the extended family was in decline during the premodern era, children in Florence who had a large network of relatives found themselves part of a loving extended-family network.[41] Florentine law recognized this fact. The sumptuary laws of 1355/6 forbade anyone to make any garment costing more than five florins for their children, their nephews or their grandchildren.[42]

How did children react to this attention? Most Florentine children of the merchant elite honored and obeyed their parents. Children were supposed to address their parents as sir (Messer padre) and madam (Madonna madre). Iris Origo saw this formality as an example of the lack of affection between parents and children in Tuscan society. But Giovanni Dominici, who had advised this formality out of respect, also said that children could and should refer to their parents as simply father and mother. Most likely, he wished to distinguish between public and private forms of address between parents and children without any particular connotation of a lack of affection in the formal address.[43] Luigi Guicciardini received a letter from his daughter Simona, written 3 December 1542, addressed to "Carisissimo e honorando padre" (dearest and honored father).[44] Accounts of children's love for their parents are also not hard to find. Benedetta Carlini was "deeply attached" to her father; Boccaccio too describes filial affection in his *Decameron*.[45] This filial respect and love is perhaps reflected in the tendency of so many Florentine sons to live close to their parents' house.[46]

Not only did Florentine children owe respect to their parents, they also did chores for them. These included household tasks, such as cleaning and cooking, and other tasks, such as running errands. One September day in 1412, for instance, Andrea Bucachi took her foster father's lunch of bread and wine to him where he was working in a forest cutting wood. San Bernardino urged mothers to teach their daughters household chores, including how to look after babies and change their diapers.[47] Giovanni Dominici suggested that parents should use little rewards, such as pieces of fruit or toys or new shoes, to encourage children to perform chores. He noted they would do them for such rewards because "a child loves gifts and presents."[48] Where there was the carrot, however, there was also the stick. As a child Catherine of Racconigi was so afraid of being punished for doing household chores improperly that she trembled with fear while washing the dishes.[49]

This stern discipline was the rule in Florentine homes according to Iris Origo. Although it is probably an exaggeration, she believed that children were treated just as harshly as slaves at Florence.[50] While Florentine parents certainly spanked their disobedient children, this was not necessarily cruel.[51] In Alberti's *Libri della Famiglia*, Adovardo mentioned that parents did have to spank their children, but he emphasized how difficult it was to do this to children one loved. He also noted how most fathers absolutely hated to see a tutor discipline their children.[52] Giovanni Dominici, who has a reputation among Florentine social historians as a stern disciplinarian, urged moderation in discipline—spankings were not to be severe.[53] Alberti had Lionardo state emphatically that a father must not punish his children when enraged.[54] In fact, most humanists were opposed to corporal punishment.[55]

In Alberti's *Libri della Famiglia* the characters discussed the theory behind discipline. All agreed that discipline was essential for the moral development of the child. Lionardo criticized those fathers who simply forgave their children's transgressions with a simple "don't do it again." He added that a father should encourage good behavior not just punish bad. But the punishment should be consistent enough so that a child could count on the certainty of it. This certainty was more instructive, he thought, than the actual imposition of the penalty. Yet Adovardo cautioned that fathers could love their children too much to discipline them properly. Disciplining children then, as always, was hard work, and a father needed help. Gianozzo said he had told his wife to monitor his performance as a father and to point out his faults. "In that way I shall know that our honor and our welfare and the good of our children are dear to your heart."[56]

In general, discipline for children in Florence was not harsh, though depending on the individual it could be strict. Francesco Datini told Piero Mazzei, one of Lapo Mazzei's sons whom Francesco had informally adopted, "You are my son. Do your duty well, and you will acquire honour and profits, and can count on me as if I were Ser Lapo. But if you do not, it will be as if I had never known you."[57] Despite this rigid warning, Lionardo's comment in Alberti's *Libri della Famiglia* is perhaps more realistic and understanding regarding parental attitudes towards their children's discipline: "some misbehavior is part of childhood."[58]

Along with educating and disciplining his children, Alberti believed a father had the duty of clothing his children well. In his study of Marco Parenti, Mark Phillips noted that as his family grew so did the number of his *ricordanze* entries for his children's expenses, especially those listing articles of clothing.[59] As in education and discipline, both parents shared the responsibility of purchasing these items. "I remember," so recorded Bernardo Machiavelli, "how on the 26th of March I bought from Benedetto di Goro, hosemaker, a pair of dark hose for Niccolò, and a pair of the same color for Totto, at a price of 4 lire and 10 soldi." Tribaldo dei Rossi recorded on 14 August 1500 that his wife, Nannina, bought a pair of hose for their son, Amerigho, at a price of four lire. Lapo Castiglionchio gave his wife money so that she could go out and buy clothing for their son.[60] Giovanni and Niccolaio Niccolini kept a detailed record of the clothing purchased for their nieces, Filippa and Tommasa, even to the ribbons, threads, and hook-and-eye fasteners. These men, not the girls' mother, actually bought the clothing; and they were extravagant. A Florentine sumptuary law of 1330 had forbidden children from wearing parti-colored cloth. Nevertheless, these men made sure to buy plenty of it for their nieces. Between 1348 and 1353 they spent, on the average, 12 gold florins per year to dress each girl.[61] Florentines who could afford it splurged on their children's clothing, despite Giovanni Dominici's admonishment to dress children modestly.[62] Charles de la Roncière noted that one child's inventory contained about 50 items of clothing; another's contained over 170 items.[63]

While it is difficult to determine what portion of the household expenses children's clothing comprised, we can get some indication of the frequency with which Florentines of the merchant elite purchased clothing for their children and what those specific items were. The *ricordanze* of Niccolò Strozzi contains a detailed listing of the clothing purchases he made for his children Simone (b.1472), Carlo (b.1473), and Lena (b. 1475). His wife, Francesca, continued the accounts in 1487 for Carlo and Lena in her *ricordanze* after Niccolò's death (see Appendix A, Table A.7).

Although examples drawn from Strozzi expenses might not be representative, Niccolò and Francesca shared one thing in common with other *ricordanze* writers who recorded clothing purchases. Shoes, including cloth slippers [*scharpette* or *sciarpetti*], leather slippers [*pianelle* (some had painted high heels, which San Bernardino thought scandalous whenever little girls wore them)],[64] wooden clogs [*zucholi,* zocholi or zoccholi], wooden-soled sandals [legniani or lengnacci], and boots [scharpelle], formed the bulk of the purchases.[65] The frequency with which the cloth slippers were purchased probably illustrates more the abrasive effect of Florence's streets on cloth than conspicuous consumption. The Strozzi children received wooden clogs in the fall and early winter, which reflects Tuscany's rainy season, a pattern paralleled in the accounts of the other ricordanze writers.

As seen above, the commune paid attention to the dress of children, especially that of little girls. Sumptuary legislation from the fourteenth century prohibited finery in dress for females over the age of ten years. In 1373 the commune declared that women and girls "of whatever age" could not wear gold, silver, jewelry, stones, or silk. If they did, they or their parents were subject to a 50-florin fine. On 10 June 1378 the Giudici degli Appelii prosecuted "Nicolosa, daughter of Niccolò Soderini, of the parish of S. Frediano, aged ten years. Nicolosa was discovered wearing a dress made of two pieces of silk with tassels and bound with various pieces of black leather, in violation of the Communal statutes." Her lawyer admitted her guilt and paid her fine of fourteen lire. The law of 1373, however, was not designed to regulate dress. According to the preamble, it was a device with which the commune would gain income. In other words, it was a luxury tax.[66] Nothing, then, prevented people from dressing their children in all sorts of finery, as long as they were willing to pay. But there may have been a practical reason why parents would not want to dress their children sumptuously—it could be dangerous:

> 1465. 10th April. A young woman, who was the daughter of Zanobi Gherucci, was tried for having killed and then thrown into a well the little girl of Bernardo della Zecca, a goldsmith, for the sake of stealing a pearl necklace and certain silver ornaments that the child wore round her neck. She was taken away in the executioner's cart and was beheaded.[67]

Dowries represented another expense relating to children, one for which, under Florentine law, the father was responsible.[68] If children's clothing expenses could be likened to a persistent leaky faucet for a family's budget, dowry expenses then were a burst main, one that increased pressure over time. Paolo Niccolini recalled that in 1350 his great aunt's dowry had been 350 florins, and in 1401 his mother's had been 1000 florins; he presented his daughter, Ginevra, with a dowry of 1770 florins.[69] The reason for this inflation, which Dante had deplored in his time, was simple, according to Francesco Guicciardini:

> Nothing in our civil life is more difficult than marrying off our daughters well. The reason is that all men think more of themselves than others do, and they begin to reach for heights which in fact they cannot attain. I have seen many fathers refuse matches which, after they had looked around, they would have accepted gratefully. Men should, therefore, measure accurately their own condition as well as that of others, and not be led astray by a higher opinion of themselves than is warranted. I know all this well, though I do not know whether I shall use this knowledge well. Nor do I know whether I shall fall into the common error of presuming more than I should. But neither ought this ricordo serve to disgust anyone so much that, like Francesco Vettori, he give his daughters to the first man who asks for them.[70]

Parents wanted the best matches they could arrange for their daughters. In Florence, they began investing for this early. By 1433 the *Monte delle Doti,* a time-deposit investment account, was in full operation. With a minimum deposit of 60 florins (later changed to 70), a depositor could choose either a five-year account at 18.47 percent interest compounded annually, a seven-and-a-half-year account at 20.96 percent, an eleven-year account at 17.84 percent, or a fifteen-year account at 15.18 percent. Not surprisingly, the average amount invested in the *Monte delle Doti* was 71 florins.[71]

According to the study that Julius Kirshner and Anthony Molho have undertaken of the *Monte delle Doti,* fathers usually invested in Monte shares for their daughters after they turned five years old. Of the girls enrolled in the Monte, 91 percent had been enrolled before their tenth birthday.[72] Some were enrolled earlier. Marco Parenti enrolled his two-year-old daughter Gostanza with an investment of 140 florins. After she turned three, he added 200 florins to her account. Paolo Niccolini enrolled his daughter when she was two; Neri di Bicci enrolled his daughter Nanina when she was four.[73] Filippo Strozzi invested 161 florins in the Monte for his daughter Lucretia three months after she was born; ten years later he added 137 florins. In 1503, Tommaso Guidetti invested in the Monte for his daughter Madalena two months after she returned from the wetnurse.[74] Considering the early age at which fathers made investments for their daughters (some of which were substantial), Kirshner and Molho concluded that, contrary to popular belief, Florentines did not send their daughters off to a convent to avoid paying for a dowry since the average age of girls entering a convent was 17 years. The dowry investment had been made years before, on the average seven years before; moreover, the convent, not the father, received the *Monte delle Doti* funds of any girl who had been enrolled and who became a nun.[75]

Considering the payments Florentines had to make concerning their children, no wonder Niccolò Ammanatini in 1442 asked the tax officials of the *popolo* to take into account his growing children when they debated whether or not to reduce his taxes. The problem of taxes and the cost of children seems to have been a constant concern of Florentines. It is not unusual to find reference to both together. In an anonymous appeal for general tax relief in 1369, someone addressed the priors: "People are living in misery since they earn little and prices have been so high for thirteen months and more. Just think about those who have three or four or five children, and who are assessed two or three florins, and who have to live from the labor of their hands and those of their wives. . . . How can they stay here and live?"[76]

Expenses for their children's clothing and their daughters' dowry funds were not the only things that Florentine parents of the merchant elite were troubled about and monitored carefully. Most parents paid close attention to their children's health and hygiene. While puberty and adolescence are outside the bounds of this study, some commentators were concerned about a child's sexual behavior even at an early age. As might be expected, these were churchmen, but their overriding concern in dealing with childhood sexuality was to help prevent the child from becoming a slave to the flesh.[77] San Bernardino warned parents not to trivialize childhood sexual experimentation as just play, since in his opinion this experimentation could lead to homosexuality. His concern with homosexuality as well as the commune's (which eventually established an office against sodomy) stemmed from the fear that God would punish all Tuscany for the sins of the few who engaged in this activity.[78] Giovanni Dominici stated that boys older than two should sleep in nightshirts reaching below their knees. This was so a boy would not fondle himself, advice that reflected Dominici's fears of masturbation. Moreover, he said a boy could sleep in bed with his sisters until he was three years old but no longer, since nature (by which he probably meant sexual desire rather than physical development) begins to develop for boys at five. His prohibition against little boys and girls sleeping together is not based so much on a fear of incest but more his prohibition against male and female sexuality as a whole. The main point of his treatise was to gather little monks, nuns, friars, and tertiaries.[79]

Not much is known about diets for Tuscan children, though it is clear that most children went from breast milk to Tuscan wine (diluted of course) with no transition. Menus for children at the Innocenti indicate that bread made up the largest portion of the meal, though wine, meat, cheese, beans, and salad were also served. Francesco Datini recalled that he loved eating turnips as a child, so much so that as an adult he had Margherita fix them for him often.[80] Florentine children certainly must have had hearty appetites (perhaps reflecting the sad reality of malnutrition in the premodern world, even for the elite) since Boccaccio observed that "children are generally fond of food."[81] One thing about children's diets is clear. Humanists and moralists alike all advised that boys should eat better and more than girls. This may not be mere chauvinism or misogyny; Paolo da Certaldo specifically said that this was so boys would grow up to be strong. Perhaps these commentators recognized that caloric requirements for male and female children (and adults) are different. Certaldo reflected that possibility since he said that little girls should not eat so much that they would become overweight.[82]

Good grooming for children was crucial for the parents from the merchant elite. Giovanni Dominici told mothers to make sure their children were kept clean. But, reflecting his denial of the vanities of the world, he also thought parents spent too much time combing their children's hair and trying to keep it blond and curled. Bartholomeus Anglicus commented, however, that once children were cleaned they would run off as soon as possible and get dirty again. He noted the difficulty in the cleaning process: "When they are washed and combed by their mothers they fight and resist like men." Lapo Niccolini avoided this problem for his wife. In 1421 he rented out a shop to two barbers, and part of their payment was to give free haircuts and baths to Lapo and his children.[83]

A child's sleep was important to parents too. Dante mentioned in *The Paradiso* how delightful it was for parents to watch their children sleep, and Alberti noted how parents would let their children fall asleep in their arms. Just as wetnurses took infants into bed with them, so parents took their young children into bed with them, despite the canonical prohibitions against taking infants into bed. Although doing this might represent the paucity of bedroom furniture in some houses, it certainly was a comfort to both parents and children.[84] Children of the merchant elite did have their own beds, and if Renaissance art is any reflection of reality, these were cut-down versions of adult beds.[85] And children would also sleep with their siblings in these beds. The sources are, however, almost silent on the bedtime rituals to which Alberti's description hints. Catherine of Siena's biographer, however, recorded that at the age of five she would say a Hail Mary at each step on her way to bed. This was not, so Rudolph Bell concluded, a sign of her religious precocity as her hagiographer thought, but a practice common among children in a culture in which religious ritual and pageantry occupied central stage.[86]

Not surprisingly, then, religious play preoccupied many children. Catherine and her little friends formed themselves into a secret flagellant society. Bell stressed how normal this sort of behavior was for children in the fourteenth century: "How many hundreds of Sienese girls had the same thoughts we cannot know . . . the most remarkable thing about them is how ordinary they are." Even with this behavior that appears odd if not deviant to us, her contemporary chroniclers all agree that she was "an obedient, happy, outgoing child." In 1377 some children of about ten years of age were seen in a flagellant procession through Florence. But here they were not playing. Florentine youth confraternities, however, did not include flagellation, perhaps because of the fear of harm. Richard Trexler noted that they concentrated on "activities more fitting to their age," such as games, though with religion permeating the culture these were probably religious games.[87] Giovanni Dominici, for instance, encouraged parents to let children play pretend games, such as a priest's saying Holy Office. He also said that children should develop imaginary friends. Joan of Orvieto (1264-1306), reflecting the religiosity of the day, would tell her playmates that an angel was her real mother.[88] Savonarola remembered that he set up little altars at home to play with when he was a child. Trexler has noted how this pretend play could even extend into the civic realm with children imitating orators.[89]

Children, of course, played outside as well—much to Franco Sacchetti's chagrin. The narrow urban valleys of Florence, according to him, echoed with the "bothersome and vain songs of those who never go down the streets quietly. Thus the cruel Herod could return, but [this time] to kill only those from four to twelve years." San Bernardino observed one children's game where they would run around shouting "bread and candles" and "candles and bread." Giovanni Dominici noted how active children were, and encouraged parents to let their children play running and jumping games. In 1505 the Arno froze over and children instantly ran out onto it to play ball.[90]

Boccaccio described children playing these running and jumping games. According to Dominici, "as long as they play these games you play with them and let them win."[91] He saw fellowship and enjoyment as more important than physical competition and development for children and their parents. Alberti too noted active games for boys, and specifically included fathers in the picture as he described them playing with their children by tossing them in the air and catching them. Parents who were wealthy enough often took their children out for horseback rides.[92] Florentine parents and children enjoyed being together. Giovanni Dominici describes parents playing hide and seek with their children, telling them foolish and scary stories, and singing songs with them.[93]

Parents, adults, and children participated together in various celebrations. At Christmas for good luck, Tuscans burned a log that had been decorated with gifts and coins; presumably they removed the coins and gifts before burning it. Children had their own miniature versions of these.[94] One of Margherita Datini's friends asked her to come to her daughter's birthday party. She added that Margherita should bring "a bowl and an ewer, such as is customary to give to girls" and some confections.[95] Women, as we saw above, would even have their friends' daughters come over to spend the night. Perhaps this was at their own daughters' requests.[96]

Some of this childhood play could have a harsh edge. One of Boccaccio's characters, angered at another, exclaims, "Do you think I'm some kind of child you can make fun of?" People like to tease children. On the other hand, children too could be cruel. In another story Boccaccio recounted how the rector of Fiesole had been caught in bed with a maid: "the Rector could never show his face outdoors without the children pointing a finger at him and saying: 'He's the one who slept with Ciutazza'; this bothered him so much that it nearly drove him insane."[97] On 27 February 1497, Savonarola and his supporters held a burning of the vanities in the Piazza della Signoria. Some boys, who obviously were not impressed with the solemnity of the occasion, threw dead cats onto the pyres.[98] Children of all classes also learned rude gestures out in the streets from their friends and others.[99] Humanists, such as Palmieri and Rucellai, urged parents not to encourage their children in these by laughing at them.[100]

Friendship among children could, of course, last until adulthood, and Morelli advised his sons to consciously seek out and gain friends with children their own age. He advised his sons that ties such as these could be very valuable in the future.[101] And from early on some of these children played together without any regard for class or gender distinctions; Florence's particular urban mixture of rich and poor in the same neighborhoods contributed to this. One of Boccaccio's stories reflects that fact. The son of a wealthy merchant, Girolamo Sighieri, "grew up with the other children of families in the neighborhood and became very friendly with a little girl of his own age, the daughter of a tailor."[102] Florentine children of the merchant elite likewise played with the young household servants and slaves, some of whom, as we have seen, had been specifically bought as playmates.[103]

Florentine children certainly played with toys, but we have very little evidence of exactly what they played with. Art provides some clues, such as in Giovanni Francesco Caroto's *Fanciullo con Pupazzetto*. Inventories of the household goods of dead fathers do at times list the presence of wooden balls.[104] In condemning the vanities of this world,

Giovanni Dominici described the toys children had: "little wooden horses, attractive cymbals, imitation birds, and a thousand different kinds of toys." He also warned parents not to give children toy banks, since that would lead to avarice. He thought play was indicative of what a child would become. He, therefore, warned parents that if they let their children play with dice they would become gamblers.[105] Francesco Datini had his friend, Domenico di Cambio, spend all day searching for a tambourine for his illegitimate daughter "so that the little girl may be happy." San Bernardino, at one point, stopped a band of children just to see how they used their slingshots.[106] Jacopo Nardi recalled that when he was a child "I saw fathers and mothers confiscating anything like a weapon from their sons' rooms in the interest of good discipline and checking their wildness."[107] Children, when the situation demanded it, could make their own toys. A snowfall that lasted five days in November 1500 let children make animals out of the snow—especially lions, one of the symbols of Florence.[108] Pets were not unknown for Florentine children; dogs, cats, and birds appear in paintings and literature as pets. Alberti, for instance, had a pet goose when he was a child and wrote an oration for his dead dog.[109]

One toy—if that is what it was—does appear in the *ricordanze*, the so called Holy Dolls. St. Veronica as a child played with a baby Jesus. But in a culture dominated by Christianity and the depictions of its central figure, a doll such as this did not necessarily mean religious precocity. It may have just been a popular toy. Miniature representations of heroes for today's age are, of course, not unknown. According to Christiane Klapisch-Zuber, these representations of the Christ Child, called *bambini* in the *ricordanze*, were for play as well as religious and ritual practice depending on the age of the owner. Savonarola even condemned them as idolatrous, which certainly reflects their popularity.[110] In the records they usually appear as part of the trousseau a wife brought to a marriage.[111] In her *ricordanze* Alessandra Strozzi noted that she possessed two wooden representations of the Virgin Mary. Whether these were icons or toys or both is unknown.[112]

Children also played with the dead, an activity that demonstrates to us our distance from the people of the past. For them it was not at all unusual to find the dead—especially the criminal dead—literally among them. Florentine officials in the fifteenth century complained that youth gangs and even children were dismembering dead criminals. In 1381 some children cut off the hands of an executed Ghibelline and used them as soccer balls for four days.[113] After Jacopo Pazzi died in the abortive Pazzi conspiracy (17 May 1478) his body was disinterred, dragged past his house, tossed in the Arno, and then hung on a tree—all by a bunch of youths, who made up songs about what they were doing to his body.[114] On 29 May 1503 the crowd at an execution stoned the executioner to death because he had not dispatched the victim with the customary alacrity. A number of youths in the crowd dragged his body to Santa Croce.[115]

And children played dead. San Bernardino witnessed a children's game, similar to ring-around-the-rosy, in which all the participants fell down, pretending to be dead. Each held a little reed cross.[116] Considering the demographic disasters of the premodern world, this was not an unusual game for children. And this highlights a facet of Florentine childhood that is likewise alien to us in the modern world. Death hung over a child's head like a sword of Damocles. It was always present and real. In fact, the death of a child was more a probability for premodern Florentine parents than the remote possibility it is for modern Western parents. Moreover, because people lacked effective medicines and medicinal techniques, childhood illnesses were much more dangerous and troubling than they are today—harder to cure, more likely fatal. What were the consequences of childhood disease and death for premodern Florentines?

†Mori Subito: The Demographic Agonies of Childhood in Premodern Florence

ON THE FIFTH DAY in Boccaccio's *Decameron,* Fiametta tells a story about lovers who achieve happiness after sorrow:

Monna Giovanna was now a widow, and every summer, as our women usually do, she would go to the country with her son to one of their estates very close by to Federigo's farm. Now this young boy of hers happened to become more and more friendly with Federigo and he began to enjoy birds and dogs; and after seeing Federigo's falcon fly many times, it made him so happy that he very much wished it were his own, but he did not dare to ask for it for he could see how precious it was to Federigo. During this time, it happened that the young boy took ill, and his mother was much grieved, for he was her only child and she loved him dearly; she would spend the entire day by his side, never ceasing to comfort him, asking time and again if there was anything he wished, begging him to tell her what it might be, for if it was possible to obtain it, she would certainly do everything in her power to get it. After the young boy had heard her make this offer many times, he said:

"Mother, if you can arrange for me to have Federigo's falcon, I think I would get well quickly."

... the love she bore her son persuaded her that she should make him happy ... so she answered her son:

"My son, cheer up and think only of getting well, for I promise you that first thing tomorrow morning I shall go fetch it for you."

The child was so happy that he showed some improvement that very day.

The next morning under the pretext of a friendly visit she went to Federigo's house to ask him for the falcon. Federigo, an impoverished nobleman, decided to hold a dinner for her; but he found that he had nothing in his larder. Nevertheless, to do her honor he decided to make a meal of his prized falcon:

> Then, having left the table and spent some time in pleasant conversation, the lady thought it time now to say what she had come to say. . . .
>
> ". . . if you had children, through whom you might have experienced the power of parental love, I feel certain that you would, at least, in part, forgive me. But just as you have no child, I do have one, and I cannot escape the laws common to all mothers; the force of such laws compels me to follow them against my own will and against good manners and duty, and to ask of you a gift which I know is most precious to you; and it is naturally so, since your extreme condition has left you no other delight, no other pleasure, no other consolation; and this gift is your falcon, which my son is so taken by that if I do not bring it to him, I fear his sickness will grow so much worse that I may lose him.

Realizing what he had done, a horrified Federigo confessed to Giovanna that they had just consumed the falcon:

> ... then having lost all hope of getting the falcon and thus perhaps improving the health of her son, she thanked Federigo both for the honor paid to her and for his good intentions, and then left in grief to return to her son. To his mother's extreme sorrow, whether in disappointment in not having the falcon, or because his illness inevitably led to it the boy passed from this life only a few days later.
>
> After the period of her mourning and her bitterness had passed, the lady was repeatedly urged by her brothers to remarry, since she was very rich and still young. . . .[1]

This was the sorrow. The happiness came when Giovanna decided to marry Federigo.

This excerpt supplies only the background to the point of the story, which is Federigo's and Giovanna's love. It is an instructive excerpt, however, for another point, one related to daily life in premodern Florence. The fate of Giovanna's son was that of many Florentine children.[2] Moreover, her reaction was that of most Florentine parents. They did as much as was in their power to aid their sick children; when faced with the death of their children they grieved and felt a deep sense of loss.

Admittedly, these are familiar reactions to us. But the world of Florentine parents is not familiar. Most of the serious childhood diseases that modern Western society sees as infrequent visitors—if even that anymore—were constant companions to premodern society. Most of the minor illnesses that modern Western society sees as occasional nuisances were major ordeals—even debilitations—to premodern society.[3] The awareness of disease was more acute in the premodern world than that of today, appearing frequently as the subject of correspondence. Alessandra Strozzi, for instance, laced her letters with her fears for her sons' and their families' health.[4] Premodern children had a greater awareness of disease than children today. Not only did they suffer its dread effects, they saw its ravages among friends, kin, and neighbors. When Leon Battista Alberti was in Padua at school, his father, Lorenzo, was in Venice. At one point, plague came to Venice. The tutor wrote to Lorenzo to tell him that his son could not sleep and cried all the time, worried about his father's health. Alberti had good reason to be worried since his mother had died of the plague.[5] Disease implied death to premodern Westerners more often that it does for modern Westerners. And for children, especially the very young, the likelihood of death resulting from disease was even greater.[6] Florentines recognized that fact. The physician Michele de Savonarola noted that diseases that killed those younger than two had little effect on those older. Florentines knew that even the most trifling illness could be a major crisis in a child. For girls enrolled in the Monte della Doti the death rate for those less than five years was three times as high as that for those between ten and fourteen years. Florentine fathers made their decisions to invest in the dowry fund based on that fact. After a girl turned two, fathers began to invest, undoubtedly figuring that now they were "a good investment risk."[7] Discussing toddlers, Alberti had his readers pause: "Consider . . . how much anguish it is to a father to think that more children perish at this age than any other." A father had to be on guard constantly when monitoring his child's health.[8] Some commentators told Florentines to prepare for the worst whenever illness struck their children. Giovanni Dominici advised his readers to have children over the age of eight go to confession and receive the sacraments whenever they became ill, even though they were not of the canonical age to partake of the sacraments. Nevertheless, this response to illness highlights how closely the premodern Florentine was touched by death. Discussing his ancestors, Giovanni Morelli concluded that they lived longer and were healthier than Florentines of the fourteenth and fifteenth centuries. This was wishful thinking to some extent, a reaction to the world he saw around himself.[9] Yet, despite the dreary reality regarding the everyday presence and consequences of childhood disease and death, Florentines did have cause for hope. Alberti pointed out how almost magically at times children recovered from illnesses, and in his *Libri della famiglia* he had Lionardo state, "As long as there is breath in a child, one should hope for the best rather than fear the worst."[10]

Despite the common historical misconception that premodern people, including physicians, took little notice of childhood diseases, Florentines at all levels recognized what diseases could afflict their children. In a summary of medical treatises from the premodern era, Luke Demaitre noted the most common childhood ailments, in descending order of their frequency, in the treatises: diarrhea, sleeplessness, worms, vomiting, wheezing, coughing, and fevers. Significantly, these form two general categories: gastrointestinal and respiratory diseases. This is understandable, considering the poor sanitation of the premodern world, the delicate nature of an infant's intestinal and respiratory systems, and the poor heating of premodern dwellings. In his *De regimine pregnantium*, Michele de Savonarola mentioned measles and smallpox as deadly childhood visitors. Alberti also mentioned them along with other childhood ailments. Writers of *ricordanze* recorded these diseases and more for their children. Morelli suffered two serious attacks of an undefined ailment at four and seven years of age; he also had smallpox at nine, and a serious bout with fever (malaria?) at twelve.[11]

Disease was not the only deadly gauntlet children had to run; the premodern world was also an accident-prone world.[12] Luca Landucci filled his diary with accounts of such accidents, giving an impressionistic picture of the dangers lurking in premodern Florence. Adovardo mentioned in the *Libri della famiglia* how sad it was for a father to see his child fall, scrape its knee, and come home crying.[13] Sad yes, but compared to some of the other accidents that could befall a child in premodern Florence the proper reaction should have been relief that it was just a scraped knee.

Florentine children needed to beware of animals, weather, construction, and humans. A scorpion almost stung Cellini when he was a child; a dog tried to drag away Benedetta Carlini when she was a child. We tend to forget how dangerous wild (or hunting) dogs were to premodern people, especially before the advent of rabies vaccine and animal control. The artist Simone Martine did a painting of the Blessed Agostino Novello on the theme of the miraculous recovery of the child killed by a wolf. Wolves for premodern people were not just storybook characters that swallowed grandmothers whole. They were real and vicious killers. And children made easy targets for them and dogs. In addition, Landucci noted accidents happening to children who got too close to trained animals in Florence.[14] These are scenes that few if any of us in the modern Western world will ever witness. Something that we still witness and fear, even though we understand it, terrified Florentines, since they did not. Luca Landucci recorded for 11 June 1510 that a "thunderbolt fell at San Domino killing a father and son, and two other children of his were frightened out of their wits and had fallen ill." Nature could be dangerously deadly. Even the urban canyons of Florence were unsafe. Simone Martine painted the blessed Agostino Novello saving a child who fell from a balcony. Tiles from roofs sometimes loosened and fell, hitting adults and children alike. Landucci recorded a boy getting a broken leg from such an accident in 1501. In 1497 a child fell from the bell tower of the Signoria and died. Florence was an unsafe place, particularly for children, because public wells stood in every square and on every street corner. Many private houses also had their own well. Children sometimes fell into these.[15] Piero della Francesco's *A Miracle of St Elizabeth* (1469) depicts such an accident. Two children pray while the mother peers into the shaft; a man runs towards the well with a grappling hook and rope. Rescuing a child from one of these wells was undoubtedly difficult business. Children also had to fear other humans. Crime touched children just as it did adults.[16] Children then, just as today, had to fear sexual abuse. The city condemned this crime since execution for it seemed to have been common.[17] Incest too occurred and seemed to be greeted with horror. Antonio di Tome was sentenced in 1412 to be burnt alive in a wooden basket for committing incest with a niece. The punishment was changed to merely decapitation.[18] The presence of troops inside the city could be troublesome as well. Landucci recorded that some French soldiers who were quartered in his house roughed up his young son.[19] The premodern urban world was a dangerous one for children, just as it was for adults.

Whether struck by disease or accident, the children of the merchant elite were commonly treated by doctors. Paolo Sassetti recorded payments of ten florins to a Maestro Giovanni, who treated his nephew. Francesco Datini's illegitimate daughter had a swollen face (perhaps resulting from a toothache?) when she was six years old, and Margherita Datini called in a physician to treat her. For the illness of his young apprentice, Francesco hired two physicians, who stayed with the boy till he died.[20] Parents could be so concerned for their children's health and so willing to turn to the medical profession that they sometimes had autopsies performed on their dead spouses just to discover whether or not the disease they had died of was hereditary (and thus threatening to their children).[21]

Sometimes, as Demaitre concluded, "the silly coexisted with the sensible in infant hygiene and regimen." Paolo Bagellardus, for instance, advised rubbing fresh calf excrement on a child's swelling stomach; he insisted that he saw this treatment work.[22] A journey through the medical or pharmacological tracts of the premodern era can turn up some odd (at least to us) concoctions. Giovanni Serapione's *Trattato delle medicine semplici* has a recipe for some sort of unguent for children that contains, among other ingredients, mouse excrement. Bartolomeo Sassetti listed "medicine da occhi" (perhaps a salve for eye infections) on the back cover of his *ricordanze;* one of the ingredients was "latte di donna." He added that if this were unavailable, goat's milk would suffice.[23]

Medicine then, as now, could be unpalatable. Giovanni Dominici advised parents to let children take small doses of medicine. This was not homeopathy, however. He just thought introducing children to the taste little by little would mean that whenever they took doses for real they would not complain as much. He even noted that parents would give children bitter substances—peach stones, horehound, or certain herbs—to acquaint them with the taste of medicine.[24] Pharmacists likewise treated children's ailments. Niccolò Strozzi recorded that he paid a pharmacist eight soldi for medicine for his three-year-old son, Carlo. He recorded later that he paid one lira five soldi to treat a child who had some sort of eye and mouth infection (perhaps measles?). The Niccolini brothers purchased medicine for their niece, Tommasa, whenever she fell ill.[25]

Parents themselves treated their children, in fact this was expected or routine, which may explain why it appears as if premodern medical writers neglected the illnesses of children.[26] Michele de Savonarola, for instance, limited his discussion of childhood diseases to those that the parents could not treat themselves. In one of his stories Boccaccio described a father who lanced a daughter's abscessed ear.[27] In many cases, however, this care consisted only of the love and attention, hugs and kisses, a parent could give to a sick child. Lapo Mazzei, for instance, frequently took his epileptic son into bed with him to comfort him.[28] Paintings of parents clustered around a child's sickbed are common in Florence.[29] Too often, premodern parents realized, this gathering could turn into a death watch. Ser Iacopo da Prato lost his son, Paulo, after a four-day illness; Manetto Dati, Gregorio's four-year-old son, died after being "very sick."[30] With this in mind, and having to serve as physician and comforter, a parent in premodern Florence was undoubtedly under considerable physical and emotional stress when dealing with a sick child. Moreover, a parent had to spend considerable time and energy nursing an ill child.[31] Some of this stress and strain would have been alleviated by the presence of servants who could help tend the child. Since the mother's role was most closely associated with the day-to-day activities of the child, she probably spent more time with an ill child than did the husband. In fact, women in general probably spent more time with the sick in Florence than did men.[32]

Despite the attention of physicians, pharmacists, and parents, childhood diseases in the premodern era were difficult to detect and cure. As Michele de Savonarola recognized, the infant obviously could not contribute to the diagnosis by explaining what was wrong or what was hurting.[33] Moreover, sometimes parents could do little for their sick children but pray for them. But this was not just an act of despair. Incantations invoking the name of Christ or the symbols of faith were thought efficacious in the cure of disease. These things actually cured the disease, so people thought, by connecting their ill children with the greatest healer and greatest healing power the world—their Christian world—had ever known.[34] And belief in the power of the heavenly supernatural helps explain why parents turned to other supernatural powers to cure their children.

At the first sign of illness, parents rushed to get brevi, which were pieces of parchment with incantations or Christ's name written on them. These were charms prepared by certain men or women and reputed to possess curative powers. There were other sources of supernatural cures. In 1376, Niccolò Consigli was burned at the stake in Florence for using sorcery to cure people, including children.[35] Incantations, however, failed to cure Datini's illegitimate child, just as medicine had failed.[36] Near Arezzo in 1425, San Bernardino tried and failed to eliminate a spring, once sacred to Apollo, called the Fonte Tecta, where parents brought sick children for cures. San Bernardino claimed that it was a haunt of witches and magicians; nevertheless, the population so respected its powers that the citizens rose up against him and expelled him. Fifteen years later he returned, desecrated the site, and dedicated a church to Santa Maria delle Grazie. The cures of children continued, this time under divine sanction.[37]

Boccaccio tells a story of a miraculous cure of a boy afflicted with worms. The main character, a friar, exorcised the child with prayer. After curing him, the friar told the father to have a life-sized wax image of the child made and placed in the Saint Ambrose chapel in Siena before the statue of the saint.[38] Worms in particular were a serious ailment for children in premodern Florence. Herlihy and Klapisch-Zuber found that they were the second-greatest cause of children's death after the plague. Worms cause diarrhea, which in children can quickly lead to dehydration and then death.[39] Giovanni Corsini received a prescription to cure worms from Maestro Iacopo da Furli. In the recipe he mentioned that more sugar could be added to make the pill easer to take for children. (Sugar itself was even thought to be medicinal; the Niccolini brothers gave it to their niece Tommasa whenever she was ill.) The existence of worms and other gastrointestinal diseases in Florence, and their dreadful effects on the childhood population, should not be all that surprising. Modern sanitary facilities were nonexistent, and the Arno was a sewer. No wonder death rates due to gastro-intestinal disorders climbed during the summer.[40] In fact the month of August, closely followed by July, had the highest percentage of deathrates by disease for the Florentine population.[41]

As we have seen, writers of *ricordanze* were prolific in the number of children they had, but they had to be. Their children died prolifically. By 1422, Gregorio Dati recorded that he had 21 children from his second and third wives. Of these only 5 were still alive: 3 boys and 2 girls. Others had similar experiences. Lapo Mazzei had 14 children; only 5 lived to adulthood. Catherine of Siena's mother had 25 children; only 8 lived to adulthood.[42] These instances could be multiplied endlessly, which highlights a particular facet of premodern parenthood.[43] Not only was there a great likelihood of any child's dying, there was also a great likelihood of many children from the same family dying. The cold dry statistic of 30 percent childhood mortality rates common for the premodern world takes on a stunning complexion when we realize that this rate or higher could occur in any individual family.[44] Moreover, 30 percent or more of the family could die in one fell swoop with a visitation from the plague.

This disease also separates premodern from modern Europe. A new arrival in 1347, the plague stayed into the eighteenth century, returning in periodic cycles (every ten years or so) to carry off people, especially the young.[45] The plague visitation at Prato in 1363-64 so ravaged the young that it was known specifically as the children's plague.[46] Between 1363 and 1400 the loss of children to plague was so astounding that the Tuscan population needed a century to recover from it.[47] The plague and its effects were uppermost in the minds of premodern people and formed the backdrop against which they had to live their lives. The introduction to Boccaccio's *Decameron,* written just after 1348, gives a fine representation of that perception. Other chroniclers, commentators, and witnesses seconded his observations on the effects of the plague. The Sienese chronicler Agnolo di Tura described the severity of the Black Death at Siena by saying that father abandoned child, an observation Boccaccio made as well for the plague at Florence.[48] What is important here is not so much whether this happened, but the fact that both chroniclers used the same motif to explain the severity of this disease in their society. And Agnolo knew what he was talking about. He recalled having to bury five of his children by himself. Giovanni Morelli's *Ricordi* is chock full of references to death in his family due to the plague.[49]

Herlihy and Klapisch-Zuber stated that the plague rarely eliminated entire families, though it did leave many severely truncated.[50] This may miss the point of the plague's effect on families. Too many writers of *ricordanze* recorded devastating losses, especially losses that occurred in a short time. Autumn 1417 was a painful time for Bernardo Strozzi. On 25 August his daughter Lisa died, on 23 September his daughter Sandra died, on 25 September his wife Antonia died, on 3 October his son Lionardo died, and on 13 October his son Niccolò died. In the summer of 1348, Francesco Durante saw four of his nine children die. Cristofano Guidini lost his wife and six of his seven children in 1390, all in the span of a month. In August 1400, Lapo Curianni lost two of his daughters within two days.[51] In July 1400 the plague struck Prato and Lapo Mazzei wrote of its effects to Francesco Datini: "I have seen two of my children die in my arms in a few hours. . . . And in the same hour Antonia was sick to death, and in the same bed with her the second boy, who died beside her. Imagine how my heart broke, as I heard the little ones weeping, and their mother not strong, and harkened to the words of the eldest. Think of it; three dead!"[52]

Truncated indeed; the plague could destroy a family in an instant. And Florentines knew that. Even if their particular families did not suffer destruction, they undoubtedly knew a family, like that of Bartolomeo Corsini, that disappeared in the aftermath of a plague visitation. His wife and child died in Florence in 1348, and he died in London on business in 1349.[53] In *Decameron,* II:8, Boccaccio relates a tale of the plague's visitation. "In the plague's wake his lord the Marshal, the Marshal's wife, one of his sons, and a number of others including brothers, grandchildren, and relatives, all perished, leaving alive only a daughter of marriageable age." This passage had a dual effect on his readers. It made the story more familiar by reflecting reality and more informative by making a true point in fiction. Plague could be deadly to a family's fortunes and future.

Awareness of this possibility affected the behavior of Florentine parents. Having many children to cover the losses was one option, but this was a decision usually made at the beginning of a marriage. More immediately, flight from Florence on the news of plague was another option. In Alberti's *Libri della famiglia,* Lionardo emphasized that the well members of a family could abandon the sick in time of plague in order to save the family. He was discussing a hard decision for a hard occasion; as immoral as it might seem, abandoning stricken family members in order to preserve the family might be a necessity. But he added, "I pray God it may never happen in our family that I shall be forced to act on it for the sake of the family's survival and welfare."[54] Giovanni Morelli advised early flight from the plague, in the spring if possible to avoid the higher mortality rates of the summer; and he said a family should not flee to some remote corner of Tuscany but to a place with good doctors and medicine. He said that the family should take especial care of the children during this time and should not economize on their medical expenses.[55]

The *ricordanze* are filled with accounts of such journeys, as if families were bobbing about Tuscany pushed on by the waves of panic.[56] In 1400, for instance, many people fled Florence for Bologna. Giovanni Morelli, however, sent his son Alberto to Mossa where his brother was podestà. He and his other son, Lionello, who was two months old, went from Florence to Volterra to Settimello and then back to Florence to a house near the church of Ognisanti. His peregrinations did him no good, for Lionello died on 3 August.[57] Valorino Curianni likewise fled this same outbreak, and this too failed him. While in flight, two of his daughters died, as did two of his servants.[58]

At times, then, whole families, including servants and wetnurses, fled. At other times parents just sent the children.[59] Bartolomeo Masi recalled being sent to Pulciano in the Mugello with two of his brothers in August 1492 when the plague struck Florence. He remembered leaving in company with many other families. He and one brother returned on 8 October; the other returned later. They had stayed with a great aunt on their mother's side.[60] Correspondence would herald not only the plague's arrival in a location but also the imminent arrival of relatives. In May 1383 the plague struck Florence, and Francesco Datini at Prato received a letter from his brother-in-law saying that they were sending his nephew Pippo to him for safe- keeping.[61] For some children, then—those who lived—flight from the plague could mean a visit—perhaps even a pleasant one—with relatives or family friends. On the other hand, for those parents without friends or family outside Florence, plague visitations and the subsequent flight to who-knew-where could be nervewracking if not deadly.

Death, then, could come quickly and in a variety of forms for Florentine children, and writers of *ricordanze* recorded that fact. Some of the *ricordanze* entries noting the death of a child can be terse. Ser Iacopo da Prato recorded the death of his four-year-old daughter, Dominica, just below that announcing her birth: "The said child died in 1400 on the tenth of July."[62] Traditionally historians have interpreted such terseness as evidence of a lack of affection in premodern parents and a sense of emotional detachment from the death of their children. A better interpretation might be that in an account book listing debits and credits, one should not expect much more than this. But we occasionally find more; not all accounts are this terse. Finding depth of emotion and sense of loss in death entries in account books signifies that parents took the death of their children to heart. They were not emotionally detached. Bernardo Torni noted that the loss of children was a difficult emotional experience for fathers, especially if the child was male. Gregorio Dati wrenchingly recorded the almost-simultaneous deaths of his four-year-old and one-year-old sons:

> Our Lord God was pleased to take to Himself the fruits which He had lent us, and He took our most beloved Stagio, our darling and blessed first born. He died of the plague on the morning of Friday, 30 July 1400 in Florence without my seeing him, for I was in the country.

Master Lionardo [Dati's brother] and Monna Ghita [Dati's wife] were
with him. May God bless him and grant that he pray for us.

On 22 August of the same year, the Divine bounty was pleased
to desire a companion for that beloved soul. God called our son Mari
to Himself and he died at eleven o'clock on Sunday, of the plague.
God grant us the grace to find favor with Him and to bless and thank
Him for all things.[63]

Dati's first line is repeated by other writers of *ricordanze*. It pleased
God to take these children, to call these children, to wish these
children, to receive these children to Himself.[64] The entries are
formulaic, but they are formulas that make a point—they are not
mindless and meaningless. These children were now with God.
Parents received psychological and emotional comfort in realizing that
their children were back with their maker. Since, in the premodern
conception, parents were more stewards and custodians of God's fruits
rather than owners, they had returned them to their rightful place, the
spiritual or real world.[65] But this did not mean that children were
transients in a family, except in the sense that all Christians were
transients in this material world. Again, parents received psychological and emotional comfort for believing the death of their children was
part of the natural order, even if it seemed they had left prematurely.[66]
Like good Christians they accepted God's will. Moreover, this acceptance was not just mere fatalism; it was part and parcel of the Christian
mental world. Acceptance of God's will—even if it meant the plague—
allowed parents to cloak themselves in the security of a thought-
system that explained the misfortunes of the world and comforted
those affected by them.[67]

The ease of transition between life and death (God called, God
received, God wished) for premodern people highlighted that for
them the dead were not gone forever. The cult of saints showed them
that there was communication with the dead. Just as the living could
pray for the dead, so could the dead pray for the living, as Dati noted.
Moreover, as Dati also noted, the dead received other family members as companions. A religious system in which the dead and living
were not completely cut off from each other offered considerable
emotional solace to the living.[68]

Writers of *ricordanze* also sent children off to God with a benediction. For some it was a simple blessing, such as may God bless her or him.[69] For others, it was a little more elaborate. Lapo Curianni asked God to bless his dead 15-year-old daughter because she was a "vergine e buona fanciulla." Lorenzo Strozzi asked that God grant peace to his dead three-month-old son Pico ("mio carissimo figlio").[70] These blessings complimented the ones that writers of *ricordanze* asked for in the birth of their children. In the births, writers of *ricordanze* usually asked God's grace and good fortune for their children. In the deaths, they asked for salvation for their children. Ser Piero Bonaccorsi asked that God grant his grace to his dead son Filippo for the salvation of his soul.[71] This final entry for their children in their *ricordanze* was communication between the living and the dead. It was also the first step in the services of the living to aid the salvation of the dead. In a sense, then, the *ricordanze* were instruments for salvation.

Writers of *ricordanze* recorded their children's death in another fashion. Usually, they placed a cross next to the birth entry. Even if the writers were unaccustomed to recording the death of adults in such a fashion, they did so with their children.[72] The crosses could be either a crude stick figure or something more elaborate, such as a Maltese cross. Sometimes they were drawn open; other times the blank spaces were colored in with ink.[73] A cross in a medieval document, such as for a signature, signified "a promise in the sight of Christ crucified."[74] Here in the *ricordanze* for a death entry, it signified Christ's specific promise of life everlasting, symbolized by the cross. It reinforced for parents the idea that their children really were with God. Again, parents received emotional comfort for the death of their children through religion. Moreover, just like three-dimensional funerary art, these crosses were two-dimensional memorials of the death of their children.

Sometimes writers of *ricordanze* signified the death of a child in a different manner. In this case the child's entire account would have two or three lines drawn through it. This was not an act of frustration or anger, though it certainly could occur under those emotions. The conventional way to show a closed *ricordanze* account was to draw a few slashes through it.[75] Ugolino Martelli, for instance, recorded the death of his daughter in 1443 and then slashed the birth and death account with lines.[76] For him the loan of his daughter by God had been completed. The goods had been returned (with profit?). The account was closed. On the surface this action could seem cold and callous. Was it? Or was it just the way to reflect in an account book a beloved soul's return to God?

In 1378, Niccolò Baldovinetti recorded the birth and baptism of his daughter Samaritana. Then "on the 23rd of September 1383 it pleased God to want for Himself her soul, may it be blessed, we placed the body in Santo Stefano at the bridge in Florence."[77] The soul returned to God, but the body remained with the living. Just as Florence was a city full of baptismal processions moving to and from San Giovanni, so it was a city full of funeral processions for children moving to and from other churches. Writers of *ricordanze* recorded the burial place for their children. Usually this place was inside whatever church the family was associated with, though some note the burial occurred outside the church in a cemetery.[78] Giovanni Corsini recorded that his six-year-old son, Giovanni, "was buried in Santo Spirito in our chapel."[79] Located so, the boy was still part of the family whenever it worshipped. At other times writers of *ricordanze* noted how family members reposed with each other in death. Niccolò Baldovinetti recorded in 1373 how he had his wife buried next to their daughter. Filippo Strozzi recorded how his dead children were placed in "mia sepultura,"[80] undoubtedly awaiting his arrival. In his will, Michele Castellani asked that a chapel be built for him at San Marco and that his dead son, Rinieri, be disinterred from where he was buried and placed with him there.[81] Family relationships continued into and beyond death.

Proximity of the family to the dead was, undoubtedly, important, even comforting. Many of the Florentine children who died at the wetnurse, however, remained there, buried away in the local church. Yet sometimes the family made efforts to have a nursling returned and placed with the family. On 11 July 1424 a daughter was born to Matteo and Alessandra Strozzi. She went off to the wetnurse, but died there 15 August 1424, and was buried in Santa Libertà in Pistoia. Matteo had her body transferred to the family's crypt in Santa Maria Novella on 20 November 1424.[82] For the Strozzi the proper burial at home of a one-month-old child was ritually important and emotionally salving. As

Sharon Strocchia observed, "Secondary burial provided an important resource for Florentines with deep roots in the city, for it ensured family honor and continuity, which undoubtedly helped these families manage the devastating experience of plague." It was also psychologically salving for the family to have a deceased loved one return to Florence.[83]

Florentines perceived death ritual as essential not only for honor and emotion but also for salvation. Lapo Curianni recorded that his granddaughter, Tessa, who was 17, had confessed before her death after an illness. He noted as well that she was contrite and had received all the sacraments of the Church. The family buried her with great honor at Santo Stefano.[84] Proper burial ensured an easy transition into the other world, but it also cost. On 20 October 1473, Carlo Strozzi paid two florins six soldi for the funeral of his son Carlo as well as for prayers "per loro animo" at Santa Maria Novella. Niccolò Baldovinetti likewise paid two florins for his daughter's funeral.[85]

Although religion provided a comfort and a way to understand the death of a child, it did not, of course, completely wash away the sadness and the sense of loss. Cellini received word that his toddler son had died at the wetnurse. "My grief was greater than any I had ever felt before. However I knelt down, and, not without tears, I thanked God in my usual fashion, saying: 'My Lord, You gave him to me, and now you have taken him away; and for all things, with all my heart, I thank You.' Then, for all that my grief had nearly crushed me, in my usual way I made a virtue out of necessity, and as best as I could tried to accustom myself to it."[86] The passage, however, leaves the impression that he never did accustom himself to it.

Although some people escaped into indifference as a way to avoid the emotional damage caused by the frequent loss of their children, expressions of grief at the death of children were common in the premodern era. Indeed, parents were emotionally crushed by the death of their children just as we are today.[87] And Florentines were no exception. One father was so distraught at the death of his son that he cursed his private devotional symbol. Dati wrote, "I was sorely grieved at her death" for his daughter, Betta, who died at seven years.[88] Fathers and mothers grieved. Sant' Antonino emphasized that it was natural for a mother to grieve for the loss of a child.[89] The loss of a grown son could also occasion much grief. Alessandra Strozzi's son Matteo died of malaria. She wrote the surviving sons, "I am deeply grieved to be deprived of my son; by his death, I have suffered a grievous blow, greater than the loss of filial love. . . . I have suffered the greatest pain in my heart that I have ever experienced."[90] And this came from a woman who had already lost her husband and another child. Whole families grieved.[91] The death of even peripheral members of a family could be the occasion of grief too. Francesco Datini was saddened at the death of his apprentice, and he wanted Margherita to go and comfort the boy's mother. He noted that at times like that "it is needful to comfort the afflicted."[92]

Humanists wrote consolations on the deaths of their children and those of others.[93] Since most humanists lost children (Filelfo, for instance, lost an astounding 20 of 24 children), this was a shared experience among these men, and they turned their learning and training to understanding their loss and comforting themselves and their friends. More specifically they used classical models of consolation for their loss when they realized that their philosophy and religion was inadequate to assuage their grief.[94] George W. McClure concluded that this was an attempt to replace the ritual of mourning with the rhetoric of mourning.[95] More likely, it was an attempt to buttress ritual with rhetoric. Humanists also traded consoling letters back and forth on the deaths of their children.[96] The humanists reaction to the death of their children did not represent some new-found perception of childhood, as some believe[97]; it was just their attempt to use their new learning to solve an ages-old problem. How does a father react to and deal with the death of his child?

Giovanni Morelli wrote a lengthy consolation on his son's death to himself, though he skipped any classical references.[98] On 5 June 1406 his nine-year-old son, Alberto, died after a 17-day illness. His parents' care and prayers had not saved him. The family left the house for a month in grief; no one used his room for the summer. Morelli was so distraught and grief-stricken that he could not enter Alberto's room for a year. He constantly referred in his *ricordi* to how cutting this loss was by making allusions to how the pain was like that caused by knives and lances. On the first anniversary of his son's death, he was still affected by the loss. He entered his son's room and feverishly prayed before the same crucifix and other ritual images that Alberto had prayed before right before he died. That night in bed doubts assailed him—he said they were put in his mind by the devil, who accused him of being a poor father to Alberto. And Morelli agonized over and over again about the negative aspects of childrearing and domestic life. He finally fell asleep to be comforted with a dream, a dream about Alberto. In the dream he remembered the positive aspects of childrearing and domestic life with Alberto. The boy's soul appeared, consoled him, and reassured him that indeed he was in heaven and at peace. Moreover, Alberto explained to him that God had called him to help in the salvation of Giovanni's soul and the family as a whole. Morelli awoke, unafraid and happy.

Clearly, this passage reflected the ritual of mourning, ritual that placed grief and loss into a Christian context. And this context had particularly salving qualities, since Christ's crucifixion meant that his father and mother lost a son. They, especially Mary, understood Giovanni's loss. In fact, reflecting on Mary's loss, Giovanni felt ashamed at his reaction to the loss of his own son. Moreover, his consolation represented communication between the living and the dead. The intent of Giovanni's prayers had been to establish a line of communication into the otherworld where the prayers would then aid in Alberto's salvation. Giovanni still felt a duty to his son. Apparently, the prayers had worked, and Alberto had even returned to comfort his father. The communication would continue since Alberto was working for the salvation of his family. This ritualistic self-consolation had assuaged some of Morelli's grief—grief that was overwhelming—at the death of his son.

The demographic agonies of the premodern world affected children in another way. Peter Laslett has concluded that a child in the premodern world had a 30 percent chance of losing a parent.[99] And with premodern mortality rates, there was a good chance a child could lose both. Orphans and their fate form the focus or background of six of Boccaccio's stories, and orphans abound in the *ricordanze*.[100] Giovanni Morelli, for instance, recalled that his father died, leaving four children behind, three of them still at the wetnurse.[101] Add to these premodern mortality rates a pattern of late marriages for men, and a Florentine child had a greater chance of remaining fatherless than motherless—25 percent of the women listed in the 1427 Catasto were widows compared to 4 percent of the men as widowers.[102] Francesco Datini, for instance, was warned by friends that if he waited too long to get married he would run a greater risk of leaving his children orphans than if he married while young.[103] Boccaccio's Monna Giovanna and her son, who were mentioned at the beginning of this chapter, therefore, were typical creatures of premodern Florence.[104] Datini, like other Tuscan fathers, knew the fate of orphans, and it was neither pleasant nor comforting.

Giovanni Morelli discussed the evils that could befall an orphan.[105] First, he said a child was left without a father at an early age. An obvious point, but all other troubles flowed from this. Florentines feared the consequences of the loss of a father. Fathers were greatly concerned about the fate of their children after their deaths, and the death of a father was concern for other family members, especially the mother. Niccolò Ammanatini recalled that when his father died he and his siblings "were in great trouble."[106] The death of a father meant that a child's prime supporter and educator was now gone. Marco Palmieri recorded in his declaration in the Catasto the fate of the daughter of Marco da Rasoio, who was left with nothing after the death of her father.[107] As a consequence of the loss of his or her father, an orphan had to depend upon others, sometimes outsiders, for sustenance, the management of his or her affairs, and education. An orphan was exposed, defenseless to the world. Francesco Datini felt honor bound to provide for the needs of his dead partner's children.[108] Guardians could be appointed or stipulated in wills. Many testators specified that their wives should perform this function.[109] Sometimes Florentines assumed responsibility for their siblings' children.[110] At other times, someone outside the family could be appointed. On 26 January 1364, Lapo Castiglionchio recorded a payment of five florins and twenty-five soldi to Doffo degli Alberti, the tutor of his dead brother's children. Sometimes, however, tutors themselves died, thus beginning the problem anew.[111]

In 1384 the commune instituted the Ufficiale dei Pupilli, which was intended to administer the financial affairs of orphans whose fathers had died intestate or without specifying a guardian. The orphan's estate was invested in state funds, and elected officers monitored it. The idea was to protect the orphan's estate from diminution (hence protecting the commune) and to prevent any one individual from gaining special advantage over the heir.[112] Bernardo Machiavelli recorded how he and the widow of Boninsegna Machiavelli entrusted the finances of her sons to the Ufficiale dei Pupilli on 22 August 1480, a year after Boninsegna had died. In 1418, after the death of his daughter, the Ufficiale dei Pupilli requested that Lapo Niccolini take in her three children—his son-in-law had died the year before. Sometimes the guardians appointed by the Ufficiale took the children in themselves. Years after they were grown Carlo and Matteo Strozzi remembered their ex-guardian by paying him back for his kindness.[113] Too often, though, as was Morelli's case, relatives could mismanage the patrimony, sometimes leaving the orphan penniless.[114] This was why wills and the Ufficiale insisted on outsiders' administering a child's inheritance. Relatives could be greedy and rapacious, but so could the state. Without dedicated protectors, as Morelli noted, a child's patrimony was at the mercy of the commune's tax policies.

An orphan's mother could remarry, said Morelli, which often led to the child's being separated from her and being raised by others, since her children often went to her deceased husband's family to be raised if she remarried.[115] A woman who did this was the so called cruel mother so much on the minds of Florentines, but orphans did not necessarily always suffer this fate.[116] In fact women in Florentine society had a number of options after the deaths of their husbands, but these options undoubtedly were limited by the widow's economic and social difficulty in maintaining an independent household in Florence. Morelli recalled that his sister was left to be a young, impoverished, single mother by the death of her husband. Like many other Florentine widows, she moved back into the family home.[117] While this was a right enshrined in Florentine law, many men felt compelled to state explicitly in their wills that their daughters would be provided for and reestablished in the paternal household if they became widowed.[118] This probably represented only a temporary expedient, and remarriage was a more economically and socially viable option. Only 3 percent of Pratese widows returned to their families. Luca Panzano's mother remarried within a year after the death of his father.[119] But remarriage carried with it its own problems, as Morelli noted. To what lineage did her children from the previous marriage belong: hers, her ex-husband's, or her current husband's? In what household would these children be reared? As could be expected, all three family groups could and would apply pressure to have control over these children.[120] Bartolomeo Salvietti recalled how it took some time before his wife's children—his stepchildren—came to live with them.[121] Moreover, the transition from orphan to stepchild was not easy.[122]

Many children recognized how confused their life could be with the death of a parent, especially the father, and feared abandonment by the remaining parent. This is an understandable response not only to the demographic agonies of the premodern era but also to how families had to react to them. Moreover, children would be more concerned about who would care for them than who would control their patrimony. This perception of abandonment and the fear of it was ever present in Florentine society—and not just in children. Bartolomeo Valori recalled how his mother at the age of 28 did not remarry after the death of his father. The reason she did this, he said, was that she did not want to abandon her children. Boccaccio mentions a widow who "reassured the little son whom she had had by Fernando that she would never abandon him; thus she remained in Fernando's house caring for the son and administering the wealth of her husband."[123] In fact, it probably was not all that unusual for the maternal family to take in the orphaned children. Maddelena Nerli kept her children, took in her daughter's orphaned children, and even took in her granddaughter's orphaned children.[124]

Fears of abandonment, mismanagement of property, loss of the natural teacher: no wonder concern for orphans was paramount in Florentine society, especially for those who lost both parents. The plight of orphans was a frequent subject for art, and orphans themselves participated in civic processions.[125] Who would care for them and rear them? The commune, through such organs as the Innocenti and the Ufficiale dei Pupilli, dealt with the problem.[126] Various charitable organizations, such as the society of Orsanmichele, distributed alms to those of the poor who took orphans in.[127] Moreover, the society placed orphans in more well-to-do homes. Supporting orphans was an act of charity; 25 percent of all orphans cared for by families not their own were held "for the love of God." Most of these families came from the wealthiest households in Florence.[128] Taking in orphans and rearing them, however, was primarily the immediate family's responsibility.[129] Marco Palmieri took in his grandchildren after his son's death, even though the mother was still alive and living elsewhere. After his death another son, Matteo, continued to rear these children at home with him. He also may have done this because he and his wife had no children. Lapo Niccolini took in his daughter's three children after she and her husband died in the plague of 1417.[130] The plague—swift, sure, and deadly—left children parentless in its wake; and Florentines recognized this fact. No wonder they fled before its onslaught: they feared for their children's lives and fate.

The demographic agonies of the premodern era—disease, plague, death—were the sources of much anxiety and grief for Florentine parents and children. They formed their outlook on life and on family life in particular; they were part of the warp and woof of daily life, as much a part of their mental world as expectation of good health is of ours. But Florentines did not just endure these agonies, they lived them: they had to live their lives in relation to them and their consequences.[131] This fact, of course, helps demonstrate how great our mental distance really is from those who lived in the past. Unlike us, people in premodern Europe were closer to death because it visited them so frequently. In 1977, John Gardner argued that the high infant-mortality rates of the premodern world probably meant that children who lived back then were more cherished and cared for than children who live today.[132] Whether we agree with this or not, we can certainly understand Giovanni Morelli's plea at the death of his son Antoniotto: "Make me worthy enough not to see the death of the others."[133] The demographic agonies of the premodern world hurt—deeply.

Epilogue: Farò Richordo Di Tutti i Figliuoli Arò Della Tita Mia Donna

IF FLORENTINE CHILDREN SURVIVED the demographic agonies of the premodern world, at approximately the age of seven they encountered a different world than they had previously known, a world that extended far beyond the house. Learning became more formal and regimented; children attended schools rather than learning at home. The world of work began to intrude on the pleasant pastimes of childhood; children participated in the family business or learned a trade from someone else as an apprentice. Moreover, at about age seven, life for little boys and girls made a radical shift and society's rules of gender became more rigid. While some little girls went to school, few went for long.[1] Similarly, few little girls helped in the family business for long, if they helped at all. Little girls learned more about the complexities of the domestic sphere, some of which they had already learned. Little boys, on the other hand, learned how to become public figures and good Florentine citizens.

The chronicler Villani's well-known estimates that nine to eleven thousand boys and girls aged six to fifteen years were in school in the year 1330 suggest that 60 percent of Florence's children attended school.[2] Paul Grendler has good evidence that this is an exaggeration and that only some 30 percent attended school. Still, this makes Florence a very literate society by premodern standards, and demonstrates that education was central for many Florentine parents.[3]

Although many children learned how to read earlier, seven years was the accepted age for children to begin learning to read, which meant learning Latin grammar.[4] After about four years of this a child, and by now we are mostly describing little boys, learned business mathematics, called *abacco* from the board and counters used to tally debits and credits and note monetary conversion. After a year or two of this a boy either went off into the business world or went back for more schooling, this time in the classics.[5] From his father's *ricordi* we can trace Niccolò Machiavelli's journey through this educational course. By the age of 12 he was reading the classics with Master Pagolo da Ronciglione.[6] Considerable research has been done on Florentine schooling. Although we know much about the educational programs of the humanists, the universities, and the organization of the Renaissance Italian school system, we know rather less about what children themselves did at school and how they felt about it.[7]

A major goal of this education was to make good businessmen. Florentine children learned business by doing it, and many started this process early. Florentines consistently listed in their *ricordanze* who carried goods or payments to the recipient. Often these were the writer's children or the children of the recipients. Manno Petrucci, for instance, recorded for 23 August 1426 that his son Iacopo, then age ten, delivered a payment, though he failed to record to whom and for what.[8] The average age of these messengers was about ten years.[9] Bernardo Machiavelli even noted that little girls acted as messengers.[10] Children thus formed part of the communication network that supported Florentine business.

Just as we know precious little about children's specific academic activity, we also know little about their specific activity in the so called real world of work. Boys would be formally apprenticed to the various trades sometime after age seven as well. Guido Antella recalled being apprenticed into a relative's shop in Genoa when he was 13 years old.[11] Not much is known about apprenticeship at Florence, and a study of it drawn from notarial records would contribute immensely to the history of Florentine childhood and economics.[12] As part of the process of introducing their sons into the world of work, fathers enrolled them in the various guilds and brought them to the meetings of their confraternities.[13] Inexorably, young Florentine males were drawn into the economic, social, and political structures of Florence. But the exact process by which boys were turned into public figures and Florentine citizens needs further elucidation.

Children also began to be drawn into the religious structures of Florence. And the exact process by which children became monks and nuns in Florence also needs further elucidation.[14] Although the average age of girls entering a nunnery was about 18 years, many entered years before this. Some commentators and historians have argued that these houses functioned as safety valves to vent the pressure on the family of maintaining unmarriageable children. Others see heart-felt religious beliefs by both the parents and the children as a prime motive in having children adopt the life of a religious.[15] Francesco Giovanni sent his daughter Gostanza to a monastery; she was nine years and three months old. In a loose collection of documents contained in his *ricordanze,* he recorded on a half slip of paper her entry into the monastery and her new name of "suora Angelicha." The handwriting is considerably better, even more formal, than that in the rest of his *ricordanze.*[16] Obviously her becoming one of those who pray was important enough to him to warrant more than a common entry in his *ricordanze.* Why? And little boys became monks.[17] What did it mean for and to Florentines when their children became monks and nuns; how did the children feel about this? More research needs to be done on these topics as well.

The Florentine Catasto of 1427 records that the average age of Florentine women when they married was 17.5 years. But 1.3 percent of the women listed as married were 13 years or younger. Obviously marriage was something contemplated by Florentine parents early in the lives of their children. And children too would have to think of marriage. When his illegitimate daughter, Ginevra, was nine years old, Francesco Datini began searching for a husband for her. When she married at age fifteen, it was to the fellow Francesco had picked out when she was nine.[18] As Anthony Molho has shown, youth was an important commodity for women in the Florentine marriage market.[19] Some males were young too. Biagio Buonaccorsi's son, Buonaccorso, married at thirteen.[20] A study of marriage and the young in Florence would highlight much about children, the family, and sex in the premodern world.[21]

Formal schooling, work, the religious life, and marriage, however, belong more properly to the world of adolescence than the world of birth and infancy. In fact, adolescence in Florence is worthy of a detailed study of its own, one that could form the sequel to this present work.[22]

As we have discovered in the preceding chapters, Florentines recognized childhood as a distinct stage in human development. Specifically, they recognized that newborns and infants had special needs, needs for which they provided willingly within the structures of their daily lives. While a serious and deadly business, the miracle of birth provided Florentines with joy and a sense of fulfillment. The many rituals surrounding birth and infancy reflect these feelings. Florentines wanted children. This desire for children coupled with the premodern reality of high infant-mortality rates led the merchant elite to have many children. They faced, however, the likely prospect that just as many of their children could die before adulthood. They did not defend themselves from the mortality of their children by becoming cold, indifferent, uncaring creatures. They accepted the emotional risk attendant with the mortality of their children and grieved for them when necessary. They coped. And in so doing they remained human. We can empathize with them for this.

Other structures of their daily life led Florentines to adopt childrearing practices that for us seem quite alien, such as wetnursing. But the parents' underlying motive in these practices—to provide the best for their children while maintaining their own duties in the world beyond the home—is quite familiar to us. In that respect there is little distance between us and them. This survey of some 300 years from approximately 1300 to 1600 has uncovered no shift in Florentine attitudes towards children let alone any shifts in practice. Florentine childhood saw no Renaissance, just an ages-old rhythm.

I began this study with a letter from Boccaccio to his friend Petrarch. I want to end with one from Petrarch to his friend Donato Albanzani, which encapsulates much of what I have been trying to illustrate. Petrarch wrote on the occasion of the death of Donato's son, which reminded him of the loss of his own grandson:

> My own dear boy was your spiritual son, since you sponsored him in baptism. Let me join my own cruel recent loss to yours, that we

may both seek wholesome balm. Do not murmur that our wounds are not comparable, that you have lost a son and I a grandson. I swear by Christ and by our friendship that I loved him more than a son. What if I did not beget him? His parents were Francesco and Francesca [Petrarch's illegitimate daughter], who as you know, are both dearer to me than my own soul. Being born of two persons much dearer to me than myself, he was dearer than if he were my son. You gave an illustrious ancient name to your boy; we gave ours a humble family name, or rather you gave them both, since you christened my boy. Your Solon augured a great career, if only fate had been kind; our child received the name of both his parents and of myself. He was the fourth Francesco, the solace of our lives, our hope, the joy of our house. And to make our grief the keener, he chanced to possess unusual beauty and intelligence. You would have called him a princely child. He promised to equal his father in good looks and surpass him in intellectual gifts. His only fault was to resemble me so much that one who did not know his mother would certainly have called me the father. So everyone alleged; and I remember that once, when he was hardly a year old, you wrote me that you could see my face in his, and thus you had somehow conceived great hopes for him. This remarkable resemblance, despite the great discrepancy of age, made him dearer to his parents and indeed to all; and it so impressed the great Lord of Liguria [Galeazzo II Visconti] that he who had shortly before watched dry-eyed the passing of his only son could hardly hear of my loss without tears.

As for me, I recognize that he has passed without trouble to everlasting felicity, and that my care for things of this world has been largely eliminated. So it may be judged that both he and I have at a single stroke gained advantage. But I admit I was profoundly shaken to see the sweet promise of his life reft away at its beginning. And if I were now what I was only few years ago, I should have assailed all my friends, and you first of all, with my moans and groans. It is irrelevant to remark that my loss was that of a mere infant. For infants may be passionately loved; not to mention natural instinct, we are captured by their innocence and purity, whereas we may be repelled by their pretensions and disobedience in later years, and our love may mingle with disfavor. . . .

Now—to let you know all my weakness—I have ordered a marble tomb in Pavia for my little boy. It is inscribed with six elegiac verses. I should hardly do this for anyone else, and I should be most unwilling that anyone should do the same for me. But suppressing my tears and lamentations, I was so overcome by my emotions that, having no other recourse, I did what I could. He is in heaven, beyond all earthly cares, and I could offer him nothing but this last vain kind of tribute. If it is useless to him, it is some solace to me. And so I wanted to consecrate something, not to evoke tears, as Virgil says, but to preserve his memory—not in me, who have no need of stones or of poems, but in chance passersby, that they may learn how dear he was to all, from the very beginning of his life. Though Cicero says in his eighth Philippic that we can pay to the dead no other tribute than tombs and statues, we know that we can render them a greater service by prayers to God for the salvation of their souls. Of such prayers my little boy has slight need; yet since in the sight of God not even the heavens are spotless and a baby may not spend a single day on earth without sin, I pray to God to have mercy upon him. Now that he is torn from my embrace, may God take him lovingly in his arms. My love for that child so filled my breast that I cannot think that I ever loved anything else on earth so much. . . .[23]

Petrarch's letter offers in the experiences and observations of one extraordinary Florentine an example of how most ordinary Florentines perceived and felt about birth and infancy in the premodern era.

In 1957, Iris Origo published a detailed examination of the private life of the merchant of Prato, Francesco Datini. In it she made a general conclusion about Florentine childhood and parental attitudes toward children, one that has held sway ever since. "There was little room left for affection or tenderness; parental authority was too absolute, too severe."[24] I prefer a different general conclusion about Florentine childhood and parental attitudes toward children, a more positive one. One that premodern Florentines, like Petrarch, talked about themselves. Alberti described the pure and simple human joy of listening to a child's laughter.[25] Boccaccio tells us that when a father came home at the end of a hard day at the shop, the marketplace, the governmental offices, or the banker's table, he would be greeted by his son, and "when the young boy saw his father, he ran toward him and, as little boys do, made a fuss over his arrival."[26] Joy. We do not need to be surprised or puzzled that Florentines loved their children deeply and cared for them responsibly.

When confronted with evidence like Petrarch's letter—clear, detailed, and to the point—I wonder why historians have been so adamant about showing how the premodern family was something and somehow less than the modern family. Considering how much birth and infancy was a shared experience between Florentine mothers and fathers I wonder if the premodern family was something and somehow more.

Appendix: Tables

TABLE 1

DATE	GODCHILD'S SEX	FATHER'S NAME	FATHER'S OCCUPATION
		BARTOLOMEO MASI'S BAPTISMAL KINSHIP NETWORK	
1505	Female	Bernardo di Cienni	Second-hand Dealer
1506-08	Male	Filippo di Santi	Second-hand Dealer
	Female	Carlo di Guglielmo	Butcher
	Female	Bernardo di Cienni	(ShD)
	Female	Filippo di Santi	(ShD)
	Female	Carlo di Guglielmo	(Btch)
1509	Male	Carlo di Guglielmo	(Btch)
1509-10	Male	Bernardo di Cienni	(ShD)
1512	Male	Paganello Falani	Unknown
1513	Female	Bernardo di Cienni	(ShD)
	Female	Zanobi di Filippo	Scissors-maker
1514	Female	Filippo di Santi	(ShD)
1515	Male	Lodovico di Chimenti	Leather Dealer
	Male	Poggino di Zanobi	Painter
	Male	Poggino di Zanobi	(Pntr)
	Female	Zanobi di Filippo	(Scmk)
1516	Male	Bernardo di Cienni	(ShD)
	Female	Lorenzo di Simone	Blacksmith

BARTOLOMEO MASI'S BAPTISMAL KINSHIP NETWORK			
1516-17	Male	Poggino di Zanobi	(Pntr)
	Female	Lodovico di Chimenti	(LD)
	Female	Lorenzo di Benedetto	Doublet Maker
1517	Female	Michele di Barnaba	Pharmicist
1517-18	Female	Pagolo di Gilio	Shoemaker
	Male	Zanobi di Filippo	Blacksmith
1519	Female	Michele di Barnaba	(Phrmst)
	Male	Fillippo di Santi	(ShD)
	Female	Giovanni di Bartolo	Notions Dealer
1521	Female	Giovanni di Michele	Pharmicist
1522	Female	Giovanni di Tommaso	Woodcutter
	Male	Nicolò di Luca	Unknown
1522-23	Male	Giovanni di Iacopo	Shoemaker
	Female	Piero di Lionardo	Unknown
1523	Male	Vanni di Cienni	Unknown
	Male	Giovanni di Piero	Shoemaker
1524	Female	Giovanni di Tommaso	(Wdctr)
	Female	Piero di Domenico	Unknown
	Female	Giovanni di Luca	Linen Worker
	Male	Giovanni di Michele	Pharmicist
	Male	Bernardo di Cienni	(ShD)
1524-25	Male	Pagolo di Gilio	(Shmkr)
1525-26	Male	Giovanni di Iacopo	(Shmkr)
	Male	Giovanni di Bartolo	(ND)
1526	Male	Giovanni di Tommaso	(Wdctr)

Twenty-six different individuals asked Bartolomeo Masi, a copper-smith, to be godfather to their child and cofather to themselves.

Bartolomeo was 29 years old the first time he recorded becoming a godfather and cofather. In 1515 he and his father had become partners in a shop, so Bartolomeo's entry into baptismal kinship networks came just after he entered the world of business. Surprisingly, no fellow coppersmith asked Bartolomeo to be cofather.

TABLE 2

Cofathers who chose Bartolomeo Masi by Status	
Artisan	20
Shopkeeper	18
Unknown	5

TABLE 3

COFATHERS WHO CHOSE BARTOLOMEO MASI BY OCCUPATION	
Second-hand Dealer	10
Shoemaker	5
Pharmicist	4
Butcher	3
Painter	3
Woodcutter	3
Scissors Maker	3
Notions Dealer	2
Leather Dealer	2
Doublet Maker	1
Linen Worker	1
Blacksmith	1
Unknown	5

TABLE 4

COFATHERS WHO CHOSE BARTOLOMEO MASI MORE THAN ONCE AS *COMPARE*		
Name of Cofather	Occupation	Frequency
Bernardo di Cienni	Second-hand Dealer	5
Filippo di Santi	Second-hand Dealer	3
Carlo di Guglielmo	Butcher	3
Zanobi di Filippo	Scissors-maker	3
Poggino di Zanobi	Painter	3
Lodovico di Chimenti	Leather Dealer	2
Michele di Barnaba	Pharmacist	2
Pagolo di Gilio	Shoemaker	2

Bartolomeo Masi's cofathers are about equally divided between artisans and shopkeepers. Second-hand dealers, however, often chose him as their cofather. Almost 25 percent of the time he became godfather for someone's child, it was for the child of a second-hand dealer. The person who most frequently asked Bartolomeo to become cofather again was a second-hand dealer. Of the eight individuals who asked him to become cofather more than once, two were second-hand dealers. Since second-hand dealers were shopkeepers, hence above Bartolomeo's status as artisan, and probably wealthier than Bartolomeo, their choosing him represents attempts to build or maintain a network of clients.

Almost half of Bartolomeo's baptismal kinship connections were repeat performances, representing maintainence or reinforcement of the baptismal kinship relationship.

TABLE 5

SEX OF GODCHILD	
Female	22
Male	21

The sex of the godchild played no part in Bartolomeo's baptismal kinship network.

TABLE 6

FREQUENCY OF COPARENT/ GODPARENT TIES OVER TIME (FIVE-YEAR INCREMENTS)	
1505-10	8
1511-15	8
1516-20	11
1521-26	16

As might be expected, as Bartolomeo became older and became acquainted with more people, he was in greater demand as a coparent.

TABLE 7

		CLOTHING LIST AND EXPENSES FOR STROZZI CHILDREN			
Child	Date	Item	Price		
			LIRE	SOLDI	DENARI
SIMONE (B. 1472)					
	15-2-1473	Blanket			
	16-8-1473	Cradle and gown			
	31-8-1473	Cape and gown			
	8-10-1473	Gown			
	21-10-1473	Cloth to make a gown			
	20-11-1473	Cloth slippers (He was still at the wetnurse for Niccolò's sister delivered them to her.)			
	28-1-1474	Cloth slippers and wooden-soled sandals			
	2-4-1474	Cloth slippers			
	30-4-1474	Cloth to make a gown			
	7-7-1474	Leather slippers			
	24-9-1474	Cloth slippers and wooden clogs			
	21-10-1474	Cloth slippers			
	6-10-1474	Hose and cloth slippers[1]			
CARLO (B. 1473)					
	16-4-1476	Unspecified		s. 6	d. 8[2]
	18-9-1477	Cloth slippers		s. 7	
	23-5-1478	Hose and white cloth slippers			
	12-6-1479	Unspecified		s. 3	
	17-6-1479	Hose and cloth slippers		s. 6	
	21-1-1480	Unspecified		s. 11	d. 8
	12-2-1487	Cloth slippers		s. 14	
	12-2-1487	Belt	l. 2		

CLOTHING LIST AND EXPENSES FOR STROZZI CHILDREN					
	15-2-1487	Leather slippers		s. 15	
	13-3-1487	Black boots		s. 6	d. 4
	24-3-1487	Cloth slippers		s. 13	
	1-5-1487	Cloth for a black doublet	l. 2	s. 14	
	1-5-1487	Cloth slippers		s. 13	
	1-5-1487	5 canne of black cloth for a gown3	l. 30		
	6-5-1487	Tailoring of a gown			
	21-5-1487	Cloth slippers		s. 12	
	21-6-1487	6 canne of black silk cloth	l. 4	s. 16	
	21-6-1487	2 canne of black silk cloth			
	28-6-1487	Cloth slippers		s. 13	
	19-7-1487	Cloth slippers		s. 13	
	13-8-1487	Hose	l. 3	s. 6	
	13-8-1487	Cloth slippers		s. 13	
	18-9-1487	Cloth slippers		s. 13	
	18-9-1487	Doublet	l. 3	s. 4	
	18-9-1487	3 canne of black cloth			
	3-11-1487	Wooden-soled sandals		s. 1	d. 4
	29-11-1487	Hose	l. 4	s. 10	
	7-12-1487	Cloth slippers and leather slippers	l. 1	s. 7	
	18-12-1487	Cloth slippers		s. 15	
	17-1-1488	Cloth for hose		s. 5	
	10-2-1488	Cloth slippers		s. 13	
	10-2-1488	4 sleeves		s. 3	
	24-2-1488	To tailor and dye hose	l. 1		
	27-3-1488	Hose	l. 1	s. 5	
	1-4-1488	Cloth for hose		s. 5	

	CLOTHING LIST AND EXPENSES FOR STROZZI CHILDREN				
	10-5-1488	Cloth slippers		s. 13	
	10-5-1488	Hose	l. 1	s. 5	
	27-5-1488	Red cloth slippers		s. 15	
	1-6-1488	Black hat	l. 1	s. 10	
	1-6-1488	Boots	l. 2	s. 2	
	10-6-1488	Doublet	l. 3	s. 17	
	10-6-1488	Cloth slippers		s. 14	
	7-7-1488	Cloth slippers		s. 14	
	1-8-1488	Cloth slippers		s. 14	
	23-8-1488	Cloth slippers		s. 14	
	13-9-1488	Wooden-soled sandals		s. 2	
	17-10-1488	Cloth slippers		s. 14	
	11-11-1488	Cloth slippers		s. 14	
	25-11-1488	Cloth slippers[4]		s. 14	
LENA (B. 1475)					
	5-2-1476	Hose and cloth	l. 2	s. 19	d. 4
	6-4-1476	Wool cloth		s. 5	
	3-8-1476	Red cloth slippers(scharpettino) toddler-sized (?)		s. 5	
	30-8-1476	Unspecified		s. 18	
	25-1-1477	Hose and cloth slippers		s. 5	
	31-1-1477	Wooden-soled sandals		s. 1	
	18-3-1477	Cloth for a gown	l. 1	s. 5	
	22-3-1477	Wool cloth for a gown		s. 3	d. 4
	10-4-1477	Unspecified	l. 1	s. 6	d. 8
	12-5-1477	Cloth slippers		s. 5	
	4-6-1477	Black cloth slippers		s. 5	
	26-9-1477	Hose and cloth slippers		s. 6	d. 8

CLOTHING LIST AND EXPENSES FOR STROZZI CHILDREN				
29-11-1477	Black cloth slippers		s. 6	d. 1
1-12-1477	Wooden clogs		s. 3	
4-4-1478	Hose and cloth slippers			
26-5-1478	Cloth slippers		s. 11	
20-7-1478	Hose and shoes			
25-8-1478	Green cloth		s. 7	
23-9-1478	Wooden clogs			
15-10-1478	Cloth slippers		s. 6	
15-3-1479	Black cloth slippers		s. 6	
27-4-1479	Red cloth slippers		s. 6	
24-5-1479	Cloth slippers		s. 6	
24-11-1479	Cloth slippers		s. 6	
2-3-1487	Unspecified		s. 7	d. 8
24-3-1487	Cloth slippers		s. 10	
24-3-1487	Leather slippers		s. 11	
3-5-1487	Cloth slippers		s. 9	
31-5-1487	1 braccio of black silk	l. 7	s. 4	
3-6-1487	Cloth slippers		s. 9	
3-6-1487	2 braccia of cloth for a gown		s. 13	
4-6-1487	1 braccio of black silk	l. 10	s. 3	
4-6-1487	Hook-and-eye fasteners		s. 2	
9-7-1487	Cloth slippers		s. 9	
19-7-1487	Cloth slippers		s. 9	
15-9-1487	Cloth slippers		s. 9	
1-11-1487	Cloth slippers		s. 10	
18-12-1487	Wooden-soled sandals		s. 1	
18-12-1487	7 braccia of rough wool cloth for one gown	l. 42		

CLOTHING LIST AND EXPENSES FOR STROZZI CHILDREN				
20-12-1487	To tailor a gown			
20-12-1487	Leather slippers		s. 14	
20-12-1487	Cloth slippers		s. 9	
29-3-1488	Cloth	l. 1	s. 15	
29-3-1488	Cloth slippers		s. 10	
25-4-1488	Cloth slippers		s. 10	
10-5-1488	Cloth slippers		s. 13	
25-5-1488	Leather slippers		s. 13	
1-8-1488	Cloth slippers		s. 10	
21-8-1488	Black silk belt		s. 13	
12-9-1488	Cloth slippers		s. 10	
13-9-1488	Long-sleeved gown		s. 14	
13-9-1488	Red surcoat		s. 6	
24-9-1488	To tailor a gown with 6 cloth bands	l. 3	s. 19	
24-9-1488	Black taffeta sleeves	l. 2	s. 10	
6-11-1488	Wooden-soled sandals		s. 1	d. 14
20-1-1489	Cloth	l. 4	s. 2	
20-1-1489	6 braccia of white cloth	l. 1	s. 17	
24-1-1489	Cloth and tailoring of a gown	l. 5	s. 8	
1-2-1489	Belt	l. 3	s. 3	
1-2-1489	Leather bag	l. 2	s. 2	
16-4-1489	Cloth slippers		s. 10	
12-2-1490	Red long-sleeved gown		s. 17	
21-2-1490	1 braccio of blue cloth for a surcoat		s. 7	
17-6-1490	Cloth and leather slippers5	l. 1	s. 5	d. 4

Notes

Unless otherwise noted, all translations from Italian and Latin are my own.

Introduction

1. Giovanni Boccaccio, *Opere latine minore*, ed. Francesco Massèra (Bari, 1928), Ep. 14 in Thomas G. Bergin, *Boccaccio* (New York, 1981), 50-51.
2. Noting the anguished reaction of a Venetian father to the death of his son, Margaret King concluded that it ran counter to "what some historians suggest is the usual pattern of family relations in this premodern era." Margaret King, "The Death of the Child Valerio Marcello: Paternal Mourning in Renaissance Venice," in *Renaissance Rereadings: Interest and Context*, ed. Maryanne C. Horowitz, Anne J. Cruz, and Wendy Furman (Urbana, 1988), 217. "Proponents of the nonexistence of childhood and adolescence in the Middle Ages," observed Barbara Hanawalt more recently, "however, have widespread support among professional historians, as well as among the general public." Barbara A. Hanawalt, *Growing Up in Medieval London: The Experience of Childhood in History* (New York, 1993), 6.
3. Philippe Ariès, *Centuries of Childhood: A Social History of Family Life* (New York, 1965); Edward Shorter, *The Making of the Modern Family* (New York, 1975); Lawrence Stone, *The Family, Sex and Marriage in England 1500-1800* (New York, 1977); Randolf Trumbach, *Rise of the Egalitarian Family: Aristocratic Kinship and Domestic Relations* (New York, 1978); Judith Schneid Lewis, *In the Family Way: Childbearing in the British Aristocracy 1760-1860* (New Brunswick, 1986); Renate Blumenfeld-Kosinski, *Not of Woman Born: Representations of Caesarean Birth in Medieval and Renaissance Culture* (Ithaca, 1990); C. John Sommerville, *The Discovery of Childhood in Puritan England* (Athens, 1992); Hugh Cunningham, *Children and Childhood in Western Society since 1500* (London, 1995).
4. Sarah B. Pomeroy, review of Suzanne Dixon's *The Roman Mother, American Historical Review* 95 (1990), 468.

5. For the best elaboration of this position see Viviana Zelizer, *Pricing the Priceless Child: The Changing Social Value of Children* (Princeton, 1994). See also: Peter N. Stearns and Carol Z. Stearns, "Emotionology: Clarifying the History of Emotions and Emotional Standards," *American Historical Review* 90 (1985), 818-19; Tamara K. Harevan, "The History of the Family and the Complexity of Social Change," *American Historical Review* 96 (1991), 121; Nancy Scheper-Hughes, "The Cultural Politics of Child Survival," in *Child Survival: Anthropological Perspectives on the Treatment and Maltreatment of Children,* ed. Nancy Scheper-Hughes (Dordrecht, 1987), 2-9.

6. Stearns and Stearns, 818; Gerda Lerner, *The Creation of Patriarchy* (New York, 1986), 39-42. The work that Nancy Scheper-Hughes has done on women and children in the *favelas* of Brazil is predicated on the concept that mother-love is a bourgeois conceit and conception that arose in the modern world. Nancy Scheper-Hughes, *Death Without Weeping: The Violence of Everyday Life in Brazil* (Berkeley, 1992).

One of the problems with defining something—be it an emotion or a practice—as a social construct is the implication that it is therefore subject to easy change, usually through education. While this implication is both hopeful and progressive, it is also incredibly naive. As we are finding out about all sorts of things labeled as social constructs, such as racism and sexism, they are incredibly resistant to change. Moreover, while emotions may be socially determined, they are determined around certain biological, physiological, and historical rules, reactions, and attitudes. Perhaps all emotionology, the historical study of the social construction of emotion, represents then are variations around themes—but real, instinctual, and deeply embedded themes nevertheless. For setting a good balance between biological determinism and social construction regarding emotions in the past see Caroline Walker Bynum, "Wonder," *American Historical Review* 102 (1997), 14-15 n. 58.

7. Richard A. Goldthwaite, *Private Wealth in Renaissance Florence: A Study of Four Families* (Princeton, 1968); F. W. Kent, *Household and Lineage in Renaissance Florence: The Family Life of the Capponi, Ginori, and Rucellai* (Princeton, 1977); David Herlihy and Christiane Klapisch-Zuber, *Les Toscans et leurs familles: Une étude du catasto florentin de 1427* (Paris, 1978) in English as *Tuscans and Their Families: A Study of the Florentine Catasto of 1427* (New Haven, 1985); Richard C. Trexler, *Public Life in Renaissance Florence* (New York, 1980); Thomas Kuehn, *Emancipation in Late Medieval Florence* (New Brunswick, 1982); Gene Brucker, *Giovanni and Lusanna: Love and Marriage in Renaissance Florence* (Berkeley, 1986).

There are some excellent surveys of Florentine family life: Charles de la Roncière, "Tuscan Notables on the Eve of the Renaissance," in *A History of Private Life* vol. 2 *Revelations of the Medieval World,* ed. Georges Duby (Cambridge, 1988), 157-310; David Herlihy, *Medieval Households* (Cambridge, 1985), 131-156, a chapter on late medieval households in Tuscany; Frances and Joseph Gies, *Marriage and the Family in the Middle Ages* (New York, 1987), 271-290, a chapter on merchant families in fifteenth- century Florence.

8. Christiane Klapisch, "L'enfance en Toscane au de'but du 15ᵉ siècle," *Annales de Démographie Historique* (1973), 99-122; James Bruce Ross, "The Middle-Class Child in Urban Italy, Fourteenth to Early Sixteenth Centuries," in *The History of Childhood,* ed. Lloyd deMause (New York, 1974), 183-228; Richard C. Trexler, "Infanticide in Florence: New Sources and First Results," *History of Childhood Quarterly* 1 (1973-4), 96-116; "The Foundlings of Florence 1395-1455," *History of Childhood Quarterly* 1 (1973-74), 259-84; "In Search of Father: The Experience of Abandonment in the Recollections of Giovanni di Pagolo Morelli," *History of Childhood Quarterly* 3 (1975), 225-52.

9. One example of how paintings exhibited a new attitude toward children in the Renaissance is the artists' emphasis on the Christ child, and especially the Christ child with Mary (Raphael's *Madonna of the Chair,* for instance, immediately springs to mind). According to Herlihy, "The cult of the Christ Child implies an idealization of childhood itself." David Herlihy, "Medieval Children," in *Essays on Medieval Civilization. The Walter Prescott Webb Memorial Lectures,* ed. B. K. Lackner and K. R. Philip (Austin, 1978), 129. See also his "The Making of the Medieval Family: Symmetry, Structure, and Sentiment," *Journal of Family History* 8 (1983), 116-30. Yet other historians have not seen any significant change in the portrayal of the Christ child-in the Renaissance or any other time period. These paintings then tell us nothing about attitudes toward children. Jack Goody, *The Development of the Family and Marriage in Europe* (Cambridge, 1983), 154; and Ilene H. Forsyth, "Children in Early Medieval Art: Ninth through Twelfth Centuries," *Journal of Psychohistory* 4 (1976), 31-70. It may be that the focus on the Christ child in paintings carries just a theological meaning (Christ as human) and not any social meaning.

10. Christiane Klapisch-Zuber, *Women, Family, and Ritual in Renaissance Italy* (Chicago, 1985), 94, 104-6, 114-16, 151, 328-29. Herlihy argued that a change was made during the Renaissance in attitudes toward children, but he placed it after 1350, when the sources begin to detail domesticity. David Herlihy, "Family Solidarity in Medieval Italian History," in *Economy, Society, and Government in Medieval Italy: Essays in Memory of Robert L. Reynolds* (Kent, 1969), 181. This may represent only an increase in the volume of written sources; it may be then that there was no fundamental change in attitudes. Some have even argued that this change was a mirage. According to Antonia Fraser, the Renaissance did not exhibit "a new consideration of children," and Renaissance people were "singularly lacking in interest in the flowering of the child." Barbara Kay Greenleaf, *Children Through the Ages: A History of Childhood* (New York, 1978), 42. According to Sommerville, "[w]e have seen nothing in the most characteristic features of the Renaissance to suggest a greater devotion to the child's welfare." C. John Sommerville, *The Rise and Fall of Childhood* (Beverley Hills, 1982), 87. Yet the debate whether or not the fifteenth century represented some sort of watershed of family affective attitudes continues. Sharon Strocchia, "Death Rites and the Ritual Family in Renaissance Florence," in *Life and Death in Fifteenth Century Florence,* ed. Marcel Tetel, Ronald Witt, and Rona Goffen (Durham, 1989), 123; and her "Remembering the Family: Women, Kin, and Commemorative Masses in Renaissance Florence," *Renaissance Quarterly* 42 (1989), 645-46.

11. Herlihy and Klapisch-Zuber, 254-56. Herlihy later expressed some dissatisfaction with the Ariès model. See his *Medieval Households*, 112, 125, 207.

12. David Herlihy, *The Family in Renaissance Italy* (St. Louis, 1974), 8.

13. Herlihy, *Medieval Households*, 158.

14. David Herlihy, *The Family in Renaissance Italy*, 11. Herlihy never explained why these fathers would have trouble communicating with their children or why these husbands and wives would have trouble creating loving relationships. He just assumed that the age difference would create barriers. In actuality, this does not seem to be the case wherever we find enough evidence to examine the phenomenon.

15. Sommerville, 78. In actuality, fathers wrote these advice manuals for their sons knowing that because of the wide disparity between their age and that of their sons a good chance existed that they would be dead before their sons matured. They intended these manuals to serve as a replacement for the advice they could offer their sons. It was not that fathers had some psychological difficulty communicating face to face with their sons but that they might not be able to communicate face to face because of death.

16. Herlihy noted that Florentine women's influence over young children (here he means male children) gave them "a taste for refined manners and elegant dress, and a high esthetic sensibility." Herlihy, *The Family in Renaissance Italy*, 11. While he does not say it, Herlihy seems to be arguing that the cultural refinement we associate with the Renaissance stemmed from the fact that Renaissance men were "mama's boys." Others, especially psychohistorians, have also attributed the Renaissance to the childhood experiences of men, especially artists, like Michelangelo and da Vinci.

17. David Herlihy, "Mapping Households in Medieval Italy," *Catholic Historical Review* 58 (1972), 17.

18. Herlihy and Klapisch-Zuber, 135.

19. Diane Owen Hughes, "Domestic Ideals and Social Behavior: Evidence from Medieval Genoa," in *The Family in History*, ed. Charles E. Rosenberg (Philadelphia, 1975), 115.

20. Trexler, *Public Life*, 88.

21. Sommerville, 80. Recently, Clarissa Atkinson concluded that the "gulf between moral ideas and social realities in the matter of wet-nursing serves as a reminder that the lively interest in children should not be misread: they were neglected and abused during the Renaissance as before [and after]." Clarissa Atkinson, *The Oldest Vocation: Christian Motherhood in the Middle Ages* (Ithaca, 1991), 158.

22. de la Roncière, 223.

23. Klapisch-Zuber, 98-101, 105-6, 109, 111-12. This view has been challenged by Anthony Molho. He argued that the Florentine tendency to underestimate daughters' ages in records like the *Catasto* did not represent parental neglect based on sex as is commonly thought. In fact, it represented a crafty attempt to manipulate the Florentine marriage market where young brides were at a premium. Rather than neglect, this reflects considerable care and concern. Anthony Molho, "Deception and Marriage Strategy in Renaissance Florence: The Case of Women's Ages," *Renaissance Quarterly* 41 (1988), 193-217.

24. Klapisch-Zuber, 112.
25. de la Roncière, 223.
26. Klapisch-Zuber, 116.
27. Greenleaf, 44.
28. Greenleaf, 44; Sommerville, 81.
29. Sommerville, 78-79.
30. Anomalies abound in the historiography of the premodern family. Lawrence Stone pegged the origins of the modern family to the mercantile elite of Florence and their rise in affluence: the modern family was thus the result of bourgeois capitalism. He then says this pattern shifted to the Dutch in the seventeenth century (their golden age) and then to the English from there. Yet Stone argues that a modern nuclear affective family did not arise in Renaissance Venice, even though it was every bit as mercantile and affluent as Florence—perhaps even more so. Lawrence Stone, *The Family, Sex and Marriage in England 1500-1800* (New York, 1977), 260-61. Perhaps the pervasiveness and power of the prevailing thesis on childhood set up these anomalies. On the one hand Blumenfeld-Kosinski said that it is "absurd" to believe that medieval people did not love children, but on the other hand she then observed that "the general spiritual climate of the age did not form ideas on childbearing as an important social function." Blumenfeld-Kosinski, 12.
31. Linda Pollock, *Forgotten Children: Parent-Child Relations from 1500-1900* (Cambridge, 1983); Steven Ozment, *When Fathers Ruled: Family Life in Reformation Europe* (Cambridge, 1983); David Nicholas, *The Domestic Life of a Medieval City: Women, Children, and the Family in Fourteenth-Century Ghent* (Lincoln, 1985); Barbara Hanawalt, *The Ties That Bound: Peasant Families in Medieval England* (Oxford, 1986); Shulamith Shahar, *Childhood in the Middle Ages* (New York, 1990); Mark Golden, *Children and Childhood in Classical Athens* (Baltimore, 1990); Suzanne Dixon, *The Roman Family* (Baltimore, 1992); Barbara Hanawalt, *Growing Up in Medieval London: The Experience of Childhood in History* (Oxford, 1993). What is historiographically interesting about these studies is that all the traits that a scholar such as Scheper-Hughes identifies as modern, bourgeois, socially constructed ideas about children and childhood can be found in abundance in premodern Europe.
32. As late as 1983 Linda Pollock could complain that "despite all the recent work on the history of childhood, we still know little about actual childhood." Pollock, 203. Miriam Slater noted that "the vagueness and complexities of parent/child relationships seem endlessly variable and relentlessly resistant to generalization." Miriam Slater, *Family Life in the Seventeenth Century: The Verneys of Claydon House* (London, 1984), 108. See also Pollock, 12; Slater, 25. Other historians have voiced these same concerns: Peter Laslett, *The World We Have Lost: England Before the Industrial Age* 2nd ed. (New York, 1971), 110; David Hunt, *Parents and Children in History: The Psychology of Family Life in Early Modern France* (New York, 1970), 19; Herlihy, "Medieval Children," 109-10; Lawrence Stone, "Family History in the 1980s: Past Achievement and Future Trends," *Journal of Interdisciplinary History* 12 (1981), 83; Kate Mertes, *The English Noble Household 1250-1600: Good Governance and Politic Rule* (Oxford,

1988), 161-62; Brucker, 6. In a survey of the Renaissance family, Barbara Diefendorf admitted that though "aiming for breadth, I have had to leave out a great deal: sexuality, for instance, and parent/child relations." Barbara Diefendorf, "Family Culture, Renaissance Culture," *Renaissance Quarterly* 40 (1987), 661-62. Peter Stearns noted that in general few historical studies of affection ever projected themselves past the nineteenth century. Peter Stearns, "Social History Update: Sociology of Emotion," *Journal of Social History* 22 (1989), 596-97.

33. Stearns and Stearns, however, warned that recent attempts to show continuities of emotions may themselves be biased toward that view because they rely heavily on diary evidence, which might be more conducive to seeing continuity rather than change. Stearns and Stearns, 830.

34. Here I mean `structures of everyday life' in a Braudelian sense: "Everyday life consists of the little things one hardly notices in time and space. [T]he everyday happening . . . characterizes ways of being and behaving which are perpetuated through endless ages . . . the more an everyday event is repeated the more it becomes a structure." Fernand Braudel, *Civilization and Capitalism 15th-18th Century* Vol. 1 *The Structures of Everyday Life: The Limits of the Possible* (New York, 1981), 29.

35. Dixon observed that "we need a good rigorous base of knowledge about families past and present if we are to make sensible comments about current developments and future plans." Dixon, xi. Others have agreed; see Adrian Wilson, "The Infancy of the History of Childhood: An Appraisal of Philippe Ariès," *History and Theory* 19 (1980), 148-49, 152.

36. When I first planned this study in the mid-1980s, I wanted to investigate childhood and adolescence in medieval England as a way to directly attack Ariès's *Centuries of Childhood.* I saw myself as a Horatius defending the bridge of true family life in the past. Little did I know then that many Horatii were already there, or headed there, which meant a considerable reshaping of my plans as the research progressed. No research plan ever survives contact with the sources and the historiography.

37. A number of authors have recently called for a more thorough study of the earliest years of a child's life, especially to view things such as attitudes towards procreation, the birth process, and birth rituals. Harevan, 119; Hanawalt, *Growing Up in Medieval London,* 42, 56; Shahar, 4; Sherrin Marshall, "Childhood in Early Modern Europe," in *Children in Historical and Comparative Perspective: An International Handbook and Research Guide,* ed. Jospeh M. Hawes and N. Roy Hiner (New York, 1991), 55; Adrian Wilson, "The Ceremony of Childbirth and its Interpretation," in *Women as Mothers in Pre-industrial England: Essays in Memory of Dorothy McLaren,* ed. Valerie Fildes (London, 1990), 94; Peter Garnsey, "Child Rearing in Ancient Italy," in *The Family in Italy: From Antiquity to the Present,* ed. Richard Saller and David I. Kertzer (New Haven, 1991), 48, 51, 64; Marie-France Morel, "Reflections on Some Recent French Literature on the History of Childhood," *Continuity and Change* 4 (1989), 325.

38. Especially by historians of the modern world. Scheper-Hughes, for instance, saw the work of Ariès, Lloyd deMause, Shorter, Stone, and Peter Laslett as providing good models to explicate premodern childhood as well as setting up good

comparative guidelines for her own studies. Nancy Scheper-Hughes, "Culture, Scarcity, and Maternal Thinking: Mother Love and Child Death in Northeast Brazil," in *Child Survival: Anthropological Perspectives on the Treatment and Maltreatment of Children*, ed. Nancy Scheper-Hughes (Dordrecht, 1987), 202. But if these models are wrong, her own conclusions about modern attitudes toward children may be in doubt. Stearns and Stearns attempted to get around this debate by investigating emotional standards, that is the social construction of emotion, not emotions themselves; but eventually they conformed to the model set out by Ariès, Shorter, and Stone: "Shifts in affection toward infants have probably occurred in Western society over the past three centuries, but they have not been as great as the shifts in emotional standards regarding infants." Stearns and Stearns, 824. See also 814, 821-24, 828-29.

Judith Bennett lamented that while medievalists had rejected Ariès, Shorter, and Stone, modern historians had not. Judith Bennett, review of Frances and Joseph Gies's *Marriage and the Family in the Middle Ages*, *Speculum* 64 (1989), 432. Yet, in concluding that medieval Germans viewed children as somehow deficient when compared to adults, James Schultz has actually offered some support for Ariès's views on childhood in the Middle Ages. James Schultz, *The Knowledge of Childhood in the German Middle Ages, 1100-1350* (Philadelphia, 1995). Bad history dies hard; therefore, another study assaulting the conclusions of scholars such as Ariès, Shorter, and Stone and their adherents is not necessarily overkill.

39. "Until many detailed, smaller-scale studies have been done, a picture of the childbirth experience in the past will remain incomplete at best." Judith Walzear Leavitt, review of Richard W. and Dorothy C. Weitz's *Lying In: A History of Childbirth in America*, *Journal of Social History* (13) 1979, 484. More recently, Shahar made a strong call for more detailed regional studies of childhood in the Middle Ages, a call that Hanawalt answered admirably well with her *Growing Up in Medieval London*. Shahar, vi.

40. Despite being a critic of Ariès's views about childhood in the Middle Ages, Shahar even concludes that "the custom of baptizing an infant several days after birth was inspired by the negative image of childhood." Shahar, 45. In fact, the custom was inspired by the parents' hope of salvation for their children; their fear of damnation or life in limbo for their children; and the need to publicly demonstrate, as soon as possible, society's acceptance of their children.

41. Richard Goldthwaite's *Private Wealth in Renaissance Florence: A Study of Four Families* (1968) was much influenced by Ariès. Diefendorf, 662. Ariès's conclusions likewise specifically inspired Trexler's work on adolescence. Charles Trinkhaus and Heiko Oberman, *The Pursuit of Holiness in Late Medieval and Renaissance Religion* vol. 10 *Studies in Medieval and Reformation Thought* (Leiden, 1974), xv, 200. To be fair to these authors, however, at the time they did their studies on childhood in Renaissance Florence, the ideas of Ariès, Shorter and Stone stood virtually unchallenged and appeared so compelling.

42. Although I do not have the room here to detail the particular reasons why I think the prevailing model on childhood in the past is in error, readers interested in my views on this subject should consult Louis Haas, "Mi naqui: Birth and Infancy in

Late Medieval and Renaissance Florence," Ph.D diss. University of Illinois, 1990, 349-403.

43. Examples of these glimpses appear in the work of authors such as Gene Brucker, Anthony Molho, and Sharon Strocchia, as I shall show throughout this study.

44. For the idea that the Renaissance is still seen as a watershed for affective attitudes toward children, see Margaret L. King, *The Death of the Child Valerio Marcello* (Chicago, 1994), 153-55.

45. On this concept, see Richard C. Trexler, *Public Life,* passim; and Mary Bergstein, "Marian Politics in Quattrocento Florence: The Renewed Rededication of Santa Maria del Fiore in 1412," *Renaissance Quarterly* 44 (1991), 673-719.

46. Since Alberti was an outsider to his family and to Florence, his analysis of the Florentine family is that much more valuable. Thomas Kuehn, "Reading Between the Patrilines: Leon Battista Alberti's *Della Famiglia* in Light of His Illegitimacy," in *I Tatti Studies: Essays in the Renaissance* vol. 1, ed. Caroline Elam and F. W Kent (Florence: 1985), 166.

47. On the *ricordanze* as historical sources see P. J. Jones, "Florentine Families and Florentine Diaries in the Fourteenth Century," *Papers of the British School at Rome* 24 (1956), 183-205; Christian Bec, *Les Marchands écrivains: affairs et humanisme à Florence, 1375-1434* (Paris, 1967); Fernando Levy, "Florentine *Ricordanze* in the Renaissance," *Stanford Italian Review* 3 (1983), 107-22; Angelo Cicchetti and Raul Mordenti, *La memoria familiare* 1, *I libri di famiglia in Italia* vol. 1 *Filologia e storiografia letteraria* (Rome, 1985); Vittore Branca, ed., *Mercanti scrittori: ricordi nella Firenze tra medioevo e rinascimento: Paolo Certaldo, Giovanni Morelli, Bonaccorso Pitti, Domenico Lenzi, Donato Velluti, Goro Dati, Francesco Datini, Lapo Niccolini, Bernardo Machiavelli* (Milan, 1986). See also the new journal, *Bollettino della ricerca sui libri di famiglia in Italia.* Giulia Calvi has recently examined a woman's *ricordanze;* see "Maddalena Nerli and Cosimo Tornabuoni: A Couple's Narrative of Family History in Early Modern Florence," *Renaissance Quarterly* 45 (1992), 312-39. For what can be done with memoirs for explicating the premodern world, see Jacques-Louis Mènètra, *Journal of My Life* (New York, 1986); and Emmanuel Le Roy Ladurie, *The Beggar and the Professor: A Sixteenth-Century Family Saga* (Chicago, 1997).

48. Klapisch-Zuber, amongst others, saw their value for family history. She developed a marvelous recreation of premodern Florentine social and familial life utilizing primarily the *ricordanze* in her collection of essays, *Women, Family, and Ritual in Renaissance Italy.* Julius Kirshner recognized that private documents like the *ricordanze*-and letters-were the best sources with which to investigate the family in the past. Julius Kirshner, "Some Problems in the Interpretation of Legal Texts *Re* the Italian City-States," *Archiv für Begriffsgeschichte* 19 (1975), 21. Herlihy and Klapisch-Zuber followed this advice in their *Tuscans and their Families.* Unfortunately, they did not carry the method far enough and only used *ricordanze* information to selectively highlight or illustrate their demographic conclusions.

49. As the *Annalistes* and microhistorians have shown, literature can unlock all sorts of secrets about social life in the past. On the use of literature as a corrective for diaries, see Stearns and Stearns, 830.

50. For a good definition and examination of who made up the Florentine elite see Anthony Molho, *Marriage Alliance in Late Medieval Florence* (Cambridge, 1994), 214, 365-410.

51. Sharon Strocchia correctly noted the need for seeing gender as a category under which to study the Florentine family-something she tried to remedy. Strocchia, "Remembering the Family," 636.

52. I am not the only one to think Klapisch-Zuber overemphasized the anti-female tendencies in Florentine society: see Diefendorf, 673-74 and 677-78; Strocchia, "Death Rites and the Ritual Family," 148 and "Remembering the Family," 636; Richard P. Saller and David I. Kertzer, "Historical and Anthropological Perspectives on Italian Family life," in *The Family in Italy: From Antiquity to the Present,* ed. Richard P. Saller and David I. Kertzer (New Haven, 1991), 13; Stanley Chojnacki, "Comment: Blurring Genders," *Renaissance Quarterly* 40 (1987), 745. Moreover, most of the review literature likewise criticizes her for this tendency; for an example see Humfrey Butters, review of Christiane Klapisch-Zuber's *Women, Family, and Ritual in Renaissance Italy, Renaissance Quarterly* 42 (1989), 299.

53. Hans Medick and David Warren Sabean, "Interest and Emotion in Family and Kinship Studies: A Critique of Social History and Anthropology," in *Interest and Emotion: Essays in the Study of Family and Kinship,* ed Hans Medick and David Warren Sabean (Cambridge, 1984), 9-12. Thomas Kuehn, the foremost scholar of Florentine law and society, observed: "Law provided a language by which lawyers, legislators, and litigants formed the discourse by which they attempted to manage strategies, resources, and social order." Thomas Kuehn, *Law, Family, & Women: Toward a Legal Anthropology of Renaissance Italy* (Chicago, 1991), 257. Law did not necessarily reflect the reality of a society, just how lawyers saw that society. On the limitations of legal sources for premodern family history see also Diefendorf, 668 and 679.

54. Dixon, 4, 36, 59; Saller and Kertzer, 3, 5, 6, 10, 14; Beryl Rawson, "Adult-Child Relationships in Roman Society," in *Marriage, Divorce, and Children in Ancient Rome,* ed. Beryl Rawson (Oxford, 1991), 7-9. These concerns are more fully elaborated in a series of articles by Richard Saller: "European Family History and Roman Law," *Continuity and Change* 6 (1991), 335-46; "*Patria Potestas* and the Stereotype of the Roman Family," *Continuity and Change* 1 (1989), 7-22; "Corporal Punishment, Authority, and Obedience in the Roman Household," in *Marriage, Divorce, and Children in Ancient Rome,* ed. Beryl Rawson (Oxford, 1991), 144-65. Other ancient historians see law as "an imperfect and at times misleading guide to reality." Barry Strauss, *Fathers and Sons in Athens: Ideology and Society in the Era of the Peloponnesian War* (Princeton, 1993), 62.

55. "Legal sources are generally not a good place to look for traces of ordinary children; they had almost no independent legal existence and were absorbed into their families." Joseph Lynch, review of *Enfant et parenté dans la France médiévale Xe-XIIIe sie`cles,* by Roland Carron *American Historical Review* 95 (1990), 1516.

56. Goldthwaite recently lamented that we still know too little of the private life of Florentines, especially the details of what went on inside their homes. Richard

A. Goldthwaite, *Wealth and the Demand for Art in Italy 1300-1600* (Baltimore, 1993), 237-38.

57. Julius Kirshner commented on the limits to demographic history for illustrating family life: "The problem here, as I see it, is that these variables form only one subsection of kinship and reflect the preoccupations of modern census-takers—not the preoccupations of families living five to seven hundred years ago." Kirshner, 21. See also Golden, 82-94, for a critique of relying solely on demography to explore reactions to the death of infants.

Chapter I

1. Leon Battista Alberti, *The Family in Renaissance Florence*, trans. Renée Neu Watkins (Columbia, 1969), 45. This attitude is common among Florentine humanists. Charles de la Roncière, "Tuscan Notables on the Eve of the Renaissance," in *Revelations of the Medieval World*, ed. Georges Duby, Vol. 2 of *A History of Private Life*, ed. Philippe Ariès and Georges Duby (Cambridge, MA, 1988), 275.

2. ASF, Consulte e Pratiche, 42, fol. 17v, in Gene Brucker, ed., *The Society of Renaissance Florence: A Documentary Study* (New York, 1971), 81. Alberti, however, put children above public life in importance. Alberti, 67.

3. Alberti, 50, 116.

4. Niccolò Machiavelli, *Mandragola*, trans. Mera J. Flaumenhaft (Prospect Heights, 1981), 36.

5. Paolo da Certaldo, *Libro di Buoni Costumi*, ed. Alfredo Schiaffini (Florence, 1945), 128.

6. Francesco Guicciardini, *Maxims and Reflections (Ricordi)*, trans. Mario Domandi (Philadelphia, 1965), 112.

7. ASF, Giudice degli Appelii, 79, 2, fol. 68r, in Brucker, 206.

8. In a letter to the Otto di Balia di Firenze dated 10 November 1466 he noted that to pay off a debt to Filippo Strozzi he had to sell two farms, and he asked them to convince themselves and Filippo of the justness of this deal. He added this sentence to his plea to help them recognize his desperate plight. Cesare Guasti, ed., *Le Carte Strozziane del R. Archivio di Stato in Firenze: Inventario Serie Prima* Vol. 1 (Florence, 1884), 575.

9. *Libro della confessione*, BNF, Landau Finlay, 288, fol. 28r.

10. Luca Landucci, *A Florentine Diary from 1450 to 1516 Continued by an Anonymous Writer Till 1542*, trans. Alice de Rosen Jervis (New York, 1927), 165; and pages 22, 81, 115, 117, 183, 239, 256-57. For the same sentiment by various authors, see *Decameron*, II:3; Brucker, 216, 271; Agnolo Firenzuolo, *Tales of Firenzuolo*, trans. anon. (New York, 1987), 3; ASF, 2, 13, fol. 18r; Francesco Barbaro, *On Wifely Duties*, trans. Benjamin G. Kohl in *The Earthly Republic: Italian Humanists on Government and Society*, ed. Benjamin G. Kohl and Ronald Witt (Philadelphia, 1978), 222; Michael Goodich, "Bartholomaeus Anglicus on Child-Rearing," *Journal of Psychohistory* 3 (1975), 82.

11. Alberti, 93.

12. ASF, CS, 4, 418, fol. 44r.

13. "Giovanni mio figliuolo nato dame e de Carmellina mia donna." ASF, CS, 2, 6, fol. 46r.

14. ASF, CS, 3, 49, fol. 41. Giovanni Morelli referred to his sister's birth as the "primo frutto" his father received from his mother. Giovanni di Pagolo Morelli, Ricordi, ed. Vittore Branca (Florence, 1969), 177. At the death of his sister he said that "no seed remained from her." Richard C. Trexler, "In Search of Father," Journal of Psychohistory 3 (1975-76), 232.

15. David Herlihy and Christiane Klapisch-Zuber, Tuscans and their Families: A Study of the Florentine Catasto of 1427 (New Haven, 1985), 256; James Bruce Ross, "The Middle-Class Child in Urban Italy, Fourteenth to Early Sixteenth Century," in History of Childhood, ed. Lloyd deMause (New York, 1974), 207; David Herlihy, The Family in Renaissance Italy (St. Louis, 1974), 8.

16. Giovanni Dominici, Regola del governo di cura familiare parte quarta: On the Education of Children, trans. and ed. Arthur Basil Coté (Washington D.C., 1927), 68. Coté, observed that his theories were "surprisingly modern." Ibid., 5; see also 15-16, 23, and 37. On Giovanni Dominici see also Ross, "The Middle-Class Child," 202-05; Christiane Klapisch-Zuber, Women, Family, and Ritual in Renaissance Florence (Chicago, 1985), 111-15, 320-22.

17. Iris Origo, The Merchant of Prato: Francesco di Marco Datini, 1335-1410 (New York, 1957), 159, 180-90, 198-200, 257, 309, 367, 374, 383-84, 387.

18. Barbaro, 180.

19. Luke Demaitre, "The Idea of Childhood and Childcare in Medical Writings of the Middle Ages," Journal of Psychohistory 4 (1977), 462-65, 469, 476; Goodich, 75-76; John Gardner, The Life and Times of Chaucer (New York, 1977), 63-64; Ross, 210.

20. Philip Gavitt, Charity and Children in Renaissance Florence: The Ospedale degli Innocenti, 1410-1536 (Ann Arbor, 1990), 274-75.

21. "Tuscan society swarmed with children." David Herlihy, "Santa Caterina and San Bernardino: Their Teachings on the Family," in Atti del simpozio internazionale Cateriniana-Bernardiniano Siena, 17-20 Aprile 1980, ed. Domenio Maffei and Paolo Nardi (Siena, 1982), 923. Florentine "family life in the fifteenth century was lived among large numbers of children." de la Roncière, 169. Men "made" the house and "filled it with children." Klapisch-Zuber, Women, Family, and Ritual, 117.

22. ASF, CS, 5, 1461, fol. 47v.

23. Luca Landucci, Diario Fiorentino dal 1450 al 1516 continuato da un anonimo fino al 1542, ed. I. Del Badia (Florence, 1883), 8; Two Memoirs of Renaissance Florence: The Diaries of Buonaccorso Pitti and Gregorio Dati, trans. Julia Martines, ed. Gene Brucker (New York, 1967), 107; For Catherine of Siena's mother see de la Roncière, 224-25.

24. For Masi see Sharon Strocchia, Death and Ritual in Renaissance Florence (Baltimore, 1992), 173; for Strozzi see Eric Cochrane and Julius Kirshner, eds., The Renaissance vol 5 of Readings in Western Civilization (Chicago, 1986), 105.

25. Donald Weinstein, "The Myth of Florence," in *Florentine Studies*, ed. Nicolai Rubinstein (London, 1968), 16.

26. Ginevra Niccolini di Camugliano, *Chronicles of a Florentine Family, 1200-1470* (London, 1933), 183-85. Lapo Niccolini had seven children from his first wife and six from his second wife. At one point his household contained him, his second wife, ten children, and his mother. Klapisch-Zuber, *Women, Family, and Ritual*, 72; Ginevra Niccolini di Camugliano, "A Medieval Florentine, his Family, and his Possessions," *American Historical Review* 31 (1925), 2.

   Florentine society and Florentine law recognized three types, or levels, of legal children: legitimate; natural, meaning those illegitimate children born during the course of a long-term affair; and *spurii*, meaning those illegitimate children born during the course of a short-term affair or even because of a one-night stand. While Florentine law and society discriminated against bastards, and especially against *spurii*, they could be legitimated—and often were—by a legal process of legitimation, by the marriage of the parents, or even by a testamentary act of their father. See Thomas Kuehn, *Law, Family, and Women: Toward a Legal Anthropology of Renaissance Italy* (Chicago, 1991), 176-93; and "Reading Between the Patrilines: Leon Battista Alberti's *Della Famiglia* in Light of His Illegitimacy," in *I Tatti Studies: Essays in the Renaissance* vol. 1, ed. Salvatore Camporeate, Caroline Elam, and F. W. Kent (Florence, 1985), 164-65.

27. Klapisch-Zuber, *Women, Family, and Ritual*, 17.

28. Alberti, 115 and 119.

29. Kuehn, *Law, Family, and Women*, 197.

30. For the canonists' development of this theory see James A. Brundage, *Law, Sex, and Christian Society in Medieval Europe* (Chicago, 1987), 51, 67, 89, 91, 197-98, 255, 280, 352. Medieval society as a whole reflected this theory. Shulamith Shahar, *Childhood in the Middle Ages* (London, 1990), 1-20. And in this, Christian attitudes just followed those of Roman society. Suzanne Dixon, *The Roman Family* (Baltimore, 1992), 62, 67-69.

31. A survey of private letters and the *ricordanze* indicates a close correlation between what humanists had to say about the family and what the Florentine elite had to say and write—thus believe—about the family. Anthony Molho, *Marriage Alliance in Late Medieval Florence* (Cambridge, MA, 1994) 234-35. Curiously, in a work that says so much about how Florentines did not use marriage (it was not intended as a device to make political alliances), it does not really tell us why Florentines married. There is no index entry for children or for the purpose of marriage.

32. Gene Brucker, *Giovanni and Lusanna: Love and Marriage in Renaissance Florence* (Berkeley, 1986), 86; Niccolò Machiavelli, 14, 16, 23-24, 27, 34, 37, 51; Alberti, 98; *Two Memoirs*, 115.

33. Niccolò Machiavelli, 34; see also Alberti, 113.

34. Benvenuto Cellini, *Autobiography*, trans. George Bull (New York, 1956), 19; Origo, 168.

35. Alberti, 211.

36. Herlihy, *The Family*, 7; ibid., "Deaths, Marriage, Births, and the Tuscan Economy," in *Population Patterns in the Past*, ed. R. D. Lee (New York, 1977),147;

Christiane Klapisch, "Household and Family in Tuscany in 1427," in *Household and Family in Past Time*, ed. Peter Laslett and Richard Wall (Cambridge, 1972), 274; Herlihy and Klapisch-Zuber, *Tuscans and their Families*, 241-45, 253, 287.

37. Klapisch-Zuber, *Women, Family, and Ritual*, 17; Herlihy and Klapisch-Zuber, *Tuscnas and their Families*, 320.

38. G. O. Corazzini, ed., *Ricordanze di B. Masi calderaio fiorentino dal 1478 al 1526* (Florence, 1906), 284-85.

39. See Herlihy, "Deaths, Marriage, Births," 146; Emmanuel Le Roy Ladurie, *Montaillou: The Promised Land of Error* (New York, 1978), 205-07; Herlihy and Klapisch-Zuber, *Tuscans and their Families*, 251-54; Jean-Louis Flandrin, *Families in Former Times: Kinship, Household and Sexuality* (Cambridge, 1979), 212-42; John Eastburn Boswell, "Expositio and Oblation: The Abandonment of Children and the Ancient and Medieval Family," *American Historical Review* 89 (1984), 12; Lawrence Stone, "Family History in the 1980s: Past Achievements and Future Trends," *Journal of Interdisciplinary History* 12 (1981), 59; Rudolph M. Bell, *Holy Anorexia* (Chicago, 1985), 166; Richard C. Trexler, *Public Life in Renaissance Florence* (New York, 1980), 379; Jack Goody, *The Development of the Family and Marriage in Europe* (Cambridge, 1983), 85, 162; Ralph A. Houlbrooke, *The English Family* (London, 1984) 128; Klapisch-Zuber, *Women, Family, and Ritual*, 158; P. P. A. Biller, "Birth-Control in the West in the Thirteenth and Early Fourteenth Centuries," *Past and Present* 94 (1982), 3-26; Niccolò Machiavelli, 31-32; Boccaccio, 28; *Decameron*, V:7, IX:3; BNF, Landau Finlay, 288, fol. 21r; St. Antoninus, *Confessionale* (Venice, 1474), fols. 33v, 54r. John T. Noonan, *Contraception: A History of its Treatment by the Catholic Theologians and Canonists* (Cambridge, MA, 1986).

Despite the work on contraception in the past, the evidence for the extent of family limitation in premodern European society is tenuous at best. Barbara Hanawalt found only one case of abortion listed in the thousands of coroners' inquests she has surveyed. Peter Laslett called it "rare" for English parish registers to list abortions. Alan Macfarlane concluded that late age of marriage and high infant mortality rates precluded the need for family limitation, including abortion, in premodern England. Barbara Hanawalt, *The Ties that Bound: Peasant Families in Medieval England* (Oxford, 1986), 100-103; Peter Laslett, *The World We Have Lost: England before the Industrial Age* 3rd ed. (New York, 1984), 129-30; Alan Macfarlane, *Marriage and Love in England 1300-1840* (Oxford, 1986), 62. Although John Riddle likewise agrees on the difficulty tracking the use of contraception in the past, he believes that people of the Renaissance knew less about this than did their medieval forbears. John Riddle, *Contraception and Abortion from the Ancient World to the Renaissance* (Cambridge, MA, 1992), 7, 11-14, 143, 157. Riddle's work is more valuable for studying this subject in the premodern era than Angus Maclaren, *A History of Contraception from Antiquity to the Present Day* (New York, 1990).

40. Herlihy and Klapisch-Zuber, *Tuscans and Their Families*, 253.

41. These proportions parallel those for modern European populations. Herlihy, "Deaths," 155; Herlihy and Klapisch-Zuber, *Tuscans and their Families*, 81, 151, 185, 240; Klapisch-Zuber, *Women, Family, and Ritual*, 98-99.

42. While it may seem obvious that every culture is child-centered, that is far from correct. Modern Chinese culture, according to some anthropologists, is not child-centered. Shulamith Heins Potter, "Birth Planning in Rural China: A Cultural Account," in *Child Survival: Anthropological Perspectives on the Treatment and Maltreatment of Children,* ed. Nancy Scheper-Hughes (Dordrecht, 1987), 33-58.

43. Ross, "The Middle-Class Child," 197; Iris Origo, "The Domestic Enemy: Eastern Slaves in Tuscany in the Fourteenth and Fifteenth Centuries," *Speculum* 30 (1955), 340. In 1348 Donato Velluti took in his deceased brother's ten-year-old illegitimate daughter. He noted that he wished to raise her as his own not only because of a family obligation but also because she reminded him so much of his brother. David Herlihy, "Family and Property in Renaissance Florence," in *The Medieval City,* ed. H. Miskimin, D. Herlihy, and A. Udovitch (New Haven, 1977), 20.

44. Patrick Geary, ed., *Readings in Medieval History* (Lewiston, 1991), 813.

45. Scholars have had some trouble deciding whether or not formal legal adoption existed in the medieval world. Shulamith Shahar reflected that confusion by saying, at one point, that the practice had disappeared and then, within pages of this, saying that it still existed. Shahar, *Childhood in the Middle Ages,* 123-25. Formal adoption was a legal process in medieval and Renaissance Florence, though Thomas Kuehn notes that he only found a few examples of it in the Florentine notarial records. Kuehn, "Reading Between the Patrilines," 173-74; on its scarcity in Florentine legal records see also his *Law, Family, and Women,* 167, 168-70, 173-74, 191, 256, and 328 nn. 57 and 58. Why formal adoption was not more popular or widespread in the premodern world is a question begging for an answer.

46. Herlihy and Klapisch-Zuber, *Tuscans and their Families,* 246; Origo, "The Domestic Enemy," 345, 348; Alberti, 129-30. Kuehn argues that the topic of adoption in Alberti's work is the "hinge on which much of the dialogue turns." Kuehn, "Reading Between the Patrlines," 172.

47. Origo, *The Merchant of Prato,* 5, 168, 177.

48. BNF, Fondo Nazionale, 2, 1, 231, fol. 1rv; Origo, *The Merchant of Prato,* 116, 166, 194-95.

49. Allessandra was very attached to her last born, a posthumous child, which might explain why he was her favorite. Mark Phillips, *The Memoir of Marco Parenti: A Life in Medici Florence* (Princeton, 1987), 81-82; Ross, "The Middle-Class Child," 201. In Genoa bequests to children whose identity is now unknown, though they were not family members, occurred frequently, perhaps representing the existence of informal adoptions. Steven Epstein, *Wills and Wealth in Medieval Genoa, 1150-1250* (Cambridge, MA, 1984), 77. Datini made such a bequest. Origo, *The Merchant of Prato,* 385. English monarchs frequently took in pauper children as an act of charity. Lorraine C. Attreed, "From *Pearl* Maiden to Tower Princes: Towards a New History of Medieval Childhood," *Journal of Medieval History* 9 (1983), 47. In ancient Rome some childless couples took in slave children, many of whom had been abandoned, and expected in return that these children would perform the requisite burial duties for them at the appropriate time. Because of

this family obligation, this act represented an adoption of sorts. Susan Dixon, *The Roman Family* (Baltimore, 1992). Perhaps some childless Florentines took in children for this same purpose.

50. Brucker, *Society of Renaissance Florence*, 31-32.
51. Boccaccio, *Decameron*, II:8, IV:1, V:7.
52. Boccaccio, *Decameron*, V:5. This imagery from war is not all that unusual in fiction or in fact. On the retreat to Corunna in January 1809 a hardbitten Highland Light infantryman recorded the following:

> I was roused by a crowd of soldiers. My curiosity prompted me to go to it; I knew it must be no common occurrence that could attract their sympathy. Judge of the feelings which I want words to express. In the centre lay a woman, young and lovely, though cold in death, and a child, apparently about six or seven months old, attempting to draw support from the breast of its dead mother. Tears filled every eye, but no one had the power to aid. While we stood around gazing on the interesting object, then on each other, none offered to speak, each heart was so full. At length one of General Moore's staff-officers came up and desired the infant to be given to him. He rolled it in his cloak, amidst the blessings of every spectator. Never shall I efface the benevolence of his look from my heart, when he said, 'Unfortunate infant, you will be my future care.'"

Christopher Hibbert, ed., *A Soldier of the Seventy-First: The Journal of a Soldier of the Highland Light Infantry 1806-1815* (Warren, 1976), 30-31.

53. Origo, "The Domestic Enemy," 365 n. 133; Phil Gavitt, *Charity and Children*, 19-20, 154, 189, 211, 226, 236, 243-58, 299, 301; John Boswell, *The Kindness of Strangers: The Abandonment of Children in Western Europe from Late Antiquity to the Renaissance* (New York, 1988), 397-427.
54. Herlihy and Klapisch-Zuber, *Tuscans and their Families*, 245-46.
55. Michael Mitterauer and Reinhard Sieder, *The European Family: Patriarchy to Partnership from the Middle Ages to the Present* (Chicago, 1982), 61.
56. Alberti, 48-49; for an explication of this see Gavitt, 290-92.
57. Guicciardini, 52. Nicia in the *Mandragola* voiced the same concerns. Niccolò Machiavelli, 21. Lapo Niccolini saw this from bitter experience; he commented ruefully that his one son (who kept getting him involved in shady business deals) gave him a great deal of trouble. Klapisch-Zuber, *Women, Family, and Ritual*, 78.
58. Alberti, 58.
59. Herlihy and Klapisch-Zuber, *Tuscans and their Families*, 232.
60. Brucker, *Society of Renaissance Florence*, 19; for other sentiments like this see de la Roncière, 143.
61. Origo, *The Merchant of Prato*, 231.
62. David Herlihy, "The Family and Religious Ideologies in Medieval Europe," *Journal of Family History* 12 (1987), 14.
63. Brucker, *The Society of Renaissance Florence*, 143. Catherine of Siena saw having children as a distraction for those who wanted to devote themselves to God.

David Herlihy, "The Making of the Medieval Family: Symmetry, Structure, and Sentiment," *Journal of Family History* 8 (1983), 125.

64. Alberti, 86; for this same sentiment see also 55.

65. Ibid., 48.

66. A mother described her daughter as "the best and most virtuous daughter in Florence." VII:8. The birth of a son to another woman "increased enormously the happiness of Messer Gentile [her lover] as well as her own." X:4. Boccaccio described the Count of Antwerp's children as "the most beautiful and sweetest children in the world." II:8. See also III:9; X:10. Fathers commonly expressed their joy about their children in letters, sometimes addressed to these same children. Most Florentine children knew how prized they were by family members. de la Roncière, 208; see also Morelli, 301.

67. These expressions are replete in the letters and *ricordanze*. Isabella Guicciardini addressed her son as dearest son (*carissimo figliuolo*) in her letters to him. ASF, CS, 1, 63, fol. 52.

68. Alberti, 50-51. In his *Libri della famiglia* Alberti tackled an ages-old dichotomy: having children while giving great joys also gave great heartaches. Klapisch-Zuber argued, incorrectly I believe, that Alberti presented a new, "modern" view of childhood to oppose the older medieval view. Klapisch-Zuber, *Women, Family, and Ritual*, 114.

69. Alberti, 112-13.

70. Alberti, 124. On the Florentine desire to have children to preserve the patriline see David Herlihy, "Medieval Children," in *Essays on Medieval Civilization: The Walter Prescott Webb Memorial Lecture XII*, ed. Bede Karl Lackner and Kenneth Day Philip (Austin, 1978), 124; Kuehn, "Reading Between the Patrilines," 170-71, 178; and Kuehn, *Law, Family, and Women*, 197.

   Sant'Antonino set providing children as one goal of marriage. Klapisch-Zuber, 186 n. 34. Other Florentines saw marriage this way too and would tie the two together by chiding their single friends to get married and have children. Alberti, 52; Origo, *The Merchant of Prato*, 26; Boccaccio, *Decameron*, V:10. A common belief among the English upper class was that wives provided a marriage first with a dowry and second with an heir. Miriam Slater, *Family Life in the Seventeenth Century: The Verneys of Claydon House* (London, 1984), 8. People in France saw marriage in this same light. Madelaine Jeay, "Sexuality and Family in Fifteenth Century France: Are Literary Sources a Mask or a Mirror?" *Journal of Family History* 4 (1979), 336.

71. Molho, 12.

72. Klapisch-Zuber, *Women, Family, and Ritual*, x.

73. Maria Teresa Sillano, ed., *Le ricordanze di Giovanni Chellini da San Miniato: medico, mercante e umanista (1425-1457)* (Milan, 1984), 187.

74. Alberti, 115; see also, Kuehn, *Law, Family, and Women*, 198. Florentines believed sons succeeded fathers not only within the family and as heirs but also as citizens and office-holders. Strocchia, *Death and Ritual*, 132-33.

75. Margherita Datini consoled a friend who had just given birth to another girl by noting that the father loved his daughters as much as his sons. But she then added that having a boy would be nice since it would perpetuate the family

name. Ross, "The Middle-Class Child," 206. On the other hand, men wished that friends and family members would have many children, both male and female. Morelli, 542; Alessandro Perossa, ed., *Giovanni Rucellai ed il suo zibaldone* (London, 1960), 63-64. There is little evidence of a preference for sons in premodern England. Alan Macfarlane, *Marriage and Love in England 1300-1840* (New York, 1980), 54. Moreover, there is little evidence of a disappointment at the birth of daughters in another patriarchal society, that of ancient Rome. Emil Eyben, "Fathers and Sons," in *Marriage, Divorce, and Children in Ancient Rome,* edited by Beryl Rawson (New York, 1991), 119; Beryl Rawson, "Adult-Child Relationships in Roman Society," in *Marriage, Divorce, and Children in Ancient Rome,* ed. Beryl Rawson (New York, 1991), 11.

76. In his will (drawn up on 6 December 1423) Giovanni Corsini recognized this demographic threat to the family's fortunes by acknowledging the possibility of his children's dying without heirs. A. Petrucci, ed., *Il libro di ricordanze dei Corsini (1362-1457)* (Rome, 1965), 121; On this demographic threat and the "baby bubbles" see Herlihy and Klapisch-Zuber, *Tuscans and their Families,* 80-83, 237; Herlihy, "Deaths, Marriages, Births," 149-53.

77. Klapisch-Zuber, *Women, Family, and Ritual,* 73; Niccolini di Camugliano, *Chronicles,* 137.

78. Gavitt, 276.

79. Herlihy and Klapisch-Zuber, *Tuscans and their Families,* 10.

80. Niccolò Machiavelli, 35.

81. Dominici, 38, 44; Gregorio Dati, for instance, noted that for the birth of his son, Stagio, "the Lord lent us a seventh child." *Two Memoirs,* 116-17.

82. On this duty, see Certaldo, 63-64; *Two Memoirs,* 115.

   For the prayers for both mothers and fathers see Matteo Palmieri, *Ricordi fiscali (1427-1474) con due appendici relative al 1474-1495,* ed. Elio Conti (Rome, 1983), 212; Corrazzini, 29; Petrucci, 137, Niccolini di Camugliano, *Chronicles,* 86; Sharon Strocchia, "Death Rites and Ritual Family in Renaissance Florence," in *Life and Death in Fifteenth-Century Florence,* ed. Marcel Tetel, Ronald Witt, and Rona Goffen (Durham, 1989), 133; ibid., *Death Rituals* 14 and 69; and ASF, CS, 2, 27, fols. 97v-98r and ASF, CS, 2, 6, fols. 4v and 58r. In the *Corbaccio* a character complained that his children could not pray for his soul as they were still too young, which may mean they were not yet of the canonical age to partake in the sacraments and hence could not offer aid to those in purgatory. Giovanni Boccaccio, *The Corbaccio,* trans. and ed. Anthony K. Cassell (Urbana, 1975), 74.

83. BNF, Landau Finlay, 288, fol. 4v.

84. Origo, *The Merchant of Prato,* 25;

85. Alberti, 58.

86. Origo, *The Merchant of Prato,* 230. Matteo Corsini recorded the death of his wife Francesca on 2 February 1397, and he noted she had given him five children: Nicolo, 24; Lodovicho, 23; Giovanni, 21; Francesca, 15; and Andrea, 11. Petrucci, 5. On wives remembered by the number of children they had had see *Two Memoirs,* 22; Landucci, *Diario,* 8; Niccolini di Camugliano, *Chronicle,* 133; Morelli, 157; Brucker, *Society of Renaissance Florence,* 44; *Decameron,* IV:3; ASF, CS, 4, 418, fol. 47v; ASF, MS, 77, fol. 40v; BNF, Panciatichiano, 134, fol. 5r;

Petrucci, 81. On daughters or daughters-in-law remembered so, see ASF, CS, 2, 17 bis, fol. 2r; BNF, 2, 10, 112, 135, fols. 25 and 36; Petrucci, 82.

87. ASF, AD, 20, fol. 76v.

88. Petrucci, 87; ASF, CS, 2, 76, fol. 491; ASF, CS, 2, 119, fol. 11r; ASF, AD, 7, fol. 132r; ASF, CS, 2, 9, fol. 90v; Camugliano, Chronicles, 86-87, 170-71; Palmieri, 212; ASF, CS, 4, 418, fol. 12r; ASF, CS, 5, 1750, fol. 180r; Boccaccio, Decameron, VII:7.

89. Morelli, 141-42, see also 184-85; Bernardo Machiavelli, Libro di Ricordi, ed. Cesare Olschki (Florence, 1954), 214; ASF, MS, 77, fol. 51v; Niccolini di Camugliano, Chronicles, 60 and 81; ASF, MS, 88, fols. 146v and 160v. San Bernardino recalled the lament and complaints of some girls sent to convents who claimed their parents placed them there so that they would not have children. Obviously, they saw being childless as an insult or as evidence that they lacked some sort of status. Iris Origo, The World of San Bernardino (New York, 1962), 64.

90. Origo, The Merchant of Prato, 166, 232.

91. ASF, MS, 77, fol. 22r. BNF, Panciatichiano, 102, fol. 10v; Brucker, Giovanni, 86-89; Boccaccio, 31. Iacopo Lanfredini, Iacapo Pucci, and Lionardo Pucci made a series of bets with each other in October 1461 over what sex various pregnant women's children would be. They had these bets notarized. BNF, 2, 13, fols. 103-4, 107-8. Anthony Molho found evidence of this practice—involving members of the Pucci family among others—recorded in the archives of the Monte delle Doti. Molho, 109.

92. Origo, The Merchant of Prato, 166, 168-89. Brucker suggests that one of the motives for Lusanna's adultery was her barrenness: by taking in lovers she could conceive. Brucker, Giovanni, 85.

93. Alberti, 121. Some canonists specified intercourse at specific points in the menstrual cycle to ensure a successful pregnancy and to prevent birth defects. Attreed, 45.

Although historians have devoted considerable attention to birth control and contraceptives, few studies have been done about or little attention has been given to the subject of conception and the desire to increase fertility in the past. Angus McLaren, Reproductive Rituals: The Perception of Fertility in England from the Sixteenth Century to the Nineteenth Century (New York, 1984) purports to be a study about fertility, but it is more interested in examining birth control and family limitation. John Riddle's interpretation of Maimonides' Treatise on Cohabitation shows how little attention historians have paid to the subject of fertility. He used a particular passage as evidence of contraceptive practices and awareness, even though the passage is more about what foods one wanted to avoid in order to get pregnant. Riddle, 139. On the other hand, we know a little bit more about fertility practices in the ancient world than we do for the medieval or Renaissance world. Nancy Demand, Birth, Death, and Motherhood in Classical Greece (Baltimore, 1994), 17-18.

94. Alberti, 120-21; de la Roncie`re, 214, 216; Jeay, 338; Dominici, 38.

95. Sillano, 185, 187; Klapisch-Zuber, *Women, Family, and Ritual*, 319, 319 n. 32, 319 n. 33; Camugliano, *Chronicles*, 64; Brucker, *Giovanni*, 19; Origo, *The Merchant of Prato*, 204; BNF, Fondo Nazionale, 2, 10, 135, fol. 96.

96. Boccaccio, *Decameron*, III:9.

97. de la Roncière, 214.

98. David Herlihy, "Tuscan Names, 1200-1530," *Renaissance Quarterly* 41 (1988), 577.

99. Klapisch-Zuber, *Women, Family, and Ritual*, 318.

100. Brucker, *Giovanni*, 9; Machiavelli, *Mandragola*, 28; Simone Baigellini, "Seven Merchants, One Dante—and an Angel," *Florenscape: The News Magazine of Florence*, 7 March 1987, 11.

101. Origo, *The Merchant of Prato*, 167.

102. Brucker, *Society of Renaissance Florence*, 267; see also Origo, *World of San Bernardino*, 170.

103. Origo, *Merchant of Prato*, 167.

104. Klapisch-Zuber, *Women, Family, and Ritual*, 317-20.

105. Machiavelli, *Mandragola*, 22, 25. For the mandrake and its powers in premodern Europe see Emmanuel Le Roy Ladurie, *Jasmin's Witch* (New York, 1987), 31-7, 58, 60. Origo, *World of San Bernardino*, 165-66; Ross, "The Middle-Class Child," 206.

106. BNF, Landau Finlay, 288, fol. 23r.

107. Origo, *Merchant of Prato*, 165-66.

108. *Two Memoirs*, 82.

109. Machiavelli, *Mandragola*, 15-22.

110. Trexler, "In Search of Father," 247.

111. Cellini, 19; Goodich, "Bartholomaeus Anglicus," 80, 85; Jeay, 342.

112. Barbaro, 221; Goodich, "Bartholomaeus Anglicus," 85; BNF, Manoscritti Palatini, 678, fol. 42v.

113. BNF, Manoscritti Palatini, 678, fol. 42v.

114. *Purgatorio*, XXV: 34-78. For a discussion of Dante's ideas and their antecedents, see Jane Fair Bestor, "Ideas about Procreation and their Influence on Ancient and Medieval Views of Kinship," in *The Family in Italy: From Antiquity to the Present*, ed. Richard P. Saller and David I. Kertzer (New Haven, 1991), 150-67. Bartholomaeus Anglicus had said the soul entered a fetus only at some indeterminate point before birth. Goodich, "Bartholomaeus Anglicus," 77.

115. Brucker, *Society of Renaissance Florence*, 147. For a similar case in nineteenth-century Bavaria see Regina Schulte, "Infanticide in Rural Bavaria in the Nineteenth Century," in *Interest and Emotion: Essays on the Study of Family and Kinship*, ed. Hans Medick and David Warren Sabean (Cambridge, 1984), 85. For a fictional rendering of this male confusion about pregnancy, see Boccaccio, *Decameron*, V:7.

116. Brucker, *Society of Renaissance Florence*, 218; Mona Fiora told Lusanna, who was faking a pregnancy, to let her touch her stomach so that she could determine whether she was lying or not. Lusanna so believed in Fiora's ability that she instantly confessed to the charade. *Idem, Giovanni*, 86. For other accounts of

faked pregnancies see Boccaccio, *Corbaccio*, 30, 110 n. 129; Firenzuolo, 55; Brucker, *Giovanni*, 85-86, 92.

117.   Alberti, 112.

118.   Alberti, 180. Actually, Alberti defined three levels of the family: household, patriline, and lineage (all patrilines combined). Kuehn, "Reading between the Patrilines," 176-78. On the conjugal family and household at Florence see Herlihy and Klapisch-Zuber, *Tuscans and their Families*, 12; Origo, *Merchant of Prato*, 205; Klapisch-Zuber, *Women, Family, and Ritual*, 18; Alberti, 185; for Genoa see Epstein, 69. Florentines perceived the household as a natural society. Herlihy "Santa Caterina," 930. This household, over the life course, would change and contract in size. Klapisch-Zuber, *Women, Family, and Ritual*, 70-80; de la Roncie`re, 158-61; Francis William Kent, *Household and Lineage in Renaissance Florence: The Family Life of the Capponi, Ginori, and Rucellai* (Princeton, 1977). In theory it was supposed to mimic the holy family, which in general it did: father, mother, and children. de la Roncière, 304.

Chapter II

1.   *The Autobiography of Benvenuto Cellini*, trans. George Bull (New York, 1956), 19.

2.   For a good comparative picture of birth in the premodern era see Barbara Hanawalt, *Growing Up in Medieval London: The Experience of Childhood in History* (New York, 1993), 42-44.

3.   ASF, CS, 2, 3, fol. 85r.

4.   Leon Battista Alberti, *The Family in Renaissance Florence: I Libri della Famiglia*, trans. Rene'e Neu Watkins (Columbia, 1969), 122.

5.   ASF, CS, V, 16, fol. 1r; ASI, 1, 4, (1843), 42-44; ASF, AD, 8, fol. 31v; A. Petrucci, ed., *Il libro dei ricordanze dei Corsini (1362-1457)* (Rome, 1965), 53.

6.   Giovanni di Pagolo Morelli, *Ricordi*, ed. Vittore Branca (Florence, 1969), 425. His other children had been born in the households of the Spini, Panteleoni, and Aliso. Ibid., 361, 358, 380, 402, 410.

7.   ASF, CS, 4, 563, fol. 1v; ASF, CS, 4, 564, fol. 30r; Petrucci, 98; *Decameron*, X:4.

8.   ASF, CS, 5, 1750, fol. 193r.

9.   ASF, CS, 2, 17bis, fol. 2r; see also Mark Phillips, *The Memoirs of Marco Parenti: A Life in Medici Florence* (Princeton, 1987), 45.

10.   On the importance of ancestral homes for the maintenance of the lineage see D. V. and F. W. Kent, "A Self Disciplining Pact Made by the Peruzzi Family of Florence (June 1433)," *Renaissance Quarterly* 34 (1981), 345-48. On the importance of ancestral homes for birth in other premodern societies see Catherine Clinton, *The Plantation Mistress: Woman's World in the Old South* (New York, 1982), 44-45.

11.   BNF, Palatino Baldovinetti, 37, fol. 32r.

12.   On tower associations and *consorzerie* in general see Daniel Waley, *The Italian City-Republics* 3rd ed. (London, 1988), 122-31, 143-44. Charles de la Roncière noted that while towers did serve as residences, sometimes temporarily, in "the

14th century these same buildings served as symbols of the lineage's strength, unity, and political influence." Charles de la Roncière, "Tuscan Notables on the Eve of the Renaissance," in *A History of Private Life,* eds. Philippe Ariès and Georges Duby, Vol. 2, *Revelations of the Medieval World,* ed. Georges Duby, trans. Arthur Goldhammer (Cambridge, MA, 1988), 189. For the existence of a version of the *consorzerie* late in Florence's history (1433) see Kent and Kent, "A Self-Disciplining Pact," 337-55.

13. BNF, Panciatichiano, 134, fol. 5v.

14. Steven Ozment, *When Fathers Ruled: Family Life in Reformation Europe* (Cambridge, MA, 1983), 115.

15. de la Roncière, 217-18.

16. Judith C. Brown, *Immodest Acts: The Life of a Lesbian Nun in Renaissance Italy* (Oxford, 1986), 21.

17. To emphasize the humbleness of Christ's birth, Sant'Antonino stated that he did not have a midwife or any other servants there present to help in his birth. St. Antoninus, *Summa Theologica* Pars 4 (Venice, 1581), 15:31. Yet the Apocrypha notes midwives present at Christ's birth. In English upper-class births in the premodern period one could expect to find midwives and physicians there as well as nursekeepers for the newborn. It was the godparents' duty to pay the nurse some 40 to 50 shillings for her services. Miriam Slater, *Family Life in the Seventeenth Century: The Verneys of Claydon House* (London, 1984), 111. See also Ralph A. Houlbrooke, *The English Family* (London, 1984), 129. A late-seventeenth-century Venetian tax survey listed midwives under the category of *artefici.* Peter Burke, *The Historical Anthropology of Early Modern Italy: Essays on Perception and Communication* (Cambridge, 1987), 37.

18. Michael Goodich, "Medieval Child-Rearing," *Journal of Psychohistory* 3 (1975), 81. Merry E. Wiesner recognized the significance of this person's role in medieval society: "The most important occupation in which women were involved during the medieval and early modern period, in terms of impact on society as a whole and recognition by government and church authorities, was midwifery." Merry E. Wiesner, "Early Modern Midwifery: A Case Study," in *Women and Work in Preindustrial Europe,* ed. Barbara Hanawalt (Bloomington, 1986), 94. For a good general survey of recent research on midwifery in the premodern world see Hilary Marland, ed., *The Art of Midwifery: Early Modern Midwives in Europe* (London, 1993); for a detailed picture of one premodern midwife's activities see Laurel Thatcher Ulrich, *A Midwife's Tale: The Life of Martha Ballard Based on Her Diary 1785-1812* (New York, 1990). See also Renate Blumenfeld-Kosinski, *Not of Women Born: Representations of Caesarian Birth in Medieval and Renaissance Culture* (Ithaca, 1990), 4-5, 15-21, 61-74, 101-04, 109-10, 116-18; and Jacques Gélis, *History of Childbirth: Fertility, Pregnancy and Birth in Early Modern Europe,* trans. Rosemary Morris (Cambridge, 1991), 32, 48-49, 91-92, 99, 102-14, 128-29, 134-37, 157-64, 172-83, 192, 227-31, 239-40.

19. In Venice one of the names by which midwives were identified, *comare* (godmother), also indicates that it was a female-dominated (if not -dominant) profession. This term likewise reflects the close ties a midwife could have with the family she served. As we shall see for Florence, midwives were a popular

choice of godmother. In Venice it must have been so too. Midwives were also called *allevatrice* in Venice. Burke, 37.

20. Rudolph M. Bell, *Holy Anorexia* (Chicago, 1985), 95, 98.

21. Nicholas Orme, *From Childhood to Chivalry* (London, 1984), 8.

22. BNF, Fondo Nazionale, 2, 2, 357, fol. 59r.

23. Bernardo Machiavelli, *Libro di Ricordi*, ed. Cesare Olschki (Florence 1954), 23; and Gene Brucker, ed., *The Society of Renaissance Florence: A Documentary Study* (New York, 1971), 218-22.

24. Matteo Strozzi, for instance, knew exactly where the midwife for his daughter Caterina's birth lived. ASF, CS, 5, 11, fol. 131v. Men's participation in this aspect of the birth process must have been common in the premodern era. In a series of letters to his father Edmund Verney discussed how he was the one who arranged for the midwife, lying-in nurse, and wetnurse for his wife's confinement. Anna Giardina Hess, "Midwifery Practice among the Quakers in Southern Rural England in the Late Seventeenth Century," in *The Art of Midwifery: Early Modern Midwives in Europe*, ed. Hilary Marland (London, 1993), 64-65.

25. Ibid., 20v and 119v.

26. ASF, CS, 4, 71, fol. 107v; ASF, CS, 5, 17, fol. 96v.

27. Luca Landucci, *A Florentine Diary from 1450 to 1516 Continued by an Anonymous Writer till 1542*, trans. Alice de Rosen Jervis (New York, 1927), 12.

28. Wiesner, 97.

29. Iris Origo, "The Domestic Enemy: Eastern Slaves in Tuscany in the Fourteenth and Fifteenth Centuries," *Speculum* 30 (1955), 347.

30. Burke, 208-9.

31. Vittore Branca, the editor of Morelli's *Ricordi*, calls her a type of midwife or nurse who assists at birth. Morelli, 337 n. 2.

32. Ibid., 380.

33. ASF, CS, 5, 22, fol. 54v.

34. Judith Schneid Lewis, *In the Family Way: Childbearing in the British Aristocracy 1760-1860* (New Brunswick, 1986), 163-64. In seventeenth-century New England certain women would come to watch over women in birth as well as afterwards and even care for their older children. Rose Lockwood, "Birth, Illness, and Death in 18th-Century New England," *Journal of Social History* 12 (1978), 119. In his description of urban working-class life in Victorian and Edwardian England, Robert Roberts noted that beyond midwives each neighborhood "had half a dozen middle-aged women with special skills who could be booked for the lying in." Robert Roberts, *The Classic Slum: Salford Life in the First Quarter of the Century* (London, 1988), 46-47. In premodern Braunschweig midwives' apprentices were called warming-women, who may have been similar to *guardadonne*. Mary Lindemann, "Professionals? Sisters? Rivals? Midwives in Braunschweig, 1750-1800," in *The Art of Midwifery: Early Modern Midwives in Europe*, ed. Hilary Marland (London, 1993), 180-87.

35. BNF, Fondo Nazionale, 2, 2, 357, fol. 111r; ASF, CS, 5, 11, fol. 20v.

36. ASF, CS, 2, 15, fol. 41r; ASF, CS, 5, 22, fol. 54v; ASF, CS, 5, 11, fol. 20v.

37. Bernardo Machiavelli, 75-76.

38. ASF, CS, 4, 71, fols. 23v and 24r.

39. Cellini, 19.
40. ASF, CS, 5, 22, fol. 54v.
41. Petrucci, 138.
42. Ozment, *When Fathers Ruled*, 102; Burke, 207; Carlo M. Cipolla, *Public Health and the Medical Profession in the Renaissance* (Cambridge, 1976); and Katherine Park, *Doctors and Medicine in Early Renaissance Florence* (Princeton, 1985).
43. Boccaccio, *Decameron*, X:4.
44. Christiane Klapisch-Zuber, *Women, Family, and Ritual in Renaissance Italy* (Chicago, 1985), 175 n. 22.
45. Brucker, 218.
46. BNF, Nuovi Acquisiti, 260, unpaginated, 4 April 1564.
47. Iris Origo, *The Merchant of Prato: Francesco di Marco Datini* (New York, 1957), 339.
48. Goodich, "Medieval Childrearing," 77 and 80.
49. ASF, AD, 11/1, fol. 11v. See also ASF, CS, 5, 11, fol. 119v.
50. Boccaccio, *Decameron*, V:7 and IX:3.
51. Madelaine Jeay, "Sexuality and Family in Fifteenth-Century France: Are Literary Sources a Mask or a Mirror?" *Journal of Family History* 4 (1979), 337.
52. ASF, MS, 88, fols. 150r and 150v. G. O. Corazzini, ed. *Ricordanze di B. Masi calderaio fiorentino dal 1478 al 1526* (Florence, 1906), 6, 7, 8, 11. His phrase is "mediante [by means of] la grazia di Dio."
53. Commenting on the legend of St. Margaret and the work of Le'vi-Strauss, Burke asked if "a legend of descent into depths works as a 'talking cure' for the Cura Indians, why should it not have been equally efficacious in sixteenth-century Italy." Burke, 211. For other accounts on the widespread popularity of St. Margaret as the patron saint of childbirth in Europe see Blumenfeld-Kosinski, 7-10, 121; and Gélis, 70-72, 143, 146-48, 265, 271.
54. Ozment, *When Fathers Ruled*, 108.
55. Judith Schneid Lewis, 193.
56. Goodich, "Medieval Childrearing," 81.
57. Ibid. Bathing the child in warm water simulated the environment of the womb that the child had just left. Michael Goodich, *From Birth to Old Age: The Human Life Cycle in Medieval Thought, 1250-1350* (London, 1989), 86. See also Shulamith Shahar, *Childhood in the Middle Ages* (London, 1990), 83-87.
58. Archivio Innocenti Firenze, XVI, 1 fol. 33v, in Richard C. Trexler, "The Foundlings of Florence," *Journal of Psychohistory* 1 (1973), 269.
59. Boccaccio, *Decameron*, V:7. For an examination of the taboos associated with birthmarks in the premodern European world, see Gélis, 14, 56-57, 203.
60. "[L]a chaterina mia donna fece una fanciula femmina naque vestita." ASF, CS, 4, 346, fols. 89v-90r.
61. Carlo Ginzburg, *Night Battles: Witchcraft and Agrarian Cults in the Sixteenth and Seventeenth Centuries* (Baltimore, 1983), 12.
62. Klapisch-Zuber, *Women, Family, and Ritual*, 292 n. 21.
63. This is not absolute, for in a painting of the birth of the Virgin, we see in the same room the father being presented with the child. Perhaps all the artist has done here is to telescope the activity in a household during birth. Nevertheless, birth

paintings point to the fact that after the birth—for a little while at least—this was women's business. Ginevra Niccolini da Camugliano, *The Chronicles of a Florentine Family 1200-1470* (London, 1933), 162.

64. Jeay, 328-46; Adrian Wilson, "The Ceremony of Childbirth and its Interpretation," in *Women as Mothers in Pre-Industrial England: Essays in Memory of Dorothy McLaren*, ed. Valerie Fildes (London, 1990), 68-107. Birth at Rome was likewise female centered, but Nancy Demand has argued forcefully that men controlled the process in ancient Greece. Beryl Rawson, "Adult-Child Relationships in Roman Society," in *Marriage, Divorce, and Children in Ancient Rome*, ed. Beryl Rawson (Oxford, 1991), 11-14; Nancy Demand, *Birth, Death, and Motherhood in Classical Greece* (Baltimore, 1994).

65. Origo, "The Domestic Enemy," 346.

66. David Herlihy and Christiane Klapisch-Zuber, *Tuscans and their Families: A Study of the Florentine Catasto of 1427* (New Haven, 1985), 277. In sixteenth- and seventeenth-century England about 25 mothers died for every 1000 births. Shahar, 35. Compare these figures to a modern (1980) rate of .069 mothers dying for every 1000 births in the United States. A. Joy Ingalls and M. Constance Salerno, *Maternal and Child Health Nursing* 5th ed. (St. Louis, 1983), 1.

67. Wiesner, 104; Alberti, 122; Houlbroke, 129; Paul S. Seaver, *Wallington's World: A Puritan Artisan in Seventeenth-Century London* (Stanford, 1983), 86; de la Roncière, 255.

68. Origo, "The Domestic Enemy," 345.

69. Boccaccio, *Decameron*, III:9.

70. ASI, 1, 4, 42-43.

71. Boccaccio, *Decameron*, X:6.

72. ASF, CS, 4, 418, fol. 10v.

73. Cellini, 19.

74. ASF, CS, 2, 23, fol. 179v. See also BNF, Panciatichiano, 134, fol. 2r.

75. "[A] dio piacia mi vivere lungho tempo chon santa del anima e del le chorpo chosi a dio piacia el detto fanciullo mi batezo questo di." ASF, MS, 96, fol. 12r.

76. Morelli, 361. He recorded other premature births in his family. Ibid., 181-82, 199. See also BNF, Nuovi Acquisiti, 260, unpaginated, undated.

77. Herlihy and Klapisch-Zuber, *Tuscans and their Families*, 266.

78. Ozment, *When Fathers Ruled*, 110. *Mirk's Festial*, ed. Theodore Erbe (London, 1905), 4.

79. *Ricette Segreti chimici e medicinale*, BNF, Manoscritti Palatini, 796, fol. 36v.

80. Brucker, 44-45. See also C. Carnesecchi, "Un fiorentino del secolo XV e le sue ricordanze domestiche," ASI, 5, 4, (1889), 158-59. During the Middle Ages and Renaissance, caesarians, which were performed on mothers who died in childbirth before the child could be delivered, were "always an act of desperation." Blumenfeld-Kosinski, 2.

81. Brucker, 45.

82. BNF, Panciatichiano, 134, fol. 5v; ASF, CS, 4, 346, fol. 90v; Petrucci, 93; ASF, CS, 2, 17, fol. 66r.

83. *Two Memoirs*, 112, 126, 135.

84. Ibid., 127.

85. Landucci, *A Florentine Diary,* 12. These monstrous births were always seen as harbingers of some sort of future doom. For an anthropological interpretation of monstrous births in the premodern era see, Gélis, 55-56, 257-69.

86. Ibid., 47, 249-50, 272.

87. Morelli, 191-92.

88. Luke Demaitre, "The Idea of Childhood and Child Care in Medical Writings of the Middle Ages," *Journal of Psychohistory* 4 (1977), 478.

89. Master Guglielmo da Piacenza, *La Cirugia,* BNF, Panciatichiano, 81, fol. 4v.

90. For this paradox elsewhere in the premodern world see Demand, 71-86; Gélis, 36, 227, 229, 233, 235-42; Atkinson, 219.

91. *Two Memoirs,* 128, 132. Lapo Curianni also made sure to record that when his wife died of the effects of a stillborn child in 1382 she too had received all the proper sacraments of the Church. ASF, MS, 77, 27.

92. Petrucci, 82, 138, 143.

93. BNF, Panciatichiano, 101, fol. 32r; BNF, Palatino Baldovinetti, 37, fol. 23v; ASF, AD, 11/1, fol. 37r; ASF, CS, 5, 22, 97r; Corrazzini, 240, 242-43.

94. ASI, 4, (1843), 55.

95. BNF, Nuovi Acquisisti, 260, unpaginated.

96. Petrucci, 93, 98.

97. Herlihy and Klapisch-Zuber, *Tuscans and their Families,* 261.

98. ASF, CS, 2, 7, fol. 2v.

99. Corrazzini, 140.

100. ASF, CS, 4, 346, fol. 90v.

101. This burial location signified a place of high honor. Origo, *Merchant of Prato,* 175.

102. de la Roncière, 247.

103. ASF, CS, 2, 15, fol. 41r. Confections were a popular gift and food with which to celebrate birth. Margaret Datini got her confections from her apothecary. Origo, *The Merchant of Prato,* 197.

104. ASF, CS, 1, 10, fol. 243. On letters announcing birth see also de la Roncière, 255.

105. *The Private Correspondence of Niccolò Machiavelli,* trans. Orestes Ferrara (Baltimore, 1929), 92. Ferrara concluded that the reference to the little girl was Marietta's to herself. Ridolfi, on the other hand, thought that this referred to a child born before Bernardo. Ridolfi, *The Life of Niccolò Machiavelli* (London, 1954), 274 n. 40. Ferrara's conclusion seems to make more sense in the context of the letter and fits most genealogists' views that Bernardo was Machiavelli's first child.

106. Translated and quoted in Ridolfi, 75.

107. Niccolò Machiavelli, *Lettere* (Florence, 1929), 222.

108. Origo, *Merchant of Prato,* 307; Cesare Guasti, ed., *Le Carte Strozziane del R. Archivio di Stato in Firenze,* Vol. 1 *Inventario Serie Prima* (Florence, 1884), 155.

109. Origo, *Merchant of Prato,* 25, 196, 328.

110. ASF, CS, 2, 3, 36r.

111. Origo, *Merchant of Prato,* 252.

112. Neri di Bicci, *Le Ricordanze (10 marzo 1453-24 aprile 1475)* ed. Bruno Santi (Pisa, 1976), 167-68, 345.

113. Origo, *Merchant of Prato*, 252.

114. de la Roncière, 166, 248.

115. Klapisch-Zuber, *Women, Family, and Ritual*, 238 n. 78. Cloth of course could go to clothing the baby. Iacopo Pandolfini sent five braccia of cloth to a friend on hearing that his wife had delivered a son. Here, as Klapisch-Zuber has so ably noted, is the reciprocity of this sort of gift giving. Pandolfini noted in his *ricordanze* that whenever he and his wife had a son that this friend and his wife would have to return the favor.

116. ASF, CS, 4, 418, fols. 8v, 11v.

117. Klapisch-Zuber, *Women, Family, and Ritual*, 237, 237 n. 77. See her pages 236-38 for a discussion of the reciprocal giving of these gifts.

118. ASF, CS, 4, 418, fol. 8v.

119. Klapisch-Zuber, *Women, Family, and Ritual*, 237.

120. Giovanni Rucellai, *Il zibaldone quaresimale*, ed. A. Perosa, Studies of the Warburg Institute 24 (London, 1960), 35.

Chapter III

1. *Two Memoirs of Renaissance Florence: The Diaries of Buonaccorso Pitti and Gregorio Dati*, trans. Julia Martines, ed. Gene Brucker (New York, 1967), 128-30.

2. The classic anthropological statement on birth rituals remains Arnold van Gennep, *The Rites of Passage* (Chicago, 1960), 50-64. For a good look at birth rituals in the ancient Greek world see Nancy Demand, *Birth, Death, and Motherhood in Classical Greece* (Baltimore, 1994), 87-101.

3. As Barbara Hanawalt concluded, "Baptism was the beginning of the development of an individual's social network." Barbara Hanawalt, *Growing Up in Medieval London: The Experience of Childhood in History* (New York, 1993), 46. On medieval baptism and children in general see Shulamith Shahar, *Childhood in the Middle Ages* (London, 1990), 45-52; and Jack Goody, *The Development of the Family and Marriage in Europe* (Cambridge, 1983), 89. With the greater secularization of the modern world, we just do not see baptism in the same light as premodern people did. For instance, in early-twentieth-century Berlin, only 25 percent of the children ever were baptized. Carter Vaughn Findley and John Alexander Murray Rothney, *Twentieth-Century World* 3rd ed. (Boston, 1994), 36. In medieval Europe that percentage would have approached 100 percent.

4. Popular folk belief in premodern Europe held that baptism turned an infant into a human. Jean-Claude Schmitt, *The Holy Greyhound: Guinefort Healer of Children Since the Thirteenth Century* (Cambridge, 1983), 82.

5. *Paradiso*, XV:134-35.

6. Giovanni di Pagolo Morelli, *Ricordi* (Florence, 1969), 195. "To make someone a Christian" was one of the popular idioms used in Florence to describe becoming a godparent. This was an idiom that implied function. There were others. Tommaso Guidetti recorded how his coparents baptized his son ["lo feci batezare"]. ASF, CS, 4, 418, fol. 33r. Cambio Petrucci used these terms "baptized

by" and "made Christian by" interchangeably to introduce his coparents. ASF, CS, 2, 10, fol. 8r.

7. Benvenuto Cellini, *La vita*, ed. Bruno Maier (Novare, 1962), 35.

8. Richard C. Trexler, *Public Life in Renaissance Florence* (New York, 1980), 368-69. San Bernardino preached a sermon in 1425 on "The Innocents": "Non di quegli che sono affogati ne privai o uccisi in corpo per forze di medicine che non ànno l'anima, non s'intende per loro, ma per quegli ch'ànno l'anima pel santo battesimo; quegli sono gl' innocenti." San Bernardino, *Prediche 4* (Florence, 1958), 412, in Trexler, *Public Life*, 369. The passage is a little troublesome. Gene Brucker had disagreed with Trexler's reading of *anima* as soul, seeing it more as some sort of life force. But Trexler argued convincingly that Bernardino used *anima* to mean "soul," and its coupling with baptism certainly implied that. *Ibid.*, n. 2.

9. ASF, CS, 2, 4, fol. 46v.

10. David Herlihy, "Medieval Children," in *Essays on Medieval Civilization*, ed. Bede Karl Lackner and Kenneth Roy Philip (Austin, 1978), 126. For a more general view of Europeans' perception of Limbo see Jacques LeGoff, *The Birth of Purgatory* (Chicago, 1984), 45, 158, 220-21, 253, 258, 265, 335-37.

11. *Inferno*, IV:35-36; *Il Purgatorio*, VII:28-33. On Dante and Limbo see LeGoff, 336-37.

12. A. Petrucci, ed., *Il Libro di Ricordanze dei Corsini (1362-1457)* (Rome, 1963), 89; BNF, Landau Finlay, 288, fol. 31r.

13. Trexler rightly concluded that the Innocenti thus was an institution for salvation. Richard C. Trexler, "The Foundlings of Florence, 1395-1455," *Journal of Psychohistory* 1 (1973), 260. If the attendants at the Innocenti received a child older than 15 days, they would have the child baptized conditionally, for fear of rebaptism. *Ibid.*, 269.

14. Morelli, 199.

15. C. Carnesecchi, "Un fiorentino del secolo XV e le sue ricordanze domestiche," *ASI*, Series 5, 4 (1889), 158; Petrucci, 93; ASF, MS, 96, fol. 12r; ASF, CS, 4, 346, fol. 90v.

16. BNF, Panchiatichiano, 134, fol. 5v. See also Petrucci, 93; Morelli, 199, 361; Gregorio Dati, *Il libro segreto di Giovanni Dati*, ed. Carlo Gargiolli (Bologna, 1869), 75.

17. Gene Brucker, ed., *The Society of Renaissance Florence: A Documentary Study* (New York, 1971), 45.

18. *Two Memoirs*, 135. Although I have no certain evidence to support this, these cases leave the strong suspicion that parents with the cooperation of the clergy baptized infants who were already dead. Midwives elsewhere in Europe frequently baptized stillborn children. Renate Blumenfeld-Kosinski, *Not of Woman Born: Representations of Caesarian Birth in Medieval and Renaissance Culture* (Ithaca, 1990), 26. In fact, the popular desire to ensure baptism for a dead child developed into a belief that some children could even return from the dead—or be made miraculously to return from the dead by saints—to receive baptism. Silvano Cavasso, "Double Death: Resurrection and Baptism in a Seventeenth-Century Rite," in *History from Crime: Selections from Quaderni Storici*, ed. Edward

Muir and Guido Ruggiero (Baltimore, 1994), 1-31. Medieval saints lives abound with these sort of miracles; Blumenfeld-Kosinski estimated that upwards of 40 percent of saintly miracles for some saints consist of this one act. Shahar, *Childhood*, 50; Blumenfeld-Kosinski, 177 n. 122.

19. Richard C. Trexler, ed., *Synodal Law in Florence and Fiesole, 1306-1518* (Vatican City, 1971), 267.

20. Petrucci, 145; Dati, 74; ASF, AD, 11/1, fol. 5r; David Herlihy and Christiane Klapisch-Zuber, *Tuscans and their Families: A Study of the Catasto of 1427* (New Haven, 1985), 167. This speed in baptism was universal in premodern Europe. In England baptism occurred on the same day as or next day after birth. Louis Haas, "Baptism and Spiritual Kinship in the North of England, 1250-1450," M.A. thesis, Ohio State University (1982), 54, 90 n. 1. According to the butcher in Erasmus' *Concerning the Eating of Fish*, "Circumcision was taken away but baptism took its place, and its features are even more severe. Circumcision was performed eight days after birth, but if during that time anything happened to the child, the vow of the rite sufficed. But now we douse children, scarcely out of the dark cavern of the mother's womb, with cold water, which has stood a long time in a stony font. If the baby chances to die on the first day or at birth, through no fault of the parent or friends, the poor babe is doomed to eternal damnation." *The Essential Erasmus*, trans. John P. Dolan (New York, 1964), 285.

21. Giovanni Dominici, *Regola del governo di cura familiare parte quarta: On the Education of Children*, trans. Arthur Basil Coté (Washington D. C., 1927), 38-39; Morelli 199; St. Antoninus, *Confessionale* (Venice, 1474), 33v; Trexler, *Public Life*, 368-69.

22. Jacques Heers, *Family Clans in the Middle Ages* (New York, 1977), 241.

23. Lauro Martines, *Power and Imagination: City-States in Renaissance Italy* (New York, 1979), 55.

24. On the importance of ritual in Florence see Trexler, *Public Life*, 1-8, 215-330.

25. Christiane Klapisch-Zuber, "Parrains et Filleuls. Une Approche Comparée de la France, l'Angleterre et l'Italie Mediévales," *Medieval Prosopography* 6 (1985) 72, n. 34.

26. Morelli, 361. Bartolomeo Masi's phrase for becoming a godfather was similar, again implying the importance of touch: "on 7 October 1505 I, Bartolomeo, found myself holding in my arms at baptism [tenere in collo a battesimo] a child the daughter of Bernardo di Cieni di Ristoro, a second hand dealer." G. O. Corrazzini, ed., *Ricordanze di Bartolomeo Masi calderaio fiorentino dal 1478 al 1526* (Florence, 1906), 66.

27. ASF, CS, 5, 17, fol. 189v. For other examples of this see ASF, CS, 4, 418, fol. 33r; ASF, MS, 77, fol. 51v.

28. In premodern Italy, only the older churches, known as *pievi*, had the right to administer baptism. San Giovanni, the baptistery, was the *pieve* for Florence. The baptistery in fact also had authority to baptize those living in the 30 rural parishes surrounding Florence. David Herlihy, "Deaths, Marriages, Births, and the Tuscan Economy," in *Population Patterns in the Past*, ed. R. D. Lee (New York, 1977), 136; Herlihy and Klapisch-Zuber, 36. Writers of *ricordanze* recorded baptisms in the country away from the baptistery; usually, they specified that this

country church was a *pieve*. ASF, MS, 77, fol. 51v; Morelli, 368; ASF, CS, 5, 175, 208r; BNF, Panciatichiano, 134, fol. 5v; BNF, Manoscritti Palatini, 1129, 43r, 44v, 108r; BNF, Palatino Baldovinetti, 42, fol. 11r.

29. Trexler, *Public Life*, 13. Herlihy and Klapisch-Zuber identified the "religious heart of the city—the cathedral and the baptistery." Herlihy and Klapisch-Zuber, 37.

30. As late as 1767 the average number of daily baptisms was still seven. David Herlihy and Christiane Klapisch-Zuber, *Les Toscans et leurs Familles: Une Etude du Catasto Florentin de 1427* (Paris, 1978), 197. Their information comes from Marco Lastri, *Ricerche sull'antica e moderna popolazione della città di Firenze per mezzo dei registri di battesimi del Battistero di San Giovanni dal 1451 al 1774* (Florence, 1775); See also Herlihy and Klapisch-Zuber, *Tuscans*, 67-68, 74-77.

31. Between 1453 and 1461 there was an average of 5.5 baptisms performed per day; between 1475 and 1483 there was an average of 6.6 baptisms per day; between 1493 and 1502 there was an average of 6.9 baptisms per day; between 1523 and 1531 there was an average of 7.3 baptisms per day. In practical terms this meant that the workload of the priests at San Giovanni increased by about one-third during this time. Herlihy and Klapisch-Zuber, *Les Toscans*, 197.

The font at San Giovanni was designed to accommodate these large crowds and to protect the priests from the crush. It was large enough for full immersion with marble tubes placed inside that were large enough for a priest to stand in and stay dry. This was the great font, which some writers of *ricordanze* noted as the location for their children's immersion. Morelli, 410. This no longer exists at San Giovanni, but the baptistery at Pisa still has its version. John Ciardi, trans., *The Inferno*, (New York, 1954), 171-72.

Dante one day came by this font and found a child wedged into one of the tubes and in danger of drowning (obviously water was entering the tube). He smashed the tube to free the child, earning a charge of sacrilege. He referred to this incident in the *Inferno*: "I saw long the walls and on the ground long rows of holes cut in the livid stone; all were cut to a size and all were round. They seemed to be exactly the same size as those in the font of my beautiful San Giovanni, built to protect the priests who come to baptize; (one of which, not so long since, I broke open to rescue a boy who was wedged and drowning in it. Be this enough to undeceive all men.)" *Inferno*, XIX:13-21. Ciardi, 171-72. There was also, apparently, a smaller font called the "ordinary font," again noted as the specific font for immersion. Corrazzini, 239.

32. The baptism of the grand duke's son on 1 August 1541 occurred with great festival and pomp. Luca Landucci, *A Florentine Diary from 1450 to 1516 continued by an Anonymous Writer till 1542*, trans. Alice de Rosen Jervis (New York, 1927), 298. Although the baptism of the heir to the ruler of Florence was no ordinary event, it reflects at a higher level what was common for the average person.

33. This was a criticism on his part, in which he railed against the pomp in baptism. Dominici, 39.

34. ASF, CS, 5, 1750, fol. 187v.

35. St. Antoninus, 49v. BNF, Fondo Nazionale, 2, 2, 357, fols. 59v and 173v. Emmanuel Le Roy Ladurie found the same sort of ritual described by Rossi in

Montaillou. Emmanuel Le Roy Ladurie, *Montaillou: The Promised Land of Error* (New York, 1978), 207.

The parish clergy in England likewise held the same ambivalent attitude about female ritual impurity after birth as Sant' Antonino. Haas, 68-69, 93 n. 40. Recently some historians have concluded that churching did not represent the cleansing of female ritual impurity so much as it represented a rite of passage that reintegrated women back into the community after their confinement for birth, and that women actually had considerable control over this process. Adrian Wilson, "The Ceremony of Childbirth and its Interpretation," in *Women as Mothers in Preindustrial England: Essays in Memory of Dorothy McLaren,* ed. Valerie Fildes (London, 1990), 68-107; and David Cressy, "Purification, Thanksgiving and the Churching of Women in Post-Reformation England," *Past and Present* 141 (1993), 106-46.

36. ASF, CS, 4, 71, fol. 42r.

37. Here I am following the ideas of Jacques LeGoff on the role of spectators at ritual events in the Middle Ages. He noted that their presence "is not merely to provide a guarantee for the performance of the ritual act in the form of witnesses. It is part of the system. The presence of spectators creates a symbolic social space in the midst of the symbolic material space." Jacques LeGoff, *Time, Work and Culture in the Middle Ages,* (Chicago, 1980), 274.

38. ASF, CS, 2, 9, fol. 28v. Agnolo Firenzuolo, *Tales of Firenzuolo* trans. anon. 2nd ed. (New York, 1987), 16. Iris Origo, *The Merchant of Prato: Francesco di Marco Datini, 1335-1410* (New York, 1957), 195.

39. In Jacob Burckhardt, *The Civilization of the Renaissance in Italy* (New York, 1860, 1954), 151.

40. Giovanni Boccaccio, *The Corbaccio,* trans. and ed. Anthony K. Cassell (Urbana, 1975), 155.

41. BNF, Fondo Nazionale 2, 2, 357, fol. 11r; ASF, CS, 5, 11, fol. 20v; ASF, CS, 4, 71, fol. 69v.

42. Niccolò Strozzi noted expenses (including that for sugar) for the dinner held after the baptism of his daughter Lena, which was held the night of 21 November 1475. Her baptism cost him almost six florins—he noted "per loro anima benedetta." ASF, CS, 4, 71, fols. 69v, 70r. In August 1454 the ill-starred lovers Giovanni and Lusanna went to a dinner to celebrate the baptism of a neighbor's new son. Gene Brucker, *Giovanni and Lusanna: Love and Marriage in Renaissance Florence* (Berkeley, 1986), 22.

43. Trexler, *Public Life,* 409. Daniel Waley believed that "Florentine sumptuary legislation originated in the commune's fears that if the rich ruined themselves by extravagance the city itself was poorer." Daniel Waley, *The Italian City-Republics* 2nd ed. (New York, 1978), 49. This may in fact be the basis for sumptuary legislation throughout history; nevertheless, a by-product of any sumptuary legislation is an attack on honor, so Trexler is essentially correct. Other states as well tried to curb the luxury displayed at birth and baptism. In Venice during the sixteenth century the Office Against Luxury tried and largely failed to curb lavish displays on such occasions. G. Bistort, *Il Magistrato alle*

Pompe in Venezia nella Republica di Venezia (Venice, 1912), 201, 205. Its failure implies that this was more of a tax.

44. Trexler, *Synodal Law,* 188-89, 272-73.

45. On godparenthood in general in the premodern world see Joseph H. Lynch, *Godparents and Kinship in Early Medieval Europe* (Princeton, 1986); Hanawalt, *Growing Up in Medieval London,* 49-51; and Goody, 31, 48, 56, 59, 74, 94, 144, 194, 201, 229, 270-71.

46. Luca Landucci, *Diario Fiorentino dal 1450 al 1516, continuato da un anonimo fino al 1542,* ed. I. Del Badia (Florence, 1883), 14.

47. Trexler, *Synodal Law,* 188; J. D. Mansi, ed., *Sacrorum conciliorum nova et amplissima collectio* 26 (Florence, 1902), 58.

48. Joseph H. Lynch, "Baptismal Sponsorship and Monks and Nuns" and "Spiritual Kinship and Sexual Prohibition in Early Medieval Europe," *Proceedings of the Sixth International Congress of Medieval Canon Law (Berkeley, California, August 1980),* Monumenta iuris canonica C/7 (1985), 271-88. For the frequent redaction of these sexual prohibitions by the bishops of medieval England see *Councils and Synods with Other Documents Relating to the English Church,* Vol. 1, ed. F. M. Powicke and C. R. Cheney, 88, 190, 234, 636. None of the Florentine synodal statutes mentioned the canon law prohibition against monks and nuns becoming godparents. Perhaps this was because the bishop had few religious under his authority. Trexler, *Synodal Law,* 86-91, 91-102.

49. Trexler, *Synodal Law,* 272.

50. Lapo Niccolini had one clerical cofather, Matteo Corsini had five clerical or religious cofathers, Giovanni di Matteo Corsini had three, Matteo di Giovanni Corsini and Buonoccorso Pitti each had two, Gregorio Dati had thirteen.

51. Mansi, 35, 250-51.

52. *Ibid.,* 250-51. At the episcopal court of Constance during the fifteenth and sixteenth centuries the impediment of spiritual kinship was the most frequently discussed of all marital impediments. Thomas M. Safley, *Let No Man Put Asunder: The Control of Marriage in the German Southwest: A Comparative Study, 1550-1600* (Kirksville, 1984), 22. Sexual regulations among baptismal kin are universal. In Latin America sexual relations between coparents or between godparents and godchildren are especially reprehensible. According to a Yucatan folk myth, coparent incest is worse than mother-son incest. In Teniá, Mexico, coparents who have sexual relations become water snakes. Charles J. Erasmus, "Current Theories on Incest Prohibitions in the Light of Ceremonial Kinship," *Kroeber Anthropological Society Papers* 2 (1950), 44-45. A medieval story told about Robert the Pious demonstrates as well "the tetralogical consequences of intermarriage" among baptismal kin. He married his comother and their first child had "a neck and head like a goose." Georges Duby, *The Knight, The Lady, and The Priest: The Making of Modern Marriage in Medieval France* (New York, 1983), 84-85.

53. San Bernardino, *Le Prediche Volgare,* ed. C. Cannarozzi, Florentine Sermons, 1424, vol. 1, (Pistoia, 1934), 200; Boccaccio, *Decameron,* I:2, IV:2, VI:10, VII:3 and 10, IX:10, and X:4. Louis Haas, "Boccaccio, Baptismal Kinship, and Spiritual Incest," *Renaissance and Reformation/Renaissance et Réforme* 13 (1989), 343-56.

54. Whether people had had sex with a coparent or godchild was one of the questions confessors were to ask regarding the sexual practices of their flock. These warnings were equally addressed to men and women. St. Antoninus, 34v; BNF, Landau Finlay, 288, fols. 20v and 25v.

55. Trexler, *Synodal Law*, 201; see also 235, 267.

56. Julian Pitt-Rivers, "Ritual Kinship in Spain," *Transactions of the New York Academy of Sciences* 20 (1957-58), 425.

57. Mansi, 35, 268.

58. Bistort, 205.

59. Boccaccio, *The Corbaccio*, 155.

60. Mansi, 35, 251; *Ricerche sull'antica e moderna popolazione della città di Firenze per mezzo dei registri di battesimi del Battistero de San Giovanni dal 1451 al 1774* (Florence, 1775), 12.

61. It was only after the Council of Trent limited the scope of baptismal kinship and set the maximum number of godparents at two—one male, one female—that Florentines followed canonical regulations. Children recorded in the Parigi *Ricordi*, written after the Council, have only two godparents recorded—one male, one female. BNF, Manoscritti Palatini, 853, fols. 43rv-44r.

62. Benvenuto Cellini, *Autobiography*, trans. George Bull (New York, 1956), 292.

63. Michael Bennet, "Spiritual Kinship and the Baptismal Name in Traditional Society," in *Principalities, Power and Estates*, ed. L. O. Frappel (Adelaide, 1979), 1-14.

64. Immigrant Italians in turn of the century United States used baptismal kinship precisely in this fashion. Gallatin Anderson, "Il Comparragio: The Italian Godparenthood Complex," *Southwestern Journal of Anthropology* 13 (1957), 32-53.

65. Francesco Guicciardini, *Maxims and Reflections (Ricordi)*, trans. Mario Domandi (1965), 44. For a brief sketch of the importance of friendship in premodern Florence see Gene Brucker, *Renaissance Florence* (1969, 1983), 91-99. Modern Italian baptismal kinship gives participants psychological benefits of affection, intimacy, and security. Anderson, 49.

66. Cellini, *Autobiography*, 35.

67. Friendship is a major component of baptismal kinship. Two of Boccaccio's stories relating baptismal kinship note how baptismal kin visit each other frequently and offer each other hospitality. Boccaccio, *Decameron*, VII:3 and 10. Lapo Niccolino referred to Ser Antonio dall'Ancisa as "Mio compare e intimo amicho e beni volo." *Il Libro degli affari proprii di casa di Lapo di Giovanni Niccolini de' Sirigatti*, ed. C. Bec (Paris, 1969), 130, in Christiane Klapisch-Zuber, *Women, Family, and Ritual in Renaissance Florence* (Chicago, 1985), 88. Lapo Mazzei and Niccolò Machiavelli each used baptismal kinship as a seal on their friendship with others. Origo, *The Merchant of Prato*, 227; Ridolfi, 117. Luca Panzano had his friend Lionardo Bruni, the historian and Florentine chancellor, stand as godfather for his first son. They were friends as well as neighbors. Carnesecchi, 157.

68. Corazzini, 6, 66, 70, 160, 215. See also ASF, CS, 2, 15, fol. 76v; ASF, CS, 2, 16, fol. 15r; ASF, CS, 2, 23, fols. 2r, 3v, 4v, 171r, 174v; ASF, CS, 5, 1461, fol. 13v; ASF,

MS, 85, fol. 99v; ASF, Acquisiti e Doni, 11/1, fols. 10rv, 11v, 17r; ASF, CS, 4, 418, fol. 18r; BNF, Panciatichiano, 134, fol. 2r; BNF, Palatino Baldovinetti, 37, fol. 8r; and BNF, Fondo Nazionale, 2, 2, 357, fol. 55r.

69. Of the 1758 Florentine godparents listed in various *ricordanze* whose identity can be determined, only 37, a mere 2.1 percent, were natural kin of their coparents. Klapisch-Zuber, "Parrains et filleuls," 57. On choices of godparents in Florence see also Louis Haas, "*Il Mio Buono Compare:* Choosing Godparents and the Uses of Baptismal Kinship in Renaissance Florence," *Journal of Social History* 29 (1995), 341-56.

70. Leonida Pandimiglio, "Giovanni di Pagolo Morelli e le strutture familiari," *Archivio Storico Italiano* 136 (1978), 7. Morello Morelli had also just moved into a different quarter. Perhaps he had no friends among the neighbors yet. Morelli, 340.

71. In modern Italian cities the custom is for parents to exchange baptismal kinship ties with friends, which "seems to foster joint social activities and to emphasize friendship bonds between families." Anderson, 38. The same custom prevailed in premodern Florence.

72. Morelli, 194.

73. *Libro degli Affari,* 47-48; Christiane Klapisch-Zuber, "Parenti, amici, vicini," *Quaderni storici* 33 (1976), 971.

74. Ronald F. E. Weissman, *Ritual Brotherhood in Renaissance Florence* (New York, 1982), 18-20. Almost all of his cofathers (87.5 percent) were urban dwellers. Ibid., 16-19.

75. Morelli, 190. For other examples of next-door neighbors as godparents see Brucker, *Giovanni and Lusanna,* 5; Klapisch-Zuber, *Women, Family, and Ritual,* 91-92.

76. D. V. Kent and F. W. Kent, *Neighbours and Neighbourhood in Renaissance Florence: The District of the Red Lion in the Fifteenth Century* (Locust Valley, NY, 1982), 89.

77. Klapisch-Zuber, *Women, Family, and Ritual,* 91.

78. ASF, AD, 11/1, fol. 7r. ASF, CS, 5, 16, fol. 3v. ASF, CS, 3, 271, fol. 37v.

79. Anderson saw this as a double-edged component of baptismal kinship choices. Anderson 49-50. Giovanni della Casa was godparent four times to each of Piero Cavicculi's children. Giovanni was Piero's employer in silk manufacturing and the two dined together frequently. Apparently, they were very close friends. Brucker, *Giovanni and Lusanna,* 96.

80. Petrucci, 93.

81. Dati, 43 and 75.

82. Ibid., 41.

83. Petrucci, 53; ASF, CS, 4, 564, fol. 30v; BNF, Palatino Baldovinetti, 37, fol. 25v.

84. Petrucci, 91. Others listed paupers as coparents. BNF, Nuovi Acquisiti, 260, unpaginated, 23 July 1566 and 12 June 1567; BNF, Palatino Baldovinetti, 37, 30r. On coparents not having to give gifts when contracted "for the love of God," see Klapisch-Zuber, *Women, Family, and Ritual,* 90. Being blind in premodern Italy, according to Peter Burke, meant more than not being able to see. It was a job title. Burke, 35. Being a pauper in premodern Italy meant more than being poor; it too was a job title. In a society dedicated to charity, beggars and the needy provided

an outlet for the exercise of that impulse. They then received a livelihood—though a marginal one at best.

85.   Lapo Mazzei for the most part chose coparents who were poor as an act of charity (it was years before he let his best friend Francesco Datini become his coparent). Origo, *The Merchant of Prato*, 226. In Florence the wealthy took in orphaned children "for the love of God." Herlihy and Klapisch-Zuber, *Tuscans*, 246.

86.   Petrucci, 93.

87.   Weissman, 18.

88.   San Bernardino, Vol. 1, 199-200. For the same practice in the High Middle Ages see Lynch, "Hugh I of Cluny's Sponsorship of Henry IV," *Speculum* 802-3, 813.

89.   Corrazzini, xviii, 6-7, 11, 33, 42, 62, 215 (See Appendix A, Table 1.); Klapisch-Zuber, "Parenti, amici, vicini," 972; *Libro degli Affari*, 18, 47-48.

90.   Pandimiglio, 43; David Herlihy, *Medieval and Renaissance Pistoia: The Social History of an Italian Town* (New Haven, 1967), 196; George Foster, "Godparents and Social Networks in TzinTzunTzan," *Southwestern Journal of Anthropology* 9 (1953), 261-78. Marco Parenti's first son was born in the Mugello, at Ronta, the ancestral home. Five of his six godfathers and five of his six godmothers were from Ronta. Mark Philips, *The Memoir of Marco Parenti: A Life in Medici Florence* (Princeton, 1987), 45; ASF, CS, 2, 17bis, fol. 2r.

91.   In 1411, for instance, Dati had all his fellow standard- bearers of the militia become his cofathers. Dati, 76. Paolo Niccolini invited his fellow priors of the Signoria and the Gonfalonier to be his daughter's godfathers in 1445; Gino Capponi had his fellow members of the Dieci della Balia to be his coparents in March, 1451; Niccolò Baldovinetti had his 13 fellow Ufficiali della Torre members become godfathers to his son. One of Machiavelli's cofathers was the first chancellor of the Republic, Marcello Virgilio. Ginevra Niccolini di Camugliano, *The Chronicles of a Florentine Family 1200-1470* (London, 1933), 129; Maria Teresa Sillano, ed., *Le Ricordanze di Giovanni Chellini da San Miniato: medico, mercante e umanista (1425-1457)* (Milan, 1984), 185; BNF, Palatino Baldovinetti, 37, fol. 33v. Ridolfi, 74-75. In July 1455, Bartolomeo Valori recorded a number of godfathers for his daughter and wrote that one man held her at baptism "come procuratore" for the others. BNF, Panciatichiano, 134, fol. 5v. Iacopo Delmanno held Gostanza Bartolomei at baptism, representing the other eight office-holders. ASF, AD, 11/1, fol. 6r.

92.   "Symbolically, if not in law," said Trexler, "the infant was sponsored by the structures of Florence." Unlike other individuals in Florence, the Medici considered the city itself their neighborhood. Trexler, *Public Life*, 428.

93.   In 1425, Luca Pitti, Buonoccorso's son, was commissioner at the town of Malespina. Luca's son, who was born during his father's term as commissioner, had citizens from Malespina as his godparents. *Cronica di Buonaccorso Pitti con annotazioni ristampata da Alberto Bacchi della Lega* (Bologna, 1905), 82. Klapisch-Zuber, ""Parrains et filleuls," 57. In 1436, while Matteo Corsini was Captain of Pistoia, his cofathers were citizens from Pistoia. While serving as administrator of Monte Spertoli, Buonaccorso Pitti had the town as his coparent. While vicar of Alpe di Firenzuola, Giovanni di Matteo Corsini had that town as his coparent. In January 1387, while vicar of Pescia, Lapo Curianni had five

townsmen representing the whole town as his cofathers. Petrucci, 138, 144; *Cronica*, 82; ASF, MS, 77, fol. 52r. In these last two instances proctors representing the town stood at the font. Ambassadors as well could represent the state in baptismal kinship. Donald E. Queller, *The Office of Ambassador in the Middle Ages* (Princeton, 1967), 49, 100.

94. Martines, *Power and Imagination*, 121.

95. American administrators in the Philippines during the late nineteenth and early twentieth centuries found the same advantage in becoming *compadres* with the Filipino elite. N. Owen, *Compadre Colonialism: Studies in the Philippines under American Rule* (Ann Arbor, 1973); D. Steinberg, "Why the Philippines are Neither Here nor There—Compadre Colonialism," *New Republic* 187 (1982), 19-23. On Douglas MacArthur's close ties with his *compadre*, Manuel Quezon, the president of the Commonwealth of the Philippines, see William Manchester, *American Caesar: Douglas MacArthur 1880-1964* (Boston, 1978), 178, 199, 264.

96. Trexler, *Public Life*, 5.

97. Ibid., 285.

98. A. Rochon, *La Jeunesse de Laurent De Médicis 1449-1476* (Paris, 1963), 203; Angelo Fabronio, *Adnotiones et Monumenta Laurentii Medicis Magnifici vitam pertinentia*, vol. 2 (Pisa, 1784), 57.

99. Trexler, *Public Life*, 18.

100. Morelli, 149-50.

101. Trexler, *Public Life*, 13; Kent and Kent, 24-47; *Cronica*, 176; Gene Brucker, *Giovanni and Lusanna*, 70.

102. Morelli, 199, 337, 380, 452. Others listed *guardadonne* as comothers (Petrucci, 139; ASF, CS, 2, 17, fol. 66r) or midwives (ASF, CS, 5, 11, fol. 131v; ASF, MS, 85, fol. 103r).

103. ASF, CS, 3, 275, fol. 7v; ASF, CS, 2, 11, fol. 48; Morelli, 359; Cellini, *La Vita*, 456.

104. One of Morello Morelli's comothers was the wetnurse of his nephew, Antonio, Giovanni's son. Morelli, 359. Lena Petrucci's godmother was her brother's wetnurse. ASF, CS, 2, 15, fol. 21v. Francesco di Tommaso Giovanni recalled that his most frequent choices for coparents were monks, midwives, and wetnurses, all "for the love of God." Klapisch-Zuber, *Women, Family, and Ritual*, 90. In premodern Spain midwives were known as *comadres de parir*, thus reflecting how often they became real comothers. Teresa Ortiz, "From Hegemony to Subordination: Midwives in Early Modern Spain," in *The Art of Midwifery: Early Modern Midwives in Europe*, edited by Hilary Marland (London, 1993), 95.

105. See below chapters IV and V in this volume; Klapisch-Zuber, *Women, Family, and Ritual*, 132-64.

106. Cellini, *La Vita*, 458.

107. San Bernardino, Vol. 1, 198-201.

108. San Bernardino, Vol. 1, 199. Boccaccio, *Decameron*, VII:3. According to Giovanni Dominici, the child at baptism does not make a virtuous act; this is done for him by the parents and godparents. Dominici, 38. Under the rubric entitled *Misericordia Spirituale* (Spiritual Charity) in a Florentine confessor's manual the priest was to ask the penitents if they had forgiven their trespassers, prayed to God for their relatives, and become godparents to children. BNF, Landau Finlay, 288, fols.

30r-31r. Niccolò Baldovinetti called his children's godfathers *nonni* (grandfathers). He is the only writer of *ricordanze* I have seen that did this. BNF, Palatino Baldovinetti, 37, fols. 7v-8r.

109. Boccaccio, *Decameron*, I:2.

110. San Bernardino, I, 198-201.

111. BNF, Landau Finlay, 288, 31r.

112. Corrazzini, iv-v. A Florentine couple discovered a foundling, took it to the Innocenti, and asked the officials if they could be its godparents. Trexler, "Foundlings of Florence," 264.

113. Klapisch-Zuber, *Women, Family, and Ritual*, 88; Cellini, *La Vita*, 197; Fabroni, 75; Origo, *Merchant of Prato*, 227, 230; Fabroni, 75; ASF, CS, 3, 49, *Libro di lettere scritte a Filippo Strozzi dalla Signora Clarice, sua moglie, Francesco del Nero ed altri*, fols. 3, 4, 6, 7, 10-11, 13-15, 17-20, 22-31.

114. Cellini, *La Vita*, 101.

115. Boccaccio, *Decameron*, IX:10.

116. Kent and Kent, 29-30; Origo, *Merchant of Prato*, 231; Klapisch-Zuber, "Parrains et filleuls," 73 n. 36.

117. Michael Herzfeld, "When Exceptions Define the Rules: Greek Baptismal Names and the Negotiation of Identity," *Journal of Anthropological Research* 38 (1982), 297.

118. Origo, *Merchant of Prato*, 226. See also Carnesecchi, 170, on gift-giving. On the concept of baptismal gift-giving and honor see Klapisch-Zuber, *Women, Family, and Ritual*, 90.

119. ASF, CS, 2, 9, fol. 11v. See also ASF, CS, 4, 418, fol. 9v; BNF, Palatino Baldovinetti, 35, fols. 33r, 35r.

120. Boccaccio, *Corbaccio*, 155.

121. *Cronica di Buonaccorso Pitti*, 29. Alessandro Perosa, ed., *Giovanni Rucellai ed il suo Zibaldone* vol. 1 *Il Zibaldone Quaresimale* (London, 1960), 35; ASF, CS, 5, 11, fol. 59r; Sillano, 185.

122. *Ricordanze di Bartolomeo Masi*, 240. Despite his contention, elsewhere in premodern Europe gift-giving among baptismal kin was common. And in Italy gift-giving is still a salient feature of baptismal kinship, as it is world wide. Anderson, 36.

123. ASF, CS, 2, 9, fol. 22v. See also NTF, 640 and BNF, Palatino Baldovinetti, 42, fol. 11r.

124. Sillano, 197. Others were just as generous. Niccolò Guidotti noted how he placed coins worth seven lire, ten soldi in one godson's swaddling cloth; and seven lire, six soldi, eight denari in another's swaddling cloth. ASF, CS, 2, 29, fol. 215r. At that time the florin-to-lira ratio would have been about one to eight. Goldthwaite, *The Building of Renaissance Florence: An Economic and Social History* (Baltimore, 1980), 430. Tribaldo Rossi only put two grossi in the swaddling cloth of his godson, Piero Guicciardini, on 14 June 1490. BNF, Fondo Nazionale, 2, 2, 357, fol. 55r. In the 1490s, Tommaso Guidetti was placing two to four grossi in his godchildren's swaddling cloth. When he became a godfather in 1501 he was able to place eight grossi in his goddaughter's swaddling cloth. ASF, CS, 4, 418, fols. 21r, 23r, 25r, 43r. See also ASF, CS, 4, 71, fol. 42r.

125. On the ritual for the bride see Origo, *Merchant of Prato*, 204; for the point that a coin as gift to a child meant its hope for riches see Jacques Gélis, *History of Childbirth: Fertility, Pregnancy and Birth in Early Modern Europe* (Cambridge, 1991), 190, 203-04.

126. Philip Gavitt, *Charity and Children in Renaissance Florence: The Ospedale degli Innocenti, 1410-1536*, (Ann Arbor, 1990), 196; Trexler, "Foundlings of Florence," 282-83 n. 68. A bag of salt around its neck meant the child had not been baptized. John Boswell, *The Kindness of Strangers: The Abandonment of Children in Western Europe from Late Antiquity to the Renaissance* (New York, 1988), 400; Trexler, "Foundlings of Florence," 269.

127. Trexler, *Public Life*, 443.

128. *Libro degli Affari*, 68; See also Klapisch-Zuber, *Women, Family, and Ritual*, 88, 90 on these instances with Lapo Niccolini.

129. F. W. Kent, *Household and Lineage in Renaissance Florence: The Family Life of the Capponi, Ginori, and Rucellai* (Princeton, 1977), 238; For Catherine of Siena see Rudolph M. Bell, *Holy Anorexia* (Chicago, 1985), 196 n. 13. Giovanni Dino Amica used his comother to make payments to his child's wetnurse. BNF, Palatino Baldovinetti, 42, fol. 11r. A coparent was often an intermediary for all sorts of things. Giovanni della Casa's cofather arranged for him to meet Lusanna. Brucker, *Giovanni and Lusanna*, 28-29.

130. Dominici, 39.

131. ASF, CS, 4, 563, fol. 1v; Morelli, 118, 172; ASF, CS, 4, 418, fol. 10v; ASF, CS, 2, 9, fol. 90v; Trexler, "Foundlings of Florence,"272. Boccaccio, *Decameron* V:7, VII:7.

132. Klapisch-Zuber, *Women, Family, and Ritual*, 288.

133. Corrazzini, 140. See also ibid., 66 and 215; BNF, Fondo Nazionale, 2, 2, 357, fol. 11r; BNF, Panciatichiano, 134, fol. 3v; ASF, CS, 5, 16, fol. 2r; ASF, AD, 11/1 fols. 9rv, 11v, 15r; ASF, AD 190, 3a, fol. 20r; ASF, CS, 2, 11, fol. 42r; BNF, Panciatichiano, 134, fol. 5v.

134. Leon Battista Alberti, *The Family in Renaissance Florence: I Libri dell famiglia*, trans. Rene'e Neu Watkins (Columbia, 1969), 122-23.

135. Klapisch-Zuber, *Women, Family, and Ritual*, 283-309. Of the 266 Florentines recorded with the names of their godparents listed, only 2.63 percent had the same name as one of the godparents. Perhaps the low status of these Florentine godparents relative to the parents explains why they had no choice in the names—a phenomenon that occurred in premodern Spanish naming patterns. Herzfeld, 296.

136. David Herlihy, "Tuscan Names, 1200-1530," *Renaissance Quarterly* 41 (1988), 565-70, 573. He argued that compound names were rare before 1427, which is erroneous. They were not rare; Florentines just did not use their second names in official records, like the *Catasto*. Herlihy, "Tuscan Names," 574. Certainly, with up to three names to choose, Florentines could name their children after a variety of things, for a variety of reasons, and pursue a variety of strategies. For an examination of naming patterns in Medieval London see Hanawalt, *Growing Up in Medieval London*, 46-49.

137. ASF, CS, 4, 418, fol. 33r. See also ASF, CS, 2, 9, fol. 22r.

138. Klapisch-Zuber *Women, Family, and Ritual*, 283-309.

139. Herlihy, "Tuscan Names," 571 n. 31. Moreover, she based her interpretation really on only one comment—and that by a child. One offhand comment does not make an anthropological ritual. In premodern Spain the remaking of the name only remade the name—not the individual. Herzfeld, 292-93.

140. ASF, CS, 4, 418, fol. 10v.

141. Morelli, 117; ASF, CS, 2, 16, fol. 8r; ASF, CS, 2, 4, fol. 16r. Giovanni Rucellai recorded that his grandson was born in 1468 and his son "ponemo nome Chosimo, per memoria di Chosimo di Giovanni de'Medici, suo bisalvo." Perosa, 35.

142. BNF, Fondo Nazionale, 2, 2, 357, fol. 73v. Philips, 48.

143. Klapisch-Zuber, Women, Family, and Ritual, 301. "To bear the name of an ancestor," said Herlihy, "was of course to commemorate him or her." Herlihy, "Tuscan Names," 570.

144. Klapisch-Zuber, Women, Family, and Ritual, 293.

145. BNF, Nuovi Acquisisti, 1207, fol. 7; Morelli, 140 and 190; ASF, AD, 190, 3a, fol. 3v; ASF, MS, 88, fol. 140r. According to Thomas Kuehn, one way to show respect for one's father was to name a son after him. Thomas Kuehn, "Honor and Conflict in a Fifteenth-Century Florentine Family," Ricerche Storiche 10 (1980), 296. ASI, 1, 4, (1843), 42; ASF, CS, 5, 22, fol. 94r; ASF, CS, 4, 71, fol. 23r; Sillano, 185; ASF, CS, 2, 13, fol. 16r.

146. BNF, Manoscritti Palatini, 1129, fols. 42v and 50r; Morelli, 195, 425; ASF, CS, 5, 11, fols. 119v, 156v; ASF, CS, 2, 16, fol. 8r; ASF, MS, 77, fol. 52r; ASF, CS, 5, 11, fol. 147r; BNF, Panciatichiano, 134, fol. 62r; ASF, MS, 77, fol. 51v; ASF, CS, 5, 22, fol. 94r; ASF, CS, 2, 3, fol. 85r; ASF, CS, 2, 16bis, fol. 4r.

147. ASF, CS, 2, 9, fols. 90v and 112r; ASF, CS, 4, 74, fol. 50v; Morelli, 380; ASF, CS, 5, 11, fol. 10v; ASI, 1, 4, (1843), 43; BNF, Manoscritti Palatini, 1129, fol. 49r; Sillano, 196.

148. According to Klapisch-Zuber, the father, not the mother chose the name of a child. If the mother chose the name this represented an "exceptional" occurrence. Women, Family, and Ritual, 288. This seems doubtful, considering evidence from the ricordanze. Moreover, although she made this bold conclusion, elsewhere in her footnotes she provides instances of wives choosing names that appear less than exceptional. Ibid., 289 n. 12. She also noted how Alessandra Strozzi tried to control the naming policies of her sons. Ibid., 308-09 n. 63. Filippo Strozzi's widow renamed their son, Giovanbatista, Filippo after the death of her husband. BNF MS Palatino 490, fol. 1r. Bartolomeo Masi even recorded this name change. Corrazzini, 14.

149. Cellini, Autobiography, 19; BNF, Fondo Nazionale, 2, 2, 357, fol. 173v.

150. BNF, Manoscritti Palatini, 1129, fol. 50r.

151. Morelli, 118, 135; Two Memoirs, 116; ASI, 1, 4, (1843), 42; ASF, MS, 77, fol. 51v; BNF, Panciatichi, 101, fol. 31r; ASF, CS, 4, 71, fol. 30v; BNF, Manoscritti Palatini, 1129, fol. 98r; ASF, CS, 2, 3, fol. 74r.

152. ASF, MS, 77, fol. 51r.

153. Two Memoirs, 115, 127. See also ASF, AD, 19, fol. 19v; Camugliano, 183; ASF, CS, 4, 564, fol. 30v; BNF, Palatino Baldovinetti, 37, fol. 30r.

154. BNF, Panciatichi, 101, fol. 20v.

155. BNF, Palatino Baldovinetti, fols. 23v, 34r.
156. Herlihy, "Tuscan Names," 571.
157. BNF, Fondo Nazionale 2, 3, 280 (Bargiacchi), fol. 10r; BNF, Panciatichiano, 134, fol. 5v.
158. Herlihy, "Tuscan Names," 572-73.
159. Klapisch-Zuber, Women, Family, and Ritual, 293-94.
160. Herlihy, "Tuscan Names," 576.
161. Ibid., 578-79; Preachers in Tuscany advised parents to place children under the protection of saints in this fashion. Klapisch-Zuber, Women, Family, and Ritual, 294, 301.
162. Two Memoirs, 127-28. For other similar accounts see Sillano, 185; ASF, CS, 5, 22, fol. 90r; ASF, CS, 5, 1461, fols. 17r, 21r; ASF, CS, 4, 71, fol. 30v; BNF, Panciatichiano, fol. 5v; ASF, CS, 5, 11, fol. 147v; BNF, Palatino Baldovinetti, fol. 8v; BNF, Manoscritti Palatini, 1129, fol.42v; Morelli, 183, 190, 195, 452, 457. On the benefit of saints' names see Herzfeld, 294.
163. Klapisch-Zuber, Women, Family, and Ritual, 294.
164. Ibid., 293. For instance, Lionara e Romola Strozzi or Barone Marco Romolo Bonaccorsi. ASF, CS, 5, 22, fol. 90r; ASF, CS, Aquisti e Doni, 19, fol. 34r.
165. Klapisch-Zuber, Women, Family, and Ritual, 293; ASF, CS, 4, 71, fol. 23r.
166. Klapisch-Zuber, Women, Family, and Ritual, 292. Almost all the children who died after baptism in the Corsini ricordanze were named Giovanni or Giovanna. Petrucci, 93.
167. Ibid., 93.
168. Judith C. Brown, Immodest Acts: The Life of a Lesbian Nun in Renaissance Italy (Oxford, 1986), 22; Boccaccio, Decameron III:8.
169. Herlihy, "Tuscan Names," 578-79, 581; Klapisch-Zuber, Women, Family, and Ritual, 301.
170. ASI, 1, 4, (1843), 40. He noted as well that he would have the boy become a Franciscan. Others were devoted to St. Francis and named a child for him. ASF, CS, 4, 346, fol. 90v.
171. Two Memoirs, 117.
172. Klapisch-Zuber Women, Family, and Ritual, 290; BNF, Manoscritti Palatini, 1129, fols. 48r, 76v, and 105v.
173. Boccaccio, Decameron, VI:8.
174. The writers for the most part noted that although the children had formal names the family would call them by their nicknames. Morelli, 172, 174, 177-78; Bell, 30, Two Memoirs, 128. ASF, CS, 2, 17bis, fol. 78r.
175. BNF, Nuovi Acquisiti, 457, fol. 196.
176. BNF, Palatino Baldovinetti, 37, fol. 33v.
177. Bell, 171.
178. ASI, 1, 4, (1843), 43-44.
179. According to Richard Trexler, "[h]aving arrived in the house, infants were promptly sent into the countryside with a wetnurse." Richard C. Trexler, "Infanticide in Florence: New Sources and First Results," Journal of Psychohistory 1 (1973), 100.

Chapter IV

1. BNF, Fondo Nazionale, 2, 2, 357, fols. 11r-12r.

2. Sussman, whose *Selling Mother's Milk* is a comprehensive study of the practice in premodern and modern France, stated that he had frequently encountered descriptions of wetnursing in the records and literature but that he "had never bothered to question the alien and antiquated custom of wet-nursing." George D. Sussman, *Selling Mother's Milk: The Wet-Nursing Business in France 1715-1914* (Urbana, 1982), ix. There is even some good evidence, including statistical, for the practice in ancient history; see Keith R. Bradley, "Sexual Regulations in Wet-nursing contracts from Roman Egypt," *Klio* 62 (1980), 321-25; "Wet-nursing at Rome: A Study in Social Relations," in Beryl Rawson, ed., *The Family in Ancient Rome: New Perspectives* (1986), 170-200. Many medieval female saints' lives contain references to their wanting to breastfeed the infant Jesus. David Herlihy, *Medieval Households* (Cambridge, MA, 1985), 120. They wanted, I think, to become his wetnurse.

3. This negative opinion is so commonplace that it has appeared at the introductory textbook level. John P. McKay, Bennett D. Hill, and John Buckler, *A History of Western Society*, 4th ed. (Boston, 1991), 634-36. In her otherwise excellent survey of childhood in the Middle Ages, Shulamith Shahar misunderstood what wetnursing was and how and why people utilized it. She wrongly saw it as a form of abandonment practiced only by the elite. Shulamith Shahar, *Childhood in the Middle Ages* (London, 1990), 53-76.

4. James Bruce Ross, "The Middle Class Child in Urban Italy, Fourteenth to Early Sixteenth Century," in Lloyd deMause, ed., *The History of Childhood* (New York, 1974), 185, 190, 194-95. Ross may have overstated her case here. See Luke Demaitre, "The Idea of Childhood and Childcare in Medical Writings of the Middle Ages," *Journal of Psychohistory* 4 (1977), 487. Historians seem to be too influenced by this negative view of wetnursing. Shulamith Shahar, for instance, after noting the positive view of wetnursing put forth by the humanist Francesco da Barberino, went on to conclude that in general wetnursing was a wretched practice. *The Fourth Estate: A History of Women in the Middle Ages* (London, 1983), 183-85.

5. Diane Owen Hughes referred to it as "nursery exile." "Domestic Ideals and Social Behavior: Evidence from Medieval Genoa," in *The Family in History*, ed. Charles E. Rosenberg (Philadelphia, 1975), 132. Barbara Kay Greenleaf observed that for the Florentine patriciate one "of the 'noble' customs they liked best was hiring wet nurses, and they didn't care a fig for the woman's supposedly polluted milk." *Children through the Ages: A History of Childhood* (New York, 1978), 42-43. Charles de la Roncière noted that "affluent Italians were the first to send their children off to a wet-nurse. Young widows in their haste to remarry abandoned infants still at the breast." "Tuscan Notables on the Eve of the Renaissance," in *A History of Private Life*, ed. Philippe Ariès and Georges Duby, vol. 2, *Revelations of the Medieval World*, ed. Georges Duby (Cambridge, MA, 1988), 275. According to Christiane Klapisch-Zuber, "with a nurse, he would be less carefully watched

over and less well cared for, he would live in hygienic conditions worse than those of the city, and his life would depend on the regularity of the family's payment to the nurse . . . the bourgeois baby, which was sent off to a nurse immediately after birth and which, if it had died in her care, would never even have been known to its parents." *Women, Family, and Ritual in Renaissance Italy* (Chicago, 1985), 105, 328. These negative views have been reiterated in some recent works on childhood in the premodern era. Clarissa Atkinson, *The Oldest Vocation: Christian Motherhood in the Middle Ages* (Ithaca, 1991), 158; Michael Goodich, *From Birth to Old Age: The Human Life Cycle in Medieval Thought, 1250-1350* (Lanham, 1989), 87.

      Herlihy and Klapisch-Zuber emphasized the physical risks inherent to wetnursing. David Herlihy and Christiane Klapisch-Zuber, *Tuscans and their Families: A Study of the Florentine Catasto of 1427* (New Haven, 1985), 147. Richard Trexler emphasized the psychological risks, especially separation anxiety, inherent to wetnursing. *Public Life in Renaissance Florence* (New York, 1980), 89, 162. This double danger—the physical and psychological risks to the child—inherent to wetnursing is examined by Randolph Trumbach, *Rise of the Egalitarian Family: Aristocratic Kinship and Domestic Relations* (New York, 1978) 187-88, 197.

6.   Richard Trexler, "Infanticide in Florence: New Sources and First Results," *Journal of Psychohistory* 1 (1973), 100.

7.   Klapisch-Zuber, *Women, Family, and Ritual,* 105. She does not provide any figures to show that these differences are statistically significant. Anthony Molho also struck a cautious note regarding reading too much into male and female differences whenever the percentage difference is low and the sample size is small: "given the relative modesty in the size of the sample, it would be hard to make much of so small a difference." Anthony Molho, *Marriage Alliance in Late Medieval Florence* (Cambridge, 1994), 248-49.

8.   San Bernardino, *Prediche Volgari,* ed. Banchi, II, 159-60, in Iris Origo, *The Merchant of Prato Francesco di Marco Datini 1335-1410* (New York, 1957), 215.

9.   Herlihy and Klapisch-Zuber, 147 n. 55.

10.   One humanist argument against wetnursing was that it was not natural. God had provided mothers with breastmilk, and even animals nursed their own offspring. Jack Goody, *The Development of the Family and Marriage in Europe* (Cambridge, 1983), 69-70. During the Enlightenment, this argument from nature influenced the scientific debate about the classification of animals. Londa Schiebinger, "Why Mammals Are Called Mammals: Gender Politics in Eighteenth-Century Natural History," *American Historical Review* 98 (1993), 382-411.

11.   Ross, "The Middle Class Child," 185. While it is commonplace to observe that humanism, to some extent, was merely mindless adoption of the precepts of classical literature, it is a concept that can explain something about the motives and even actions of the humanists. Much of the rhetoric in the Enlightenment's critique of wetnursing stemmed from the classics and humanists. Sussman noted that the underlying motive for the Enlightenment critique of wetnursing came from a desire to decrease infant mortality "to reverse the depopulation which they perceived to be the trend of their time, and thereby to promote the economic

and military strength of the nation." Sussman, 3, 28-29. Florence in the fourteenth, fifteenth, and sixteenth centuries too was faced with severe depopulation, economic woes, and military crises, which likewise may explain the humanists' critique of wetnursing.

12. Francesco Barbaro, *On Wifely Duties*, trans. Benjamin G. Kohl, in *The Earthly Republic: Italian Humanists on Government and Society*, ed. Benjamin G. Kohl and Ronald Witt (Philadelphia, 1978), 221-22. On this see also Herlihy, *Medieval Households*, 120. On Barbaro and the family see Margaret Leah King, "Caldiera and the Barbaros on marriage and the family: humanist reflections of Venetian realities," *The Journal of Medieval and Renaissance Studies* 6 (1976), 19-50. Barbaro argued that mothers nursing their children followed nature's laws. Barbaro, 223. When humanists cited nature (animal mothers nursing their own offspring) as a reason for maternal breastfeeding, they relied on the opinions of classical authors, who also used the argument from nature in support of maternal breastfeeding. Barbaro, for instance, relied on Plutarch's life of Marius to argue for maternal breastfeeding. Barbaro, 222-23.

13. Leon Battista Alberti, *The Family in Renaissance Florence: I Libri della famiglia*, trans. Renée Neu Watkins (Columbia, 1969), 53-54.

14. Giovanni Dominici noted how close the wetnurse was to her charge by observing that she was the one "out of whose hands he is never taken." Giovanni Domenici, *Regola del Governo di Cura Familiare Parte Quarte: On the Education of Children*, trans. Arthur Basil Coté (Washington D. C., 1927), 41. The fact that the verb *nutrire* could mean both suckle and educate during the medieval and Renaissance period implies this as well. Shahar, *Children in the Middle Ages*, 278 n. 16.

15. San Bernardino of Siena, *Sermons*, selected and ed. Don N. Orlandi, trans. H. J. Robbins (Siena, 1920), 89-90; in Ross, "The Middle Class Child," 186.

16. Ross, "The Middle Class Child," 188.

17. Matteo Palmieri even feared the great numbers (in his mind) of non-Florentines, including Tartars and even Saracens, who served as wetnurses. de la Roncière, 279. Alberti's critique of wetnursing stemmed on the whole from the fact that the wetnurse did not have the same character and morality as did the mother. Alberti, 53-54. See also Barbaro, 223. Margaret King, in her survey of Venetian humanists' opinions on the family, concluded that their arguments for maternal breastfeeding or for hiring an excellent nurse were designed "to guarantee the moral as well as physical health" of the child. King, "Caldiera and the Barbaros," 45.

18. Samuel Kline Cohn, Jr., *The Laboring Classes in Renaissance Florence* (New York, 1980), 108-10. Alberti exhibited both a dislike and a distrust of the peasantry. Alberti, 189.

19. On the misogynist tendency of the Renaissance see Joan Kelly-Gadol, "Did Women have a Renaissance?" in Renate Bridenthal and Claudia Koontz, eds., *Becoming Visible: Women in European History* (1977), 137-61.

20. Ross, "The Middle Class Child," 185-86; Donald R. Kelley, *The Beginning of Ideology: Consciousness and Society in the French Reformation* (Cambridge, 1981), 73. This sort of sexism continues within the present-day historical literature. For as nuanced and refined an approach to family history as they put forth, Richard

Saller and David Kertzer still interpret wetnursing as evidence of maternal—not paternal—detachment. Richard P. Saller and David I. Kertzer, "Historical and Anthropological Perspectives on Italian Family Life," in *The Family in Italy: From Antiquity to the Present*, ed. Richard P. Saller and David I. Kertzer (New Haven, 1991), 16.

21. David Hunt, *Parents and Children in History: The Psychology of Family Life in Early Modern France* (New York, 1970), 102; Goody, 68. Sussman also concluded that the Enlightenment critique of wetnursing had very little effect on actual practices as well. Francesco da Barberino, *Del reggimento e de' costumi delle donne*, ed. Guglielmo Manzi (Milan, 1842), 223-37. The Venetian Barbero said it was alright to hire a wetnurse if there were "compelling reasons," which he left undefined. Barbero, 225. Ross, "The Middle Class Child," 183-85, 187.

22. Sussman, 22-25, 207-8; Goody, 69, 71; David Ransel, *Mothers of Misery: Child Abandonment in Russia* (Princeton, 1988), 207-8, 235, 301; Linda Pollock, *Forgotten Children: Parent-Child Relations from 1500 to 1900* (Cambridge, 1983), 212-13; Miriam Slater, *Family Life in the Seventeenth Century: The Verneys of Claydon House* (London, 1984), 19; James R. Lehning, "Family Life and Wetnursing in a French Village," *Journal of Interdisciplinary History* 12 (1982), 645-56. Wetnursing was widespread elsewhere in Europe before World War I; see Valerie Fildes, *Wet Nursing: A History from Antiquity to the Present* (Oxford, 1988). We also find wetnurses in the homes of Roman elite and non-elite and even in the households of slaves. Susan Dixon, *The Roman Family* (Baltimore, 1992), 8.

23. For an opposing view to the ubiquity of wetnursing in Florence see Demaitre, 487.

24. Richard C. Trexler, "The Foundlings of Florence, 1395-1455," *Journal of Psychohistory* 1 (1973), 284; *Idem*, "Infanticide in Florence," 103, 106.

25. David I. Kertzer, *Sacrificed for Honor: Italian Infant Abandonment and the Politics of Reproductive Control* (Boston, 1993), 82, 113-14, 145.

26. Klapisch-Zuber *Women, Family, and Ritual,* 156; Giovanni Boccaccio, *The Corbaccio,* trans. and ed. Anthony K. Cassell (Urbana, 1975), 161-64; Iris Origo, "The Domestic Enemy: Eastern Slaves in Tuscany in the Fourteenth and Fifteenth Centuries," *Speculum* 30 (1955), 338; Boccaccio, *The Decameron,* trans. Mark Musa and Peter Bondanella (New York,1982), 98, 234; Alberti, 215; Diana Robin, "Review of Robert Black, *Benedetto Accolti and the Florentine Renaissance,*" *Renaissance Quarterly* 40 (1987), 762; Origo, *Merchant of Prato,* 125; Richard A. Goldthwaite, "The Florentine Palace as Domestic Architecture," *The American Historical Review* 77 (1972), 1009; ASF, CS, 5, 15, fol. 100r; ASF, CS, 1, 60, fol. 44; Hughes, "Domestic Ideals," 131-32.

27. ASI, 1, 4, 43, and 45.

28. ASF, CS, 2, 17bis, fols. 18v, 28v, 33v, 35r, 39v, 41v, 45v. On the other hand, writers of *ricordanze* could be very haphazard in their wetnursing accounts. Luca Panzano recorded in the birth account of his children that he sent them off to a wetnurse. He left a blank space in this announcement to record the folio number where he would list the details of their stay at the wetnurse. He only filled this in for his first child—the details of his other children's stay at the wetnurse were

unrecorded, though he did mention that he had recorded the payment schedules in another journal. ASF, CS, 2, 9, fols. 28v and 38rv. Ser Piero Bonaccorsi also noted the existence of wetnurses for his children but did not always record the account. ASF, AD, 21, fols. 6rv and 72v. Many *ricordanze* that list births have no evidence of hiring a wetnurse. A. Petrucci, ed., *Il Libro di Ricordanze dei Corsini (1362-1457)*, (Rome, 1965), 147; ASF, MS, 88 *passim.* Typically, historians who have looked at wetnursing practices in Florence have used this as proof that not all children went to the wetnurse or that not all parents utilized wetnursing. While these propositions may be true, this evidence does not necessarily prove it. The absence of wetnursing accounts in the *ricordanze* may just mean the absence of a record rather than the absence of the practice. Moreover, some writers of *ricordanze* recorded payments to a wetnurse without having made any note of having children. NTF, 307; BNF, Nuovi Acquisiti, 495, 5v.

29. ASF, MS, 89, fol. 18r; ASF, CS, 5, 12, fol. 37v; ASF, CS, 5, 11, index; Giovanni di Pagolo Morelli, *Ricordi,* ed. Vittore Branca (Florence, 1969), 159.

30. Klapisch-Zuber, *Women, Family, and Ritual,* 133.

31. Kertzer noted how foundlings represented an increase in a rural household's size; they became, temporarily, members of the family. Kertzer, *Sacrificed for Honour,* 152. So too would nurslings.

32. ASF, CS, 4, 564, 30r.

33. Ross, "The Middle Class Child," 186; Judith Schneid Lewis, *In the Family Way: Childbearing in the British Aristocracy 1760-1860* (New Brunswick, 1986), 209-13; Alberti, 53. This method, of course, was not foolproof. Catherine of Siena's mother noted that except for Catherine all her attempts at nursing her own children ended because she had become pregnant again. Rudolph M. Bell, *Holy Anorexia* (Chicago, 1985), 30. And as we will see, the most frequent cause for broken nursing contracts was the pregnancy of the nurse.

34. ASF, CS, 2, 10, fols. 8r, 10v, 16v, 17v, 24r, 30v, 46r, 77v. See also ASF, CS, 2, 7, 122v.

35. Alberti, 53. Alessandro Perosa, ed., *Giovanni Rucellai ed il suo Zibaldone* (London, 1960), 13; Ross, "The Middle Class Child," 186, 188; Boccaccio, *Decameron,* V:7.

36. David Hunt, 120; Ross, "The Middle Class Child," 185-86; Sussman, 3, 80, 86.

37. Francesco da Barberino, for one, thought the colostrum unhealthy for children. Ross, "The Middle Class Child," 185. Klapisch-Zuber, *Women, Family, and Ritual,* 137 n. 19; Valerie A. Fildes, *Breast, Bottles and Babies: A History of Infant Feeding* (Edinburgh, 1986), 201; J. E. Goldthorpe, *Family Life in Western Societies: A Historical Sociology of Family Relationships in Britain and North America* (Cambridge, 1987), 18. In reality, of course, colostrum is extremely healthy and helpful for the child.

38. ASI, 1, 4, (1843), 55.

39. Gene Brucker, ed., *The Society of Renaissance Florence: A Documentary Study* (New York, 1971), 19.

40. Bell, 159. St. Veronica (b. 1660) would not nurse her own children on fast days but would nurse the children of the poor. Bell, 58-59. A Colonial New England diarist noted that for three days his wife could not express any breastmilk so her friends offered to breastfeed their son. Rose Lockwood, "Birth, Illness, and Death in 18th-Century New England," *Journal of Social History* 12 (1978), 122.

Difficulty in breastfeeding seems to have been common in the premodern world, and is certainly related to the mother's poor nutrition. Pollock, 213-14.

41. Alberti, 54. Italian folklore describes old women who suddenly begin to lactate to feed their grandchildren whose parents had died in the plague. Fildes, *Breasts, Bottles and Babies*, 53.

42. Origo, *The Merchant of Prato*, 177.

43. C. Carnesecchi, "Un fiorentino del secolo XV e le sue ricordanze domestiche," ASI, 5, 4, (1889), 155.

44. Origo, *The Merchant of Prato*, 212-13.

45. Bernardo Machiavelli, *Libro di Ricordi*, ed. Cesare Olschki (Florence, 1954), 24.

46. Ross, "The Middle Class Child," 186; Perosa, 13.

47. Having a wetnurse could then become a symbol of high status. David Hunt, 105.

48. Barbaro, 221.

49. Demaitre, 474.

50. David Hunt, 107.

51. Lewis, 212.

52. Sommerville, *The Rise and Fall*, 80.

53. Judith C. Brown, *Immodest Acts: The Life of a Lesbian Nun in Renaissance Italy* (Oxford, 1986), 25; Lawrence Stone, *The Family, Sex and Marriage in England 1500-1800* (New York, 1977), 64. Shahar, like Brown, argued that medieval people utilized wetnursing to avoid the taboo associated with having sex with a lactating woman. Shahar, *Children in the Middle Ages*, 73-74. Some problems, however, exist with historians' attempts to see some sort of sexual taboo associated with lactation. Neither Brown nor Shahar, for instance, cited a contemporary source regarding this taboo. Moreover, while Pope Gregory the Great in the early Middle Ages had forbidden sexual relations between parents during the breastfeeding period and condemned parents who hired wetnurses so they could avoid this taboo, many other later canonists apparently failed to reiterate these taboos. Gratian, for instance, considered them of secondary importance to the conjugal debt, and even argued that if a husband demanded sex during this time, the wife had to fulfill his needs because of the conjugal debt. Brundage commented on how curious it was that this stricture revived to some extent in the late Middle Ages, but I wonder how prevalent in the popular mentality this taboo—if it was that—really was, especially after Gratian had diminished it so much. James Brundage, *Law, Sex, and Christian Society in Medieval Europe* (Chicago, 1987), 157, 199, 242, 508. Also, Gregory may not have even developed his strictures from actual cases. He may have just been looking to eliminate occasions of sex for pleasure; and this was one of them, since lactating women are less fertile. Thus the taboo probably stemmed not from a sense of ritual female impurity (a concept that seems to have mesmerized modern historians) but from a desire to keep the purpose of sex within its canonical bounds.

54. Klapisch-Zuber, *Women, Family, and Ritual*, 159. See also David Hunt, 103.

55. Origo, *The Merchant of Prato*, 178-82. According to Rudolph Bell, Catherine of Siena's mother was keenly interested in the business success of her husband and sons. She eventually sent all her children, save Catherine, to a wetnurse. Bell, 32.

The contribution of women, particularly wives, in the medieval Italian wool industry and Genoese commerce is well known. Hughes, "Domestic Ideals," 47-48. See also Steven Ozment, *Magdalena and Balthazar: An Intimate Portrait of Life in 16th Century Europe Revealed in the Letters of a Nuremberg Husband and Wife* (New York, 1986), for a German example; and Ralph A. Houlbrooke, *The English Family, 1450-1700* (London, 1984), 132, for an English example. On how a woman's household duties in premodern and modern France was a cause for wetnursing see Sussman, 59.

56. Origo, *The Merchant of Prato*, 61; For a fictional rendition of women working see Boccaccio, *Decameron*, VIII:2.

57. Merry E. Wiesner, *Working Women in Renaissance Germany* (New Brunswick, 1986); Martha C. Howell, *Women, Production, and Patriarchy in Late Medieval Cities* (Chicago, 1986). Jean-Louis Flandrin, *Families in Former Times: Kinship, Household, and Sexuality* (Cambridge, 1979), 205. Barbara Diefendorf, "Family Culture, Renaissance Culture," *Renaissance Quarterly* 40 (1987), 676.

58. Emmanuel Le Roy Ladurie, *Montaillou: The Promised Land of Error* (New York, 1978), 207.

59. Sussman, 24-25. Roman slave children had wetnurses "to release their mothers for work." Suzanne Dixon, *The Roman Family* (Baltimore, 1992), 128.

60. Klapisch-Zuber, *Women, Family, and Ritual*, 158; Boccaccio, *Decameron*, IX:6; Brucker, 145; Brown, *Immodest Acts*, 24-25.

61. Trexler, *Public Life*, 88; Klapisch-Zuber, 134 n. 10. This does not mean that the rich did not try to get a tax deduction based on their wetnursing expenses; they did. Matteo Palmieri, *Ricordi fiscali (1427-1474) con due appendici relative al 1474-1495*, ed. Elio Conti (Rome, 1983), 270; Mark Phillips, *The Memoirs of Marco Parenti: A Life in Medici Florence* (Princeton, 1987), 29.

62. Klapisch-Zuber, *Women, Family, and Ritual*, 164; see also G. O. Corrazzini, ed., *Ricordanze di B. Masi calderaio fiorentino dal 1478 al 1526* (Florence, 1906), 40, 140.

63. ASF, AD, 8, fol 31v.

64. Andrea Zorzi, "The Florentines and their Public Offices in the Early Fifteenth Century: Competition, Abuses of Power, and Unlawful Acts," in *History from Crime: Selections from Quaderni Storici*, ed. Edward Muir and Guido Ruggiero (Baltimore, 1994), 121.

65. The fact that most of these families expected to recover these children at some point reinforces the hypothesis that foundlings hospitals in the premodern era functioned as some sort of sponsored day care facilities, though of course they were never intended for such purposes. Drawing on the work of Volker Hunecke and David Kertzer, Tamara Harevan noted that foundlings hospitals did not represent a means for family limitations so much as a way to ease a family's economic pressures temporarily, since the family expected to bring the child back into the fold at some point. Tamara K. Harevan, "The History of the Family and the Complexity of Social Change," *American Historical Review* 96 (1991), 116.

66. It could serve as a "year-round" part of the family economy. Lehning, 649. Lehning does an excellent job of showing the family dilemma involved in

adopting wetnursing as a family enterprise. On the one hand the income was essential for the family's maintenance; on the other hand this may have placed their own children at greater risk by early weaning and may have resulted in some emotional neglect of their own children. They did not, however, choose to do this; economics dictated this course of action. Lehning found though that the vast majority of women who participated in this activity had already weaned their own children. *Idem*, 651. On the poor economic condition of many Tuscan peasants see Vito Caiati, "The Peasant Household under Tuscan Mezzadria: A Socioeconomic Analysis of some Sienese Mezzadri Households, 1591-1640," *Journal of Family History* 9 (1984), 111-26.

67. Klapisch-Zuber, *Women, Family, and Ritual*, 137-38.

68. Archivio Innocenti Firenze, 9a 1433, 1435 in Trexler, The Foundlings of Florence," 274-75.

69. Ibid., 260.

70. On the harsh realities of the premodern world see Peter Laslett, *The World We Have Lost: England Before the Industrial Age*, 3rd Edition (New York, 1984).

71. Barberino called them nurses *di casa* and nurses *di fuori*. Barberino, 233.

72. Klapisch-Zuber, *Women, Family, and Ritual*, 135. During the disturbances on 8 April 1498, when urban mobs were running about looking for Savaranola's adherents, a crowd pillaged Francesco Valori's house, injuring his children and their *in casa* wetnurses. Luca Landucci, *A Florentine Diary from 1450 to 1516 Continued by an Anonymous Writer till 1542*, trans. Alice de Rosen Jervis (New York, 1927), 137.

73. Klapisch-Zuber, *Women, Family, and Ritual*, 136, 143. This did not always work. Guido Antella sourly noted on 8 July 1377 that his *in casa* nurse had been giving his son, Lorenzo, "latte pregno" for a number of months. He bluntly noted that "she left us." He owed her 4 lire 9 soldi, which he refused to pay since he had been paying for pregnant milk for a while. ASI, 1, 4, (1843), 16.

74. Klapisch-Zuber, *Women, Family, and Ritual*, 139.

75. ASF, CS, 2, 17bis, fol. 56r; ASF, MS, 96, fol. 13r; ASF, AD, 83, fol. 52r.

76. Klapisch-Zuber, *Women, Family, and Ritual*, 137.

77. BNF, Palatino Baldovinetti, 37, 11r. To mention a better- known example of this, Juliet's nurse was a servant as well.

78. Iris Origo, *The Merchant of Prato*, 214.

79. ASF, CS, 4, 563, fol. 6r; ASF, MS, 96, fol. 7v. Though it was infrequent, a father would at times have to pay for a wetnurse for the child of his outside nurse. An occurrence like this represents either a shrewd deal made by the wetnurse or more likely the immediate and pressing need the child's parents had for wetnursing. ASF, CS, 5, 10, fol. 19v.

80. ASF, CS, II, 17bis, 49r.

81. ASF, CS, 3, 275, fols. 15r, 16r, 16v.

82. ASF, AD, 11/1, 8v; ASI, 1, 4, (1843), 16-17

83. This act, freeing slave wetnurses on one's death, was mandated by law, which hints at the ubiquity of wetnursing in the premodern world. Susan Mosher Stuard, "Urban Domestic Slavery in Medieval Ragusa, *Journal of Medieval History* 9 (1983), 162, 167.

84. Origo, "The Domestic Enemy," 366.

85. Origo, "The Domestic Enemy," 334, 347, 351, 362.

86. Klapisch-Zuber, *Women, Family, and Ritual*, 136-37. Premodern Paris was likewise surrounded by villages whose women hired out as wetnurses. Sussman, 2, 51.

87. Klapisch-Zuber, *Women, Family, and Ritual*, 137; Origo, *The Merchant of Prato*, 214; Biagio di Buonaccorso recorded that he sent a child to wetnurse "to Salvestro di Maso, one of Bernardo di Iacopo's workers, living in the valley of the Mugello." BNF, Panciatichi, 101, fol. 36r. Niccolò Busini recorded payments to the wetnurse for his *in casa* wetnurse's child in the Mugello. ASF, CS, IV, 563, fol. 6r.

88. Origo, *The Merchant of Prato*, 231.

89. Alberti, 64. Gianozzo, another character in the dialogue, likewise said that if he could he would raise children in the country. Alberti, 190-93. Boccaccio reflected this humanist praise of the country too: "Besides all this, the country air is much fresher and the necessities for living in such times as these are plentiful." Boccaccio, *Decameron*, I:Introduction. Morelli, 87, 144. Trexler, "Foundlings of Florence," 276. The officials of foundlings hospitals preferred rural nurses, for they saw the country as more salutary for the children. They were also cheaper than urban nurses and not as likely to leave the position for other jobs. Kertzer, *Sacrificed for Honour*, 145.

90. BNF, Palatino Baldovinetti, 42, fols. 39r, 46r; ASF, CS, 3, 275, fol. 2v; BNF, Fondo Nazionale, 2, 2, 357, fol. 60r. Sussman found that rural wetnurses came from all social levels in the village community. Sussman, 51. See also Hughes, "Domestic Ideals," 131.

91. Leah Lydia Otis, "Municipal Wet Nurses in Fifteenth-Century Montpellier," in *Women and Work in Preindustrial Europe*, ed. Barbara Hanawalt (Bloomington, 1986), 85.

92. Bernardo Masi, a coppersmith, sent his daughter Margherita, to a scissorsmaker's wife who wetnursed her. Corrazzini, 140. Origo, *The Merchant of Prato*, 174-75, Ross, "The Middle Class Child," 189.

93. Boccaccio, *Decameron*, II:6.

94. Barberino, 191-92, in Ross, "The Middle Class Child," 190. These same qualities appear in an 1836 guide for finding a good wetnurse, which says something about the structural nature of wetnursing in the premodern world. Kertzer, *Sacrificed for Honour*, 148.

95. Ross, "The Middle Class Child," 191. Margherita Datini also thought that the wetnurse should resemble the mother. Origo, *The Merchant of Prato*, 215.

96. Origo, *The Merchant of Prato*, 215. Perosa, 13. Alberti likewise emphasized the health of the wetnurse. Alberti, 51. Production of breastmilk is dependent on a woman's weight—low body weight inhibits the production of breast milk.

97. Origo, *The Merchant of Prato*, 215.

98. Alberti, 51, 53-54. Others described the desired character of a wetnurse much as Barberino described it. Dominici, 41; Rucellai, 13; Origo, *The Merchant of Prato*, 215.

99. Alberti, 51; Paolo da Certaldo, *Libro di Buoni Costumi*, ed. Alfredo Schiaffini (Florence, 1945), 233.
100. Fildes, *History of Wetnursing*, 74, 91, 146, 149, 217, 238, 240; David L. Ransel, *Mothers of Misery: Child Abandonment in Russia* (Princeton, 1988), 181, 193, 195-96, 258, 278-83, 286-89, 298.
101. Certaldo, 234. According to Bartholomaeus Anglicus, "For good milk produces good progeny and bad milk bad progeny. The corruption of the nurse's blood necessarily harms the little body of the child or infant." Michael Goodich, "Bartholomaeus Anglicus on Child-Rearing," *Journal of Psychohistory* 3 (1975), 77. ASF, CS, 2, 4, fol. 22r. Paulus Bagellardus advised that to test for the quality of breast milk a parent was to place a drop of it on a fingernail, piece of marble, or piece of glass to see how well it beaded up. Fildes, *Breasts, Bottles, and Babies*, 67.
102. Certaldo, 234. He said that a child fed animal milk "doesn't have perfect wits like one fed on women's milk, but always looks stupid and vacant and not right in the head." Certaldo, 234, in Ross, "The Middle Class Child," 187. See also Sommerville, *The Rise and Fall*, 88; Fildes, *Breasts, Bottles, and Babies*, 53-55. Unpasteurized animal milk is dangerous, carrying, amongst other germs, the tuberculosis bacillus. Greenleaf, 30. Their complaints about this practice implies, of course, that it did happen. Vasari, for instance, knew of a child that had been nursed by a goat. Ross, 187. Barbaro claimed that cross nursing in nature resulted in oddities: lambs that suckled goat's milk had coarse fleeces. Barbaro, 223.
103. Ross, "The Middle Class Child," 187.
104. Klapisch-Zuber, *Women, Family, and Ritual*, 159; Fildes, *Breasts, Bottles, and Babies*, 68.
105. Klapisch-Zuber, *Women, Family, and Ritual*, 140. Bartholomeus Anglicus warned that bad breast milk could cause "mouth ulcers, vomiting, fever, spasms, and flux." Goodich, "Bartholomaeus Anglicus," 77. In premodern France whenever medical manuals discussed wetnursing they concentrated primarily on the quality of the nurse's milk. On 17 December 1762 the police of Paris issued an ordinance defining the minimum requirements for a wetnurse's milk. Sussman, 2, 40-41.
106. ASF, CS, 2, 11, fols. 42r, 48r.
107. Alberti, 51.
108. Ibid.
109. Ross, "The Middle Class Child," 186. Despite the vast numbers of women who applied at the Moscow and St. Petersburg foundling homes to serve as wetnurses, the officials of these homes had great difficulty finding suitable wetnurses during the summer months when rural women were busy with the harvest. Ransel, 199.
110. Certaldo, 234.
111. Tribaldo dei Rossi, for instance, recorded payments to the *balio* for some of his children, payments to the *balia* for others. BNF, Fondo Nazionale, 2, 2, 357, 32v. Other writers of *ricordanze* followed suit. ASF, AD, 190, fols. 3v, 9r; ASF, CS, 5, 10, fols. 120v, 121r; ASF, CS, 4, 75, fols. 93v-94r. Sometimes, though, the wetnurse was paid directly with no mention of the husband's involvement. ASF, CS, 2, 4, fols. 21r-22r.

112. "20 October 1424, I received from Niccolò dei Ricci a child of his to be put to nurse; he will give me two *fiorini* per month." *Ricordanze A e memoriale G* di Piero di Francesco Puro da Vecchio. Archivio degli Innocenti, *Estranei*, 714, fol. 4r, in Klapisch-Zuber, *Women, Family, and Ritual,* 163.

113. ASF, CS, 2, 17bis, fol. 28v; ASF, Carte del Bene, 24, fol. 15v. In Tudor England household servants frequently carried their master's children to a village wet-nurse. Ivy Pinchbeck and Margaret Hewitt, *Children in English Society* (London: 1969), 8.

114. ASF, MS, 96, fol. 5v.

115. Tommaso Guidetti, for instance, consistently paid the son of the wetnurse in one of his wetnursing contracts. ASF, CS, 4, 418, fol. 44r.

116. Commenting about the letters, Iris Origo said, "The letters exchanged between husband and wife on this subject are too monotonous and repetitive to be quoted at length." Origo, *The Merchant of Prato,* 216. I do not think Origo really understood the meaning or the dimensions of the wetnursing business in the premodern world and tended to be bored and maybe even embarrassed by it. But finding an international businessman involved in the wetnursing business implies that this was something crucial—certainly something profitable—for the premodern world.

117. Perhaps because so many Florentine nurses were rural, distance prevented so called milk brothers (and milk sisters) from being overly familiar with each other, for no *ricordi* and *ricordanze* writer subsequently mentioned his or his children's relationship with the wetnurse's children. Klapisch-Zuber argued that there was no relationship; I think the bond was just weak or had atrophied due to time and distance. Klapisch-Zuber, *Women, Family, and Ritual,* 137. Elsewhere in medieval records, we read about milk brothers. Richard I, for instance, had one in the person of Alexander Neckham, who became an abbot. Nicholas Orme, *From Childhood to Chivalry,* (London, 1984), 11. See also Origo, *The Merchant of Prato,* 214-16.

118. Elsewhere in the premodern world, in France and Russia, priests helped their parishioners find wetnurses. Sussman, 56-57; Ransel, 177.

119. Klapisch-Zuber, *Women, Family, and Ritual,* 140.

120. Premodern Russia possessed just such a large network. Ransel, 300. "Because thousands of foundlings were sent to the Italian countryside each year, wetnursing and foster care were important industries in impoverished rural areas." Kertzer, *Sacrificed for Honour,* 152.

121. Klapisch-Zuber, *Women, Family, and Ritual,* 143. Sussman concluded the same for wetnursing in premodern France. Sussman, 80-81.

122. Klapisch-Zuber, *Women, Family, and Ritual,* 140. ASF, CS, 2, 10, fol. 10v.

123. Elaine G. Rosenthal, "The Position of Women in Renaissance Florence: neither Autonomy nor Subjection," in *Florence and Italy: Renaissance Studies in Honor of Nicolai Rubinstein,* ed. Peter Denley and Caroline Elam (London, 1988), 376-77. She provided a more balanced evaluation of the position of women in Florentine society in this article than did Klapisch-Zuber in her *Women, Family, and Ritual.*

124. Ricciardo del Bene and Niccolò del Buono Busini both noted that an *in casa* nurse came to stay with "us." ASF, Carte del Bene, 37, 81r-82r; ASF, CS, 4, 563, fol. 6r.

Tommaso di Guidetti referred to "our wetnursing contractor of our daughter." ASF, CS, 4, 418, fol. 27rv; see also 28v, 44r.

125. Klapisch-Zuber, *Women, Family, and Ritual*, 163-64.

126. ASF, CS, 4, 74, fol. 27v. The existence of the *balio* was another reason Klapisch-Zuber saw wetnursing as a male-dominated business. But the term may just mean the husband of the wetnurse without any implication of his control of the business, much like how the term *father of companions* referred to the husband of the *mother of companions*, the woman who organized the living conditions, jobs, and social relations of journeymen in premodern France. Here the woman was in charge and the husband was her subordinate. It may have been so for the *balio*. For an extended commentary on the mother of companions see Jacques-Louis Ménétra, *Journal of My Life* (New York, 1986).

127. Klapisch-Zuber, *Women, Family, and Ritual*, 144 n. 46. Gentile Sasseti's *Libro del dare e dell'avere* for 1298 lists perhaps the only exception that proves the rule; he notes that the wetnursing agreement between him and Chorso, "our *balio*," was notarized by Ser Latino. NTF, 345.

128. ASF, CS, 5, 1750, 17r, 20v, 21r, 34v, 43v, 44r, 66r, 81v, 82r, 126v, 127r, for the wetnursing contracts; 185v, 187v, 191r, 193r, 196v, 203r, 208r, for the births.

129. ASF, CS, 2, 17, 48r.

130. NTF, 17-18.

131. ASF, CS, 2, 9, fol. 22v. This to me reflects poor (or perhaps common) accounting practices of the past rather than neglect of children.

132. Klapisch-Zuber, *Women, Family, and Ritual*, 144.

133. ASF, CS, 2, 17bis, fol. 18v.

134. Hughes, "Invisible Madonnas," 48.

135. ASF, CS, 2, 9, fol. 38r.

Chapter V

1. "Canzona delle balie," no. XXIX of "Trionfi e canzone anonimi," and no. XCIV in *Canti carnascialeschi del Rinascimento*, ed. C. S. Singleton (Bari, 1936), 39, 125-26. In James Bruce Ross, "The Middle Class Child in Urban Italy, Fourteenth to Early Sixteenth Century," in Lloyd deMause, ed. *The History of Childhood* (New York, 1974), 190, 192-94; Christiane Klapisch-Zuber, *Women, Family, and Ritual in Renaissance Italy* (Chicago, 1985), 105 n. 25; Valerie Fildes, *Wet Nursing: A History from Antiquity to the Present* (Oxford, 1988), 50-52.

2. Neri di Bicci, *Le ricordanze (10 marzo 1553-24 aprile 1475)*, ed. Bruno Santi (Pisa, 1976), 71; ASF, CS, 2, 23, fols., 171v, 173rv, 177v, 179v; BNF, Palatino Baldovinetti, 37, fol. 65v; Klapisch-Zuber, 151 n 67.

3. ASF, AD, 21, fol. 6r.

4. Klapisch-Zuber, *Women, Family, and Ritual*, 152, Table 7.6.

5. ASF, CS, 2, 4, fol., 24v.

6. Ross, "The Middle Class Child," 187.

7. Rudolph M. Bell, *Holy Anorexia* (Chicago, 1985), 31; Ross, 185.

8. Boccaccio, *Decameron*, II:6.
9. Giovanni Serapione, *Trattato delle Medicine Semplice*, BNF, Panciatichiano, 80, fols. 26r-27r, 178r.
10. Klapisch-Zuber, *Women, Family, and Ritual*, 144.
11. Ross, "The Middle Class Child," 183; Giovanni di Pagolo Morelli, *Ricordi*, ed. Vittore Branca, 2nd ed. (Florence, 1969), 143-45; For a comparative and instructive example from premodern France that demonstrates family contact with a child out to wetnurse, Jacques-Louis Ménétra in his autobiography recalled that his grandmother and godfather monitored his stay at the wetnurse. Jacques-Louis Ménétra, *Journal of My Life*, ed. Daniel Roche (New York, 1986), 18.
12. ASF, CS, 2, 9, fol. 22r.
13. ASF, CS, 4, 75, fol. 121v.
14. ASF, CS, 4, 418, fols. 27r, 33r, 35r.
15. ASF, CS, 5, 11, fols. 19v, 38v, 63v, 88v, 120v, 131v, 146v-147r, 148v, and 157v; BNF, Panciatichi, 101, fol. 20r.
16. "A di ultimo del decto mese andai a vedere el decto mio fanciullo a Brolio, e dei a la detta Monna Andrea sua balia due fiorini." ASI, 1, 4, (1843), 45. See also ASF, CS, 2, 7, fol. 123v.
17. BNF, Magliabecchiano, 7, 1014, fol. 67v. See also BNF, Panciatichi, 101, fol. 20v; or NTF, 307, for other examples of wetnurses' traveling to their employers' house to receive payment or to visit with the child.
18. "In idle hours, or when some festal day/ Wakes to rude mirth the giddy and the gay,/ She brings your infant child—nor yours alone/ But all she feeds, another's or her own.—/ With smiles and kindness you the flock receive/." Luigi Tansilo, *The Nurse*, trans. William Roscoe (Liverpool, 1804), 60-61.
19. "Portai a mona Lena sopradetta [he then lists the goods] e port'gliele a chasa sua a Prato." Neri di Bicci, 102. He referred to going to see the wetnurse rather than his child because this is an entry in his account book listing expenses.
20. ASF, CS, 2, 9, fol. 22v.
21. ASF, CS, 2, 15, fol. 12r. See also ASF, CS, 5, 10, fols. 19v, 20rv, 21r, 39v, 42r, 45v, 60r, 65r; ASF, CS, 4, 74, fol. 43v. ASF, CS, 2, 9, fol. 38r; BNF, Palatino Baldovinetti, 42, fol. 46r; NTF, 261, 264.
22. ASF, CS, 4, 75, fol. 35v.
23. Iris Origo, *The Merchant of Prato: Francesco di Marco Datini* (New York, 1957), 175. Orestes Ferrara, *The Private Correspondence of Niccolò Machiavelli* (Baltimore, 1929), 99-100. Sources from premodern France provide abundant evidence that wetnurses communicated with families about the health of their children. George D. Sussman, *Selling Mother's Milk: The Wet-Nursing Business in France 1715-1914* (Urbana, 1982), 73-79.
24. Benvenuto Cellini, *Autobiography*, trans. George Bull (New York, 1956), 332-33. As Cellini was an unmarried father and busy as well, it would have been difficult for him to raise the child by himself. A 1516 rape case from a village in the diocese of Troyes illustrates as well that people visited children at the wetnurse just to be with them. An urban woman had sent her son to the wife of a winegrower at the village of Barberey. One day she visited the child and spent the

night there, where some local rowdy raped her. Jean-Louis Flandrin, "Repression and Change in the Sexual Life of Young People in Medieval and Early Modern Times," *Journal of Family History* 2 (1977), 208.

25. Philip Gavitt, *Charity and Children in Renaissance Florence: The Ospedale degli Innocenti, 1450-1536* (Ann Arbor, 1990), 193, 200, 201-02, 205, 277. Richard C. Trexler, "The Foundlings of Florence, 1395-1455," *Journal of Psychohistory* 1 (1973), 272.

26. Paolo da Certaldo, *Libro di Buoni Costumi* ed. Alfredo Schiaffini (Florence, 1945), 234; Ross, "The Middle Class Child," 190. Klapisch-Zuber did say that fathers (though, significantly, not mothers) visited their children at the wetnurse, but she tried to minimize that contact, forgetting that a good portion of children out to wetnurse were only a few hours away from Florence. Klapisch-Zuber, *Women, Family, and Ritual*, 144. Yet, as I showed above, women did visit their children at the wetnurse.

27. Certaldo, 233-34; Klapisch-Zuber, *Women, Family, and Ritual*, 144.

28. Klapisch-Zuber, *Women, Family, and Ritual*, 145; Table 7.5, 147. In noting the number of nurses hired and fired in the wetnursing business in premodern France, David Hunt commented that surely this must reflect the family's care and oversight of the child's welfare. David Hunt, *Parents and Children in History: The Psychology of Family Life in Early Modern France* (New York, 1970), 114-15.

29. ASF, CS, 5, 418, fols. 28rv, 33r, 35r; ASF, CS, 2, 11, fols. 11r, 14r; Ross, "The Middle Class Child," 191; Klapisch-Zuber, *Women, Family, and Ritual*, 154.

30. Klapisch-Zuber's figures show 36 percent of contracts were broken for this reason.

31. Bicci, 272.

32. Klapisch-Zuber, *Women, Family, and Ritual*, 145. This of course relates to the initial concern parents had about the quality of the nurse's milk.

33. That he discovered the nurse was pregnant by two months implies that he monitored his child rather closely. ASF, CS, 2, 21, fol. 3r. The Verney family quickly fired their wetnurses whenever they discovered that they had become pregnant, again implying a close monitoring of the wetnurse. Miriam Slater, *Family Life in the Seventeenth Century: The Verneys of Claydon House* (London, 1984), 114.

34. ASI, 1, 4, (1843), 45. Manno stayed with this wetnurse for a year and five months, when he again returned because the wetnurse became pregnant. Gherardo also returned early from his first wetnurse because she became pregnant. *Ibid.*, 42-46. Lady Verney, at times, had great difficulties finding replacement nurses. Slater, 114.

35. Klapisch-Zuber, *Women, Family, and Ritual*, 145, Table 7.4, 146.

36. "Richordo chome a dì 7 di luglio in venerdì matina Santi di Nanni del Pretto balio di Bicci sopradetto, chontro a la mia voglia mi rimenò Bicci mio figliuolo e più no llo volle tenere," Neri di Bicci, 72.

37. Klapisch-Zuber, *Women, Family, and Ritual*, 145; Ross, "The Middle Class Child," 184-85; Shulamith Shahar, *Childhood in the Middle Ages* (London, 1990), 95.

38. Valerie A. Fildes, *Breasts, Bottles and Babies: A History of Infant Feeding* (Edinburgh, 1986), 203; Sussman, 67; Slater, 109.

39. Jean-Claude Schmitt, *The Holy Greyhound: Guinefort Healer of Children Since the Thirteenth Century* (Cambridge, 1983), 74. This fear is certainly reflected as well in the charms and amulets in the trousseaus that were for the baby's protection. As far as the parents were concerned, there were dangers out there.

40. Gene Brucker, *Giovanni and Lusanna: Love and Marriage in Renaissance Florence* (Berkeley, 1986), 86. Other things could happen to a child at the wetnurse's house. Sir Ralph Verney believed his son developed rickets because of the nurse's poor milk. As syphilis spread throughout Europe in the premodern period there was the problem of syphilitic children's infecting nurses who then could infect other children. See David L. Ransel, *Mothers of Misery: Child Abandonment in Russia* (Princeton, 1988), 279-85 on this in premodern and modern Russia.

41. Klapisch-Zuber, *Women, Family, and Ritual*, 146, 151; Jean-Louis Flandrin, *Families in Former Times: Kinship, Household and Sexuality* Cambridge, 1979), 204. Kertzer noted the extremely high infant-mortality rates in premodern Florence for foundlings at the Innocenti—something on the order of 66 percent dead within two years. While he alluded to it, he perhaps missed the real reason for these high infant-mortality rates: the immense pressure that ever increasing numbers of foundlings put upon the system in the premodern era. Foundling homes could never find enough nurses to handle their in-house children. Moreover, he notes that once the children went to outside nurses, who were more available and settled, the mortality rates dropped. David I. Kertzer, *Sacrificed for Honour: Italian Infant Abandonment and the Politics of Reproductive Control* (Boston, 1993), 133-39.

42. Flandrin, *Families in Former Times*, 203; Sussman, 65-66.

43. Origo, *The Merchant of Prato*, 175; Morelli, 193. Though rare, some of these infant deaths occurred because the child could not nurse. Ann G. Carmichael, *Plague and Poor in Renaissance Florence* (Cambridge, 1986), 51.

44. Ross, "The Middle Class Child," 192.

45. BNF, Panciatichiano, 101, fol. 36r.

46. ASF, AD, 18, fol. 53r; ASF, CS, 2, 4, fol. 6r; ASF, CS, 2, 22, fol. 2r.

47. ASF, CS, 2, 14, fol. 19r.

48. "pensammo l'affogasse." For others see BNF, Panciatichi, 101, fol. 36r; ASF, CS, 2, 11, fol. 34r; ASF, CS, 5, 22, fol. 9r; G. O. Corazzini, ed., *Ricordanze di B. Masi calderaio fiorentino dal 1478 al 1526* (Florence, 1906), 140.

49. Ross, "The Middle Class Child," 195-96; Klapisch-Zuber, *Women, Family, and Ritual*, 148 n. 58.

50. Luke Demaitre, "The Idea of Childhood and Childcare in Medical Writings of the Middle Ages," *Journal of Psychohistory* 4 (1977), 471-72.

51. The *Confessionale* of Sant' Antonino warned mothers and nurses that overlaying was homicide. St. Antoninus, *Confessionale* (Venice, 1474) fol. 33v. As late as the eighteenth century French diocesan statutes threatened parents and nurses with excommunication for sleeping in the same bed as infants less than one year of age. Sussman, 40.

52. ASF, CS, 5, 22, 9r.

53. Ross, "The Middle Class Child," 196; Klapisch-Zuber, *Women, Family, and Ritual*, 104; Shahar, *Childhood in the Middle Ages*, 129-30. All discount overlaying as

deliberate death, but see it as accidental. Klapisch-Zuber even states that; "A deliberate suffocation would be difficult to explain, what is more, since nurses were paid at regular intervals." Klapisch-Zuber, 148. On the other hand, and this is why study of overlaying is so problematical, some historians see it as presumptive infanticide. Carmichael, 51-53; Richard C. Trexler, "Infanticide in Florence: New Sources and First Results," *Journal of Psychohistory* 1 (1973), 109. To strengthen his hand that overlaying was infanticide, Trexler argued for a female bias in these cases. Carmichael discounted this, finding the exact opposite in a sample of cases from 1444-57 that she drew from the Florentine Books of the Dead. Unfortunately, as she herself admits, her sample size is "quite small" (only 44 cases with 23 boys dying and 11 girls dying). Carmichael, 53. In fact, it is so small that I would argue that it is virtually worthless for any solid conclusions to be drawn from it. This again highlights the difficulty of drawing conclusions from medieval data that are too fragmentary and too disparate. We must be very cautious here with numbers from the Middle Ages.

54.   Gavitt, 237-38; Elsewhere, Gavitt strengthens his position that overlaying actually represented crib death. Philip Gavitt, "Infant Death in Late Medieval Florence: The Smothering Hypothesis Reconsidered," in *Medieval Family Roles,* ed. Cathy Jorgensen Itnyre (New York, 1995), 137-56. Modern evidence of overlaying that actually are cases of SIDS seems to support Gavitt's contention. Nancy Scheper-Hughes, "The Cultural Politics of Child Survival," in *Child Survival: Anthropological Perspectives on the Treatment and Maltreatment of Children,* ed. Nancy Scheper-Hughes (Dordrecht, 1987), 6. Carmichael, however, discounted the connection between SIDS and overlaying since the accounts only surfaced in the fifteenth century. Carmichael, 51-54.

     Confusion about these cases was standard for the premodern world. Cotton Mather in his diary recorded that his daughter Mehetebel, "dyed suddenly, in its nurses Arms; not known to bee dying, till it was dead; of some sudden stoppage by Wind. . . . (Alas, the Child was overlaid by the Nurse!)" Cotton Mather, *Diary of Cotton Mather* Vol. 1. (New York, n. d.), 179. Which was it: crib death or overlaying?

55.   BNF, Panciatichi, 101, fol. 36r; Klapisch-Zuber, *Women, Family, and Ritual,* 146-89.

56.   A. Petrucci, ed., *Il Libro di Ricordanze dei Corsini (1362-1457)* (Rome, 1965), 147.

57.   Klapisch-Zuber, *Women, Family, and Ritual,* 147 n. 52.

58.   Michael Goodich, "Bartholomaeus Anglicus on Child-Rearing," *Journal of Psychohistory* 3 (1975), 81.

59.   Despite his minute study of daily life in Montaillou, Emmanuel Le Roy Ladurie concluded with resignation, "There is virtually no information on natal and prenatal practices in Montaillou." Emmanuel Le Roy Ladurie, *Montaillou: The Promised Land of Error* (New York, 1978), 207.

60.   Demaitre translates this as "baby pacifier." Demaitre, 470-71.

61.   Bell, 30.

62.   Sussman, 54.

63.   Fildes, *Breasts, Bottles and Babies,* 68. Maestro Guglielmo da Piancenza, *La Cirugia,* BNF, Panciatichiano, 81, fols. 24rv.

64. Piero di Giovanni da Corella, *Trattato di Medicina*, BNF, Manoscritti Palatini, 796, fol. 108r.

65. Barbara Kay Greenleaf, *Children through the Ages: A History of Childhood* (New York, 1978), 26.

66. Goodich, "Bartholomaeus Anglicus," 77; Ross, "The Middle Class Child," 193-94; Demaitre, 475.

67. Leon Battista Alberti, *The Family in Renaissance Florence* trans. Renée Neu Watkins, (Columbia, 1969), 113.

68. Soranus, *Gynecology* (c. 130 AD), a standard text on childcare into the eighteenth century, included a section on swaddling. C. John Sommerville, *The Rise and Fall of Childhood* (Beverley Hills, 1982), 44-45.

69. Lawrence Stone, *The Past and the Present* (Boston, 1981), 219. In his model of unaffective personal and familial relationships in the past, swaddling then served as the mechanism for creating this coldness. When swaddling ceased, people became more caring and loving. See also Sommerville, 82; Greenleaf, 44.

70. Bell, 136.

71. Demaitre, 471-72; Ralph A. Houlbrooke, *The English Family* (London, 1984), 132; See also Barbara A. Hanawalt, "Childrearing Among the Lower Classes of Late Medieval England," *The Journal of Interdisciplinary History* 8 (1977), 15; Greenleaf, 29-30; Shahar, *Childhood in the Middle Ages*, 85-88.

72. Sommerville, *Rise and Fall*, 23.

73. Demaitre, 471-73; Ross, "The Middle Class Child," 194.

74. Goodich, "Bartholomaeus Anglicus," 77-78; Ross, "The Middle Class Child," 184; Demaitre, 472. David Hunt argued that swaddling in the premodern era kept infants warm and away from harm. David Hunt, 127.

75. In Richard Trexler, *Public Life in Renaissance Florence* (New York, 1980), 462.

76. Ross, "The Middle Class Child," 194.

77. Goodich, "Bartholomaeus Anglicus," 77; Alberti, 63; Klapisch-Zuber, *Women, Family, and Ritual*, 148; Boccaccio, *Decameron*, 583; BNF, Palatino Baldovinetti, 42, fols. 39r-41v.

78. Klapisch-Zuber, *Women, Family, and Ritual*, 326.

79. Demaitre, 471-73; Alberti, 61-63; Ross, "The Middle Class Child," 184; Agnolo Firenzuolo, *Tales of Firenzuolo* (New York, 1987), 21.

80. Shulamith Shahar, *The Fourth Estate: A History of Women in the Middle Ages* (New York, 1983), 184; Ross, 195.

81. Klapisch-Zuber, *Women, Family, and Ritual*, 105 n. 25, 149; Houlbrooke, 131; Shahar, *The Fourth Estate*, 184.

82. Fildes, *Breasts, Bottles and Babies*, 66; Goodich, "Barthomaeus Anglicus," 77. A trip to the rural wetnurse exposed urban children to a number of germs or diseases for which they had no initial immunity since their mothers were urban-dwellers. Yet these children would eventually benefit from the antibodies in the nurse's milk. Fildes, *Breasts, Bottles and Babies*, 199-201. On the other hand, it was possible for a child to carry disease to its wetnurse. Donato Velluti's son, for instance, made all his nurses ill. Klapisch-Zuber, *Women, Family, and Ritual*, 148.

83. Demaitre, 470. Undoubtedly, folk remedies too played a part in premodern childcare. In premodern England, for instance, rhubarb was thought beneficial for soothing a teething child. Slater, 116.
84. Goodich, "Bartholomaeus Anglicus," 78.
85. Paolo Certaldo, 126; Shahar, *The Fourth Estate*, 184; Fildes, *Breasts, Bottles and Babies*, 126. Premodern Italian bread censuses omitted unweaned children from their tabulations because the enumerators assumed that they had their own food supply in the wetnurse or mother. Peter Burke, *The Historical Anthropology of Premodern Italy* (Cambridge, 1988), 30.
86. Klapisch-Zuber, *Women, Family, and Ritual*, 154. By contrast, in present day England children are weaned between six and twelve months. Linda Pollock, *Forgotten Children: Parent-Child Relations from 1500 to 1900* (Cambridge, 1983), 219.
87. In Bell, 33.
88. Fildes, *Breasts, Bottles and Babies*, 66; Alberti, 122; Shahar, 184; Greenleaf, 31.
89. Pollock, *Forgotten Children*, 221.
90. ASF, San Paolo, 129, 71v, in Klapisch-Zuber, *Women, Family, and Ritual*, 158.
91. Goodich, "Bartholomaeus Anglicus," 78.
92. Fildes, *Breasts, Bottles, and Babies*, 392-93, 401.
93. Sommerville, *Rise and Fall*, 80; Greenleaf, 30; Fildes, *Breasts, Bottles and Babies*, 141-42. Despite the strictures against drinking animal milk, this certainly occurred. In a *Birth of the Virgin* by Bernardo Daddi there is a woman standing off to the side holding one of these cow-horn drinking utensils. Ibid., 308.
94. Klapisch-Zuber, *Women, Family, and Ritual*, 153, 158. She found from her evidence that girls were weaned on the average sooner than boys—at 18 versus 19.4 months—and concluded that this was evidence that Florentines favored their male over their female children. Klapisch-Zuber, *Women, Family, and Ritual*, 155. The difference in numbers here, however, may be statistically insignificant due to her small sample size. Nevertheless, Michele Savonarola did advise that boys should be nursed longer than girls. Demaitre, 474. This may not be so much an anti-female bias as a realization of the fact that boys have a higher metabolic rate than girls and need more calories, which became translated in premodern terms to a perceived need to breastfeed longer. See Table 5, "Basal Metabolism from Birth to Maturity," in Newton Kugelmass, *The Newer Nutrition in Pediatric Practice* (Philadelphia, 1940), 18. Even today recommended daily caloric levels for boys and men are higher than those for girls and women beginning at about age eight.
95. In Klapisch-Zuber, *Women, Family, and Ritual*, 155 n. 80.
96. ASF, CS, 5, 563, fol. 1v.
97. Stone, *Past and Present*, 217.
98. Klapisch-Zuber, *Women, Family, and Ritual*, 154; Table 7.8, 157.
99. Leah L. Otis, "Municipal Wet Nurses in Fifteenth-Century Montpellier," in Barbara Hanawalt, ed., *Women and Work in Preindustrial Europe* (Bloomington, 1986), 88-89.

100. Alessandro Perosa, ed., *Giovanni Rucellai ed il suo zibaldone* (London, 1960), 13; Origo, 231; ASF, CS, 2, 4, fol. 22r; ASF, CS, 2, 17bis, fol. 18v; ASF, CS, 4, 346, fols. 3r, 31r, 38r; ASF, CS, 5, 10, fol. 128v; ASF, CS, 5, 17, fols. 199v-200r.

101. BNF, Palatino Baldovinetti, 42, fol. 46; ASF, CS, 2, 7, fols. 122v, 125v; ASF, CS, 3, 271, fols. 20rv, 43r; ASF, CS, 2, 17, fol. 66v.

102. James R. Lehning, "Family Life and Wetnursing in a French Village," *The Journal of Interdisciplinary History* 12 (1982), 656.

103. Origo, *The Merchant of Prato*, 198. Boccaccio noted in one of his stories how the characters had affection for their wetnurse. *Decameron*, II:6. Some wetnurses and their families decided to adopt their charges from the Innocenti. Gavitt, *Charity and Children*, 235-37. In premodern Venice it was "especially common" for wetnurses to leave bequests to their nurslings. In fact, the bequests usually were larger than those for other blood relatives (though not for one's own children), which implies that these wetnurses saw themselves connected to their nurslings like family members. Dennis Romano, "Aspects of Patronage in Fifteenth- and Sixteenth-Century Venice," *Renaissance Quarterly* 46 (1993), 725-26.

Chapter VI

1. Niccolò Machiavelli, *Lettere familiari*, ed. Edoardo Alvisi (Florence, 1883), 206. In Roberto Ridolfi, *The Life of Niccolò Machiavelli* (London, 1963), 117.

2. Unfortunately, we know little about the private life of Florentine children. James Bruce Ross noted that concerning "the homely activities of the child, where and how he ate, slept, defecated, played, we know very little." James Bruce Ross, "The Middle-Class Child in Urban Italy, Fourteenth to Early Sixteenth Century," in *History of Childhood*, ed. Lloyd deMause (New York, 1974), 183-228, especially 205. Sources for the study of the private life of children in the premodern era are rare, scanty, and uninformative. Linda Pollock, for instance, found little evidence on the day-to-day activities of children in English diaries before the nineteenth century. Linda Pollock, ed., *A Lasting Relationship: Parents and Children over Three Centuries* (Hanover, 1987), 135.

3. Benvenuto Cellini, *Autobiography*, trans. George Bull (New York, 1956), 19-22. Soderini and a counsellor advised Cellini's father to teach him the other arts. Cellini's father, however, was adamant that he should become "the greatest musician in the whole world." Cellini, much to the disappointment of his father, refused to become a musician, professing a love for design instead. This caused some tension between the two of them. Nevertheless, Cellini said, "For all this, I remembered to cheer up my lovable old father now and then by playing the flute or the cornet. He used to weep and sigh his heart out whenever he heard me play. So out of filial affection I very often used to give him pleasure in this way, even pretending to enjoy it myself." Cellini, 23-24. Father-and-son conflict in premodern Florence thus did not necessarily only stem from a father's economic control over his son via *patria potestas* as some, such as Thomas Kuehn, have claimed. Thomas Kuehn, "Honor and Conflict in a Fifteenth-

Century Florentine Family," *Ricerche Storiche* 10 (1980), 299. And father-and-son conflict in premodern Florence did not necessarily have to be long-lasting, as Cellini's account indicates.

4. Ross, "The Middle Class Child," 202; Christiane Klapisch-Zuber, "Le Chiavi Fiorentine di Barbablù: L'Apprendimento della lettura a Firenze nel XV secolo," *Quaderni Storici* 57 (1984), 769; Richard C. Trexler, *Public Life in Renaissance Florence* (New York, 1980), 166; Judith C. Brown, *Immodest Acts: The Life of a Lesbian Nun in Renaissance Italy* (Oxford, 1986), 24. For a broader examination of maternal and paternal roles in childrearing see Shulamith Shahar, *Childhood in the Middle Ages* (London, 1990), 112-17.

    The question of feminine influence on children in premodern Florence presents a larger issue than just discovering which parent had the primary childrearing responsibilities. Some implicitly and others explicitly attribute the vibrant cultural achievement of the Renaissance to female influence on the artists and patrons when they were children. David Herlihy, for instance, claimed that the age discrepancy between a child's relatively young mother and relatively aged father in premodern Florence meant that the mother "became a prime mediator in passing on social values from old to young." David Herlihy, *The Family in Renaissance Italy* (St. Louis, 1974), 11. This concept falters at two points: first, female influence was not a new concept for the era 1300-1600; second, female influence was not absolute for the era 1300-1600.

5. Leon Battista Alberti, *The Family in Renaissance Florence: I Libri della famiglia*, trans. Renée Neu Watkins (Columbia, 1969), 210. In ancient Rome both parents were expected to see to a child's moral and educational development. Suzanne Dixon, *The Roman Family* (Baltimore, 1992), 131. For a competent survey of select humanists' views on childrearing see Philip Gavitt, *Charity and Children in Renaissance Florence: The Ospedale degli Innocenti, 1410-1536* (Ann Arbor, 1990), 273-306.

6. Giovanni Dominici, *Regola del governo di Cura familiare parte quarta: On the Education of Children*, trans and ed. Arthur Basil Coté (Washington, D. C., 1927), 42, 47; Alessandro Perosa, ed., *Giovanni Rucellai ed il suo zibaldone*, vol. 1 *Il zibaldone quaresimale* (London, 1960), 13. Charles de la Roncière concluded that despite the differences in age, "[p]arents in Tuscany and indeed throughout all Italy probably appeared to their children as a couple, a tutelary pair enveloped in an aura of joint authority that obscured differences and tended to equalize the partners in a marriage." Charles de la Roncière, "Tuscan Notables on the Eve of the Renaissance," in *A History of Private Life*, eds. Philippe Ariès and Georges Duby, vol. 2 *Revelations of the Medieval World* ed. Georges Duby, trans. Arthur Goldhammer (Cambridge, MA, 1988), 211.

7. Alberti, 49. There seemed to be some appreciation by Florentine men of the existence of particular and unique ties between mothers and daughters. For instance, in their wills the husbands of Maddelena Nerli tried "to safeguard the mother/daughter emotional bond." Giulia Calvi, "Maddelena Nerli and Cosimo Turnabuoni: A Couple's Narrative of Family History in Early Modern Florence," *Renaissance Quarterly* 45 (1992), 330-32.

8. Gene Brucker, ed. *The Society of Renaissance Florence: A Documentary Study* (New York, 1971), 173.

9. Giovanni Boccaccio, *The Corbaccio*, trans. and ed. Anthony K. Cassell (Urbana, 1975), 61; Kuehn, "Honor and Conflict," 296; Gavitt, *Charity and Children*, 278. Miriam Slater recognized that a father from the gentry of premodern England "was not only the dispenser of financial support but also the source of family influence which he could give or withdraw as he saw fit." Miriam Slater, *Family Life in the Seventeenth Century: The Verneys of Claydon House* (London, 1984), 7.

10. Alberti, 36, 62. According to Alberti, speaking through Lionardo, "Fathers should not fail, in every discussion they have in the presence of children, to extol the virtues of other men. They should also clearly condemn the wickedness of such as are wicked." Alberti, 79.

11. Trexler, 165.

12. Cellini, 26. Years before, Alberti had written that "[f]rom your father you have your being and many principles to guide you." Alberti, 40.

13. Alberti, 84. On how diligent the humanists thought a father should be see Gavitt, 280-89.

14. Alberti, 49, 112. At one point he (using the voice of Gianozzo) mentioned that all household members were to be at specific tasks during the day and the mother was to be "watching over the children." Alberti, 180. This division of labor is, of course, not surprising in a patriarchal society. See Steven Ozment, *When Fathers Ruled: Family Life in Reformation Europe* (Cambridge, MA, 1983).

15. Michael Goodich, "Bartholomaeus Anglicus on Child-Rearing," *Journal of Psychohistory* 3 (1975), 80.

16. Trexler, 166. He also made the point that the mother was the best woman to raise a child as well, versus wetnurses, stepmothers or grandmothers.

17. C. Carnesecchi, "Un fiorentino del secolo XV e le sue ricordanze," ASI 5, 4 (1889), 147.

18. Boccaccio, *The Corbaccio*, 31. He drew this conceit from Juvenal's Satire Number 6, but he believed it applied to his own era. In the *Decameron* he noted a more positive version of maternal education. Boccaccio, *The Decameron*, VII:8. Alberti too noted the mother's role in education. Alberti, 63.

19. Trexler, 91-92. Luke Demaitre, "The Idea of Childhood and Childcare in Medical Writings of the Middle Ages," *Journal of Psychohistory* 4 (1977), 481. Shahar argued that a woman who used wetnurses did not bond with her children. Shahar, *Childhood in the Middle Ages*, 74. This seems to see mothering as only the function of biology; but it is social as well, if not more so, and development can occur at a later stage than infancy.

20. Alberti, 56. Matteo Palmieri echoed these sentiments. Gavitt, *Charity and Children*, 281. Alberti noted the popular belief that a parent could predict a career by observing the reactions of an infant to certain stimuli. For instance, delight in listening to parents snap their fingers meant a boy was destined for a military career; a child who liked to listen to songs was suited for the contemplative life. Alberti, 61.

21. Paul F. Grendler, *Schooling in Renaissance Italy: Literacy and Learning, 1300-1600* (Baltimore, 1989). Commentators as diverse as Boccaccio and Palmieri all

recorded this Florentine practice of carving letters in fruit. Boccaccio, *Decameron*, VIII:9; Rucellai, 14; Dominici, 35; Alberti, 81; de la Roncière, 204, 279; Gavitt, *Charity and Children*, 281. A wetnurse who did this, then, was also a Tuscan child's first teacher. For a survey of children's first educational experiences elsewhere in the Middle Ages see Shahar, *Childhood in the Middle Ages*, 162-82.

22. Iris Origo, *The Merchant of Prato: Francesco di Marco Datini 1335-1410* (New York, 1957), 305; de la Roncière, 204.

23. Cellini, 21; *Paradiso*, XXV:124-26. The conclusion that mothers were the teachers of a child's vernacular is Christiane Klapisch-Zuber's. "Le Chiavi Fiorentine," 769.

24. Alberti, 65.

25. Alberti, 66, 68-69; Maria Teresa Sillano, ed., *Le ricordanze di Giovanni Chellini da San Miniato: medico, mercante, e umanista (1425-1457)* (Milan, 1984),88; BNF Fondo Nazionale 2, 2, 357, fol. 53v; *Decameron*, II:8, V:1; Ginevra Niccolini di Camugliano, *The Chronicles of a Florentine Family 1200-1470* (London, 1933), 182, 185.

26. Klapisch-Zuber, "Le Chiavi Fiorentine," 772; Dominici, 34, 64.

27. Francesco da Barberino, *Del reggimento e costumi di Donna* ed. C. Baudi di Vesme (Bologna, 1875), 33, in Trexler, 91-92.

28. Dominici, 59.

29. St. Antoninus, *Confessionale* (Venice, 1474), 33r.

30. Dominici, 34, 64.

31. Boccaccio, *The Decameron*, 153.

32. St. Antoninus, *Summa Theologica* Part 4 (Venice, 1581), 15.

33. Niccolini di Camugliano, *The Chronicles*, 187. For the trials, tribulations, and rewards of childrearing for medieval Londoners, see Barbara Hanawalt, *Growing Up in Medieval London: The Experience of Childhood in History* (New York, 1993), 69-78.

34. Peter Burke, *The Historical Anthropology of Early Modern Italy: Essays on Perception and Communication* (Cambridge, 1987), 117. For the Niccolini see Niccolini di Camugliano, *The Chronicles*, 185. Burke thought it significant that children used their father's first name in address. Letters between husband and wife discussing their children come from diverse places such as Venice and Mantua. Burke, 116-17. For other examples from Florence see ASF, Mediceo Avanti il Principato, 106, *Lettere di Magdalena Cibo de Medici a Lorenzo di Piero di Lorenzo de Medici*, 48, letter of 8 March 1516; ASF, CS III, 104, *Strozzi lettere varie: lettere di Albiera di Giunta moglie di Simone Strozzi*, 72 letter of 22 June 1555, which notes that the children are well [state bene]; and 74 letter of 12 August 1555. Burke's survey of family letters from Renaissance Italy led him to conclude that it "should be clear that the ʾsense of childhood', as the late Philippe Ariès (1966) called it, was not a discovery of the seventeenth and eighteenth centuries, at least not in Italy." Burke, 117.

35. Iris Origo, "The Domestic Enemy: Eastern Slaves in Tuscany in the Fourteenth and Fifteenth Centuries," *Speculum* 30 (1955), 333.

36. Boccaccio, *Decameron*, V:7.

37. For an example see BNF, Manoscritti Palatini, 1129, fols. 86v-87r.

38. de la Roncière, 244-45; Boccaccio, Decameron, II:2; Alessandra Strozzi, Lettere di una gentildonna fiorentina, ed. C. Guasti (Florence, Sansoni, 1877), 591, letter of 8 May 1469 to Filippo Strozzi, her son, in Gavitt, Charity and Children, 287; Boccaccio, Decameron, II:8; Ross, "The Middle Class Child," 198 220 n. 89.

39. Klapisch-Zuber, Women, Family, and Ritual, 44; Trexler, Public Life, 161, 425-26; Ross, The Middle Class Child," 198; Giovanni di Pagola Morelli, Ricordi, ed. Vittore Branca (Florence, 1969), 205; Alberti, 200; David Herlihy, "Forward," in Klapisch-Zuber, Women, Family, and Ritual, x; Gavitt, Children and Charity, 285.

40. Mark Phillips, The Memoir of Marco Parenti: A Life in Medici Florence (Princeton, 1987), 50. On these joint households in general see Francis William Kent, Household and Lineage in Renaissance Florence: The Family Life of the Capponi, Ginori and Rucellai (Princeton, 1977).

41. de la Roncière, 275. On the supposed decline of the nuclear family in premodern Florence see Richard A. Goldthwaite, Private Wealth in Renaissance Florence: A Study of Four Families (Princeton, 1968), since superseded by Kent's study of extended families, Household and Lineage. See Alan MacFarlane, The Family Life of Ralph Josselin: A Seventeenth-Century Clergyman (New York, 1970), 153-60, on the utility of extended kin for premodern families; and Barbara Hanawalt, "Childrearing among the Lower Classes of Late Medieval England," Journal of Interdisciplinary History 8 (1977), 7, on how children at any time were members of both a nuclear and extended family.

42. Boccaccio, The Corbaccio, 155.

43. Dominici, 48-49, 51; Origo, The Merchant of Prato, 189. Sant' Antonino talked of a "timore filiali" a filial fear, which he said was based on the respect and reverence due parents because of their benevolence. St. Antoninus, Summa Theologica, 14:13.

44. ASF, CS, 1, 63, Lettere a Luigi Guicciardini, Commissario di Castro Caro 1542, fol. 29.

45. Brown, 125; Decameron, II:5.

46. Richard A. Goldthwaite, "The Florentine Palace as Domestic Architecture," American Historical Review 77 (1972), 1000; Phillips, 27.

47. de la Roncière, 225; Brucker, 152; Iris Origo, The World of San Bernardino (New York, 1962), 64.

48. Dominici, 35, 59, 326: 211. Palmieri, however, warned that giving sweets to children would only encourage them to ask for more. Gavitt, Charity and Children, 278. Alberti disapproved of an allowance for a child since anything that would contribute to one's learning how to spend money was bad. Alberti, 241-42.

49. Bell, 159.

50. "There was little room left for affection or tenderness; parental authority was too absolute, too severe." Origo, The Merchant of Prato, 189. Comments from Florentines, like the one from Lapo Mazzei to the employer of his 16-year-old son, led her to this conclusion. Lapo told him to beat his son like a dog and put him in prison if he did not obey. This may be more rhetoric than true feelings, since in the same letter Lapo told the employer to watch over his child and care

for him as his own because he was so far away from Lapo and still seemed like a little boy to him. Origo, *The Merchant of Prato*, 127.

Many social historians of ancient Rome have likewise argued that children there were treated like slaves. Richard Saller has recently refuted that notion. Richard Saller, "Corporal Punishment, Authority, and Obedience in the Roman Household," in *Marriage, Divorce, and Children in Ancient Rome*, ed. Beryl Rawson, 144-65 (Oxford, 1991).

51. Children who get spanked for various offenses appear in Boccaccio's *Decameron*, II:8, IV:1, IV:8, V:1. Catherine of Siena remembered receiving spankings from her mother; Niccolò Ammanatini remembered receiving them from his employer. Bell, 36; Brucker, 20. On spanking see also Goodich, "Bartholomaeus Anglicus," 82; Origo, *The Merchant of Prato*, 117.

52. Alberti, 66. Boccaccio noted how fathers did not like to see their second wives discipline their children. Boccaccio, *The Corbaccio*, 38.

53. Dominici, 43, 48. Alberti too urged moderation in discipline. In three of *The Decameron's* stories Boccaccio criticized fathers who imposed too harsh a punishment on their children. *Decameron*, II:6, V:7, X:10.

54. Alberti, 69-70.

55. David Herlihy, "Medieval Children," in *Essays on Medieval Civilization: The Walter Prescott Webb Memorial Lecture* 12, ed. Bede Karl Lackner; Kenneth Day Philip (Austin, 1978), 125. Giovanni Rucellai, for instance, opposed it. Gavitt, 284. Matteo Palmieri and Maffeo Vegio both thought corporal punishment was inappropriate in a school setting since it was against nature, smacked of servility, caused resentment and hatred of the teacher, and was pedagogically unsound. Herlihy, "Medieval Children," 125; Grendler, 35-36. Their criticisms are equally valid for the inappropriateness of corporal punishment at home considering the pedagogical roles of the father and mother.

56. Alberti, 70-80, 211.

57. Origo, *The Merchant of Prato*, 116.

58. Alberti, 69.

59. Alberti, 194-95; Philips, 46. Other *ricordanze* show the same pattern, for instance the *ricordanze* of Paliano di Falco Falcucci. ASF, CS, 2, 7. Iris Origo saw the same pattern in the letters between Francesco and Margherita Datini. Origo, *The Merchant of Prato*, 296.

60. Bernardo Machiavelli, *Libro di Ricordi*, ed. Cesare Olschki (Florence, 1954), 203; BNF, Fondo Nazionale, 2, 2, 357, fol. 151r; ASF, CS, 2, 3, fol. 36r.

    For purposes of illustration here the average daily wage rate between 1472 and 1488 for an unskilled worker was about ten soldi, for a skilled worker about sixteen soldi. Between 1491 and 1501 the average price per libra of veal was about two soldi, beef about one soldo, pork about one-and-a-half soldi, and fish three-and-a-half to four soldi. Twenty soldi equaled one lira. During the course of the fifteenth century the florin-to-lire ratio inflated from four to seven lire per florin. Goldthwaite, *Building Renaissance Florence*, 429-30, 436-37, 443.

61. Niccolini di Camugliano, *The Chronicles*, 38-40, 52, 56-57, 66.

62. Dominici, 37. He also advised rough cloths. Once again his theme was not how to raise children in general but how to raise children in particular to make them into little monks, friars, and nuns.

63. de la Roncière, 222-24. He notes, of course, that the inventories of poorer Florentines included fewer items of clothing for children.

64. Origo, *The World of San Bernardino*, 48, 268.

65. In 1488, Francesca Strozzi recorded purchasing 48 items of clothing for Carlo, 19 were pairs of shoes. She recorded purchasing 43 items of clothing for Lena; 14 were pairs of shoes. ASF, CS, 4, 72, fols. 2v-4r. Giovanni Niccolini specifically noted that shoes and stockings were major clothing expenses for a child. Niccolini di Camugliano, *The Chronicles*, 66. For similar clothing expense accounts see: NTF, 390, 401-02, 410, 414-15, 432-33, 439, 444, 447; Neri di Bicci, *Le Ricordanze (10 marzo 1453-24 aprile 1475)*, ed. Bruno Santi (Pisa, 1976), 9-10, 102-3, 152-53, 200, 341; BNF, Fondo Nazionale, 2, 2, 357, fols. 61r, 112v-113r, 151r; NTF, 252-55; Machiavelli, 91, 203; Sillano, 78, 93, 133-34; ASF, CS, 2, 4, fol. 41v; ASF, CS, 2, 15, fol. 29v; ASF, CS, 2, 17, fol. 20v; ASF, CS, 4, 353, fol. 63v; ASF, Magistrato dei Pupilli Repubblica, 2, fol. 12r; ASF, Acquisiti e Doni, 190/3, fol. 1v; ASF, CS, 2, 27, fol. 42r; ASF, CS, 4, 418, fol. 11v; ASF, CS, 5, 11, fol. 20v; ASF, CS, 2, 30, fols. 2r-2v, 6rv, 19rv, 23rv, 28rv. Bene Bencivenni kept what looks like a running account for hose with Neri the hosemaker, who rented a shop from him. NTF, 425. Paliano Falcucci kept up a constant account of shoes, hose, and other articles of clothing in his *ricordanze* until the sudden death of his children in 1390. ASF, CS, 2, 7.

66. ASF, Bagni, 15, p. 185. The laws from 1355/56 specifically set the age limit at ten. Boccaccio, *The Corbaccio*, 154, 159. Brucker, 179-81.

67. Luca Landucci, *A Florentine Diary from 1450 to 1516 continued by an Anonymous Writer till 1542*, trans. Alice de Rosen Jervis (New York, 1927), 4.

68. Julius Kirshner and Anthony Molho, "The Dowry Fund and the Marriage Market in Early *Quattrocento* Florence," *Journal of Modern History* 50 (1978), 413. See also Julius Kirshner, *Pursuing Honor While Avoiding Sin: The Monti delle Doti of Florence*, Quaderni di "Studi Senesi, 41 (Milan, 1978) and Anthony Molho, *Marriage Alliance in Late Medieval Florence* (Cambridge, 1994). Florentine jurists argued that grandfathers were legally bound to provide their granddaughters with a dowry if their fathers had died or were unable to provide it. Thomas Kuehn, *Law, Family, & Women: Toward a Legal Anthropology of Renaissance Italy* (Chicago, 1991), 251. One should, perhaps, apply a little caution in viewing the interaction between fathers and daughters over dowries. Daughters and dowries were not mere tools for the cynical game of marital alliance in premodern cultures. Donald E. Queller and Thomas F. Madden, "Father of the Bride: Fathers, Daughters, and Dowries in Late Medieval and Early Renaissance Venice," *Renaissance Quarterly* 46 (1993): 685-711.

69. Niccolini di Camugliano, *The Chronicles*, 130.

70. Francesco Guicciardini, *Maxims and Reflections (Ricordi)* trans. Mario Domandi (Philadelphia, 1965), 68.

71. Kirshner and Molho, 437. The Monte delle Doti came about during a fiscal crisis in 1425 while Florence was at war with Milan. The aim of this fund was to help

pay off the communal debt and assure girls of a suitable dowry. Only the woman's husband or his representative received the money on payment of a tax and presentation of proof of marriage. In theory, of course, the money was the woman's. If a girl who had money invested in the Monte delle Doti became a nun, the money reverted to the convent. Kirshner and Molho, 406-9. For a survey of the financial ups and downs of the dowry fund, see Molho, 28-79.

72. Kirshner and Molho, 413; Molho, 86.
73. Phillips, 46-47; Niccolini di Camugliano, The Chronicles, 138; Neri di Bicci, 565.
74. ASF, CS, 5, 22, fol. 2r; ASF, CS, 4, 418, fol. 46r.
75. Kirshner and Molho, 409. There are, of course, isolated cases of Florentines' placing daughters in a monastery to avoid paying a dowry. For the view that Florentines generally sent daughters off to the monastery to avoid paying the dowry see Niccolini di Camugliano, The Chronicles, 130. For an early opposing view (without the benefit of Kirshner and Molho's studies) see Ross, "The Middle Class Child," 206. Kirshner and Molho's data are drawn only from the girls who had shares enrolled for them in the Monte della Doti. The average age of marriage for these girls was 18. A decision to send a girl to a monastery may represent the realistic appraisal that this particular daughter did not have much of a prospect for marriage. Kirshner and Molho, 427. On the other hand, young women chose willingly to be nuns. Kirshner and Molho found no apparent significant link between birth order and Monte enrollment. Florentines simply enrolled all their daughters. Luca Panzano on 18 December 1445 enrolled his daughters, Mattea, Antonia, and Bartolomea, all at once in the Monte for 15 years. ASF, CS, 2, 9, fol. 123r.
76. Brucker, 20, 234.
77. For the early development of Christian attitudes toward sexuality see Peter Brown, The Body and Society: Men, Women, and Sexual Renunciation in Early Christianity (New York, 1988); Elaine Pagels, Adam, Eve, and the Serpent (New York, 1988). For how the medieval Church tried to regulate and control the sexual practices of its members see James A. Brundage, Law, Sex, and Christian Society in Medieval Europe (Chicago, 1987).
78. Trexler, 379, 381.
79. Dominici, 41. Shahar misread Dominici's intent here. Shahar, Childhood in the Middle Ages, 101.
80. Origo, The Merchant of Prato, 215, 323; Gavitt, Children and Charity, 160, 170-77, 307-09. Gavitt estimates that children at the Innocenti usually ate a pound of bread a day in addition to meat, cheese, wine, beans, and salad. He was unable to determine how much of these foodstuffs each child received. We do know, however, that bread formed 60 percent of the caloric content for the average Florentine. Goldthwaite, Building Renaissance Florence, 343-47.
81. Boccaccio, The Corbaccio, 97.
82. Paolo Certaldo, Libro di Buoni Costumi, ed. Alfredo Schiaffini (Florence, 1945), 127. Shahar, a feminist scholar, even argued that what Paulo da Certaldo was arguing was not misogynist but based on a position of perceived biological differences between girls and boys. Shahar, Childhood in the Middle Ages, 81. Prior to the 1960s pediatricians advised different caloric levels for male and

female infants and children. Newton Kugelmass, *The Newer Nutrition in Pediatric Practice* (Philadelphia, 1940), 25-27. More recently, pediatric advice distinguishes different caloric levels for infants and children based on weight, not sex. Yet, since female infants and children weigh on average less than males, a practical distinction of different caloric levels by sex is still reasonable.

83. Dominici, 45; de la Roncière, 201; Goodich, "Bartholomaeus Anglicus," 79; Ginevra Niccolini di Camugliano, "A Medieval Florentine, His Family and His Possessions," *American Historical Review* 31 (1925), 5-6.

84. *Paradiso*, XV:121-23; Alberti, 50. Mothers frequently took daughters into bed with them. de la Roncière, 195. These sleeping arrangements were common in the premodern era as Emmanuel Le Roy Ladurie discovered in the village of Montaillou. Emmanuel Le Roy Ladurie, *Montaillou: The Promised Land of Error*, trans. Barbara Bray (New York, 1978), 214.

85. See, for example, the child's bed in Filippo Lippi's *Miracle of St. Ambrose*.

86. Bell, 35.

87. Bell, 36-37; de la Roncière, 241; Trexler, 357, 373-74.

88. Dominici, 42-43; Bell, 131.

89. Klapisch-Zuber, *Women, Family, and Ritual*, 322; Trexler, 377.

90. Sacchetti, *Opere*, ed. A. Chiari (Bari 1938), in Trexler, 368; Origo, *The World of San Bernardino*, 61; Dominici, 42; Landucci, 272.

91. Boccaccio, *Decameron*, II:8; Dominici, 42-43. Froissart had described more than 50 children's games. Shahar, *Childhood in the Middle Ages*, 103. For a good description of the games medieval London children played see Hanawalt, *Growing Up*, 78-80.

92. Alberti, 50, 83-84; Trexler, 445.

93. Here he was complaining about what parents were doing instead of concentrating on their children's spiritual well- being. He said that instead of concentrating on a child's religious education parents "take pains in making them beautiful, healthy, cheerful, laughing, and wholly content according to the sensual." Dominici could be sourly critical whenever play interfered with God. Dominici, 45.

94. Origo, *The World of San Bernardino*, 166.

95. Origo, *The Merchant of Prato*, 196. Frequent references in the literature to children's receiving gifts of nuts and sweets (Dominici typically cautioned against children's getting too many of these) reflects their attendance at celebrations, including those for birthdays.

96. Boccaccio describes one of these sleepovers as background in one of his stories. *Decameron*, II:9. Dominici told parents not to let their children go on sleepovers. He might have feared sexual abuse or more likely, since this is a major theme in his work, he feared the loss of parental supervision over the child in this instance. Dominici, 42.

97. Boccaccio, *Decameron*, VIII:5, IX:9.

98. Landucci, 130-31. Savonarola did make use of children, more properly adolescents, in his various processions and demonstrations. While analysis of the meaning of this is beyond the scope of my investigation, see Trexler's *Public Life in Renaissance Florence* for a preliminary examination.

99. de la Roncière, 303.
100. Gavitt, *Charity and Children*, 284-85.
101. de la Roncière 241; Trexler, 169-70.
102. de la Roncière, 240; Boccaccio, *Decameron*, IV:8. That children formed themselves into informal groups (called *brigate* like the informal groupings of adults) which sometimes got themselves involved in mischief, seems to lend an "Our Gang" sort of flavor to what Florentine childhood must have been like. de la Roncière 165; Ross, "The Middle Class Child," 204.
103. Origo claims that even shopkeepers and notaries could have slaves. Origo, "The Domestic Enemy," 321, 333; Origo, *The Merchant of Prato*, 199.
104. ASF, Magistrato dei Pupilli, 1, fols. 62rv, 275rv. While I am assuming that these are the children's toys, they might be the fathers' toys for something resembling bocce ball. Niccolò Busini included a list of household goods at the end of his ricordanze. No toys were listed. This might just reflect the fact that the children were grown or that toys were not that significant an item in cost to be recorded. ASF, CS, 4, 564.
105. Dominici, 42, 45, 53. San Bernardino likewise thought the types of toys children had and the play they engaged in dictated future behavior. Origo, *The World of San Bernardino*, 147.
106. Origo, *The Merchant of Prato*, 199; Origo, *The World of San Bernardino*, 61.
107. Obviously, parents' concerns about violent toys is nothing new. J. R. Hale, *War and Society in Renaissance Europe 1450-1620*, 102.
108. Landucci, *A Florentine Diary*, 56.
109. de la Roncière, 195.
110. Klapisch-Zuber, *Women, Family, and Ritual*, 310-30; Bell, 60.
111. Nannina Medici brought one to her marriage to Bernardo Rucellai in 1466, and Tommaso Guidetti lists one in his wife's trousseau. Perosa, 33; ASF, CS, 4, 418, fol. 4v.
112. ASF, CS, 5, 15, fol. 80rv.
113. Trexler, 367; de la Roncière, 243.
114. Luca Landucci tells us that this "was considered an extraordinary thing, first because children are usually afraid of dead bodies." Landucci, *A Florentine Diary*, 19. Yet the other examples tend to belie this observation. Moreover, coming in contact with the dead, especially the criminal dead, certainly has an air of bravado about it that could have conferred peer approval on children by making them some of the more daring members of their *brigata*.
115. Landucci, *A Florentine Diary*, 256.
116. Origo, The World of San Bernardino, 61.

Chapter VII

1. Boccaccio, *Decameron*, V:9.
2. By one estimate, half of all Florentine children died before their tenth birthday. Ann G. Carmichael, *Plague and the Poor in Renaissance Florence* (Cambridge,

1986), 41. See also Alan S. Morrison, Julius Kirshner, and Anthony Molho, "Epidemics In Renaissance Florence," *American Journal of Public Health* 75 (1983), 531-33.

3. Today, for instance, smallpox has been eradicated. Yet for the premodern world it "is easy to forget that even toothache, however trivial as a disease, could be excruciating." Miriam Slater, *Family Life in the Seventeenth Century: The Verneys of Claydon House* (London, 1984), 117. For the premodern fear of toothache as a point of past *mentalité* see Robert Darnton, *The Great Cat Massacre and Other Episodes in French Cultural History* (New York, 1984), 4.

4. Philip Gavitt, *Charity and Children in Renaissance Florence: The Ospedale degli Innocenti, 1410-1536,* (Ann Arbor, 1990), 290. In one letter Allessandra advised her sons to take a light purgative and get plenty of fresh air because "your health is more important than your property." Gene Brucker, ed., *The Society of Renaissance Florence: A Documentary Study* (New York, 1971), 49. The Datini correspondence includes accounts of Francesco's illegitimate daughter's sore throats and accidents. Iris Origo, *The Merchant of Prato: Francesco di Marco Datini 1335-1410* (New York, 1957), 198. Florentines recognized that all age groups had their specific diseases. Leon Battista Alberti, *The Family in Renaissance Florence: I Libri della famiglia,* trans. Renée Neu Watkins (Columbia, 1969), 85. For children and disease elsewhere in medieval Europe see Shulamith Shahar, *Childhood in the Middle Ages* (London, 1990), 145-48.

5. Alberti, 11. Daniel Roche cautioned readers that they have to put the premodern violence, sickness, and death that Jacques-Louis Ménétra witnessed as a child into context. For us it is excessive; for him it was part of the structures of everyday life. Jacques-Louis Ménétra, *Journal of My Life,* trans. Daniel Roche (New York, 1986), 253. Third-world countries today—especially the poorest and least industrialized ones—experience and perceive disease much as premodern Western Europe did.

    In fact, some of these people experience a life that is worse than that in premodern Western Europe. High birth rates and high disease rates, coupled with superurbanization, malnutrition, and the effects of predatory capitalism, have created in the *favelas,* the slums surrounding Latin American megalopoleis, horrible living conditions in which even the maternal instinct is suppressed by the simple instinct for human survival. Nancy Scheper-Hughes, *Death Without Weeping: The Violence of Everyday Life in Brazil* (Berkeley, 1992).

6. On the incidence of death for children in premodern Europe see Barbara Hanawalt, *Growing Up in Medieval London: The Experience of Childhood in History* (New York, 1993), 23, 57-58, 66; Margaret King, *The Death of the Child Valerio Marcello* (Chicago, 1994), 151.

7. Luke Demaitre, "The Idea of Childhood and Childcare in Medical Writings of the Middle Ages," *Journal of Psychohistory* 4 (1977), 465. Alberti, 52. Julius Kirshner and Anthony Molho, "The Dowry Fund and the Marriage Market in Early Quattrocento Florence," *Journal of Modern History* 50 (1978), 416, 423, and 427. Whenever grain prices soared in Florence the first to be found dead of starvation were the children of the poor. Luca Landucci, *A Florentine Diary from 1450 to*

1516 Continued by an Anonymous Writer till 1542, trans. Alice de Rosen Jervis (New York, 1927), 117.

8.   Alberti, 52, 124.

9.   Giovanni Dominici, *Regola del governo di cura familiare: parte quarta: On the Education of Children,* trans. and ed. Arthur Basil Coté (Washington D.C., 1927), 68; Giovanni di Pagolo Morelli, *Ricordi,* ed. Vittore Branca (Florence, 1969), 112, 160.

10. Alberti, 54.

11. Demaitre, 477; Alberti, 52; Christiane Klapisch-Zuber, *Women, Family, and Ritual in Renaissance Italy* (Chicago, 1985), 153 n. 70. James Bruce Ross, "The Middle Class Child in Urban Italy, Fourteenth to Early Sixteenth Century," in *History of Childhood,* ed. Lloyd deMause (New York, 1974), 209. Smallpox wreaked havoc upon the child population of Florence. David Herlihy and Christiane Klapisch-Zuber, *Tuscans and their Families: A Study of the Florentine Catasto of 1427* (New Haven, 1985), 278.

The Florentine books of the dead, which are the accounts of gravediggers, list causes of death, and include descriptions of various childhood diseases. Ibid; Carmichael, 95, 41-52. The *catasto* of 1427 even recorded childhood illnesses. Klapisch-Zuber, *Women, Family, and Ritual,* 98. Medieval London children suffered from the same two categories of diseases, Hanawalt, *Growing Up in Medieval London,* 19, 20-24, 29, 34, 57-58, 67, 94-96, 113, 135, 137, 140, 164, 175-76, 196, 219.

For the connection between accident hypothermia (that associated with long-term exposure to moderately cold indoor temperatures), respiratory infections, and infants in premodern Europe see John D. Post, *Food Shortage, Climactic Variability, and Epidemic Disease in Preindustrial Europe: The Mortality Peak in the Early 1740s* (Ithaca, 1985), 202-26. On poor sanitation, dysentery, and children see ibid., 260-69.

12. In England before 1349, 24 percent of the accident victims who died were children; after 1349, 31 percent of the accident victims who died were children. Barbara Hanawalt and George Sussman argued based on such evidence that premodern people may have given less adequate care to their children than we do today. Barbara A. Hanawalt, "Childrearing among the Lower Classes of Late Medieval England," *Journal of Interdisciplinary History* 8 (1977), 5, 14-17; George D. Sussman, *Selling Mother's Milk: The Wet-Nursing Business in France 1715-1914* (Urbana, 1982), 55-56. Perhaps, but our age is accident prone as well, though the quality and quantity of our accidents are different from those of premodern accidents. Hanawalt noticed how little girls were more likely to suffer burns and scalds than little boys. Hanawalt, 15-16. Of course, for women in the past cooked over open flames in hearths, and girls learned their roles from their mothers by doing. Just as we accept traffic accidents as a consequence of modern society, so did they accept certain accidents, such as those caused by open flames. For more on medieval children and accidents see Shahar, *Childhood in the Middle Ages,* 139-44.

13. Alberti, 52.

14. Benvenuto Cellini, *Autobiography,* trans. George Bull (New York, 1956), 19; Judith C. Brown, *Immodest Acts: The Life of a Lesbian Nun in Renaissance Italy* (Oxford, 1986), 26. On 12 November 1487 a fourteen-year-old boy went with a lion tamer into the lions' cage (the city kept a cage of them near the Signoria as a symbol of the city). A lion mauled him and he died. On 9 May 1486 a trained bear in the piazza Tornaquinci retaliated against its childish tormenters by attacking a little girl. Bystanders freed her; she later recovered. Landucci, *A Florentine Diary,* 43-44. On the perception of the dangers of the premodern world, including those from animals, see Darnton, 9-72.

15. Landucci, *A Florentine Diary,* 123, 186, 239. See also Sharon T. Strocchia, *Death and Ritual in Renaissance Florence* (Baltimore, 1992), 166.

16. Landucci noted the robbery and murder of a little girl. Luca Landucci, *Diario Fiorentino dal 1450 al 1516, continuato da un anonimo fino al 1542,* ed. I. Del Badia (Florence, 1883), 4.

17. Landucci, *A Florentine Diary,* 218; Samuel Kline Cohn, *The Laboring Classes in Renaissance Florence* (New York, 1980), 196. Landucci recorded that the rapist of a twelve-year-old girl was beheaded. Landucci, *A Florentine Diary,* 11. Piero di Jacopo was executed at the stake for molesting a ten-year-old boy, though another child molester was only fined and whipped. Brucker, 207-8. My evaluation of the city's severity is impressionistic, since no detailed statistical study of sex crimes in Florence has been done.

18. "On several occasions during these months, and in various places, he committed the abominable crime of sodomy with his niece Margherita, against the instincts and norms of nature, against her will, and to her grave harm, opprobrium, and shame, and against both human and divine law, and in the greatest violation of the divine majesty and human nature." Brucker, 152-53. There is, as yet, no good study of incest in either Florence or premodern Europe as a whole.

19. Landucci, *A Florentine Diary,* 71-72. Boccaccio noted the problems of what happened to children in a sacked town. Boccaccio, *Decameron,* V:5.

20. ASF, CS, 2, 4, fol. 102r; Origo, *The Merchant of Prato,* 112, 177.

21. Katherine Park, "The Criminal and the Saintly Body: Autopsy and Dissection in Renaissance Italy," *Renaissance Quarterly* 47 (1994), 8-9.

22. Demaitre, 476.

23. BNF, Panciatichiano, 80, fol. 177r; ASF, CS, 5, 1751.

24. Dominici, 67.

25. ASF, CS, 4, 71, fols. 40v and 51r; Ginevra Niccolini di Camugliano, *The Chronicles of a Florentine Family 1200-1470* (London, 1933), 59.

26. Ancient Roman doctors' relative ignorance regarding young children and their diseases may imply that the medical profession saw them as the province of midwives, nurses, and mothers, and not that society as a whole refused to recognize them. Suzanne Dixon, *The Roman Family* (Baltimore, 1992), 100.

27. Demaitre, 476. Boccaccio, *Decameron,* V:5.

28. Origo, *The Merchant of Prato,* 231. Epilepsy was particularly a disease of children. More than 75 percent of those dying from epilepsy in Florence were children; in Arezzo they were all children. Herlihy and Klapisch-Zuber, 278.

29. Simone Martini's *St Louis of Toulouse Crowning King Robert* (1317) and Ambrogio Lorenzetti's *Scenes from the Life of Saint Nicholas* (1330-32) are examples of this. See Charles de la Roncière, "Tuscan Notables on the Eve of the Renaissance," in *A History of Private Life*, ed. Philippe Ariès and Georges Duby, Vol. 2 *Revelations of the Medieval World*, ed. Georges Duby (Cambridge, MA, 1988), 269.

30. BNF, Manoscritti Palatini, 1129, fol. 48r; *Two Memoirs of Renaissance Florence: The Diaries of Buonaccorso Pitti and Gregorio Dati*, trans. Julia Martines, ed. Gene Brucker (New York, 1967), 128.

31. Boccaccio recognized this in *Decameron*, II:8.

32. Slater, 116. Elaine G. Rosenthal, "The Position of Women in Renaissance Florence: neither Autonomy nor Subjection," in *Florence and Italy: Renaissance Studies in Honor of Nicolai Rubinstein*, ed. Peter Denley and Caroline Elam (Exeter, 1988), 369-82.

33. Demaitre, 476.

34. Fra Domenico da Pescia, a colleague of Girolamo Savonarola, healed a man's crippled knee through prayer and by making the sign of the cross on it. Iris Origo, *The World of San Bernardino* (New York, 1962), 167-68. San Bernardino himself was reputed to have healed many, including children, just by his presence. *Ibid.*, 179-80. In fact, throughout Europe about one-third of the miracles associated with saints involved the healing of children. Shahar, *Childhood in the Middle Ages*, 146.

35. *Ibid.*, 164; Brucker, 261-66.

36. Ross, "The Middle Class Child," 209. Datini even had the child brought home from the wetnurse, but to no avail.

37. Origo, *The World of San Bernardino*, 176. A sacred place with the same curative powers was located near Romans in the sixteenth century. Emmanuel Le Roy Ladurie, *Carnival in Romans* (New York, 1979), 25. On these as Europe-wide phenomena associated with shrines to a holy dog see Jean-Claude Schmitt, *The Holy Greyhound: Guinefort Healer of Children since the Thirteenth Century* (Cambridge, 1983).

38. Boccaccio, *Decameron*, VII:3. In fact, the cure described here, which certainly reflects Tuscan folkloric practices, paralleled the rite for baptism. Rosario Ferrere, "Rito battesimale e comparatico nelle novelle senesi della VII giornata," *Studi sul Boccaccio* 16 (1987): 307-14.

39. Herlihy and Klapisch-Zuber, 278-79; Carmichael, 41-45.

40. A. Petrucci, ed., *Il Libro di Ricordanze dei Corsini (1362-1457)*, (Rome, 1965), 113-14; Camugliano, 60-61. It has not been that long ago in America that the summer months were seen as killer months for children. American parents in the 1930s, 1940s, and 1950s dreaded the outbreak of polio during the summer in ways that are hard to understand today; and midwesterners in the 1920s, 1930s, and 1940s were aware of the dangers of "Summer Complaint," a combination of spoiled food and poor sanitation, that could kill children.

41. May had the fewest. Klapisch-Zuber, *Women, Family, and Ritual*, 153. See also Morrison, 532; Carmichael, 50.

42. *Two Memoirs*, 134-35; Origo, *The Merchant of Prato*, 229; David Herlihy, "Santa Caterina and San Bernardino: Their Teachings on the Family," in *Atti del simposio*

internazionale Cateriniana-Bernardiniano Siena, 17-20 Aprile 1980, ed. Domenio Maffei and Paolo Nardi (Siena, 1982), 922.

43. Giovanni Morelli recalled that his sister Mea had four children, none of whom lived more than two years. Morelli, 181. Luca Landucci recalled how he and his wife lost five of their twelve children. Landucci, *A Florentine Diary*, 7-8. Matteo Corsini ruefully noted how he had had "many" children born but only three "remained." *Il Libro*, 4. Guido Antella lost so many children that it appears he was stocking a charnel house. NTF, 803-6.

44. Between 1433 and 1453 the death rate for girls five years and under enrolled in the Monti dell Doti was 37.4 percent. Kirshner and Molho, 421.

45. Florentines recognized that their children were especially at risk. Naddo Montecatini recorded that in the visitation of July and August 1383 "mori grandissima quantita di gente in Firenze. . . . Inanzi sono molti fanciulli e fanciulle piccole." BNF, 2, 150, fol. 102. Florentine physicians recognized that the plague struck children with unusual severity. Herlihy and Klapisch-Zuber, 257, 274; Klapisch-Zuber, *Women, Family, and Ritual*, 16; Herlihy, "Santa Caterina," 919-22. Carmichael noted that while children are not necessarily more susceptible to the plague, they are more vulnerable to other effects and consequences of it. Carmichael, 90-94. Of course, the people of the era would not have been medically sophisticated to have noted the distinction.

46. Klapisch-Zuber, *Women, Family, and Ritual*, 26. A Sienese chronicler stated that so many children died only a few remained. Herlihy, "Santa Caterina," 922.

47. Herlihy and Klapisch-Zuber, 80, 195. Other visitations sometimes had little effect on the child population of urban Florence, perhaps because so many of the children were in the countryside at the wetnurse. *Ibid.*, 275. Throughout Herlihy's works the plague figures as a structure for family life in Tuscany. Anthony Molho, *Marriage Alliance in Late Medieval Florence* (Cambridge, 1994), 2.

48. Anthony Molho, ed., *Social and Economic Foundation of the Italian Renaissance* (New York, 1969), 92.

49. *Ibid.*, 92; Morelli, 159, 167, 368, 369.

50. Herlihy and Klapisch-Zuber, 91.

51. ASF, CS, 4, 346, fol. 85v; BNF, 2, 3, 280, fol. 10r; ASI, 1, 4, (1843), 40; ASF, MS, 77, fol. 36r.

52. Origo, *The Merchant of Prato*, 372-73. Losses to other *ricordanze* writers' families, while tragic, were not as devastating. ASF, CS, 2, 4, fols. 24v, 68v; BNF, Manoscritti Palatini, 1129, fols. 13v, 49r.

53. Petrucci, 37.

54. Alberti, 124-27.

55. Ross, "The Middle Class Child," 210.

56. Flight from the plague also explains why so many Florentines were born outside Florence in the country. *Two Memoirs*, 64; Mark Phillips, *The Memoir of Marco Parenti: A Life in Medici Florence* (Princeton, 1987), 45. Other cities, for instance Milan, saw the same ebb and flow of populations during the plague. Ann G. Carmichael, "Contagion Theory and Contagion Practice in Fifteenth-Century Milan," *Renaissance Quarterly* 44 (1991): 213-56. For similar effects of the

plague on family and children see Hanawalt, *Growing Up in Medieval London*, 58, 95, 113, 135, 137, 140, 164, 175-76, 196, 219.

57. Morelli, 368-69. Others too suffered the agony of futile flight. Origo, *The Merchant of Prato*, 350; Ross, "The Middle Class Child," 210.

58. Strocchia, *Death and Ritual*, 107.

59. Morelli, 168; *Two Memoirs*, 87-88; Bernardo Machiavelli, *Libro di Ricordi*, ed. Cesare Olschki (Florence, 1954), 91-92.

60. G. O. Corazzini, ed. *Ricordanze di B. Masi calderaio fiorentino dal 1478 al 1526*, (Florence, 1906), 35.

61. Origo, *The Merchant of Prato*, 349.

62. BNF, Manoscritti Palatini, 1129, fol. 52r.

63. For Torni see Park, 9; *Two Memoirs*, 116. The death of their children deeply affected Roman parents. Dixon, xiiii.

64. Marco Parenti recorded how "iddio abbia riceiuto la pura anima sua" of his four daughters when they died at eight, two, one, and less than one years of age. ASF, CS, 2, 17bis, fols. 2r-2v. Niccolò Busini noted how "a ore 15 piaque a dio chimare ase la detta Alessandra." ASF, CS, 4, 564, fol. 30r. See also BNF, Palatino Baldovinetti, 37, fols. 8v, 64r; ASF, CS, 5, 1461, fols. 19v, 47r; BNF, Panciatichi, 101, fol. 6r. Bartolomeo Salvetti noted, "Richordo oggi questo di 11 di luglio 1487 piaque al dio di tirare ase la benedetta anima di Lionardo mio figliuolo." ASF, MS, 96, fol. 12r. See also ASF, AD, 8, fols. 19v, 51v; ASF, CS, 3, 215, fol. 174v. Bartolomeo Sassetti recorded that on "di 22 daprile 1468 a ore 23 sonato piacque a idio volalo asse" his son Lorenzo. ASF, CS, 5, 1750, fol. 193r.

65. The belief that children were a loan to the parent from God was common. When a child died, according to Alberti, "I think it is the father's duty rather to recall and to render thanks for the many joys and delights which the child has given him rather than to sorrow because the one who lent them to you has in his own time claimed them again." Alberti, 54. Alessandra Strozzi echoed this sentiment. Brucker, 48. Lapo Mazzei noted his mixed feelings at the death of a son. On the one hand, he was saddened by his loss and the boy's pain; on the other hand, the child was leaving the material world before being corrupted by it. Origo, *The Merchant of Prato*, 231. In fact, this belief was common across premodern Europe. Shahar, *Childhood in the Middle Ages*, 13.

66. Even with the high mortality rates of the premodern world and the shortened life spans, Florentines thought death before 35 years of age "untimely and tragic." Herlihy and Klapisch-Zuber, 83.

67. Luca Landucci made sense of an assault upon his son by putting the random particular act into a larger conception, a Christian conception. This was not mere rationalization; it helped make sense of the senseless while at the same time reaffirming his family's relationship with their deity. After Luca's world had been temporarily halted by this misfortune, this mental outlook allowed it once again to start spinning. Benedetto, he recorded, who was only twelve, was stabbed in the face: "we cannot think by whom. We believe it must have been a mistake, as he has never offended anyone or suspected anyone of having a grudge against him: it happened in punishment of our other sins. I freely pardon the aggressor,

as I hope that the Lord may pardon me, and I pray God to pardon him and not send him to hell for this." Landucci, *A Florentine Diary*, 77.

68. Marsiglio Ficino's mother saw her mother in a dream, where she was crying. She understood that her mother was trying to communicate something to her. The next day her own child came back from the wetnurse, dead. Ross, "The Middle Class Child," 196. The dead knew they were going to receive a companion, and they wanted to and were able to tell the living about it. On how the dead were not really gone in the eyes of family members see Sharon Strocchia, "Death Rites and the Ritual Family in Renaissance Florence," in *Life and Death in Fifteenth-Century Florence*, ed. Marcel Tetel, Ronald Witt, and Rona Goffen (Durham, 1989), 123; "Remembering the Family: Women, Kin, and Commemorative Masses in Renaissance Florence," *Renaissance Quarterly* 42 (1989), 636.

69. Camugliano, 129; *Ricordanze di Bartolomeo Masi*, 140.

70. ASF, MS, 77, fol. 51r; ASF, CS, 3, 215, fol. 178v.

71. "Iddio gli dia gratia che lui salvi lanima suo." ASF, AD, fol. 36r.

72. Matteo Corsini marked all his children's deaths with a cross but none of the deaths of other relatives was so marked. Petrucci, 89-95.

73. BNF, Panciatichiano, 134, fol. 5v; ASF, CS, 5, 1461, fol. 19v; ASF, CS, 3, 275, fol. 20v; ASF, CS, 2, 17bis, fols. 2r-2v; BNF, Panciatichi, 101, fols. 4v, 5r, 6r, 11v, ASF, CS, 2, 16, fol. 5r; ASF, AD, 19, fol. 19v. Ser Iacopo da Prato did not place a cross next to his death entries. BNF, Manoscritti Palatini, 1129.

74. M. T. Clanchy, *From Memory to Written Record: England, 1066-1307* (Cambridge, MA, 1979), 184.

75. Maria Teresa Sillano, ed., *Le ricordanze di Giovanni Chellini da San Miniato: medico, mercante e umanista (1425-1457)* (Milan, 1984), *passim*.

76. ASF, CS, 5, 1461, fol. 47r.

77. BNF, Palatino Baldovinetti, 37, fol. 30r.

78. ASF, AD, fols. 6r, 36r; ASF, CS, 5, 22, fols. 90r, 97r.

79. Petrucci, 144.

80. BNF, Palatino Baldovinetti, 37, fol. 21v; ASF, CS, 5, 22, fol. 90r.

81. Brucker, 55.

82. ASF, CS, 5, 11, fol. 20v; also recorded in ASF, CS, 5, 10, 20v.

83. Strocchia, *Death and Ritual*, 58, 66, 168.

84. "Ricordanze sia che chome fu piacere di dio la sopradetta Tessa figliuola del sopradetta la pozo essendo deta d'anni 17 e bella e buona fanciulla mori in firenze la notte vengiente i di 7 di luglio 1429 e ben confessa e contrita e debbe tutti i sagramenti dell Santa Chiesa e detto di fuo sepellata con grande honore in Santo Stefano a ponte." ASF, MS, 77, fol. 41r. Alessandra Strozzi was relieved to hear that her son Matteo had received the last rites and had confessed before his death. She said his death could have been worse, since those who died suddenly without these things lost "both body and soul." Brucker, 48.

85. ASF, CS, 4, 71, fol. 41r; BNF, Palatino Baldovinetti, 37, fol. 35r.

86. Cellini, 333.

87. Commenting on a parent's reaction to the high infant- mortality of seventeenth-century England, Paul Seaver concluded, "Doubtless some became callous in the face of such a slaughter and found in indifference an antidote to the predictable

loss. For Wallington [a puritan artisan], however, each new child was an endless source of anxiety, a being to be cherished and prayed over, and each death, however expected, was a crushing blow." Paul S. Seaver, *Wallington's World: A Puritan Artisan in Seventeenth-Century London* (Stanford, 1985), 86-87. According to Martine Segalen, "The false problem of maternal indifference to the infant in past times can be disposed of at once. No woman and no couple can undergo the shock of repeated births and rapid deaths—whether in a matter of hours, days or months—without trauma. A whole range of popular prophylactics and remedies surround the most dangerous moments of the infant's life." Martine Segalen, *Historical Anthropology of the Family* (Cambridge, 1986), 174. See also Lockwood, 116-17; Linda Pollock, *Forgotten Children: Parent-Child Relations from 1500 to 1900* (Cambridge, 1983), 134-41; and Shahar, *Childhood in the Middle Ages*, 149-55.

88. Richard Trexler, *Public Life in Renaissance Florence* (New York, 1980), 120. *Two Memoirs*, 127.

89. Rudolph M. Bell, *Holy Anorexia* (Chicago, 1985), 97; Boccaccio, *Decameron*, II:6, III:8, X:10; Ross, "The Middle Class Child," 226 n. 191.

90. Brucker, 48.

91. Origo, *Merchant of Prato*, 25; BNF, Manoscritti Palatini, 853, fol. 30v; ASF, MS, 77, fol. 40r; ASF, CS, 2, 4, fol. 22v.

92. Origo, *Merchant of Prato*, 112.

93. These consolations reveal a deep and emotional sense of loss at the death of a child. George W. McClure, "The Art of Mourning: Autobiographical Writings on the Loss of a Son in Italian Humanist Thought," *Renaissance Quarterly* 39 (1986), 446-47, 452-53, 456, 462-63, 471-72. For a more complete study of this phenomenon see Idem, *Sorrow and Consolation in Italian Humanism* (Princeton, 1991). Gianozzo Manetti wrote an oration on the death of his son, which in its intensity of emotion serves as evidence that he "had formed a web of bonds with his eight year-old son, and that the child's death deprived him of essential benefits." James R. Banker, "Mourning a Son: Childhood and Paternal Love in the Consolateria of Gianozzo Manetti," *Journal of Psychohistory* 3 (1975-76), 352. According to Strocchia, "Bartolomeo Dei's more meditative reflection on the fragility of fortune and the brevity of life, written on the death of Lorenso de' Medici's young daughter Luigia in 1488, still retains the power to move the reader five centuries later." Strocchia, *Death and Ritual*, 186; see also 105-48. For an example of Venetian consolation literature see Margaret L. King, *The Death of the Child Valerio Marcello* (Chicago, 1994).

94. McClure, "The Art of Mourning," 471; Coluccio Salutati, for instance, explained in a letter to a friend that even philosophy was no consolation for the death of his son. Klaus Arnold, *Kind und Gesellschaft in Mittelalter und Renaissance* (Paderborn, 1980), 41.

95. McClure, "The Art of Mourning," 442.

96. Arnold, 40-41.

97. Banker, 352. Banker noted the lack of such literature in the Middle Ages. But this is understandable since writers of the Renaissance had adopted a different form of rhetoric and use of sources than had medieval writers.

98. See Richard C. Trexler, "In Search of Father: The Experience of Abandonment in the Recollections of Giovanni di Pagolo Morelli," *Journal of Psychohistory* 3 (1975-76), 225-52, which translates pages 142-57, 177-83, 194-99, 202-83, 358, 455-58, 475-91, 491-516, and 542 of Branca's edition of Morelli's *Ricordi.* Trexler called Morelli's reaction to his son's death "unique;" Ross called it "excessive." Trexler, "In Search of Father," 225; Ross, "The Middle Class Child," 198-99. Morelli's passage is unique in that it survived. The grief described and the ritual demonstrated were common for premodern Florentines. His reaction is excessive only if we assume people in the past did not grieve for their children. But they did, and his reaction is thus human. Charles de la Roncière read this passage correctly when he noted that Morelli "never got over the experience of watching his son Alberto die." de la Roncière, 270.

Trexler devoted considerable time and effort to this account, though he fell into the same trap Ross did since he assumed that Morelli was motivated in his reaction to his son's death by guilt, not grief. Trexler argued that Morelli felt guilty because he did not have his son confessed at his death. But, as Trexler even pointed out, Alberto was not of the canonical age to require confession before death. Trexler, *Public Life,* 172-85. Morelli's concern for the salvation of Alberto's soul stemmed from his Christian duty to the dead—especially those of the family—not from having forgotten a rite. That the dead needed earthly prayers for their transition from Purgatory to Heaven was a well-established fact in the premodern world.

99. Peter Laslett, "Parental Deprivation in the Past: A Note on Orphans and Stepparenthood in English History," in *Family Life and Illicit Love in Earlier Generations: Essays in Historical Sociology,* ed. Peter Laslett (Cambridge, 1977), 170. Stone argued that this fact, coupled with apprenticing, meant that the premodern world did not witness the conflict between parents and their adolescent children that is such a common feature of modern family life today. Lawrence Stone, *The Past and the Present* (Boston, 1981), 218.

100. Boccaccio, *Decameron,* II:3, III:9, IV:3 and 8, V:5 and 9. Most of the *ricordanze* accounts are of grandchildren or nieces and nephews left behind: "Il detto Rinaldo [a brother] mori rimasene Biagio suo figliuolo." ASF, MS, 79, fol. 60r. See also ASF, CS, 2, 59, fol. 195; Matteo Palmieri, *Ricordi fiscali (1427-1474) con due appendici relative al 1474-1495,* ed. Elio Conti (Rome, 1983), 9; ASF, MS, 77, fol. 41r; Machiavelli, 97; Petrucci, 5. Bartolomeo Valori recorded the marriage of his sister on 24 January 1369. "E a di XVI di novembre ano mccclxxxiiii piacque a dio chiamare asse la detta franciescha rimasene due fanciulli maschi." ASF, BNF, Panciatichiano, 134, fol. 1v. See also ASF, MS, 89, fol. 18r.

101. Morelli, 159. Santo Dietsalvi recorded a like occurrence in his own family, in which the death of his father in 1417 left him and his one-year-old brother behind. BNF, Nuovi Acquisti, 1241, fol. 25.

102. Klapisch-Zuber, *Women, Family, and Ritual,* 120.

103. Origo, *The Merchant of Prato,* 23-24.

104. For widows in other stories see Boccaccio, *Decameron,* II:6, III:9, IV:1 and 8. He also described widowers: II:8, IV:Introduction.

105. Morelli's fate in particular mirrors the possible general fate of Florentine orphans. Trexler, "In Search of Father," 234-38; Morelli, 202-83. For orphans elsewhere in medieval society see Shahar, *Childhood in the Middle Ages*, 155-61; Hanawalt, *Growing Up in Medieval London*, 14, 19, 47, 48-49, 53, 55, 57-58, 60, 77, 89-107, 113, 159, 175, 205, 223-25.

106. Alberti, 33-34; Brucker, 20.

107. As he put it, Marco da Rasoio at his death left behind "una fanciulla non à nulla." Palmieri, 14.

108. Origo, *The Merchant of Prato*, 372.

109. Bartolomeo Sassetti noted how his new wife, Rosa, served as guardian of her son by her previous husband. ASF, CS, 5, 1750, fol. 215rv; ASF, CS, 5, 1751, 161v. See also Brucker, 51. Manno Petrucci and his brother Giovanni became guardians of their brothers. ASF, CS, 2, 17, fol. 8r.

110. This was common practice in two generations of the Niccolini family. Niccolini di Camugliano, *The Chronicles*, 37, 48; Klapisch-Zuber, *Women, Family, and Ritual*, 71, 77.

111. ASF, CS, 2, 3, fol. 6r. In 1444, Antonio Masi's brother died and a guardian was appointed over the children; in 1454 the guardian died. ASF, MS, 89, fol. 15r.

112. ASF, Magistrato dei Pupilli-Republica, 1, fols. 1r-5r. In medieval London, the lord mayor and city council oversaw the fate and property of orphans. Hanawalt, *Growing Up in Medieval London*, 89-108.

113. Machiavelli, 116-17; Niccolini di Camugliano, *The Chronicles*, 79-80; Christiane Klapisch, "Household and Family in Tuscany in 1427," in *Household and Family in Past Time*, ed., Peter Laslett and Richard Wall (Cambridge, 1972), 271; ASF, CS, 3, 215, fol. 3r.

114. Boccaccio noted how often a relative would greedily waste a ward's property. Giovanni Boccaccio, *The Corbaccio*, trans. and ed. Anthony K. Cassell (Urbana, 1975), 29, 74-75.

115. Morelli and his siblings, however, were raised by his maternal grandparents after the death of their father.

116. Klapisch-Zuber emphasized the fear of this as common in Florence, *Women, Family, and Ritual*, 117-31. For an opposing viewpoint see Rosenthal.

117. Morelli noted specifically that she had no dowry. Morelli, 188. Antonio Rustichi recorded how his widowed sister came to live with his family in 1417, bringing her five-year-old son and four-year-old daughter with her. ASF, CS, 2, 11, fol. 12v. See also Neri di Bicci, *Le Ricordanze (10 marzo 1453-24 aprile 1475)*, ed. Bruno Santi (Pisa, 1976), 103; ASF, CS, 3, 271, fol. 52v; Klapisch-Zuber, *Women, Family, and Ritual*, 71. Giulia Calvi observed that Klapisch-Zuber's description of the cruel mother may be too static of a model, for she concluded that widows had "a wide range of variables" when they contemplated their and their family's future. Giulia Calvi, "Maddalena Nerli and Cosimo Turnabuoni: A Couple's Narrative of Family History in Early Modern Florence," *Renaissance Quarterly* 45 (1992), 334.

118. This right was called the *tornata*. Klapisch-Zuber, *Women, Family, and Ritual*, 122. Brucker, 52-53, 57-58. In fact, "marriage," as Thomas Kuehn noted, "did not bring to an end the *patria potestas* over the women." Thomas Kuehn, *Law,*

Family, & Women: Toward a Legal Anthropology of Renaissance Italy (Chicago, 1991), 200.

119. Klapisch-Zuber, *Women, Family, and Ritual,* 32; C. Carnesecchi, "Un fiorentino del secolo XV e le sue ricordanze domestiche," ASI, 5, 4 (1889), 148.

120. Klapisch-Zuber, *Women, Family, and Ritual,* 117-31; Trexler, *Public Life,* 165.

121. ASF, MS, 96, fol. 6v. Bartolomeo Sassetti also made reference to his stepdaughter. ASF, CS, 5, 1751, fol. 92v.

122. San Bernardino observed the antipathy of stepchildren for stepparents, and noted that it was reciprocated. Ross, "The Middle Class Child," 197; Origo, *The World of San Bernardino,* 39. See also Carnesecchi, 157; Origo, *The Merchant of Prato,* 195.

123. BNF, Panciatichiano, 134, fol. 4r; Boccaccio, *Decameron,* III:8. Trexler argued convincingly that the dominant theme in Morelli's *Ricordi* relative to his personal history is that of abandonment. His father abandoned him by death; his mother abandoned him by remarriage; his son abandoned him by death. Trexler, *Public Life,* 159-86.

124. Calvi, 321.

125. Trexler called them "framed innocents." Trexler, *Public Life,* 369-70.

126. Some hospitals even housed widows about to give birth. William M. Bowsky, *A Medieval Italian Commune: Siena under the Nine, 1287-1355* (Berkeley, 1981), 15.

127. An entry from October 1356 lists alms given to "Monna Dolce, a poor, old, and infirm woman who lives in the Piazza d'Ogni Santi, and who takes care of a girl who was recommended to her by the society, 15 soldi." Brucker, 233.

128. Brucker, 233. Herlihy and Klapisch-Zuber, 12-13, 246. If these children were not blood relatives, the foster family did not receive an exemption from their Catasto assessment. At Genoa people left money in their wills to children not their own, who may have been orphans. Steven Epstein, *Wills and Wealth in Medieval Genoa, 1150-1250* (Cambridge, MA, 1984), 77. Boccaccio notes such an act of charity in which someone took in a little orphan girl. Boccaccio, *Decameron,* V:5.

129. Even peasant households took in their relatives' children. Richard R. Ring, "Early Medieval Peasant Households in Central Italy," *Journal of Family History* 4 (1979), 18-19. See also Gene Brucker, *Giovanni and Lusanna: Love and Marriage in Renaissance Florence* (Berkeley, 1986), 119; Ibid., *Society of Renaissance Florence,* 53, 152. The Venetian Catasto gave exemptions to households that held related orphans; the Florentine did so haphazardly. Herlihy and Klapisch-Zuber, 9.

130. The Palmieri orphans appear in Marco's Catasto declaration of 1427 and they appear in Matteo's declarations for 1430, 1433, 1447, and 1458. ASF, CS, Acquisti e Doni, 7, fols. 19r, 26r, 41r, 76v; Palmieri, 10, 177; For the Niccolini see Klapisch-Zuber, *Women, Family, and Ritual,* 72, 74-75; Ginevra Niccolini di Camugliano, "A Medieval Florentine, His Family and His Possessions, *American Historical Review* 31 (1925), 3.

131. Herlihy concluded that the high mortality rates and periodic assaults of disease in the premodern world "undermined the durability and stability of the basic familial relations—between husband and wife, and parents and children." David Herlihy, *The Family in Renaissance Italy* (St. Louis, 1974), 8. He later modified

this view: "The Tuscan of the fourteenth century endured the frequent, usually painful sundering of close social bonds with a child, sibling, spouse, with parent, relative or friend." Herlihy, "Santa Caterina," 922.

132. John Gardner, *The Life and Times of Chaucer* (New York, 1977), 61-62. Mark Golden argued that one reason we tend to miss the emotion and grieving of premodern parents at the death of their children is because the process was so wrapped up in rituals that are alien to us. When one is able to penetrate these rituals one finds that "the weight of the evidence seems overwhelmingly to favor the proposition that the Athenians loved their children and grieved for them deeply when they died." Mark Golden, *Children and Childhood in Classical Athens* (Baltimore, 1990), 89; see also 85.

133. Morelli, 542.

Chapter VIII

1. Obviously, many went to school long enough to learn how to read and write as the evidence of their letters attests. In a letter to her husband, Lorenzo di Piero di Lorenzo de' Medici, Magdalena de' Medici signed it "Magdalena Cibo [her maiden name] de' Medici manu propria [that is, done in her own hand]." ASF, Mediceo Avanti il Principato, 106, fol. 44. Clarice Strozzi also signed herself with her maiden name (de' Medici) in her letters to her husband Filippo. ASF, CS, 3, 49, fols. 34, 35, 36, 38, 39, 40, 41, 42, 43, 45. See also ASF, CS, 1, 63, fols. 28, 46, 51, 84, 92, 99, 100; Gene Brucker, ed., *The Society of Renaissance Florence: A Documentary Study* (New York, 1971), 39; Judith C. Brown, *Immodest Acts: The Life of a Lesbian Nun in Renaissance Italy* (Oxford, 1986), 25-26; Ginevra Niccolini di Camugliano, *The Chronicles of a Florentine Family 1300-1470* (London, 1933), 41.

   We also have sketchy evidence of the existence of female teachers. Paul F. Grendler, *Schooling in Renaissance Italy: Literacy and Learning, 1300-1600* (Baltimore, 1989), 90-93. Doffo Spini listed a Mattia di Iacopa da Firenze who taught singing to his daughter, Sveva, in 1419. ASF, CS, 2, 13, fol. 31r. Francesco Datini in 1401 got a newly minted florin to give to his illegitimate daughter to pay the woman who taught her how to read. Iris Origo, *The Merchant of Prato: Francesco di Marco Datini 1335-1410* (New York, 1957), 199.

2. Christiane Klapisch-Zuber, *Women, Family, and Ritual in Renaissance Italy* (Chicago, 1985), 108; David Herlihy, "Medieval Children," in *Essays on Medieval Civilization. The Walter Prescott Webb Memorial Lectures*, eds. B. K. Lackner and K. R. Philip, (Austin, 1978), 122.

3. Grendler, 71-77. Christiane Klapisch-Zuber, "Le chiavi Fiorentine di Barbablù: L'Apprendimento della lettura a Firenze nel XV secolo," *Quaderni Storici* 57 (1984), 765. Parents created the educational structure of Renaissance Italy. Grendler, 2; see also 3-110.

4. Alessandro Perosa, ed., *Giovanni Rucellai ed il suo zibaldone* (London, 1960), 13-14; Paolo da Certaldo, *Libro di Buoni Costumi,* ed. Alfredo Schiaffini (Florence, 1945), 126; Klapisch-Zuber, "Le chiavi," 770.

5. James Bruce Ross, "The Middle Class Child in Urban Italy, Fourteenth to Early Sixteenth Century," in *History of Childhood,* ed. Lloyd deMause (New York, 1974), 212; Klapisch-Zuber, "Le Chiavi," 771, 773; BNF, Fondo Nazionale, 2, 2, 357, *passim;* G. O. Corazzini, ed., *Ricordanze di B. Masi calderaio fiorentino dal 1478 al 1526* (Florence, 1906), 13-15; Neri di Bicci, *Le ricordanze (10 marzo 1453-24 aprile 1475),* ed. Bruno Santi (Pisa, 1976), 38, 200, 285.

6. Bernardo Machiavelli, *Libro di Ricordi,* ed. Cesare Olschki (Florence, 1954), 31, 34, 45, 103, 117, 138; Grendler, 76-77, 309.

7. Grendler's book is a good synthesis punctuated with much original research on schooling as a whole in Renaissance Italy. For what students did see pages 42-110, 142-61, 306-32.

8. ASF, CS, 15, fol. 10r.

9. Bernardo Machiavelli, 31, 34, 46, 49-50, and 54; ASF, CS, 2, 16bis, fol. 4r; ASF, CS, 4, 342, fols. 27v and 32v; ASF, CS, 4, 82, fol. 63r; ASF, CS, 3, 271, fol. 35r; ASF, CS, 2, 17, fols. 39v, 57v, 58r.

10. Bernardo Machiavelli, 197.

11. NTF, 804. *Ricordanze* writers recorded their sons' becoming apprentices. ASF, AD, 83, fol. 6v; Mark Phillips, *The Memoir of Marco Parenti: A Life in Medici Florence* (Princeton, 1987), 81; ASF, MS, 88, fol. 141v; C. Carnesecchi, "Un fiorentino del secolo XV e le sue ricordanze domestiche," *ASI,* 5:4, (1889), 148; BNF, Manoscritti Palatini, 1129, fol. 51; ASF, CS, 4, 353, fol. 138r; Neri di Bicci, 200; Origo, *The Merchant of Prato,* 119-20, 232; Brucker, 17.

12. In 1986, Marvin Becker wrote and suggested this to me as a topic for future study.

13. Richard C. Trexler, *Public Life in Renaissance Florence* (New York, 1980), 372; ASF, CS, 5, 12, fol. 32r; ASF, AD, 11/1, fol. 13r; ASF, CS, 2, 16, fol. 10v; ASF, MS, 88, fol. 141v.

14. Benedetta Carlini was nine years old when she became a nun. See Brown, *passim,* for an introduction to this subject.

15. On the question of parents' motives in sending children to a monastery at an early age see Trexler, 36; Julius Kirshner and Anthony Molho, "The Dowry Fund and the Marriage Market in Early Quattrocento Florence," *Journal of Modern History* 50 (1978), 425. ASF, CS, 5, 1751, fol. 165v; ASF, AD, 11/1, fols. 19r, 21rv, 24r, 27r; ASF, CS, 4, 418, fols. 27r, 47r; Brown, 27.

16. ASF, CS, 2, 16bis. This is number five in a loose collection of letters, records of accord, and lists of goods tucked away inside this *ricordanze.*

17. ASF, CS, 4, 353, fol. 138r.

18. Klapisch-Zuber, *Women, Family, and Ritual,* 110; Origo, *The Merchant of Prato,* 200. *Ricordanze* writers noted the marriages of their daughters at ages 13, 14, and 15. ASF, CS, 3, 270, fol. 11r; ASF, CS, 2, 59, 20 fol. 201.

19. Anthony Molho, "Deception and Marriage Strategy in Renaissance Florence," *Renaissance Quarterly* 41 (1988), 193-217.

20. BNF, Panciatichi, 101, fol. 6r.

21. For some preliminary work on the significance of marriage in Florence see Klapisch-Zuber, *Women, Family, and Ritual*, 178-282. For an examination of marriage and family strategies see Anthony Molho, *Marriage Alliance in Late Medieval Florence* (Cambridge, 1994).

22. Some initial work has, of course, already been done on this. Richard C. Trexler, "Ritual in Florence: Adolescence and Salvation in the Renaissance," in *The Pursuit of Holiness in Late Medieval and Renaissance Religion*, ed. Charles Trinkhaus and Heiko Oberman (Leiden, 1974), 200-64. See also Trexler, *Public Life*, 11, 16, 29, 89, 314, 367-87, 395, 398, 432-35, 456, 458, 475-83.

23. Morris Bishop, trans., *Letters from Petrarch* (Bloomington, 1966), 274-76.

24. Origo, *The Merchant of Prato*, 189. Her conclusion is very odd. Her accounts of the Datini's relations with Francesco's illegitimate daughter, Ginevra, are full of affection and care. She disregarded this particular evidence, noting that "just as Monna Margherita and her friends appear to have led a freer, more amusing life than the conventional picture of young women of their time, so Ginevra was brought up more indulgently than most children." *Ibid.*, 198-99. Ginevra's example was the norm, however, and so perhaps was Monna Margherita's.

25. Leon Battista Alberti, *The Family in Renaissance Florence: I Libri della famiglia*, trans. Renée Neu Watkins (Columbia, 1969), 50.

26. Boccaccio, *Decameron*, VII: 3.

Appendix

1. ASF, CS, 4, 71, fols. 34v, 38v, 39r, 40v, 41r, 41v, 44v, 45v, 46r, 48r, 51r, 52v, 67v.

2. Here l. stands for lire, s. stands for soldi, and d. stands for denari--the standard monetary units in medieval and Renaissance Florence. Twelve denari equaled one soldo, and twenty soldi equalled one lira.

3. A *canna* of cloth equaled between 3 and 4 *braccia*; a woman's gown could contain between 14 and 32 *braccia* of cloth. Iris Origo, *Merchant of Prato: Fancesco di Marco Datini, 1335-1410* (New York, 1957), 391. She has considerable information on Tuscan clothing; see pages 175, 285-303.

4. ASF, CS, 4, 71, fols. 74v, 107v, 121v, 121v, 122r, 129v; ASF, CS, 4, 72, fol. 2v.

5. ASF,CS, 4, 71, fols. 72r, 74r, 80v, 81r, 88v, 90v, 91r, 91v, 93v, 94v, 100r, 103r, 107r, 107v, 111r, 112v, 113v, 114r, 117r, 119r, 120v, 127r; ASF, CS, 4, 72, fol. 3r.

Bibliography

Abbreviations

AD	Acquisti e Doni
ASF	Archivio di Stato di Firenze
ASI	*Archivio Storico Italiano*
BNF	Biblioteca Nazionale Centrale di Firenze
CS	Carte Strozziane
MS	Manoscritti
NTF	*Nuovi testi fiorentini del dugento.* Edited by A.Castellani. Florence: Sansoni, 1952.

PRIMARY SOURCES

I. Manuscript Sources

ASF, AD, 7. Libro di ricordi, di portate e altre memorie diverse di Matteo di Marco Palmieri (1427-1474).

ASF, AD, 8. Ricordanze di Iacopo di Niccolò Melocchi (1497-1517).

ASF, AD, 11/1. Ricordanze di Ser Antonio di Ser Battista Bartolomei (1448-1494).

ASF, AD, 17. Quaderni A di Ser Piero di Ser Domenico Bonaccorsi (1497-1544).

ASF, AD, 18. Ricordi di Ser Piero di Ser Domenico Bonacorsi (1502-1512).

ASF, AD, 19. Ricordanze di Ser Piero di Ser Domenico Bonacorrsi (1512-1517).

ASF, AD, 20. Ricordanze di Ser Piero di Ser Domenico Bonacorrsi (1517-1524).

ASF, AD, 21. Ricordanze di Ser Piero di Ser Domenico Bonacorrsi (1524-1529).

ASF, AD, 83. Ricordanze di Cipriano Guidicci (1417-1469).

ASF, AD, 190/3. Ricordi di Giovanni Baldovinetti (1440-1463).

ASF, AD, 190, 3A. Ricordi di Giovanni di Guido Baldovinetti (1475-1496).

ASF, AD, 190, 3B. Ricordi di Guido Baldovinetti (1440-1467).

ASF, AD, 190, 3C. Libro di memoriale di Francesco di Giovanni Baldovinetti (1493-1509).

ASF, Bagni, 15. Libro di debitori e creditori e ricordanze di Tommaso di Zanobi Ginori (1486-1498).

ASF, Carte Del Bene, 24. Ricordanze di Francesco Bencivenni Del Bene (1298-1321).

ASF, Carte Del Bene, 37. Ricordanze di Ricciardo di Francesco Del Bene (1395-1399).

ASF, Carte Del Bene, 49. Lettere.

ASF, Carte Ricciardi, 521. Ricordanze di Paolo di Baccuccio Vettori (1331-1377).

ASF, CS, 1, 10. Documenti relativi al principato di Cosimo I.

ASF, CS, 1, 27. Memorie di Giovanni del Maestro, maestro di casa del Gran Duca, del battesimo del Gran Principe Cosimo e della Principessa Leonora, e della nozze della regina Maria di Francia.

ASF, CS, 1, 60. Lettere a Luigi Guicciardini, Commissario di Pistoia (1537).

ASF, CS, 1, 61. Lettere a Luigi Guicciardini, Commissario d'Arezzo (1534-1535).

ASF, CS, 1, 63. Lettere a Luigi Guicciardini, Commisario di Castro Caro (1542).

ASF, CS, 2, 2. Ricordanze di Niccolò di Ventura Monachi (1348-1380).

ASF, CS, 2, 3. Ricordanze di Lapo Castiglionchio (1363-1383).

ASF, CS, 2, 4. Ricordanze di Paolo di Alessandro Sassetti (1363-1400).

ASF, CS, 2, 7. Ricordanze di Paliano di Falco Falcucci (1382-1406).

ASF, CS, 2, 9. Ricordanze di Luca di Matteo da Panzano (1406-1461).

ASF, CS, 2, 10. Ricordanze di Cambio di Tano Petrucci (1407-1426).

ASF, CS, 2, 11. Ricordanze di Antonio di Lionardo Rustichi (1412-1436).

ASF, CS, 2, 12. Ricordanze di Dino del Nero Petrucci (1409-1440).

ASF, CS, 2, 13. Ricordanze di Doffo di Nepo Spini (1415-1439).

ASF, CS, 2, 14. Ricordanze di Terrino di Niccolò Manovelli (1421-1434).

ASF, CS, 2, 15. Libro di dare e avere di Manno di Cambio Petrucci (1426-1435).

ASF, CS, 2, 16. Ricordanze di Francesco di Tommaso Giovanni (1409-1443).

ASF, CS, 2, 16 bis. Ricordanze di Francesco di Tommaso Giovanni (1444-1458).

ASF, CS, 2, 17. Ricordanze di Manno di Cambio di Tanno Petrucci (1441-1450).

ASF, CS, 2, 17 bis. Ricordanze di Marco di Parente, Piero di Marco, and Marco di Piero Parenti (1448-1520).

ASF, CS, 2, 21. Ricordanze di Virgilio d'Andrea Adriani (1463-1492).

ASF, CS, 2, 22. Ricordanze di Cambio di Giovanni di Manno Petrucci (1492-1520).

ASF, CS, 2, 23. Ricordi di Giovanni di Girolamo Buongirolami (1492-1505).

ASF, CS, 2, 27. Libro di amministrazione di Niccolò Guidotti (1545-1564).

ASF, CS, 2, 28. Libro di amministrazione di Niccolò Guidotti (1556-1558).

ASF, CS, 2, 29. Ricordanze di Alessandro di Niccolò Guidotti (1554-1590).

ASF, CS, 2, 30. Libro di debitori e creditori di Bernardo di Domenico degli Ogli (1568-1584).

ASF, CS, 2, 59. Ricordanze di Paolo di Guido (1378) and Ricordanze di Guccio di Cino di Bartolino de' Nobili (1362-1444).

ASF, CS, 2, 76. Libro di debitori e creditore e ricordi di Tommaso di Bernardo di Federigo Sassetti (1383-1384).

ASF, CS, 2, 76. Libro della famiglia de' Peruzzi (1300-1305).

ASF, CS, 2, 76. Ricordanze di Giovanni di Ser Caciotti Sensale (1416-1436).

ASF, CS, 2, 76. Ricordi di Ser Davanzato di Iacopo da San Gemignano (1399).

ASF, CS, 2, 76. Ricordi di Paolo di Alessandro Sasseti (1364-1399).

ASF, CS, 2, 119. Registro di memorie domestiche degli Alessandri (1579).

ASF, CS, 3, 49. Libro di lettere scritte a Filippo Strozzi dalla Signora Clarice, sua moglie, Francesco del Nero ed altri.

ASF, CS, 3, 104. Strozzi lettere varie.

ASF, CS, 3, 215. Ricordi di Carlo e Matteo di Lorenzo di Matteo di Simone Strozzi (1491-1541) and Lorenzo di Matteo di Lorenzo Strozzi (1526-1547).

ASF, CS, 3, 270. Ricordanze di Rosso d'Ubertino Strozzi (1317-1340).

ASF, CS, 3, 271. Ricordanze di Rossello d'Ubertino Strozzi (1402-1416).

ASF, CS, 3, 275. Ricordanze di Giovanni di Iacopo Strozzi (1443-1474).

ASF, CS, 4, 71. Ricordanze di Niccolò di Carlo Strozzi (1467-1480).

ASF, CS, 4, 72. Libro di debitori e creditori e ricordi familiari di Francesca Strozzi, vedova di Niccolò di Carlo Strozzi (1486-98).

ASF, CS, 4, 74. Ricordanze di Carlo di Niccolò Strozzi (1492-1505).

ASF, CS, 4, 75. Libro di debitori e creditori di Carlo di Niccolò di Carlo di Marco Strozzi (1501-1526).

ASF, CS, 4, 82. Libro di debitori e creditori e ricordi di Daniello di Carlo di Niccolò Strozzi (1523-1546).

ASF, CS, 4, 342. Libro di ricordi di denari, entrata e uscita e giornale di debitori e creditori di Palla di Palla Strozzi (1409-1442).

ASF, CS, 4, 346. Ricordanze di Bernardo di Tommaso Strozzi (1412-1426).

ASF, CS, 4, 348. Libro di debitori e creditori di Tommaso di Tommaso Strozzi (1428-1453).

ASF, CS, 4, 351. Ricordi per debitori e creditori di Giannozo di Giovanni Strozzi (1439-1461).

ASF, CS, 4, 353. Libro giornale de'debitori e creditori di Marco di Giovanni di Iacopo Strozzi (1486-1525).

ASF, CS, 4, 418. Ricordanze di Tommaso di Iacopo Guidetti (1481-1515).

ASF, CS, 4, 563. Ricordanze di Niccolò del Buono Busini (1394-1406).

ASF, CS, 4, 564. Ricordanze di Niccolò del Buono Busini (1400-1413).

ASF, CS, 5, 10. Libro di debitori e creditori e ricordi di Matteo di Simone Strozzi (1424-1433).

ASF, CS, 5, 11. Debitori e creditori A di Matteo di Simone Strozzi (1424-1434).

ASF, CS, 5, 12. Ricordanze di Matteo di Simone Strozzi (1424-1435).

ASF, CS, 5, 15. Libro di ricordi A di Alessandra di Filippo Macinghi, widow of Matteo di Simone Strozzi, (1453-1473).

ASF, CS, 5, 16. Ricordanze di Piero di Carlo Strozzi (1456-1490).

ASF, CS, 5, 17. Ricordanze di Filippo di Matteo Strozzi (1466-1471).

ASF, CS, 5, 22. Libro di tutti i suoi fatti di Filippo di Matteo Strozzi (1471-1483).

ASF, CS, 5, 41. Libro di debitori e creditori di Filippo di Matteo Strozzi (1484-1490).

ASF, CS, 5, 50. Giornale e ricordi di Filippo di Matteo Strozzi (1489-1491).

ASF, CS, 5, 59. Ricordanze A di eredi di Filippo Strozzi (1492-1516).

ASF, CS, 5, 1461. Ricordanze di Ugolino di Niccolò Martelli (1433-1483).

ASF, CS, 5, 1750. Ricordi di Bartolomeo di Tommaso di Federigo Sassetti (1455-1471).

ASF, CS, 5, 1751. Ricordanze di Bartolomeo di Tommaso di Federigo Sassetti (1471-1477).

ASF, Magistrato dei Pupilli Repubblica, 1. Carriscione di testamenti tutele inventori dei pupilli e adulti (1384-1390).

ASF, Magistrato dei Pupilli Repubblica, 2. Deliberazioni (1384-1390).

ASF, Magistrato dei Pupilli Repubblica, 246. Statuti per gli ufficiali dei pupilli (1384-1473).

ASF, Mediceo avanti il Principato, 99, 7. Ricordanze di Lucrezia di Francesco Tornabuoni.

ASF, Mediceo avanti il Principato, 106. Lettere di Magdalena Cibo de' Medici a Lorenzo di Piero di Lorenzo de' Medici (2 April 1514-8 March 1515).

ASF, Mediceo avanti il Principato, 153, 1. Libro di dare e avere e ricordanze di Giovanni di Bicci e Cosimo di Giovanni de' Medici (1397-1427).

ASF, Mediceo avanti il Prinicipato, 153, 2. Libro di dare e avere e ricordanze di Cosimo e Lorenzo di Giovanni de' Medici (1420-1434).

ASF, Mediceo avanti il Principato, 153, 3. Libro di dare e avere e ricordanze di Cosimo e Lorenzo di Giovanni de' Medici (1435-1450).

ASF, Mediceo avanti il Principato, 163. Ricordi di Piero di Cosimo de' Medici (1464-1468).

ASF, MS, 74. Ricordanze di Guido di Filippo Antella (1298-1312).

ASF, MS, 75. Ricordanze di Lippo di Fede Sega (1304-1362).

ASF, MS, 76. Memoriale di Franciesco Baldovinetti (1314-1338).

ASF, MS, 77. Libro de conti e memorie e ricordi di Lapo di Valore Curianni (1325-1429).

ASF, MS, 79. Ricordanze de figliuoli di Lapo da Castiglionchio (1378-1386).

ASF, MS, 80. Ricordanze de Bernardo di Lapo da Castiglionchio (1382-1384).

ASF, MS, 81. Libro di entrata e d'uscita e die carte memorie de figliuoli di Lapo da Castiglionchio (1382-1397).

ASF, MS, 85. Ricordanze di Dietsalvi di Nerone Dietsalvi (1429-1439).

ASF, MS, 86. Ricordi di Giovanni di Iacopo Venturi (1439-1441).

ASF, MS, 88. Ricordi di Piero di Bernardo Masi (1452-1513).

ASF, MS, 89. Ricordanze di Antonio di Ser Tommaso Masi (1455-1459).

ASF, MS, 96. Ricordi di Bartolomeo di Niccolaio Salvetti (1481-1494).

ASF, MS, 99. Ricordanze di Gianfigliazzi Bongianni (1528-1538).

ASF, Tratte, 39. Descrizione dell'eta' dei cittadini Fiorentini (1429-1456).

ASF, Tratte, 1093. Quaderno dell'età. (1388-1430).

BNF, Fondo Ginori Conti, 9. Libro di conti e ricordi di Bernardo di Giovanni Cambi (1470-1494).

BNF, Fondo Nazionale, 2, 13. Lettere varie.

BNF, Fondo Nazionale, 2, 150. Ricordanze di Naddo di Nepo da Montecatini (1374-1398).

BNF, Fondo Nazionale, 2, 1, 231. Memorie autobiografiche di Raffaello di Bartolomeo Sinibaldi (1515-1538).

BNF, Fondo Nazionale, 2, 2, 357. Ricordanze di Tribaldo dei Rossi (1481-1501).

BNF, Fondo Nazionale, 2, 3, 280. Ricordanze di Francesco di Giovanni di Durante (1330-1348).

BNF, Fondo Nazionale, 2, 9, 146. Ricordi di Michelangelo di Francesco Tanagli (1549-1566).

BNF, Fondo Nazionale, 2, 10, 112, 135. Ricordanze di Borghino di Taddeo (1318-1348).

BNF, Fondo Nazionale, 2, 10, 112, 135. Ricordanze di Luca di Totto da Panzano (1343-1363).

BNF, Fondo Nazionale, 2, 10, 135. Leggi di vesti (1292).

BNF, Landau Finlay, 92. Libro di ricordi di Palla di Nofri Strozzi (1423-1425).

BNF, Landau Finlay, 288. Libro della confessione.

BNF, Magliabechiani, 7, 1014. Libro e ricordi di Filippo di Bernardo Manetti (1429-1456).

BNF, Magliabechiani, 8, 1439. Zibaldone e ricordi di Iacopo di Niccolò Donati (1466).

BNF, Magliabechiani, 25, 555. Ricordi di Giambattista Betti (1509, 1521-1532).

BNF, Magliabechiani, 25, 555. Diario d'incerto (1529-1530).

BNF, Manoscritti Palatini, 678. Compendio dello zibaldone di Antonio Pucci (1484-1485).

BNF, Manoscritti Palatini, 796. Piero di Giovanni da Corella. Trattato di medicina.

BNF, Manoscritti Palatini, 796. Libro di Rasis (Rhazes).

BNF, Manoscritti Palatini, 796. Ricette segreti chimici e medicinali.

BNF, Manoscritti Palatini, 853. Ricordi di cose pubbliche e private dall' anno 1547 all'anno 1660 di Alfonso, Giulio e Alfonso iunore Parigi.

BNF, Manoscritti Palatini, 1068. Manuale miscellane di chirugia e medicina. 1516.

BNF, Manoscritti Palatini, 1129. Ricordanze di Ser Iacopo di Lando da Prato (1380-1417).

BNF, Nuovi Acquisti, 235. Libro di ricordanze di Bartolomeo di Caroccio Alberti (1349-1367).

BNF, Nuovi Acquisti, 260. Ricordanze di Mariotto di Bernardo Alberghi (1557-1571).

BNF, Nuovi Acquisti, 261. Giornale di spese di un anonimo (1525-27).

BNF, Nuovi Acquisti, 368. Libro di ricordi e conti di Bartolomeo di Ser Simone del Compagnio (1363-1371).

BNF, Nuovi Acquisti, 457. Libro di ricordi di Marietta degli Albizzi (1519-1579).

BNF, Nuovi Acquisti, 495. Libro di conti e ricordi di Giovanni di Niccolò Villi.

BNF, Nuovi Acquisti, 1207. Libretto di ricordi di Niccolò di Giovanni Franchini Faviani (1555).

BNF, Nuovi Acquisti, 1239. Libro dell'amministrazione di Tommaso di Piero Bardi (1400-1404).

BNF, Nuovi Acquisti, 1241. Ricordanze di Niccolò di Gualterotto Dietsalvi (1234-1347).

BNF, Palatino Baldovinetti, 35. Ricordi di Zanobi e Iacobo degli Uffizi (1446-1456).

BNF, Palatino Baldovinetti, 37. Ricordanze segrete di Niccolò d'Alesso Baldovinetti (1354-1391).

BNF, Palatino Baldovinetti, 42. Ricordanze di Giovanni di Bernardo di Dinoamico (1449-1485).

BNF, Palatino Baldovinetti, 70. Ricordanze di Maso di Bartolomeo detto Masaccio (1447-1455).

BNF, Palatino Baldovinetti, 152. Ricordi di Biagio Buonaccorsi (1498-1512).

BNF, Panciatichiano, 80. Giovanni Serapione. Trattato delle medecine semplice.

BNF, Panciatichiano, 81. Maestro Guglielmo da Piancenza. La cirugia (1464).

BNF, Panciatichiano, 101. Libro di ricordi di Biagio di Buonaccorso Buonaccorsi (1495-1525).

BNF, Panciatichiano, 102. Ricordi di Finali Cammillo (1597-1605).

BNF, Panciatichiano, 134. Ricordanze di Bartolomeo di Filippo Valori (1427-1476).

BNF, Panciatichiano, 147. Zibaldone di Lorenzo Ridolfi (1386-1388).

The Newberry Library, Chicago, Illinois. Special Collections. Case Manuscript, 27. Ricordanze di Peppo d'Antonio degli Albizzi (1339-1356).

II. Printed Sources

Alberti, Leon Battista. *The Family in Renaissance Florence: I libri della famiglia.* Translated by Renée Neu Watkins. Columbia: University of South Carolina Press, 1969.

Antoninus. *Confessionale.* Venice, 1474.

———. *Summa Theologica.* Pars 4. Venice, 1581.

Barbaro, Francesco. *On Wifely Duties.* Translated by Benjamin G. Kohl. In *The Earthly Republic: Italian Humanists on Government and Society,* edited by Benjamin G. Kohl and Ronald Witt, 179-230. Philadelphia: University of Pennsylvania Press, 1978.

Barberino, Francesco da. *Del reggimento e de' costumi delle donne.* Edited by Guglielmo Manzi. Milan: Giovanni Silvestri, 1842.

Bec, Christian., ed. *Il libro degli affari proprii di casa di Lapo di Giovanni Niccolini de' Sirigatti.* Paris: SEVPEN, 1969.

Bernardino, San. *Le Prediche Volgare.* Edited by C. Cannarozzi. Pistoia and Florence: Banchi, 1934, 1948.

Bicci, Neri di. *Le ricordanze (10 marzo 1453-24 aprile 1475).* Edited by Bruno Santi. Pisa: Edizioni Marlin, 1976.

Bishop, Morris, trans. *Letters from Petrarch.* Bloomington: Indiana University Press, 1966.

Bistort, G. *Il Magistrato alle pompe in Venezia nella Republica di Venezia.* Venice: Regia Deputazione Veneto di Storia Patria, 1912.

Boccaccio, Giovanni. *The Corbaccio.* Translated and edited by Anthony K. Cassell. Urbana: University of Illinois Press, 1975.

———. *The Decameron.* Translated by Mark Musa and Peter Bondanella. New York: New American Library, Inc., 1982.

Brucker, Gene, ed. *The Society of Renaissance Florence: A Documentary Study.* New York: Harper and Row, 1971.

Cellini, Benvenuto. *Autobiography.* Translated by George Bull. Middlesex: Penguin Books, 1956.

Certaldo, Paolo da. *Libro di buoni costumi.* Edited by Alfredo Schiaffini. Florence: Felice Le Monnier, 1945.

Ciardi, John, trans. *The Inferno,* by Dante Alighieri. New York: Mentor, 1954.

Ciardi, John, trans. *The Purgatorio,* by Dante Alighieri. New York: Mentor, 1957.

Ciardi, John, trans. *The Paradiso,* by Dante Alighieri. New York: Mentor, 1961.

Corazzini, G. O., ed. *Ricordanze di B. Masi calderaio fiorentino dal 1478 al 1526.* Florence: Sansoni, 1906.

Credi, Oderigo d'Andrea di. *Ricordanze dal 1405 al 1425*. Edited by F. L. Polidori. ASI, 1, 4, (1843): 50-116.

Cronica di Buonaccorso Pitti con annotazioni ristampata da Alberto Bacchi della Lega. Bologna: Romagnoli-Dall' Acqua, 1905.

Dati, Gregorio. *Il Libro segreto di Gregorio Dati*. Edited by Carlo Gargiolla. Bologna: Gaetano Romagnoli, 1869).

Dolan, John P., trans. and ed. *The Essential Erasmus*. New York: New American Library, Inc., 1964.

Dominici, Giovanni. *Regola del governo di cura familiare parte quarta: On the Education of Children*. Translated and edited by Arthur Basil Coté. Washington, D.C.: Catholic University of America, 1927.

Estratti notarili dal libro del dare e dell'avere di Castro Gualfredi e compagnie dei Borghesi (1253-1267). NTF: 207-11.

Ferrara, Orestes, ed. *The Private Correspondence of Niccolò Machiavelli*. Baltimore: Johns Hopkins University Press, 1929.

Firenzuolo, Agnolo. *Tales of Firenzuolo*. Translated by anon. New York: Italica Press, 1987.

Guasti, Cesare, ed. *Inventario serie prima*. Vol. 1 of *Le Carte Strozziane del R. Archivio di Stato in Firenze*. Florence: M. Cellini, 1884.

Guicciardini, Francesco. *Maxims and Reflections (Ricordi)*. Translated by Mario Domandi. Philadelphia: University of Pennsylvania Press, 1965.

Guidini, Cristofano. *Ricordi (1362-1396)*. Edited by Carlo Milanesi. ASI, 1st ser., 4 (1843): 25-47.

Landucci, Luca. *Diario fiorentino dal 1450 al 1516, continuato da un anonimo fino al 1542*. Edited by I. Del Badia. Florence: Sansoni, 1883.

———. *A Florentine Diary from 1450 to 1516 Continued by an Anonymous Writer Till 1542*. Translated by Alice de Rosen Jervis. New York: J. M. Dent and Sons, 1927.

Libro di amministrazione dell'eredità di Baldovino Iacopi Riccomanni (1272-78). NTF: 249-83.

Libro del dare e dell'avere di Gentile de' Sassetti e suoi figli (1274-1310). NTF: 286-382.

Libro del dare e dell'avere, e di varie ricordanze di Lapo di Ricomanno Riccomanni (1281-1297). NTF: 516-55.

Machiavelli, Bernardo. *Libro di Ricordi*. Edited by Cesare Olschki. Florence: Felice Le Monnier, 1954.

Machiavelli, Niccolò. *Lettere*. Edited by Giuseppe Lesca. Florence: Società Editrice Rinascimento del Libro, 1929.

Mansi, J. D., ed. *Sacrorum conciliorum nova et amplissima collectio*. Paris: Hubert Welter, 1902.

Ménétra, Jacques-Louis. *Journal of My Life*. Introduction and Commentary by Daniel Roche. Translated by Arthur Goldhammer. New York: Columbia University Press, 1986.

Molho, Anthony, ed. *Social and Economic Foundations of the Italian Renaissance*. New York: Wiley, 1969.

More, Thomas. *Utopia*. Translated by Paul Turner. London: Penguin Books, 1961.

Morelli, Giovanni di Pagolo. *Ricordi*. Edited by Vittore Branca. Florence: Felice Le Monnier, 1969.

Niccolini di Camugliano, Ginevra. *The Chronicles of a Florentine Family, 1200-1470*. London: Jonathan Cape, 1933.

Palmieri, Matteo. *Ricordi fiscali (1427-1474) con due appendici relative al 1474-1495*. Edited by Elio Conti. Studie Storici, vols. 132-35. Rome: Istituto Storico Italiano per il Medio Evo, 1983.

Perosa, Alessandro, ed. *Il zibaldone quaresimale*. Vol. 1 of *Giovanni Rucellai ed il suo zibaldone*. London: Warburg Institute, 1960.

Petrucci, Armando. *Il libro di ricordanze dei Corsini (1362-1457)*. Rome: Istituto Storico Italiano per il Medio Evo, 1965.

Primo libricciolo di crediti di Bene Bencivenni (1262-1275). NTF: 212-28.

Ricordanze di Guido Filippo dell'Antella con aggiunto di un suo figliolo (1299-1328). NTF: 804-13.

Ricordi di compere e prestiti in Val d'Orme e vicinanze (1264-1284). NTF: 229-48.

Ricordi di Guido di Filippo di Ghidone dell'Antela e dei suoi figlioli e discendenti (1298-1405). Edited by F. L. Polidori and G. Canestrini. ASI, 1st ser., 4 (1843): 3-24.

Sacchetti, Franco. *Il Trecentonovelle*. Edited by Antonio Lanza. Florence: Sansoni, 1984.

Secondo libricciolo di credito di Bene Bencivenni (1277-1296). NTF: 363-458.

Sillano, Maria Teresa, ed. *Le ricordanze di Giovanni Chellini da San Miniato: medico, mercante e umanista (1425-1457)*. Milan: Franco Angeli, 1984.

Tansillo, Luigi, *The Nurse, a Poem*. Translated by William Roscoe. Liverpool: Cadell and Davies, 1904.

Two Memoirs of Renaissance Florence: The Diaries of Buonaccorso Pitti and Gregorio Dati. Translated by Julia Martines and edited by Gene Brucker. New York: Harper and Row, 1967.

Secondary Works

Anderson, Michael. *Approaches to the History of the Western Family.* London: MacMillan, 1980.

Annales de Démographie Historique 1973: Enfant et Sociétés. Edited by Jacques DuPaquier. The Hague: Mouton, 1973.

Anselmi, Gian-Mario, Fulvio Pezzarossa, and Luisa Avellini, eds. *La "Memoria" dei mercatores: Tendenze ideologiche, ricordanze, artigianoti in versi nelle Firenze del Quattrocento.* Bologna: Pàtron Editore, 1980.

Ariès, Philippe. *Centuries of Childhood: A Social History of Family Life.* Translated by Robert Baldick. New York: Alfred A Knopf, 1962.

Arnold, Klaus. *Kind und Gesellschaft in Mittelalter und Renaissance: Beiträge und Texte zur Geschichte der Kindheit.* Paderborn: Schöningh, 1980.

Atkinson, Clarissa W. *The Oldest Vocation: Christian Motherhood in the Middle Ages.* Ithaca: Cornell University Press, 1991.

Attreed, Lorraine, C. "From *Pearl* Maiden to Tower Princes: Towards a New History of Medieval Childhood." *Journal of Medieval History* 9 (1983): 43-58.

Banker, James R. "Mourning a Son: Childhood and Paternal Love in the Consolateria of Giannozzo Manetti." *Journal of Psychohistory* 3 (1976): 351-62.

Barbagli, Marzio. *Sotto lo stesso tetto: Mutamenti della famiglia in Italia dal XV al XX secolo.* Bologna: Il Mulino, 1984.

Baron, Francis Xavier. "Children and Violence in Chaucer's *Canterbury Tales.*" *Journal of Psychohistory* 7 (1979): 77-103.

Bec, Christian. *Les marchands écrivains à Florence, 1375-1434.* Civilisations et Sociétés, vol. 9. Paris: Mouton, 1967.

Bell, Rudolph M. *Holy Anorexia.* Chicago: University of Chicago Press, 1985.

Bergstein, Mary. "Marian Politics in Quattrocento Florence: The Renewed Rededication of Santa Maria del Fiore in 1412." *Renaissance Quarterly* 44 (1991): 673-719.

Berkner, Lutz K. "Recent Research on the History of the Family in Western Europe." *Journal of Marriage and the Family* 35 (1973): 395-405.

Bestor, Jane Fair. "Ideas about Procreation and their Influence on Ancient and Medieval Views of Kinship." In *The Family in Italy: From Antiquity to the Present,* edited by Richard P. Saller and David I. Kertzer, 150-67. New Haven: Yale University Press, 1991.

Biller, P. P. A. "Birth-Control in the West in the Thirteenth and Early Fourteenth Centuries." *Past and Present* 94 (1982): 3-26.

Billigmeier, Jon-Christian. "Studies in the Family in the Aegean Bronze Age and in Homer." In *Family History*, edited by Patricia J. F. Rosof and William Zeisel, 9-18. Trends in History, vol. 3, nos. 3-4. New York: Haworth, 1985.

Blumenfeld-Kosinski, Renate. *Not of Woman Born: Representations of Caesarian Birth in Medieval and Renaissance Culture.* Ithaca: Cornell University Press, 1990.

Boas, George. *The Cult of Childhood.* Vol. 29 of *Studies of the Warburg Institute.* London: The Warburg Institute, 1966.

Bossy, John. *Dispute and Settlement.* Cambridge: Cambridge University Press, 1983.

Boswell, John Eastburn. "Expositio and Oblation: The Abandonment of Children and the Ancient and Medieval Family." *American Historical Review* 89 (1984): 10-33.

———. *The Kindness of Strangers: The Abandonment of Children in Western Europe from Late Antiquity to the Renaissance.* New York: Pantheon Books, 1988.

Bowsky, William M. *A Medieval Italian Commune: Siena under the Nine, 1287-1355.* Berkeley: University of California Press, 1981.

Bradley, Keith R. "Sexual Regulations in Wet-Nursing Contracts from Roman Egypt." *Klio* 62 (1980): 321-25.

———. "Wet-nursing at Rome: A Study in Social Relations." In *The Family in Ancient Rome: New Perspectives*, edited by Beryl Rawson, 170-200. New York: Cornell University Press, 1986.

Branca, Vittore. "Mercanti Scrittori: Ricordi nella Firenze tra Medioevo e Rinascimento." In *Mercanti Scrittori: Ricordi nella Firenze tra Medioevo e Rinascimento, Paolo Certaldo, Giovanni Morelli, Bonaccorso Pitti, Domenico Lenzi, Donato Velluti, Goro Dati, Francesco Datini, Lapo Niccolini e Bernardo Machiavelli*, edited by Vittore Branca, x-lxxvii. Milan: Rusconi, 1986.

Braudel, Fernand. *The Structures of Everyday Life: The Limits of the Possible.* Vol. 1 of *Civilization and Capitalism, 15th-18th Century*, by Fernand Braudel. Translated by Siân Reynolds. New York: Harper and Row, 1981.

Breisach, Ernst. *Historiography: Ancient, Medieval and Modern.* Chicago: University of Chicago Press, 1983.

Breitscher, J. K. "'As a Twig is Bent': Children and their Parents in an Aristocratic Society." *Journal of Medieval History* 2 (1976): 181-91.

Broström, Göran, Anders Brändström, and Lars-Ake Persson. "The Impact of Breastfeeding Patterns on Infant Mortality in a 19th Century Swedish

Parish." *Demograhic Data Base Newsletter*, no. 1. Umea, Sweden: Umea University, nd.

Brown, Judith C. *Immodest Acts: The Life of a Lesbian Nun in Renaissance Italy.* Oxford: Oxford University Press, 1986.

———. "A Woman's Place was in the Home: Women's Work in Renaissance Tuscany." In *Rewriting the Renaissance: The Discourses of Sexual Difference in Early Modern Europe*, edited by Margaret W. Ferguson, Maureen Quilligan, and Nancy Vickers. Women in Culture. Chicago: University of Chicago Press, 1986.

Brucker, Gene. *Giovanni and Lusanna: Love and Marriage in Renaissance Florence.* Berkeley: University of California Press, 1986.

Brundage, James A. *Law, Sex, and Christian Society in Medieval Europe.* Chicago: University of Chicago Press, 1987.

Burckhardt, Jacob. *The Civilization of the Renaissance in Italy.* Translated by S. G. C. Middlemore. New York: Random House, 1954.

Burke, Peter. *The Historical Anthropology of Early Modern Italy: Essays on Perception and Communication.* Cambridge: Cambridge University Press, 1987.

Bynum, Caroline Walker. "Wonder." *American Historical Review* 102 (1997): 1-26.

Caiati, Vito. "The Peasant Household under Tuscan Mezzadria: A Socioeconomic Analysis of Some Sienese Mezzadria Households, 1591-1640." *Journal of Family History* 9 (1984): 111-26.

Calvi, Giulia. "Maddelena Nerli and Cosimo Turnabuoni: A Couple's Narrative of Family History in Early Modern Florence." *Renaissance Quarterly* 45 (1992): 312-39.

Carmichael, Ann G. "Contagion Theory and Contagion Practice in Fifteenth-Century Milan." *Renaissance Quarterly* 44 (1991): 213-56.

———. "The Health Status of Florentines in the Fifteenth Century." In *Life and Death in 15th Century Florence*, edited by Marcel Tetel, Ronald Witt, and Rona Goffen, 28-45. Duke Monographs in Medieval and Renaissance Studies, no. 10. Durham: Duke University Press, 1989.

———. *Plague and the Poor in Renaissance Florence.* Cambridge: Cambridge University Press, 1986.

Carnesecchi, C. "Un fiorentino del secolo XV e le sue ricordanze domestiche." *Archivio Storico Italiano* 5th ser., 4 (1889): 145-73.

Carron, Roland. *Enfant et parenté dans la France mediévale, Xe-XIIIe siècles.* Geneva: Droz, 1989.

Cavozzo, Silvano. "Double Death: Resurrection and Baptism in a Seventeenth-Century Rite." In *History from Crime: Selections from Quaderni Storici*, edited by Edward Muir and Guido Ruggiero, 1-31. Baltimore: Johns Hopkins University Press, 1994.

Casey, James. *The History of the Family*. New York: Oxford University Press, 1989.

Censer, Jane Turner. *North Carolina Planters and their Children, 1800-1860*. Baton Rouge: Louisiana State University Press, 1984.

Chartier, Roger, ed. *Passions of the Renaissance*. Vol. 3 of *A History of Private Life*, edited by Philippe Ariès and Georges Duby. Translated by Arthur Goldhammer. Cambridge, MA: Harvard University Press, 1989.

Chojnacki, Stanley. "Comment: Blurring Genders." *Renaissance Quarterly* 40 (1987): 743-51.

Chojnacki, Stanley, ed. "Recent Trends in Renaissance Studies: The Family, Marriage, and Sex." *Renaissance Quarterly* 40 (1987): 636-761.

Cicchetti, Angelo and Raul Mordenti. *I Libri di famiglia in Italia*. Vol. 1 of *La Memoria familiare*. Filologia e Storiografia Letteraria, vol. 1. Rome: Edizioni di Storia e Letteratura, 1985.

Clanchy, M. T. *From Memory to Written Record: England, 1066-1307*. Cambridge, MA: Harvard University Press, 1979.

Cohn, Samuel Kline, Jr. *The Laboring Classes in Renaissance Florence*. Studies in Social Discontinuity, edited by Charles Tilly and Edward Shorter. New York: Academic Press, 1980.

Coontz, Stephanie. *The Social Origins of Private Life: A History of American Families, 1600-1900*. New York: Verso, 1988.

Cressy, David. "Kinship and Kin Interaction in Early Modern England." *Past and Present* 113 (1986): 38-69.

———. "Purification, Thanksgiving and the Churching of Women in Post-Reformation England," *Past and Present* 141 (1993): 106-46.

Cunningham, Hugh. *Children and Childhood in Western Society since 1500*. London: Longmans, 1995.

de la Roncière, Charles. "Tuscan Notables on the Eve of the Renaissance." In *Revelations of the Medieval World*, edited by Georges Duby and translated by Arthur Goldhammer, 157-310. Vol. 2 of *A History of Private Life*, edited by Philippe Ariès and Georges Duby. Cambridge: Harvard University Press, 1988.

Demaitre, Luke. "The Idea of Childhood and Childcare in Medical Writings of the Middle Ages." *Journal of Psychohistory* 4 (1977): 461-90.

Demand, Nancy. *Birth, Death, and Motherhood in Classical Greece.* Baltimore: Johns Hopkins University Press, 1994.

deMause, Lloyd. "The History of Childhood: The Basis for Psychohistory." *History of Childhood Quarterly* 1 (1973): 1-3.

deMause, Lloyd, ed. *The History of Childhood.* New York: Harper and Row, 1975.

Demos, John. *A Little Commonwealth: Family Life in Plymouth Colony.* New York: Oxford University Press, 1970.

————. *Past, Present, and Personal: The Family and the Life Course in American History.* New York: Oxford University Press, 1986.

Demos, John and Sarane Spence Boocock, eds. *Turning Points: Historical and Sociological Essays on the Family.* Chicago: University of Chicago Press, 1978.

Diefendorf, Barbara. "Family Culture, Renaissance Culture." *Renaissance Quarterly* 40 (1987): 661-81.

Dixon, Suzanne. *The Roman Family.* Baltimore: The Johns Hopkins University Press, 1992.

————. *The Roman Mother.* Norman: University of Oklahoma Press, 1988.

————. "The Sentimental Ideal of the Roman Family." In *Marriage, Divorce, and Children in Ancient Rome,* edited by Beryl Rawson, 99-113. Oxford: Oxford University Press, 1991.

Duby, George, ed. *Revelations of the Medieval World.* Vol 2 of *A History of Private Life,* edited by Philippe Ariès and Georges Duby. Translated by Arthur Goldhammer. Cambridge: Harvard University Press, 1988.

Dugan, Eileen Theresa. "Images of Marriage and Family Life in Nördlingen: Moral Preaching and Devotional Literature, 1589-1712." Ph.D. diss. The Ohio State University, 1987.

Dyhouse, Carol. "Working Class Mothers and Infant Mortality in England 1895-1914." *Journal of Social History* 12 (1978), 248-67.

Elder, Glen H., Jr. "Approaches to Social Change and the Family." In *Turning Points: Historical and Sociological Essays on the Family,* edited by John Demos and Sarane Spence Boocock, 1-38. Chicago: University of Chicago Press, 1978.

Elder, Glen H. Jr., John Modell, and Ross B. Parke. *Children in Time and Place: Developmental and Historical Insights.* Cambridge: Cambridge University Press, 1993.

Ende, Aurel. "Children In History: A Personal Review of the Past Decade's Published Research." *Journal of Psychohistory* 11 (1983): 65-88.

Enfance abandonée et société en Europe, XIVe-XXe siècle: Actes du colloque international, Rome 30 et 31 janvier 1987. Collection de l'Ecole Francaise de Rome. Volume 140. Rome: Ecole Francaise de Rome, 1991.

Epstein, Steven. *Wills and Wealth in Medieval Genoa, 1150-1250.* Cambridge: Harvard University Press, 1984.

Eyben, Emiel. "Fathers and Sons." In *Marriage, Divorce, and Children in Ancient Rome,* edited by Beryl Rawson, 106-43. Oxford: Oxford University Press, 1991.

Fauve-Chamoux, Antoinette. "Innovation et comportement parental en milieu urbain (XVe-XIXe)." *Annales Economies, Sociétés, Civilisations* 40 (1985): 1023-39.

Family and Society: Selections from the Annales Economies, Sociétés, Civilisations, edited by Robert Forster and Orest Ranum. Translated by Elborg Forster and Patricia M. Ranum. Baltimore: The Johns Hopkins University Press, 1976.

Ferreri, Rosario. "Rito battesimale e comparatico nelle novelle senesi della VII giornata." *Studi sul Boccaccio* 16 (1987): 307-14.

Fildes, Valerie A. *Breasts, Bottles and Babies: A History of Infant Feeding.* Edinburgh: Edinburgh University Press, 1986.

———. *Wet Nursing: A History from Antiquity to the Present.* Oxford: Basil Blackwell, 1988.

Fildes, Valerie, ed. *Women as Mothers in Preindustrial England: Essays in Memory of Dorothy McLaren.* New York: Routledge, 1990.

Flandrin, Jean-Louis. *Families in Former Times: Kinship, Household and Sexuality.* Cambridge: Cambridge University Press, 1979.

———. "Repression and Change in the Sexual Life of Young People in Medieval and Early Modern Times." *Journal of Family History* 2 (1977): 196-211.

Forsyth, Ilene, H. "Children in Early Medieval Art: Ninth through Twelfth Centuries." *Journal of Psychohistory* 4 (1976): 31-70.

Fothergill, Robert, A. *Private Chronicles: A Study of English Diaries.* London: Oxford University Press, 1974.

Fox, Vivian and Martin H. Quitt. *Loving, Parenting, and Dying: The Family Cycle in England and America, Past and Present.* New York: Psychohistory Press, 1981.

French, Valerie. "Children in Antiquity." In *Children in Historical and Comparative Perspective: An International Handbook and Research Guide,* edited by N. Roy Hiner and Joseph M. Hawes, 14-29. New York: Greenwood Press, 1991.

Gardner, John. *The Life and Times of Chaucer.* New York: Alfred A. Knopf, 1977.

Garnsey, Peter. "Child Rearing in Ancient Italy." In *The Family in Italy: From Antiquity to the Present,* edited by Richard P. Saller and David I. Kertzer, 48-65. New Haven: Yale University Press, 1991.

Gavitt, Philip. *Charity and Children in Renaissance Florence: The Ospedale degli Innocenti, 1410-1536.* Ann Arbor: University of Michigan Press, 1990.

————. "Infant Death in Late Medieval Florence: The Smothering Hypothesis Reconsidered." In *Medieval Family Roles: A Book of Essays,* edited by Cathy Jorgensen Itnyre, 137-56. New York: Garland Publishing, 1996.

Gay, Peter. *Education of the Senses.* Vol. 1 of *The Bourgeois Experience.* Oxford: Oxford University Press, 1984.

Gélis, Jacques. *History of Childbirth: Fertility, Pregnancy and Birth in Early Modern Europe.* Translated by Rosemary Morris. Cambridge: Basil Blackwell, 1991.

van Gennep, Arnold. *The Rites of Passage.* Chicago: University of Chicago Press, 1960.

Gies, Frances and Joseph. *Marriage and the Family in the Middle Ages.* New York: Harper and Row, 1987.

Gillis, John R. *For Better, for Worse: British Marriages, 1600 to the Present.* New York: Oxford University Press, 1985.

Golden, Mark. *Children and Childhood in Classical Athens.* Baltimore: Johns Hopkins University Press, 1990.

Goldthorpe, J. E. *Family Life in Western Societies: A Historical Sociology of Family Relationships in Britain and North America.* Cambridge: Cambridge University Press, 1987.

Goldthwaite, Richard A. *The Building of Renaissance Florence: An Economic and Social History.* Baltimore: The Johns Hopkins University Press, 1980.

————. "The Florentine Palace as Domestic Architecture." *American Historical Review* 77 (1972): 977-1012.

————. *Private Wealth in Renaissance Florence.* Princeton: Princeton University Press, 1971.

Goodich, Michael. "Bartholomaeus Anglicus on Child-Rearing." *Journal of Psychohistory* 3 (1975): 75-84.

————. *From Birth to Old Age: The Human Life Cycle in Medieval Thought, 1250-1350.* Lanham: University Press of America, 1989.

Goody, Jack. *The Development of the Family and Marriage in Europe.* Cambridge: Cambridge University Press, 1983.

Gottlieb, Beatrice. *The Family in the Western World: From the Black Death to the Industrial Age.* New York: Oxford University Press, 1993.

Greenleaf, Barbara Kay. *Children through the Ages: A History of Childhood* New York: McGraw Hill, 1978.

Greilsammer, M. "The Midwife, the Priest, and the Physician: The Subjugation of Midwives in the Low Countries at the End of the Middle Ages." *Journal of Medieval and Renaissance Studies* 21 (1991): 285-329.

Grendler, Paul F. *Schooling in Renaissance Italy: Literacy and Learning, 1300-1600.* The Johns Hopkins University Studies in Historical and Political Science Series, no. 107. Baltimore: The Johns Hopkins University Press, 1989.

Grendler, Paul F., ed. "Education in the Renaissance and Reformation." *Renaissance Quarterly* 43 (1990): 774-824.

Greven, Philip. *Child-Rearing Concepts, 1628-1861.* Itasca: F. I. Peacock Publishers, 1973.

———. *The Protestant Temperament Patterns of Child- Rearing, Religious Experience, and the Self in Early America.* New York: Alfred A. Knopf, 1977.

Hale, J. R. *War and Society in Renaissance Europe, 1450-1620.* Baltimore: Johns Hopkins University Press, 1985.

Haas, Louis. "Baptism and Spiritual Kinship in the North of England, 1250-1450." M.A. thesis, The Ohio State University, 1982.

———. "Boccaccio, Baptismal Kinship and Spritual Incest." *Renaissance and Reformation* 13 (1989): 343-57.

———. "*Il Mio Buono Compare*: Choosing Godparents and the Uses of Baptismal Kinship in Renaissance Florence." *The Journal of Social History* 29 (1995):341-56.

———. Review of *Growing Up in Medieval London: The Experience of Childhood in History* by Barbara Hanawalt, *Journal of Social History* 28 (1994): 230-32.

———. "Social Connections between Parents and Godparents in Late Medieval Yorkshire," *Medieval Prosopography* 10 (Spring 1989): 1-21.

———. "Women and Childbearing in Medieval Florence." In *Medieval Family Roles: A Book of Essays*, edited by Cathy Jorgensen Itnyre, 87-100. New York: Garland Publishing, 1996.

Hampsten, Elizabeth. *Read this Only to Yourself: The Private Writings of Midwestern Women, 1880-1910.* Bloomington: Indiana University Press, 1982.

Hanawalt, Barbara A. "Childrearing among the Lower Classes of Late Medieval England." *Journal of Interdisciplinary History* 8 (1977): 1-22.

———. *Growing Up in Medieval London: The Experience of Childhood in History.* New York: Oxford University Press, 1993.

———. *The Ties that Bound: Peasant Families in Medieval England.* Oxford: Oxford University Press, 1986.

Harevan, Tamara K. "Cycles, Courses, and Cohorts: Reflections on Theoretical and Methodological Approaches to the Historical Study of Family Development." *Journal of Social History* 12 (1978), 97-109.

———. "Family History at the Crossroads." *Journal of Family History* 12 (1987): ix-xxiii.

———. *Family Time and Industrial Time.* Cambridge: Cambridge University Press, 1982.

———. "The History of the Family and the Complexity of Social Change." *The American Historical Review* 96 (1991): 95-124.

Hawes, Jospeh M. and N. Ray Hiner, eds. *Children in Historical and Comparative Perspective: An International Handbook and Research Guide.* New York, Greenwood Press, 1991.

Herlihy, David. "Deaths, Marriages, Births, and the Tuscan Economy (ca. 1300-1550)." In *Population Patterns in the Past*, edited by Ronald Demos Lee, 135-64. New York: Academic Press, 1977.

———. "Family." *The American Historical Review* 96 (1991): 1-16.

———. "Family and Property in Renaissance Florence." In *The Medieval City*, edited by H. Miskimin, D. Herlihy, and A. Udovitch, 3-24. New Haven: Yale University Press, 1977.

———. "The Family and Religious Ideologies in Medieval Europe." *Journal of Family History* 12 (1987): 3-17.

———. *The Family in Renaissance Italy.* St. Louis: Forum Press, 1974.

———. "Family Solidarity in Medieval Italian History." In *Economy, Society, and Government in Medieval Italy: Essays in Memory of Robert L. Reynolds*, edited by David Herlihy, Robert S. Lopez, and Vsevolod Slessarev, 173-84. Kent: Kent State University Press, 1969.

———. "The Making of the Medieval Family: Symmetry, Structure, and Sentiment." *Journal of Family History* 8 (1983): 116-30.

———. "Mapping Households in Medieval Italy." *The Catholic Historical Review* 58 (1972): 1-24.

————. "Medieval Children." In *Essays on Medieval Civilization*, edited by Bede Karl Lackner and Kenneth Ray Philip, 109-42. Volume 12 of The Walter Prescott Webb Memorial Lectures. Austin: University of Texas Press, 1978.

————. *Medieval Households*. Cambridge: Harvard University Press, 1985.

————. *Medieval and Renaissance Pistoia: The Social History of an Italian Town*. New Haven: Yale University Press, 1967.

————. "Santa Caterina and San Bernardino: Their Teachings on the Family." In *Atti del simpozio internazionale Cateriniana-Bernardiniano Siena, 17-20 aprile 1980*, edited by Domenico Maffei and Paolo Nardi, 917-33. Siena: Accademia Senese degli Intronati, 1982.

————. "Tuscan Names, 1200-1530." *Renaissance Quarterly* 51 (1988): 561-82.

Herlihy, David and Christian Klapisch-Zuber. *Les toscans et leurs familles. Une étude du catasto florentin de 1427*. Paris: Presses de la fondation nationale des sciences politiques, 1978.

————. *Tuscans and their Families: A Study of the Florentine Catasto of 1427*. New Haven: Yale University Press, 1985.

Herzfeld, Michael. "When Exceptions Define the Rules: Greek Baptismal Names and the Negotiation of Identity." *Journal of Anthropological Research* 38 (1982): 288-302.

Hess, Ann Giardina. "Midwifery Practice Among the Quakers in Southern Rural England in the Late Seventeenth Century." In *The Art of Midwifery: Early Modern Midwives in Europe*. Edited by Hilary Marland, 49-76. London: Routledge, 1993.

Heywood, Colin. *Childhood in Nineteenth-Century France: Work, Health, and Education among the classes populaires*. Cambridge: Cambridge University Press, 1988.

Hoffer, Peter C. and N. E. H. Hull. *Murdering Mothers: Infanticide in England and New England, 1558-1803*. New York University School of Law Series in Legal History, no. 2. New York: New York University Press, 1981.

Holt, J. C. "Feudal Society and the Family in Early Medieval England: I The Revolution of 1066." *Transactions of the Royal Historical Society*, 5th ser. 32 (1982): 193-212.

Houlbrooke, Ralph A. *The English Family, 1450-1700*. London: Longman Inc., 1984.

Hughes, Diane. "Domestic Ideal and Social Behavior: Evidence from Medieval Genoa." In *The Family in History*. Edited by Charles E. Rosenberg, 115-43. Philadelphia: University of Pennsylvania Press, 1975.

———. "Invisible Madonnas? The Italian Historiographical Tradition and the Women of Medieval Italy." In *Women in Medieval History and Historiography*. Philadelphia: University of Pennsylvania Press, 1987.

———. "Representing the Family: Portraits and Purposes in Early Modern Italy." *Journal of Interdisciplinary History* 17 (1986): 7-38.

Hunecke, Volker. *I trovatelli di Milano: Bambini esposti e famiglie espositrici dal XVII al XIX secolo*. Bologna: Il Mulino, 1989.

Hunt, David. *Parents and Children in History: The Psychology of Family Life in Early Modern France*. New York: Basic Books, Inc., 1970.

Hunt, Lynn. *The Family Romance of the French Revolution*. Berkeley: University of California Press, 1992.

Hyde, J. K. "Italian Social Chronicles in the Middle Ages." *Bulletin of the John Rylands Library* 49 (1966-67): 107-32.

Jacks, Philip J. "The Composition of Giorgio Vasari's *Ricordanze*: Evidence from an Unknown Draft." *Renaissance Quarterly* 45 (1992): 739-84.

Jeay, Madeleine. "Sexuality and Family in Fifteenth-Century France: Are Literary Sources a Mask or a Mirror?" *Journal of Family History* 4 (1979): 328-46.

Johansson, S. Ryan. "Centuries of Childhood/Centuries of Parenting: Philippe Ariès and the Modernization of Privileged Infancy." *Journal of Family History* 12 (1987): 343-65.

Jones, Philip J. "Florentine Families and Florentine Diaries in the Fourteenth Century." *Papers of the British School at Rome* 24 (1956): 183-205.

Jordan, William Chester. *Women and Credit in Pre-Industrial and Developing Societies*. Philadelphia, University of Pennsylvania Press, 1993.

Jütte, Robert. "Household and Family Life in Late Sixteenth Century Cologne: The Weinsberg Family." *Sixteenth Century Journal* 17 (1986): 165-82.

Kelley, Donald R. *The Beginning of Ideology: Consciousness and Society in the French Reformation*. Cambridge: Cambridge University Press, 1981.

Kent, Dale. *The Rise of the Medici: Faction in Florence, 1426-1434*. Oxford: Oxford University Press, 1978.

Kent, Francis W. *Household and Lineage in Renaissance Florence: The Family Life of the Capponi, Ginori, and Rucellai*. Princeton: Princeton University Press, 1971.

Kent, D. V. and F. W. Kent. *Neighbours and Neighbourhood in Renaissance Florence: The District of the Red Lion in the Fifteenth Century*. Locust Valley: J. J. Augustin, 1982.

Kertzer, David I. "Anthropology and Family History." *Journal of Family History* 9 (1984): 201-16.

————. *Sacrificed for Honour: Italian Infant Abandonment and the Politics of Reproductive Control.* Boston: Beacon Press, 1993.

King, Margaret Leah. "Caldiera and the Barbaros on Marriage and the Family: Humanist Reflections of Venetian Realities." *Journal of Medieval and Renaissance Studies* 6 (1976): 19-50.

————. *The Death of the Child Valerio Marcello.* Chicago: University of Chicago Press, 1994.

————. "The Death of the Child Valerio Marcello: Paternal Mourning in Renaissance Venice." In *Renaissance Rereadings: Intertext and Context*, edited by Maryanne C. Horowitz, Anne J. Cruz, and Wendy A. Furman, 205-24. Urbana: University of Illinois Press, 1988.

————. "An Inconsolable Father and His Humanist Consolers: Jacopo Antonio Marcello, Venetian Nobleman, Patron, and Man of Letters." In *Supplementum Festivum: Studies in Honor of Paul Oskar Kristeller*, edited by James Hankins, John Monfasani, and Frederick Purnell, Jr., 221-46. Binghamton: Medieval and Renaissance Texts and Studies, 1987.

————. *Women of the Renaissance.* Chicago: University of Chicago Press, 1991.

Kingdon, Robert M. *Myths about the St. Bartholomew's Day Massacres, 1572-1576.* Cambridge: Harvard University Press, 1988.

Kirshner, Julius. "Some Problems in the Interpretation of Legal Texts *Re* the Italian City-States." *Archiv für Begriffsgeschichte* 19 (1975): 16-27.

Kirshner, Julius and Anthony Molho. "The Dowry Fund and the Marriage Market in Early *Quattrocento* Florence." *Journal of Modern History* 50 (1978): 403-38.

Kittelson, James M. "Visitations and Popular Religious Culture: Further Reports from Strasbourg." In *Pietas et Societas: New Trends in Reformation Social History*, edited by Kyle C. Sessions and Philip N. Bebb, 89-101. Vol. 4 of *Sixteenth Century Essays and Studies*. Kirksville: Sixteenth Century Publishers, 1985.

Klapisch, Christiane. "Household and Family in Tuscany in 1427." In *Household and Family in Past Time*, edited by Peter Laslett and Richard Wall, 267-81. Cambridge: Cambridge University Press, 1972.

Klapisch-Zuber, Christiane. "Le chiavi fiorentine di Barbablù: L'apprendimento della lettura a Firenze nel XV secolo." *Quaderni Storici* 57 (1984): 765-92.

————. "Compérage et clientélisme à Florence (1360-1520)." *Ricerche Storiche* 15 (1985): 61-76.

———. "Kinship and Politics in Fourteenth-Century Florence." In Richard P. Saller and David I. Kertzer, eds. *The Family in Italy: From Antiquity to the Present*, 208-28. New Haven: Yale University Press, 1991.

———. "Parrains et filleuls: Une approche comparée de la France, l'Angleterre et l'Italie médiévales." *Medieval Prosopography* 6 (1985): 51-77.

———. *Women, Family, and Ritual in Renaissance Italy*. Translated by Lydia G. Cochrane. Chicago: University of Chicago Press, 1985.

Kuefler, Matthew S. "'A Wryed Existence': Attitudes toward Children in Anglo-Saxon England." *Journal of Social History* 24 (1990-91): 823-34.

Kuehn, Thomas. *Emancipation in Late Medieval Florence*. New Brunswick: Rutgers University Press, 1980.

———. "Honor and Conflict in a Fifteenth-Century Florentine Family." *Ricerche Storiche* 10 (1980): 287-310.

———. "Law, Death, and Heirs in the Renaissance: Repudiation of Inheritance in Florence." *Renaissance Quarterly* 45 (1992): 484-516.

———. *Law, Family, and Women: Toward a Legal Anthropology of Renaissance Italy*. Chicago: University of Chicago Press, 1992.

———. "Reading Between the Patrilines: Leon Battista Alberti's *Della Famiglia* in Light of His Illegitimacy." In *I Tatti Studies: Essays in the Renaissance*. Vol 1., edited by Salvatore Comporeate, Caroline Elam, and F. W. Kent, Florence: Villa i Tatti, 1985, 161-87.

Laslett, Peter. "The Character of Familial History, its Limitations and the Conditions for its Proper Pursuit." *Journal of Family History* 12 (1987): 263-84.

———. "Characteristics of the Western Family Considered over Time." *Journal of Family History* 2 (1977): 89-116.

———. *Family Forms in Historical Europe*. Cambridge: Cambridge University Press, 1983.

———. *Family Life and Illicit Live in Earlier Generations: Essays in Historical Sociology*. Cambridge: Cambridge University Press, 1977.

———. *The World We have Lost: England before the Industrial Age*. 2nd ed. New York: Charles Scribner's Sons, 1971.

———. *The World We have Lost further Explored: England before the Industrial Age*. 3rd ed. New York: Charles Scribner's Sons, 1984.

Laslett, Peter and Richard Wall, eds. *Household and Family in Past Time*. Cambridge: Cambridge University Press, 1972.

Laslett, Peter, Karla Oosterveen and Richard M. Smith, eds. *Bastardy and its Comparative History: Studies in the History of Illegitimacy and Marital*

Nonconformism in Britain, France, Germany, Sweden, North America, Jamaica, and Japan. Cambridge: Harvard University Press, 1980.

Le Goff, Jacques. *The Birth of Purgatory.* Translated by Arthur Goldhammer. Chicago: Chicago University Press, 1981.

Lehmberg, Stanford E. "Review of Nicholas Orme, *From Childhood to Chivalry.*" *Renaissance Quarterly* 38 (1985): 708-09.

Lehning, James R. "Family Life and Wetnursing in a French Village." *Journal of Interdisciplinary History* 12 (1982): 645-56.

Lepowsky. Maria. "Food Taboos and Child Survival: A Case Study from the Coral Sea." In *Child Survival: Anthropological Perspectives on the Treatment and Maltreatment of Children*, edited by Nancy Scheper-Hughes. Dordrecht: D. Reidel Publishing Co., 1987.

Le Roy Ladurie, Emmanuel. *Carnival In Romans.* Translated by Mary Feeney. New York: George Braziller, Inc., 1979.

———. *Montaillou: The Promised Land of Error.* Translated by Barbara Bray. New York: George Braziller, Inc., 1978.

Levy, Barry. "Tender Plants: Quaker Farmers and Children in the Delaware Valley." *Journal of Family History* 3 (1978): 116-35.

Levy, Fernando. "Florentine *Ricordanze* in the Renaissance." *Stanford Italian Review* 3 (1983): 107-22.

Lewis, Jan. *The Pursuit of Happiness: Family and Values in Jefferson's Virginia.* Cambridge: Cambridge University Press, 1983.

Lewis, Judith Schneid. *In the Family Way: Childbearing in the British Aristocracy, 1760-1860.* New Brunswick: Rutgers University Press, 1986.

Lockwood, Rose. "Birth, Illness, and Death in 18th-Century New England." *Journal of Social History* 12 (1978): 110-128.

Lindemann, Mary. "Professionals? Sisters? Rivals? Midwives in Braunschweig, 1750-1800." In *The Art of Midwifery: Early Modern Midwives in Europe.* Edited by Hilary Marland, 176-91. London: Routledge, 1993.

Lynch, Joseph H. *Godparents and Kinship in Early Medieval Europe.* Princeton: Princeton University Press, 1986.

Lynch, Katherine A. *Family, Class, and Ideology in Early Industrial France: Social Policy and the Working Class Family 1825-1848.* Madison: University of Wisconsin Press, 1988.

McLaren, Angus. *A HIstory of Contraception from Antiquity to the Present Day.* New York: Basil Blackwood, 1990.

———. *Reproductive Rituals: The Perception of Fertility in England from the Sixteenth Century to the Nineteenth Century.* New York: Methuen, 1984.

McClure, George W. "The Art of Mourning: Autobiographical Writings on the Loss of a Son in Italian Humanist Thought." *Renaissance Quarterly* 39 (1986): 440-75.

————. *Sorrow and Consolation in Italian Humanism.* Princeton: Princeton University Press, 1991.

MacFarlane, Alan. *The Family Life of Ralph Josselin, A Seventeenth-Century Clergyman: An Essay in Historical Anthropology.* Cambridge: Cambridge University Press, 1970.

————. *Marriage and Love in England: Modes of Reproduction, 1300-1840.* New York: Basil Blackwell, 1986.

————. *The Origins of English Individualism: The Family, Property and Social Transition.* London: Basil Blackwell, 1978.

Marland, Hilary, ed. *The Art of Midwifery: Early Modern Midwives in Europe.* London: Routledge, 1993.

Marshall, Sherrin. "Childhood in Early Modern Europe." In *Children in Historical and Comparative Perspective: An International Handbook and Research Guide,* edited by Joseph M. Hawes and N. Roy Hiner, 53-70. New York: Greenwood Press, 1991.

Martin, John. "Out of the Shadow: Heretical and Catholic Women in Renaissance Venice." *Journal of Family History* 10 (1985): 21-33.

Martines, Lauro. "Forced Loans: Political and Social Strain in *Quattrocento* Florence." *Journal of Modern History* 60 (1988): 300-11.

McMillen, Sally G. *Motherhood in the Old South: Pregnancy, Childbirth, and Infant Rearing.* Baton Rouge: Louisiana State University Press, 1990.

Meckel, Richard Alan. "Childhood and the Historians: A Review Essay." *Journal of Family History* 9 (1984): 415-24.

Medick, Hans and David Warren Sabean, eds. *Interest and Emotion: Essays in the Study of Family and Kinship.* Cambridge: Cambridge University Press, 1984.

————. "Interest and Emotion in Family and Kinship Studies: A Critique of Social History and Anthropology." In *Interest and Emotion: Essays in the Study of Family and Kinship,* Hans Medick and David Warren Sabean, 9-27. Cambridge: Cambridge University Press, 1984.

Mertes, Kate. *The English Noble Household, 1250-1600: Good Governance and Politic Rule.* Oxford: Oxford University Press, 1988.

Mitterauer, Michael. *A History of Youth.* Cambridge, MA: Blackwell, 1992.

Mitterauer, Michael and Reinhard Sieder. *The European Family: Patriarchy to Partnership from the Middle Ages to the Present.* Translated by Karla

Oosterveen and Manfred Ho"rzinger. Chicago: Chicago University Press, 1982.

Modell, John. *Into One's Own: From Youth to Adulthood in the United States.* Berkeley: University of California Press, 1989.

Molho, Anthony. *Marriage Alliance in Late Medieval Florence.* Cambridge, MA: Harvard University Press, 1994.

Morrison, Alan S., Julius Kirshner, and Anthony Molho. "Epidemics in Renaissance Florence." *American Journal of Public Health* 75 (1985): 528-35.

Morel, Marie-France. "Reflections on some recent French Literature on the History of Childhood." *Continuity and Change* 4 (1989): 323-37.

Mount, F. *The Subversive Family: An Alternative History of Love and Marriage.* London: Jonathan Cape, 1982.

Muir, Edward and Ronald F. E. Weissman. "Social and Symbolic Places in Renaissance Venice and Florence." In *The Power of Place: Bringing Together Geographical and Sociological Imaginations,* edited by John A. Agnew and James S. Duncan, 81-103. Boston: Routledge, Chapman and Hall, 1989.

Mulder, Monique Borgerhoof. "Factors Affecting Infant Care in the Kipsigis." *Journal of Anthropological Research* 41 (1985): 231-62.

Myres, Sandra L. *Westering Women and the Frontier Experience, 1800-1915.* Albuquerque: University of New Mexico Press, 1982.

Niccolini di Camugliano, Ginevra. "A Medieval Florentine, his Family and his Possessions." *American Historical Review* 31 (1925): 1-19.

Nicholas, David. "Childhood in Medieval Europe." In *Children in Historical and Comparative Perspective: An International Handbook and Research Guide,* edited by Jospeh M. Hawes and N. Roy Hiner, 32-52. New York: Greenwood Press, 1991.

———. *The Domestic Life of a Medieval City: Women, Children, and the Family in Fourteenth-Century Ghent.* Lincoln: University of Nebraska Press, 1985.

Origo, Iris. "The Domestic Enemy: Eastern Slaves in Tuscany in the Fourteenth and Fifteenth Centuries." *Speculum* 30 (1955): 321-66.

———. *The Merchant of Prato: Francesco di Marco Datini, 1335-1410.* New York: Alfred A. Knopf, 1957.

———. *The World of San Bernardino.* New York: Harcourt, Brace and World, 1962.

Orme, Nicholas. *From Childhood to Chivalry: The Education of the English Kings and Aristocracy, 1066-1530.* New York: Methuen, 1984.

Ortiz, Teresa. "From Hegemony to Subordination: Midwives in Early Modern Spain." In *The Art of Midwifery: Early Modern Midwives in Europe*, edited by Hilary Marland, 77-94. London: Routledge, 1993.

Otis, Leah L. "Municipal Wet Nurses in Fifteenth-Century Montpellier." In *Women and Work in Preindustrial Europe*, edited by Barbara A. Hanawalt, 83-93. Bloomington: Indiana University Press, 1986.

Ozment, Steven. "The Family in Reformation Germany: The Bearing and Rearing of Children." *Journal of Family History* 8 (1983): 159-76.

———. *Magdalena and Balthazar: An Intimate Portrait of Life in 16th-Century Europe Revealed in the Letters of a Nuremberg Husband and Wife*. New York: Simon and Schuster, 1986.

———. *When Fathers Ruled: Family Life in Reformation Germany*. Studies in Cultural History. Cambridge, MA: Harvard University Press, 1983.

Pandimiglio, Leonida. "Giovanni di Pagolo Morelli e le strutture familiari." *Archivio Storico Italiano* 136 (1978): 3-88.

Park, Katherine. "The Criminal and the Saintly Body: Autopsy and Dissection in Renaissance Italy." *Renaissance Quarterly* 47 (1994): 1-33.

———. *Doctors and Medicine in Early Renaissance Florence*. Princeton: Princeton University Press, 1985.

Park, Katherine and Lorraine J. Daston. "Unnatural Conceptions: The Study of Monsters in Sixteenth- and Seventeenth-Century France and England." *Past and Present* 92 (1981): 20-54.

Pezzarossa, Fulvio. "La memorialistica fiorentina tra Medioevo e Rinascimento." *Lettere Italiane* 31 (1979): 96-138.

Phillips, Mark. *The Memoir of Marco Parenti: A Life in Medici Florence*. Princeton: Princeton University Press, 1987.

Pinchbeck, Ivy and Margaret Hewitt. *Children in English Society*. London: Routledge and Paul, 1969.

Plumb, J. H. "The New World of Children in the 18th Century." *Past and Present* 67 (1975): 64-95.

Pollock, Linda. *Forgotten Children: Parent-Child Relations from 1500 to 1900*. Cambridge: Cambridge University Press, 1983.

Pollock, Linda, ed. *A Lasting Relationship: Parents and Children over Three Centuries*. Hanover: University Press of New England, 1987.

Pomeroy, Sarah B. "The Family in Classical and Hellenistic Greece." In *Family History*, edited by Patricia J. F. Rosof and William Zeisel, 19-26. Trends in History, vol. 3, nos. 3-4. New York: Haworth Press, 1985.

Poos, L. R. "The Historical Demography of Renaissance Europe." *Renaissance Quarterly* 42 (1989): 794-811.

Potter, Shulamith Heins. "Birth Planning in Rural China: A Cultural Account." In *Child Survival: Anthropological Perspectives on the Treatment and Maltreatment of Children*, edited by Nancy Scheper-Hughes, 33-58. Dordrecht: D. Reidel Publishing Co., 1987.

Pounds, Norman J. G. *Hearth and Home: A History of Material Culture.* Bloomington: Indiana University Press, 1989.

Queller, Donald E. and Thomas F. Madden. "Father of the Bride: Fathers, Daughters, and Dowries in Late Medieval and Early Renaissance Venice." *Renaissance Quarterly* 46 (1993): 685-711.

Quinn, Patricia A. *Better than the Sons of Kings: Boys and Monks in the Middle Ages.* New York: Peter Lang, 1989.

Ransel, David L. *Mothers of Misery: Child Abandonment in Russia.* Princeton: Princeton University Press, 1988.

Rawson, Beryl. "Adult-Child Relationships in Roman Society." In *Marriage, Divorce, and Children in Ancient Rome*, edited by Beryl Rawson. Oxford: Oxford University Press, 1991.

———. "Family Life among the Lower Classes at Rome in the First Two Centuries of the Empire." *Classical Philology* 61 (1966): 71-83.

———, ed. *Marriage, Divorce, and Children in Ancient Rome.* Oxford: Oxford University Press, 1991.

Riddle, John M. *Contraception and Abortion from the Ancient World to the Renaissance.* Cambridge, MA: Harvard University Press, 1992.

Ridolfi, Roberto. *The Life of Niccolò Machiavelli.* Translated by Cecil Grayson. London: Routledge and Kegan Paul, 1963.

Ring, Richard R. "Early Medieval Peasant Households in Central Italy." *Journal of Family History* 4 (1979): 2-21.

Romano, Dennis. "Aspects of Patronage in Fifteenth- and Sixteenth-Century Venice." *Renaissance Quarterly* 46 (1993): 712-33.

Roper, Lyndal. *The Holy Household: Women and Morals in Reformation Augsburg.* New York: Oxford University Press, 1989.

Rosenthal, Elaine G. "The Position of Women in Renaissance Florence: neither Autonomy nor Subjection." In *Florence and Italy: Renaissance Studies in Honor of Nicolai Rubinstein*, edited by Peter Denley and Caroline Elam, 369-81. Westfield Publications in Medieval Studies, vol. 2. London: Committee for Medieval Studies, Westfield College, University of London, 1988.

Rosof, Patricia J. F. and William Zeisel. *Family History.* Trends in History, vol. 3, nos. 3-4. New York: Haworth Press, 1984.

Ross, James Bruce. "The Middle Class Child in Urban Italy, Fourteenth to Early Sixteenth Century." In *History of Childhood*, edited by Lloyd deMause, 183-228. New York: Harper and Row, 1975.

―――. "Venetian Schools and Teachers, Fourteenth to Early Sixteenth Century: A Survey and a Study of Giovanni Battista Egnazio." *Renaissance Quarterly* 29 (1976): 521-66.

Ruggiero, Guido. *The Boundaries of Eros: Sex Crime and Sexuality in Renaissance Venice*. Oxford: Oxford University Press, 1985.

Ruggles, Steven. "The Transformation of American Family Structure." *The American Historical Review* 99 (1994): 103-28.

Russell, Josiah Cox. "Populations in Europe, 500-1500." In *The Middle Ages*, edited by Carlo M. Cipolla, 25-70. Vol. 1 of *The Fontana Economic History of Europe*, edited by Carlo M. Cipolla. London: Collins/ Fontana Books, 1972.

Sabean, David W. *Property, Production, and Family in Neckerhausen 1700-1870*. Cambridge: Cambridge University Press, 1991.

Saller, Richard P. "Corporal Punishment, Authority, and Obedience in the Roman Household." In *Marriage, Divorce, and Children in Ancient Rome*, edited by Beryl Rawson, 144-65. Oxford: Oxford University Press, 1991.

―――. "*Familia, Domus*, and the Roman Conception of the Family." *Phoenix* 38 (1984): 336-55.

―――. "European Family History and Roman Law." *Continuity and Change* 6 (1991): 335-46.

―――. "*Patria Potestas* and the Stereotype of the Roman Family." *Continuity and Change* 1 (1986): 7-22.

―――. *Patriarchy, Property, and Death in the Roman Family*. Cambridge: Cambridge University Press, 1995.

Saller, Richard P. and David I. Kertzer, eds. *The Family in Italy: From Antiquity to the Present*. New Haven: Yale University Press, 1991.

―――. "Historical and Anthropological Perspectives on Italian Family Life." In *The Family in Italy: From Antiquity to the Present*, edited by Richard P. Saller and David I. Kertzer, 1-19. New Haven: Yale University Press, 1991.

Saller, Richard P. and Brent D. Shaw. "Tombstones and Roman Family Relations in The Principate: Civilians, Soldiers and Slaves." *Journal of Roman Studies* 74 (1984): 124-56.

Scheper-Hughes, Nancy. "The Cultural Politics of Child Survival." In *Child Survival: Anthropological Perspectives on the Treatment and Maltreat-*

ment of Children, edited by Nancy Scheper-Hughes, 1-29. Dordrecht: D. Reidel Publishing Co., 1987.

―――. "Culture, Scarcity, and Maternal Thinking: Mother Love and Child Death in Northeast Brazil." In *Child Survival: Anthropological Perspectives on the Treatment and Maltreatment of Children*, edited by Nancy Scheper-Hughes, 187-208. Dordrecht: D. Reidel Publishing Co., 1987.

―――. *Death Without Weeping: The Violence of Everyday Life in Brazil*. Berkeley: University of California Press, 1992.

Scheper-Hughes, Nancy., ed. *Child Survival: Anthropological Perspectives on the Treatment and Maltreatment of Children*. Dordrecht: D. Reidel Publishing Co., 1987.

Schimmelpfennig, Bernhard. "Zölibat und Lage der 'Priestersöhne' vom 11. bis 14. Jahrhundert." *Historische Zeitschrift* 227 (1978): 1-44.

Schmitt, Jean-Claude. *The Holy Greyhound: Guinefort, Healer of Children since the Thirteenth Century*. Translated by Martin Thom. Cambridge: Cambridge University Press, 1983.

Schulte, Regina. "Infanticide in Rural Bavaria in the Nineteenth Century." In *Interest and Emotion: Essays on the Study of Family and Kinship*, edited by Hans Medick and David Warren Sabean, 77-102. Cambridge: Cambridge University Press, 1984.

Schultz, James A. *The Knowledge of Childhood in the German Middle Ages*. Philadelphia: University of Pennsylvania Press, 1995.

Seaver, Paul S. *Wallington's World: A Puritan Artisan in Seventeenth-Century London*. Stanford: Stanford University Press, 1985.

Segalen, Martine. *Historical Anthropology of the Family*. Translated by J. C. Whitehouse. Cambridge: Cambridge University Press, 1986.

Shaffer, John W. *Family and Farm: Agrarian Change and Household Organization in the Loire Valley, 1500-1900*. European Social History Series. Albany: State University of New York Press, 1982.

Shahar, Shulamith. *Childhood in the Middle Ages*. London: Routledge, 1990.

―――. *The Fourth Estate: A History of Women in the Middle Ages*. Translated by Chaya Galai. London: Methuen, 1983.

Sheehan, Michael and Kathy Scardellato, comps. *Family and Marriage in Medieval Europe: A Working Bibliography*. Vancouver: Medieval Studies Committee, Faculty of Arts, University of British Columbia, 1976.

Shorter, Edward. *The Making of the Modern Family*. New York: Basic Books, 1975.

Slater, Miriam. *Family Life in the Seventeenth Century: The Verneys of Claydon House*. London: Routledge and Kegan Paul, 1984.

Smith, Daniel Blake. *Inside the Great House: Planter Life in Eighteenth-Century Chesapeake Society.* Ithaca: Cornell University Press, 1980.

Smith, R. M. "Kin and Neighbors in a Thirteenth-Century Suffolk Community." *Journal of Family History* 4 (1979): 219-56.

Soliday, Gerald L., ed. *History of Family and Kinship: A Select International Bibliography.* New York: Kraus International Publications, 1980.

Sommerville, C. John. *The Discovery of Childhood in Puritan England.* Athens: University of Georgia Press, 1992.

——. *The Rise and Fall of Childhood.* Beverley Hills: Sage, 1982.

——. "Toward a History of Childhood and Youth." *Journal of Interdisciplinary History* 3 (1972-73): 439-47.

Stearns, Peter N. "Girls, Boys, and Emotions: Redefinitions and Historical Change." *Journal of American History* 80 (1993): 36-74.

——. "Social History Update: Sociology of Emotion." *Journal of Social History* 22 (1989): 592-99.

Stearns, Peter N. and Carol Z. Stearns. "Emotionology: Clarifying the History of Emotions and Emotional Standards." *American Historical Review* 90 (1985): 813-36.

Stone, Lawrence. "Children and the Family." In *The Past and the Present,* edited by Lawrence Stone, 216-231. Boston: Routledge and Kegan Paul, 1981.

——. "Family History in the 1980s: Past Achievements and Future Trends." *Journal of Interdisciplinary History* 12 (1981): 51-87.

——. *The Family, Sex and Marriage in England, 1500-1800.* New York: Harper and Row, 1977.

——. "The Rise of the Nuclear Family in Early Modern England: The Patriarchal Stage." In *The Family in History.* Edited by Charles E. Rosenberg, 13-57. Philadelphia: University of Pennsylvania Press, 1975.

——. *Uncertain Unions: Marriage in England 1660-1753.* New York: Oxford University Press, 1992.

Stow, Kenneth R. "The Jewish Family in the Rhineland in the High Middle Ages: Form and Function." *American Historical Review* 92 (1987): 1085-1110.

Strauss, Barry S. *Fathers and Sons in Athens: Ideology and Society in the Era of the Peloponnesian War.* Princeton: Princeton University Press, 1993.

Strocchia, Sharon. "Death Rites and the Ritual Family in Renaissance Florence." In *Life and Death in Fifteenth-Century Florence,* edited by

Marcel Tetel, Ronald Witt, and Rona Goffen, 120-45. Durham: Duke University Press, 1989.

———. *Death and Ritual in Renaissance Florence.* Baltimore: The Johns Hopkins University Press, 1992.

———. "Remembering the Family: Women, Kin, and Commemorative Masses in Renaissance Florence." *Renaissance Quarterly* 42 (1989): 635-54.

Stuard, Susan Mosher. "Urban Domestic Slavery in Medieval Ragusa." *Journal of Medieval History* 9 (1983): 173-78.

Sussman, George D. *Selling Mothers' Milk: The Wet-Nursing Business in France, 1715-1914.* Urbana: University of Illinois Press, 1982.

Tamassia, Nino. *La famiglia italiana nei secoli decimoquinto e decimosesto.* Rome: Multigrafica Editrice, 1911, 1971.

Taylor, Michael D. "Gentile da Fabriano, St. Nicholas, and an Iconography of Shame." *Journal of Family History* 7 (1987): 321-32.

Tenenti, Alberto. "Témoignages Tuscans sur la mort des enfants autour de 1400." *Annales de Demographie Historique: Enfant et sociétés* (1973): 131-32.

Tentler, Thomas. "Review of Gerald Strauss, *Luther's House of Learning: Indoctrination of the Young in the German Reformation.*" *Renaissance Quarterly* 33 (1980): 427-29.

Tetel, Marcel, Ronald G. Witt, and Rona Goffen, eds. *Life and Death in Fifteenth-Century Florence.* Durham: Duke University Press, 11989.

Trexler, Richard C. "The Foundlings of Florence, 1395-1455." *Journal of Psychohistory* 1 (1973): 259-84.

———. "Infanticide in Florence: New Sources and First Results." *Journal of Psychohistory* 1 (1973): 98-116.

———. *Public Life in Renaissance Florence.* Studies in Social Discontinuity, edited by Charles Tilly and Edward Shorter. New York: Academic Press, 1980.

———. "In Search of Father: The Experience of Abandonment in the Recollections of Giovanni di Pagolo Morelli." *Journal of Psychohistory* 3 (1975): 225-52.

Trumbach, Randolf. *Rise of the Egalitarian Family: Aristocratic Kinship and Domestic Relations.* Studies in Social Discontinuity, edited by Charles Tilly and Edward Shorter. New York: Academic Press, 1978.

Tuchman, Barbara W. *A Distant Mirror: The Calamitous 14th Century.* New York: Ballantine Books, 1978.

Tucker, Nicholas. "Boon or Burden? Baby Love in History." *History Today* (September, 1993): 28-35.

Ulrich, Laurel Thatcher. *A Midwife's Tale: The Life of Martha Ballard, Based on Her Diary 1785-1812.* New York: Alfred Knopf, 1990.

Vann, Richard T. "Wills and the Family in an English Town: Bamburg, 1550-1800." *Journal of Family History* 4 (1979): 346-67.

Veyne, Paul, ed. *From Pagan Rome to Byzantium.* Vol. 1 of *A History of Private Life*, edited by Philippe Ariès and George Duby. Translated by Arthur Goldhammer. Cambridge, MA: Harvard University Press, 1987.

Weinstein, Donald. "The Myth of Florence." In *Florentine Studies*, edited by Nicolai Rubinstein, 15-44. London: 1968.

Weissman, Ronald F. E. *Ritual Brotherhood in Renaissance Florence.* Population and Social Structure: Advances in Historical Demography, edited by E. A. Hammel. New York: Academic Press, 1982.

Wemple, Suzanne F. "The Medieval Family: European and North American Research Directions." In *Family History*, edited by Patricia J. F. Rosof and William Zeisel. Trends in History, vol. 3, nos., 3-4. New York: Haworth Press, 1984.

Wertz, Richard W. and Dorothy C. *Lying-In: A History of Childbirth in America.* New York: The Free Press, 1977.

West, Elliot. *Growing Up with the Country: Childhood on the Far Western Frontier.* Albuquerque: University of New Mexico Press, 1989.

West, Elliot and Paula Petrik, eds. *Small Worlds: Children and Adolescents in America 1850-1950.* Lawrence: University of Kansas Press, 1992.

Wheaton, Robert. "Images of Kinship." *Journal of Family History* 121 (1987): 389-405.

Wiedemann, Thomas. *Adults and Children in the Roman Empire.* New Haven: Yale University Press, 1989.

Wiesner, Merry E. "Early Modern Midwifery: A Case Study." In *Women and Work in Preindustrial Europe*, edited by Barbara A. Hanawalt, 94-113. Bloomington: Indiana University Press, 1986.

———. "The Midwives of South Germany and the Public/Private Dichotomy." In *The Art of Midwifery: Early Modern Midwives in Euroupe*, edited by Hilary Marchand, 77-94. London: Routledge, 1993.

———. *Working Women in Renaissance Germany.* New Brunswick: Rutgers University Press, 1986.

Wilson, Adrian. "The Ceremony of Childbirth and its Interpretation." In *Women as Mothers in Pre-Industrial England: Essays in Memory of*

Dorothy McLaren, edited by Valerie Fildes, 68-107. London: Routledge, 1990.

———. "The Infancy of the History of Childhood: An Appraisal of Philippe Ariès." *History and Theory* 19 (1980): 132-53.

———. "Participant or Patient? Seventeenth-Century Childbirth from the Mother's Point of View." In *Lay Perceptions of Medicine in Pre-Industrial Society*, edited by Roy Porter, 129-44. Cambridge: Cambridge University Press, 1985.

Wolf, Arthur P. and Chieh-Shan-Huang. *Marriage and Adoption in China, 1845-1945*. Stanford: Stanford University Press, 1980.

Wooden, Warren W. "Childhood and Death: A Reading of John Skelton's Philip Sparrow." *Journal of Psychohistory* 7 (1980): 403-14.

Zorzi, Andrea. "The Florentines and their Public Offices in the Early Fifteenth Century: Competition, Abuses of Power, and Unlawful Acts." In *History from Crime: Selections from Quaderni Storici*, edited by Edward Muir and Guido Ruggiero, 110-34. Baltimore: Johns Hopkins University Press, 1994.

Index